This is the last page.

In keeping with the original Japanese comic format, this book reads from right to left, so action, sound effects, and word balloons are completely reversed. This preserves the orientation of the original artwork. Check out the diagram below to get the hang of things, then turn to the other side of the book to get started!

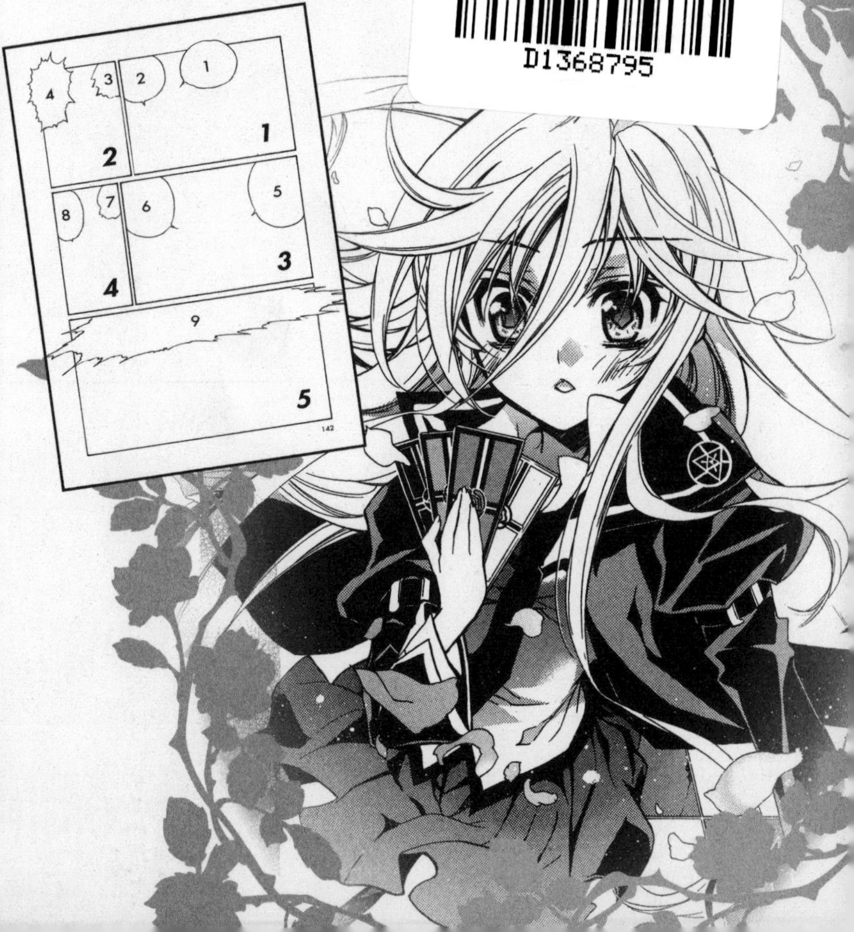

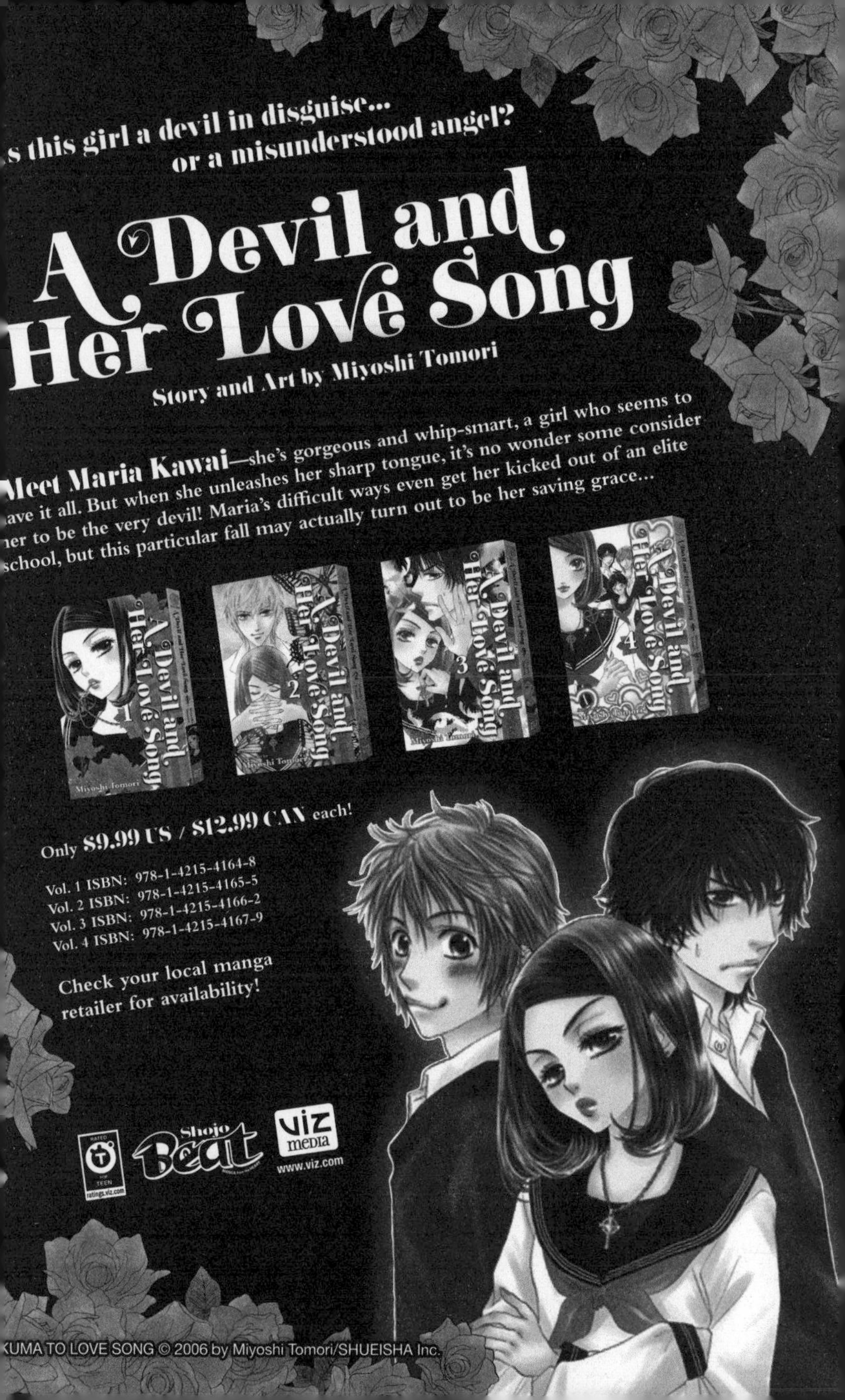
s this girl a devil in disguise...
or a misunderstood angel?
A Devil and Her Love Song
Story and Art by Miyoshi Tomori
Meet Maria Kawai—she's gorgeous and whip-smart, a girl who seems to ave it all. But when she unleashes her sharp tongue, it's no wonder some consider ner to be the very devil! Maria's difficult ways even get her kicked out of an elite school, but this particular fall may actually turn out to be her saving grace...
A Devil and Her Love Song 1
Miyoshi Tomori
A Devil and Her Love Song 2
Miyoshi Tomori
A Devil and Her Love Song 3
Miyoshi Tomori
A Devil and Her Love Song 4
Only $9.99 US / $12.99 CAN each!
Vol. 1 ISBN: 978-1-4215-4164-8
Vol. 2 ISBN: 978-1-4215-4165-5
Vol. 3 ISBN: 978-1-4215-4166-2
Vol. 4 ISBN: 978-1-4215-4167-9
Check your local manga retailer for availability!
RATED T TEEN ratings.viz.com
Shojo Beat
VIZ MEDIA
www.viz.com
KUMA TO LOVE SONG © 2006 by Miyoshi Tomori/SHUEISHA Inc.

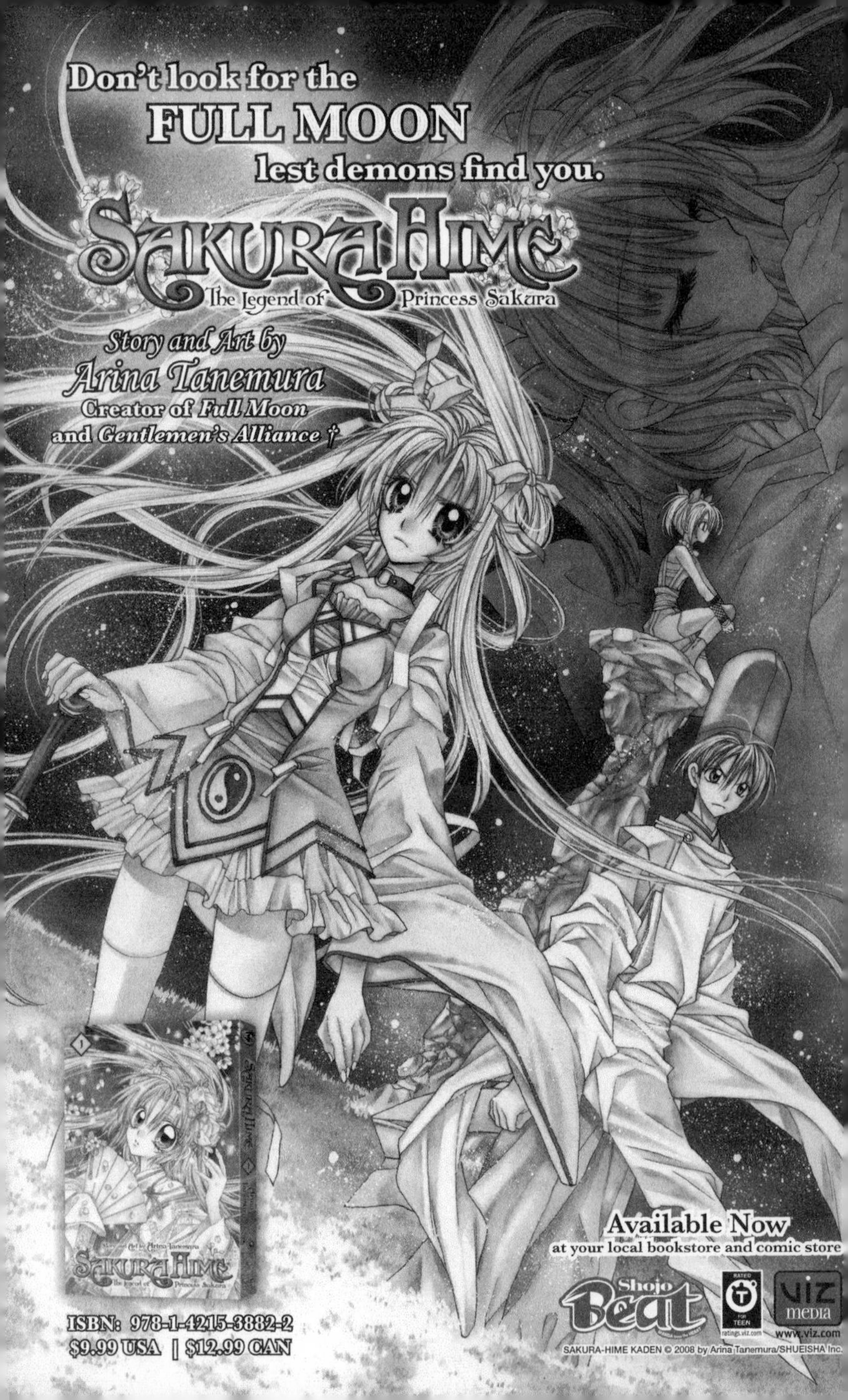
Don't look for the
FULL MOON
lest demons find you.
SAKURA HIME
The Legend of Princess Sakura
Story and Art by
Arina Tanemura
Creator of Full Moon
and Gentlemen's Alliance †
SAKURA HIME
The Legend of Princess Sakura
ISBN: 978-1-4215-3882-2
$9.99 USA | $12.99 CAN
Available Now
at your local bookstore and comic store
Shojo Beat
RATED T FOR TEEN
ratings.viz.com
VIZ media
www.viz.com
SAKURA-HIME KADEN © 2008 by Arina Tanemura/SHUEISHA Inc.

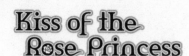

Kiss of the Rose Princess

Volume 7
Shojo Beat Edition

YA
Graphic Novel

STORY AND ART BY
AYA SHOUOTO

Translation/Tetsuichiro Miyaki
Touch-up Art & Lettering/Inori Fukuda Trant
Design/Yukiko Whitley
Editor/Nancy Thistlethwaite

KISS OF ROSE PRINCESS Volume 7
© Aya SHOUOTO 2011
Edited by KADOKAWA SHOTEN
First published in Japan in 2011 by KADOKAWA CORPORATION, Tokyo.
English translation rights arranged with KADOKAWA CORPORATION, Tokyo.

The stories, characters and incidents mentioned in this publication
are entirely fictional.

Printed in the U.S.A.

Published by VIZ Media, LLC
P.O. Box 77010
San Francisco, CA 94107

10 9 8 7 6 5 4 3 2 1
First printing, November 2015

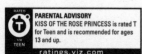

www.viz.com

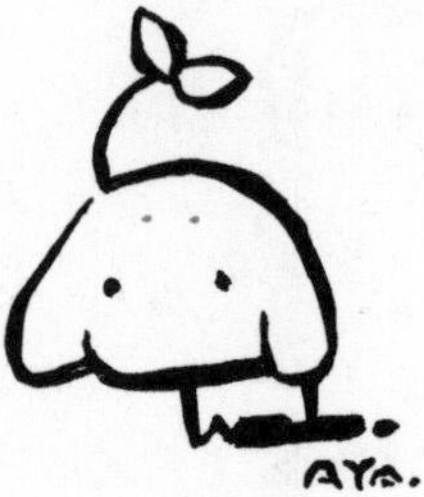
AYA.

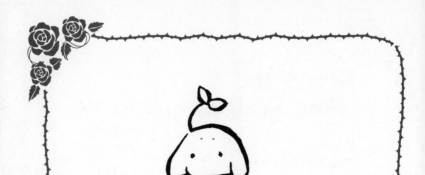

I have started taking care of a betta (fighting fish) at my new office. A cute blue boy with frills. He wriggles around and dances for me when I feed him. But when I show him a mirror, he takes on a threatening attitude towards his own reflection. I never get bored watching him.

-Aya Shouoto

Aya Shouoto was born on December 25. Her hobbies include traveling, staying at hotels, sewing and daydreaming. She currently lives in Tokyo and enjoys listening to J-pop anime theme songs while she works.

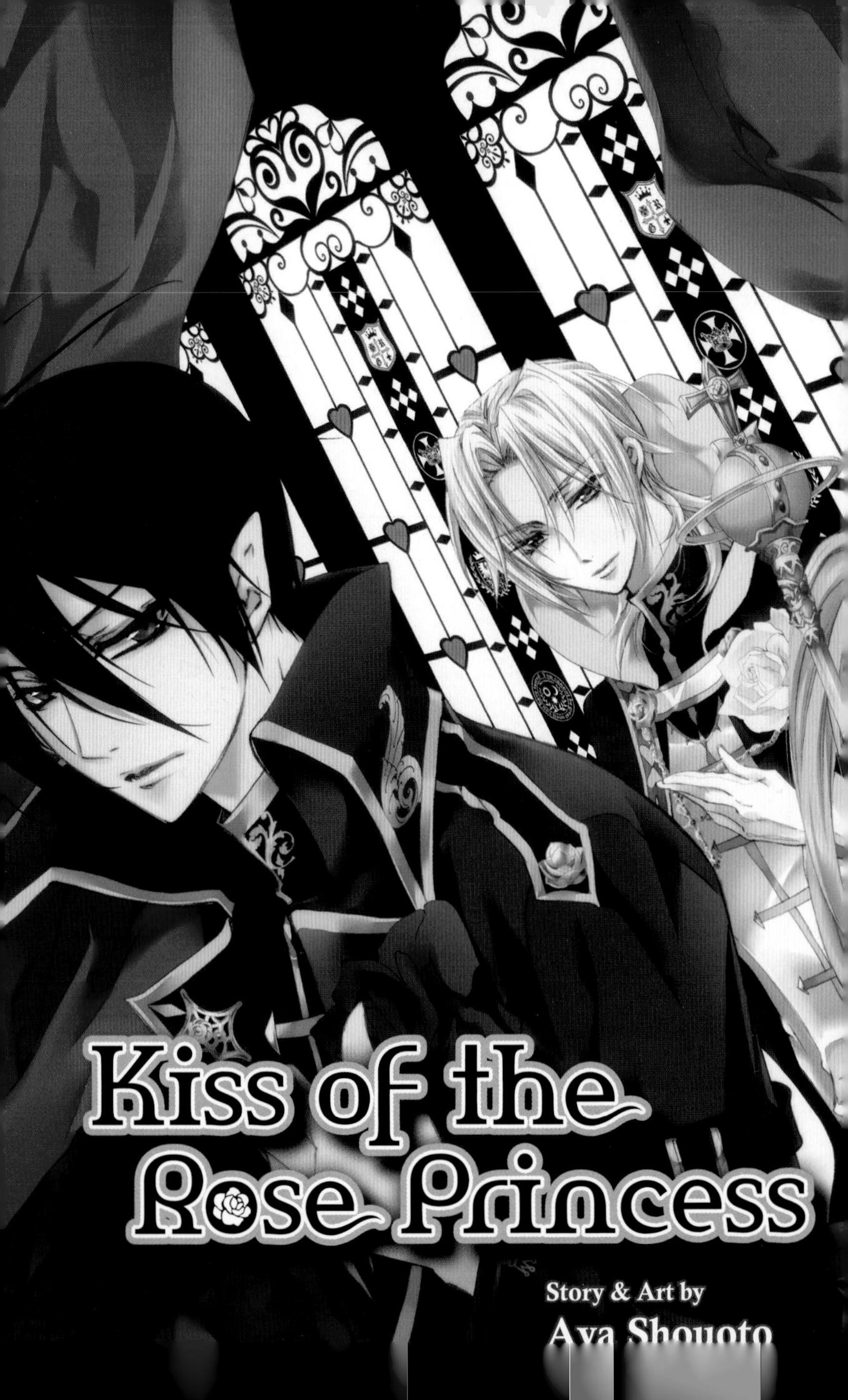
Kiss of the Rose Princess
Story & Art by
Aya Shouoto

Kiss of the Rose Princess

Contents

Characters

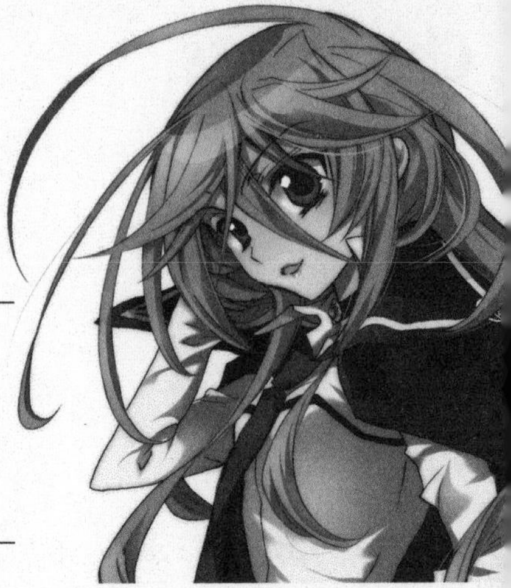

Rose Knights

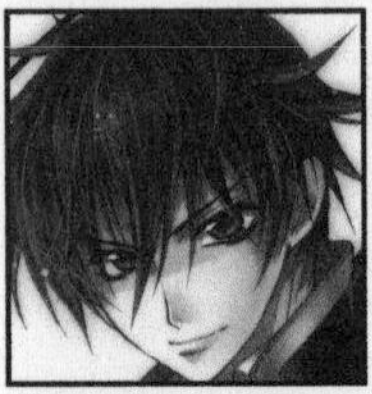

Kaede Higa (Red Rose)

Anise's classmate. He is an excellent athlete who often teases Anise.
Specialty: Offence

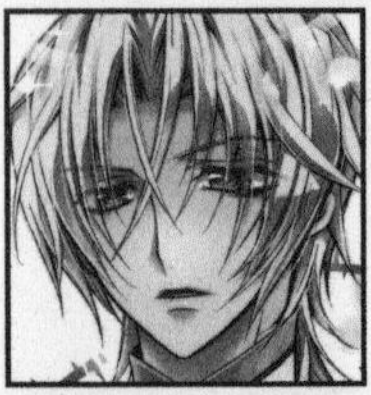

Mitsuru Tenjo (White Rose)

Third-year and Student Council President. He is revered by both male and female students. Super-rich.
Specialty: Healing, Defense

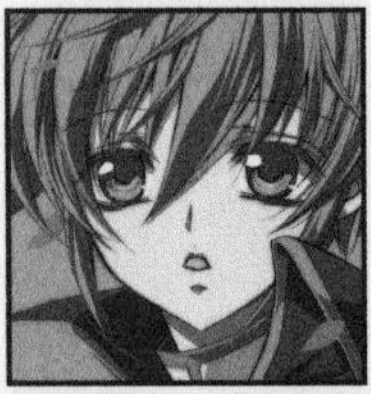

Seiran Asagi (Blue Rose)

First-year. This boy is cuter than any girl at school, and he doesn't know he's the school idol. He's well-versed in a wide range of topics.
Specialty: Alchemy, Science

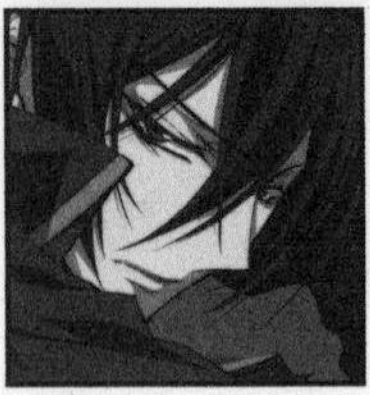

Mutsuki Kurama (Black Rose)

Second-year. There are many frightening rumors about this mysterious student. Apparently he lives in the basement of Tenjo's house.
Specialty: Discovery, Capture

Anise Yamamoto

First-year at Shobi Academy. She was an ordinary girl who became the Rose Princess after her choker was removed from her neck.

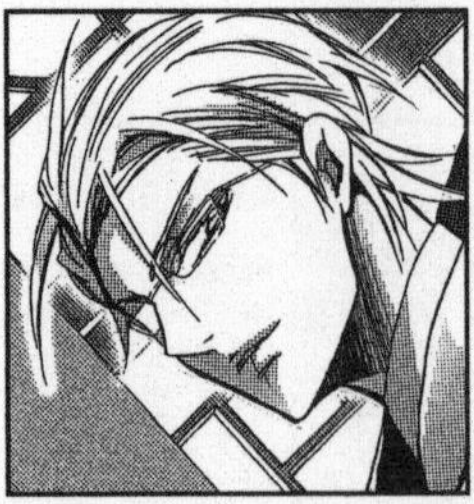

Schwarz Yamamoto

Anise's father. It seems he had a motive in putting the rose choker on Anise.

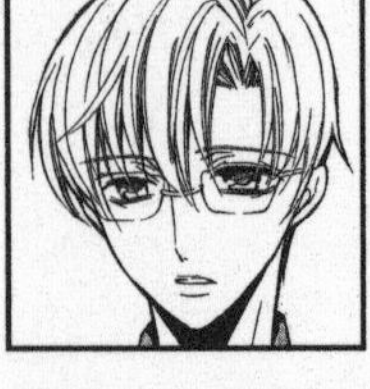

Itsushi Narumi (Classics Teacher)

He is the most knowledge-able about the "Sovereign," her "Rose Knights" and the "Rose Contract" that binds them...

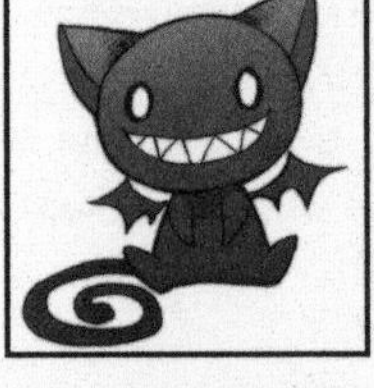

Ninufa (Guardian)

The guardian who has been protecting the cards since ancient times.

Characters

Fake Rose Princess

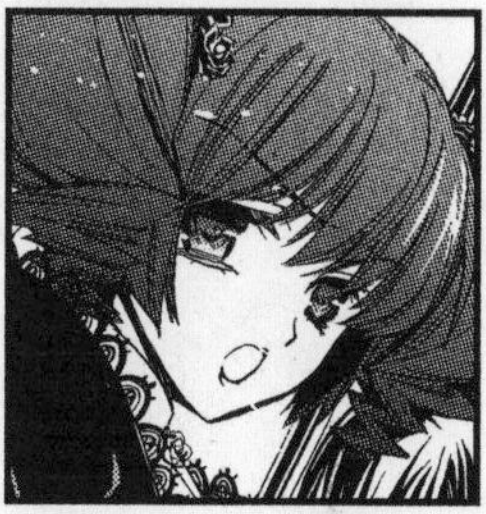

Ella

She has a strong obsession with Anise. She commands four Fake Rose Knights.

Fake Rose Knights

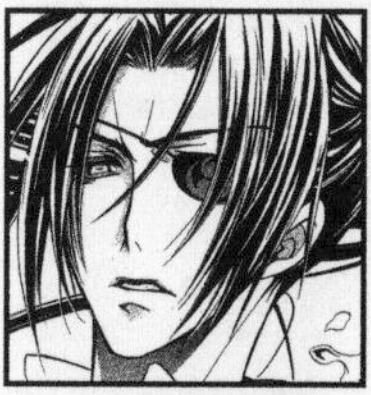

Shiden Fujinomiya (Purple Rose)

A loyal follower of Ella. He controls water to attack his enemies.

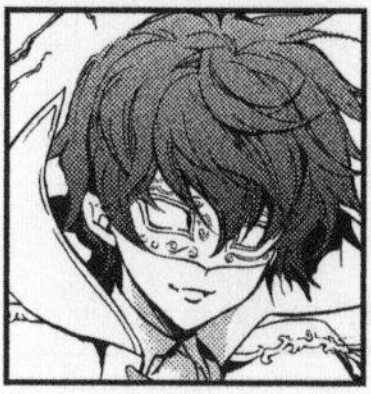

Yocto (Gray Rose)

Mutsuki's older brother. His dream is to reestablish Dark Stalkers in the world.

Rhodecia

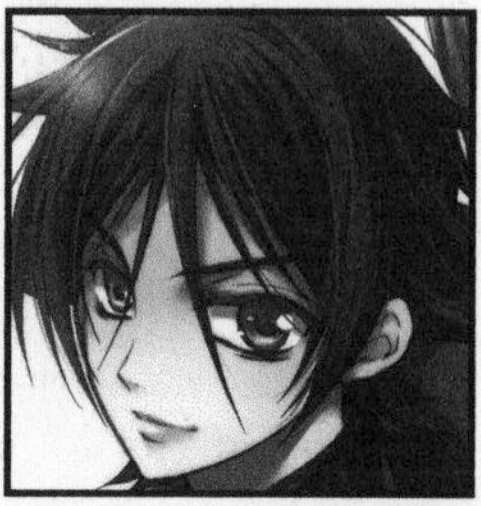

Idel Suzumura (Orange Rose)

An active and optimistic student at Shobi Academy. He can attack using sound waves.

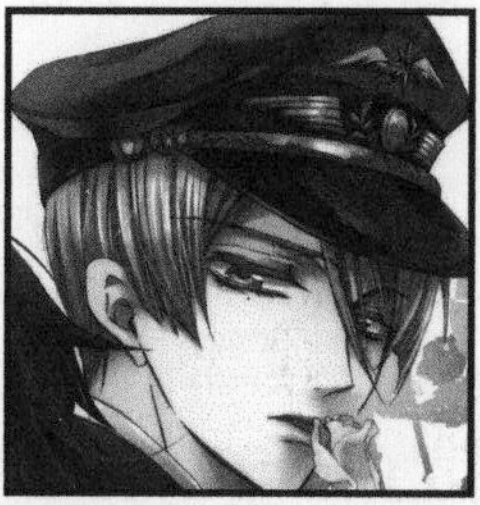

Yako Hasuzaki (Lime Rose)

A student at Shobi Academy. He uses the power of scent to hypnotize people.

Story Thus Far

The Gray Rose appears before Anise and Mutsuki. This Fake Rose Knight is Mutsuki's older brother, whom Mutsuki had killed in the past. When Anise learns about Mutsuki's tragic past, she decides to come up with a new Rose Contract for her Rose Knights. Meanwhile, Seiran heads out on his own to search for an Arcana Card, but he encounters the Fake Knight Shiden Fujinomiya. Seiran is no match for Shiden's awesome powers and is about to be killed when Anise protects him. Seiran experiences his first awakening, but...?!

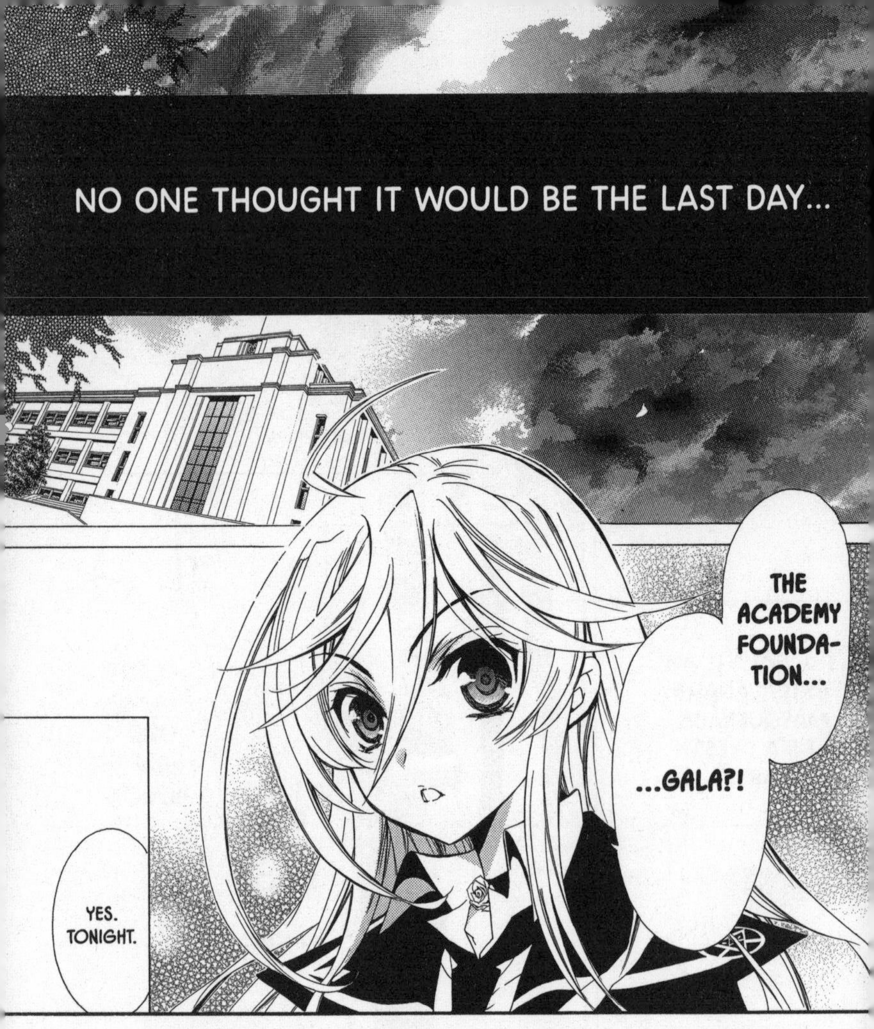
NO ONE THOUGHT IT WOULD BE THE LAST DAY...
THE ACADEMY FOUNDATION...
...GALA?!
YES. TONIGHT.

Rose Kiss Poem Corner

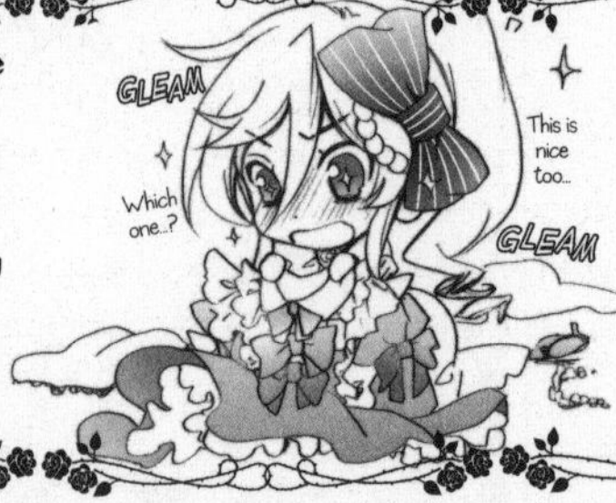
GLEAM
This is nice too...
Which one..?
GLEAM

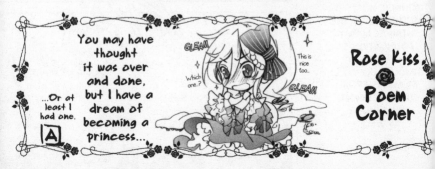

You may have thought it was over and done, but I have a dream of becoming a princess...

...Or at least I had one.

A

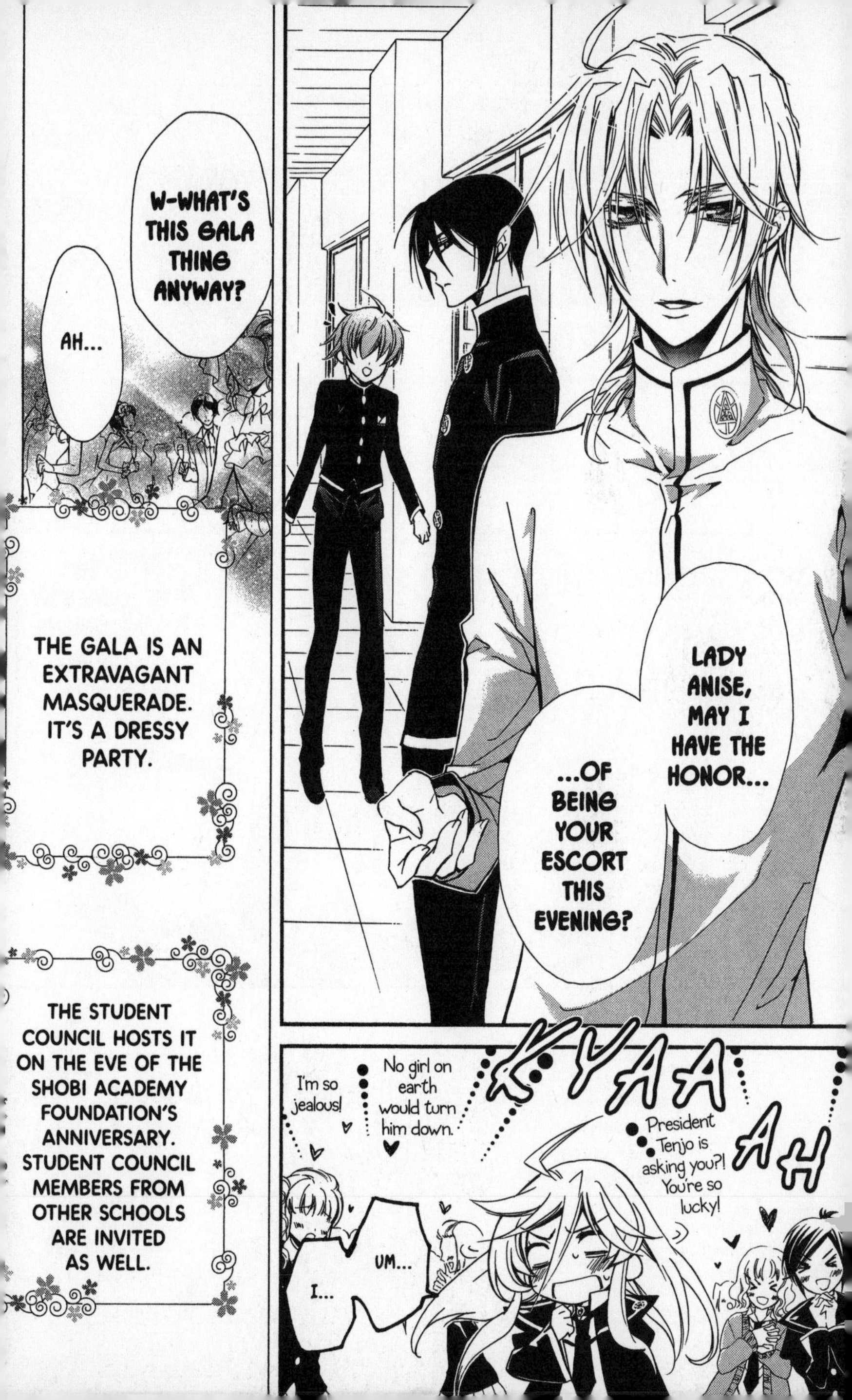
LADY ANISE, MAY I HAVE THE HONOR...
...OF BEING YOUR ESCORT THIS EVENING?
KYAAAH
President Tenjo is asking you?! You're so lucky!
No girl on earth would turn him down.
I'm so jealous!
UM...
I...
W-WHAT'S THIS GALA THING ANYWAY?
AH...
THE GALA IS AN EXTRAVAGANT MASQUERADE. IT'S A DRESSY PARTY.
THE STUDENT COUNCIL HOSTS IT ON THE EVE OF THE SHOBI ACADEMY FOUNDATION'S ANNIVERSARY. STUDENT COUNCIL MEMBERS FROM OTHER SCHOOLS ARE INVITED AS WELL.

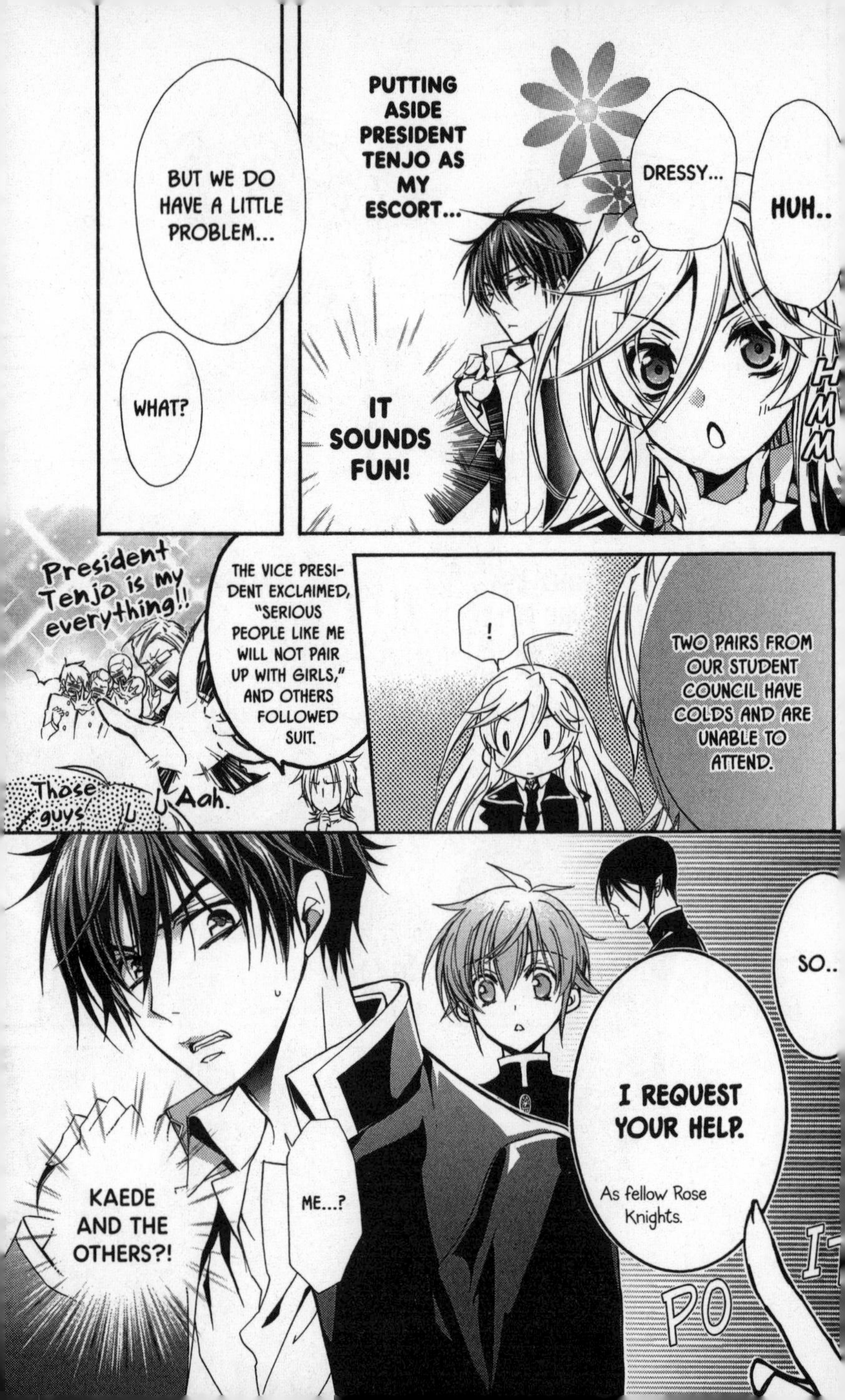
HUH..
DRESSY...
HMMM
PUTTING ASIDE PRESIDENT TENJO AS MY ESCORT...
IT SOUNDS FUN!
BUT WE DO HAVE A LITTLE PROBLEM...
WHAT?
TWO PAIRS FROM OUR STUDENT COUNCIL HAVE COLDS AND ARE UNABLE TO ATTEND.
!
THE VICE PRESIDENT EXCLAIMED, "SERIOUS PEOPLE LIKE ME WILL NOT PAIR UP WITH GIRLS," AND OTHERS FOLLOWED SUIT.
President Tenjo is my everything!!
Aah.
Those guys
SO..
I REQUEST YOUR HELP.
As fellow Rose Knights.
PO
ME...?
KAEDE AND THE OTHERS?!

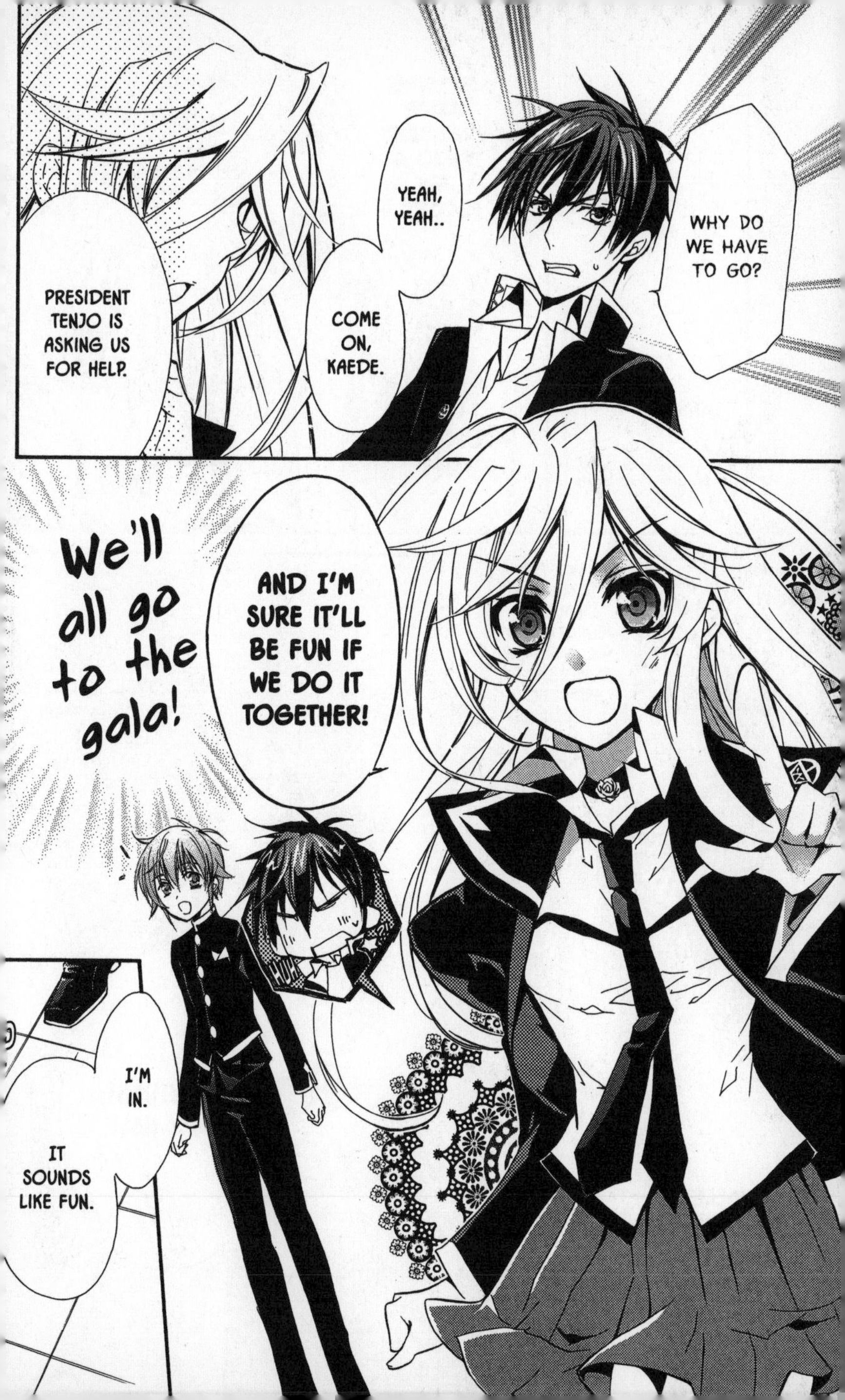
WHY DO WE HAVE TO GO?
YEAH, YEAH..
COME ON, KAEDE.
PRESIDENT TENJO IS ASKING US FOR HELP.
AND I'M SURE IT'LL BE FUN IF WE DO IT TOGETHER!
We'll all go to the gala!
I'M IN.
IT SOUNDS LIKE FUN.

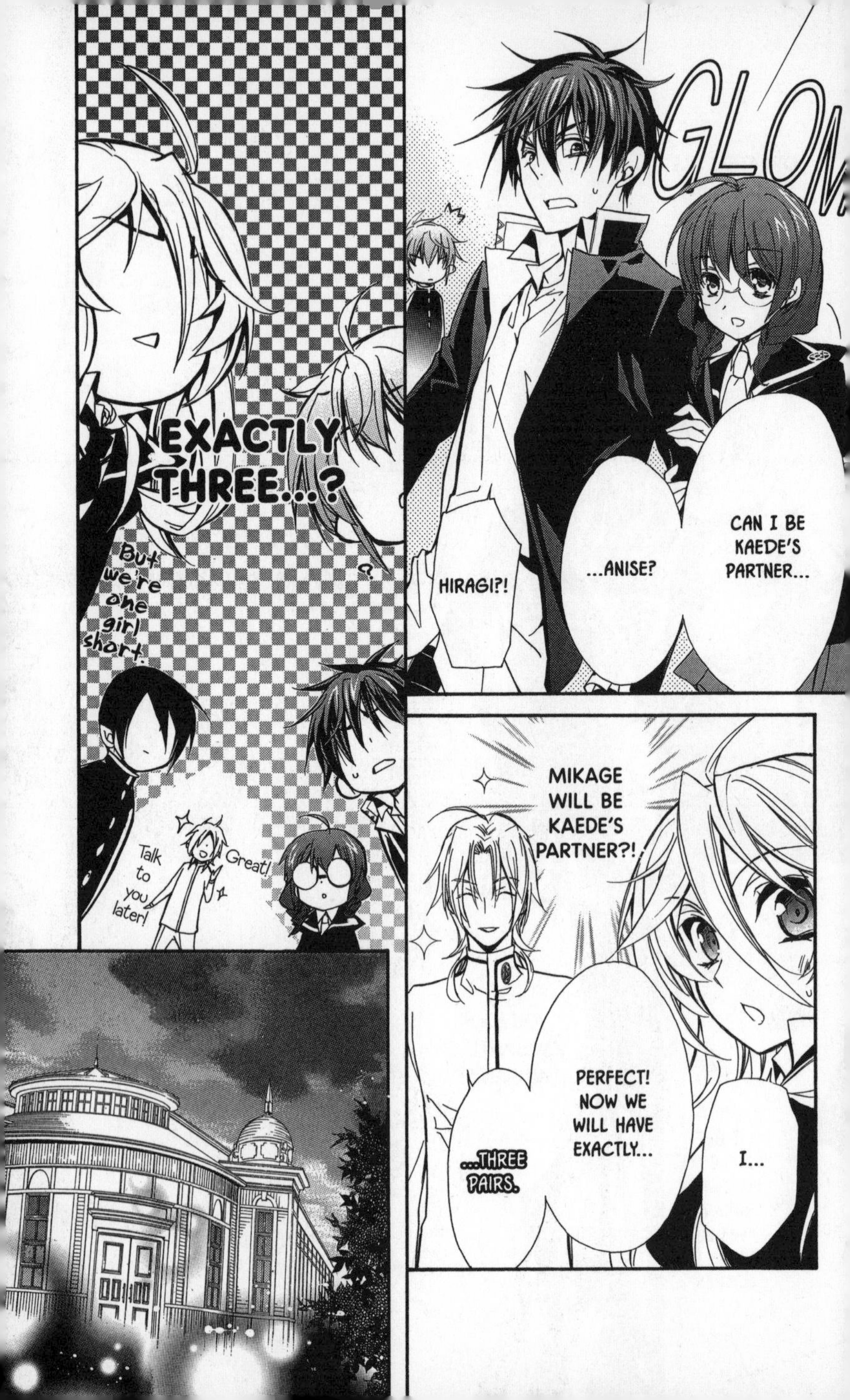
GLOM
CAN I BE KAEDE'S PARTNER...
...ANISE?
HIRAGI?!
MIKAGE WILL BE KAEDE'S PARTNER?!
I...
PERFECT! NOW WE WILL HAVE EXACTLY...
...THREE PAIRS.
EXACTLY THREE...?
?
But we're one girl short.
Great!
Talk to you later!

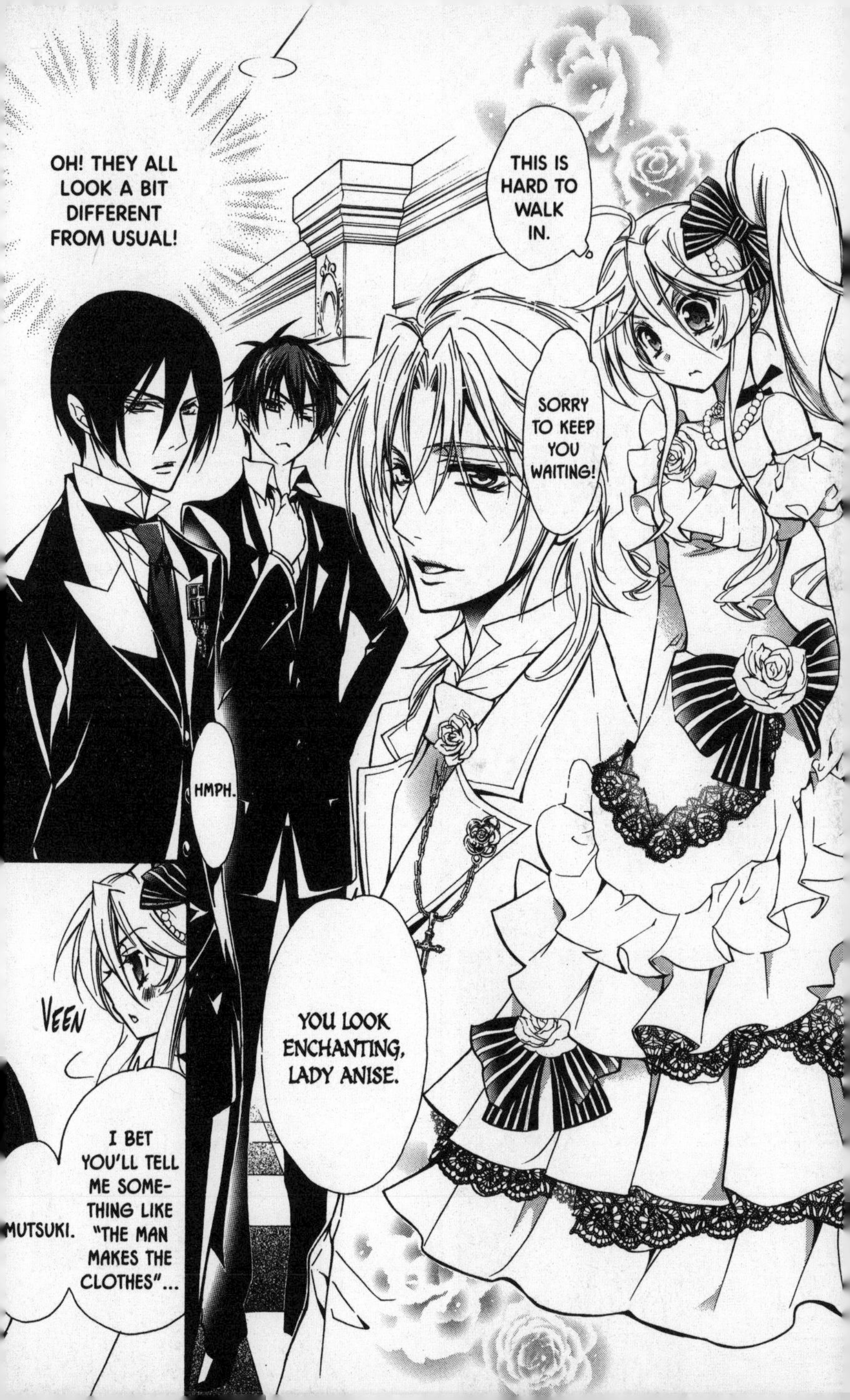
THIS IS HARD TO WALK IN.
SORRY TO KEEP YOU WAITING!
OH! THEY ALL LOOK A BIT DIFFERENT FROM USUAL!
HMPH.
YOU LOOK ENCHANTING, LADY ANISE.
VEEN
I BET YOU'LL TELL ME SOME-THING LIKE "THE MAN MAKES THE CLOTHES"...
MUTSUKI.

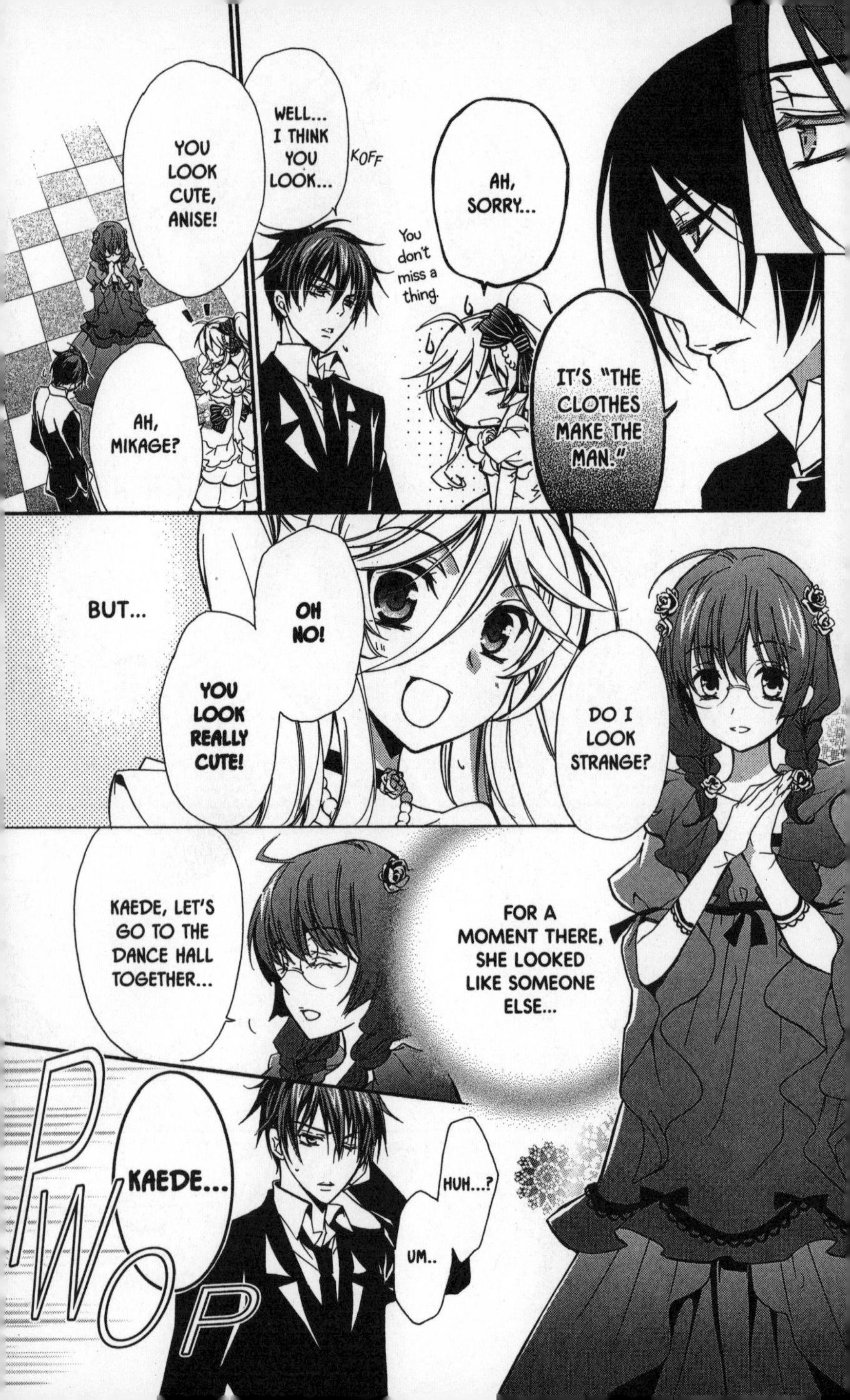
IT'S "THE CLOTHES MAKE THE MAN."
AH, SORRY...
You don't miss a thing.
WELL... I THINK YOU LOOK...
KOFF
YOU LOOK CUTE, ANISE!
AH, MIKAGE?
DO I LOOK STRANGE?
OH NO!
YOU LOOK REALLY CUTE!
BUT...
FOR A MOMENT THERE, SHE LOOKED LIKE SOMEONE ELSE...
KAEDE, LET'S GO TO THE DANCE HALL TOGETHER...
HUH...?
UM..
KAEDE...
PWOP

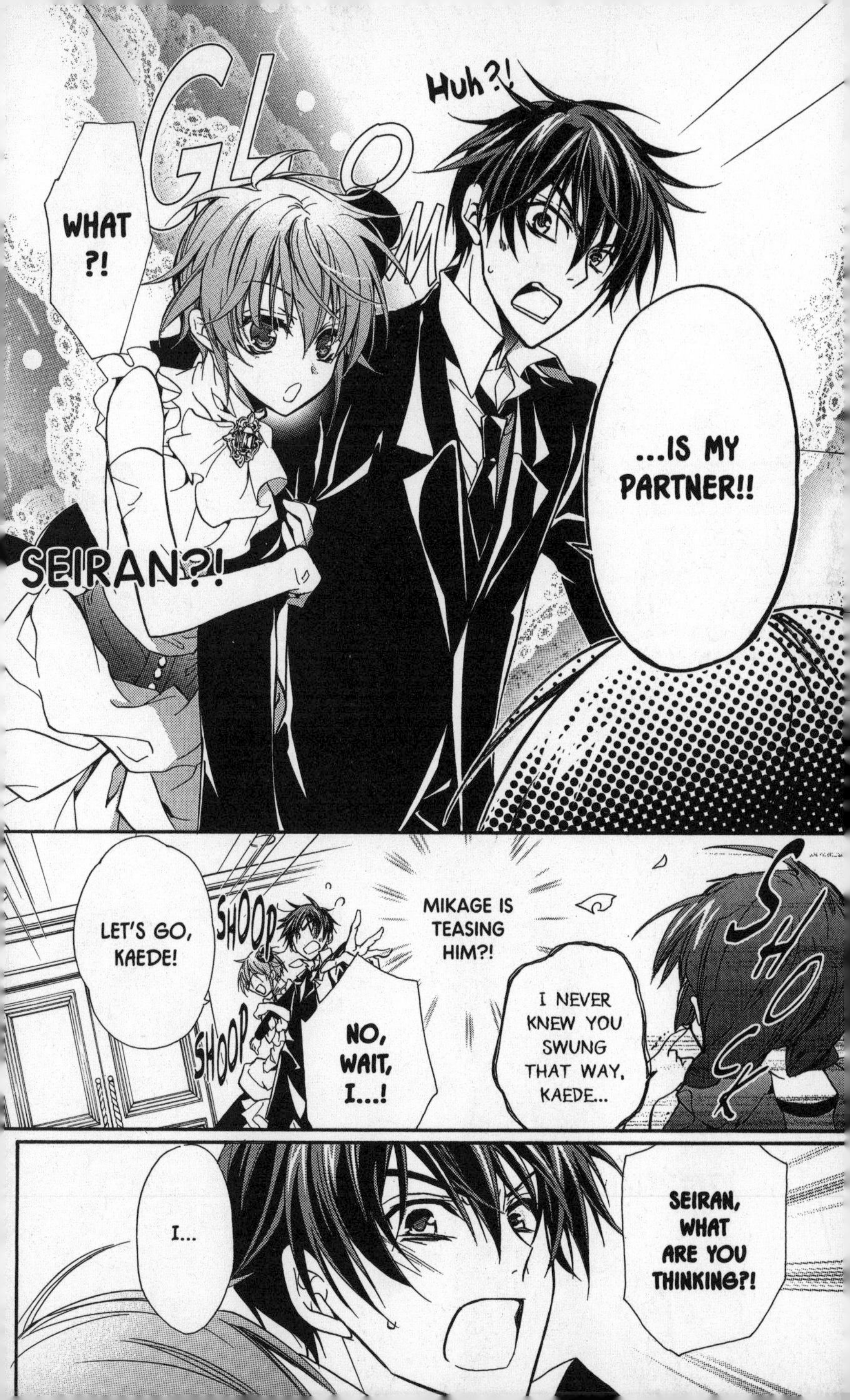
...IS MY PARTNER!!
Huh?!
GLOOM
WHAT ?!
SEIRAN?!
SHOCK
I NEVER KNEW YOU SWUNG THAT WAY, KAEDE...
MIKAGE IS TEASING HIM?!
NO, WAIT, I...!
SHOOP
SHOOP
LET'S GO, KAEDE!
SEIRAN, WHAT ARE YOU THINKING?!
I...

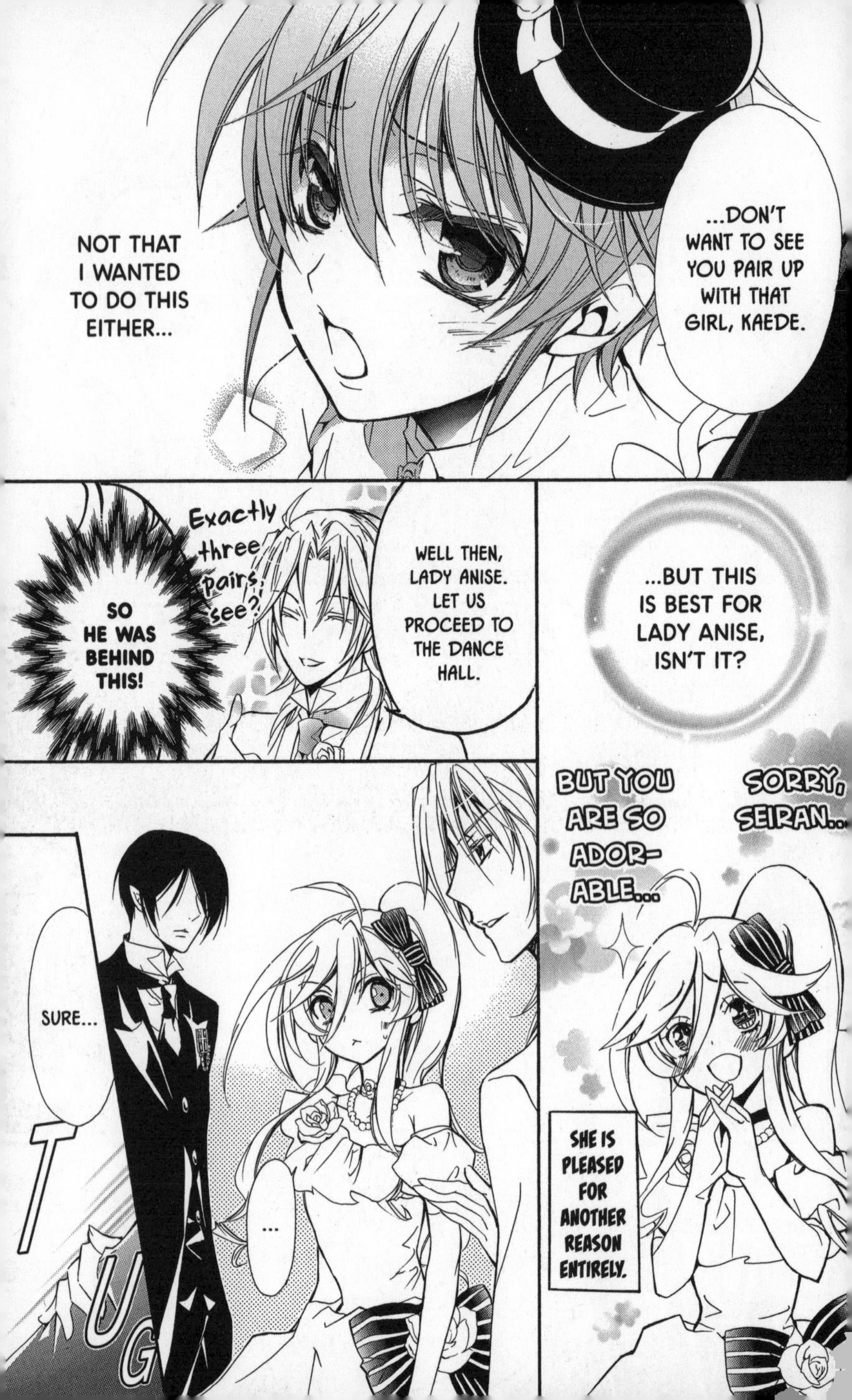
...DON'T WANT TO SEE YOU PAIR UP WITH THAT GIRL, KAEDE.
NOT THAT I WANTED TO DO THIS EITHER...
...BUT THIS IS BEST FOR LADY ANISE, ISN'T IT?
WELL THEN, LADY ANISE. LET US PROCEED TO THE DANCE HALL.
Exactly three pairs, see?
SO HE WAS BEHIND THIS!
SORRY, SEIRAN...
BUT YOU ARE SO ADOR-ABLE...
SHE IS PLEASED FOR ANOTHER REASON ENTIRELY.
...
SURE...
TUG

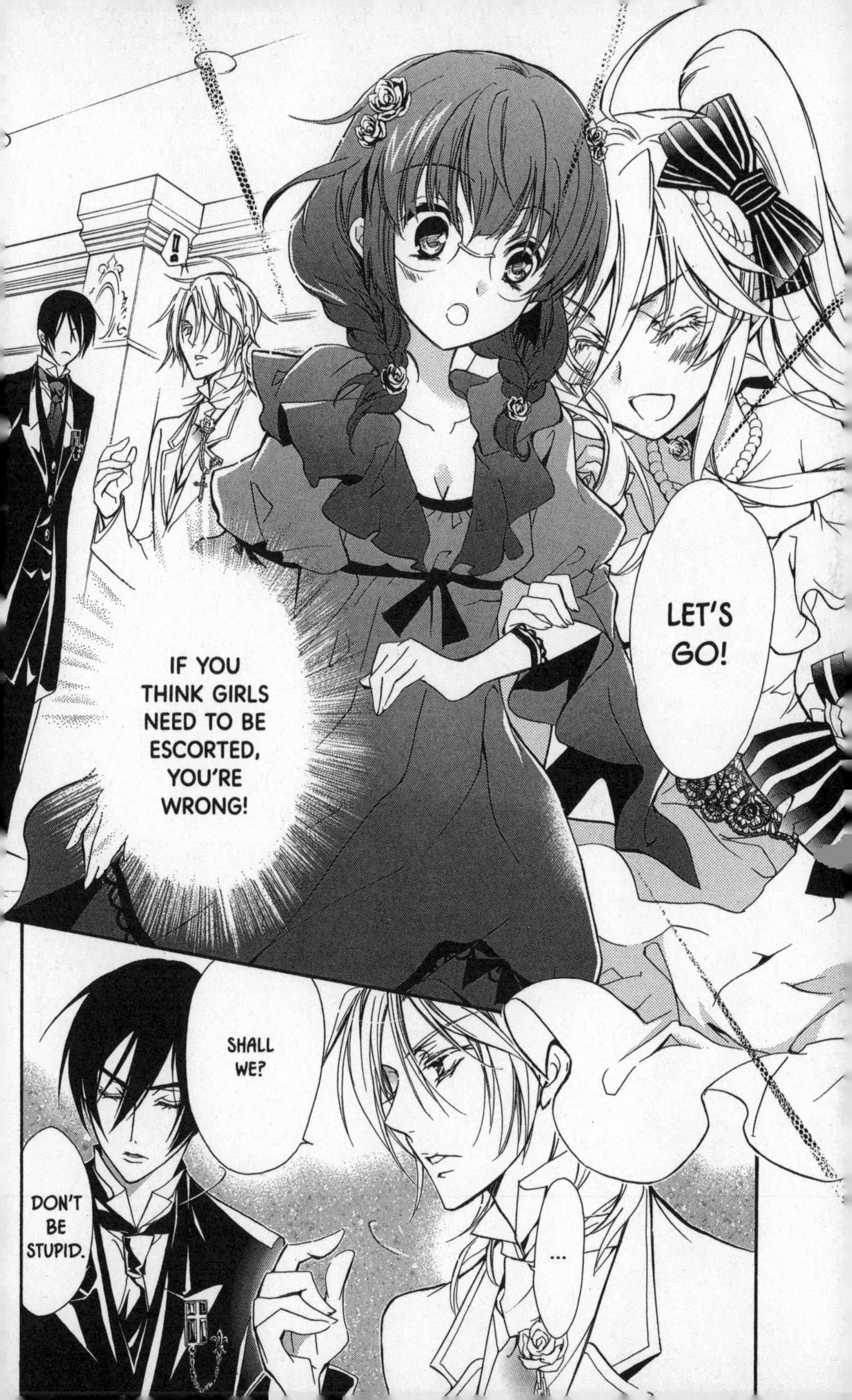
LET'S GO!
!
IF YOU THINK GIRLS NEED TO BE ESCORTED, YOU'RE WRONG!
SHALL WE?
DON'T BE STUPID.
...

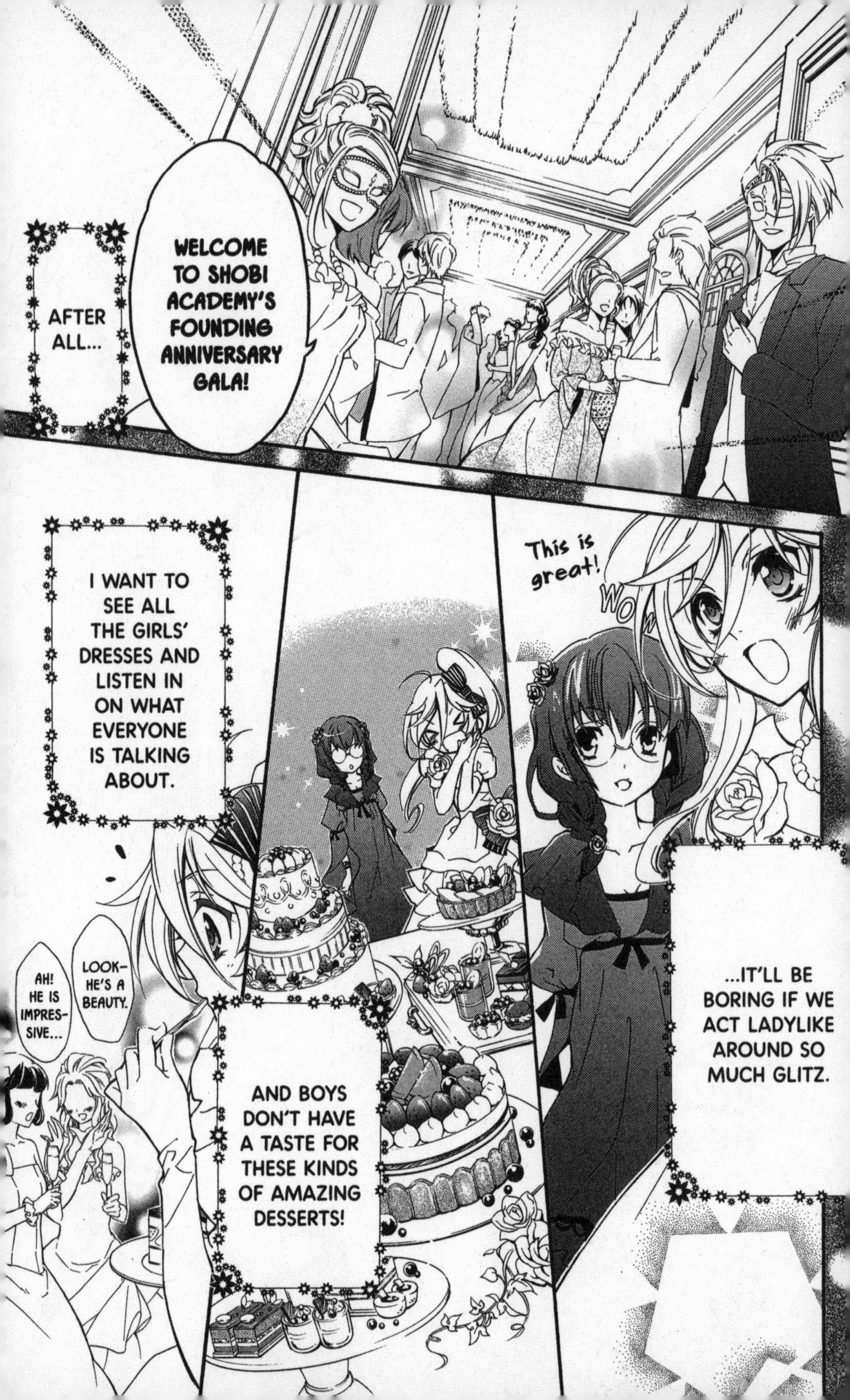
WELCOME TO SHOBI ACADEMY'S FOUNDING ANNIVERSARY GALA!
AFTER ALL...
This is great!
WOW
...IT'LL BE BORING IF WE ACT LADYLIKE AROUND SO MUCH GLITZ.
I WANT TO SEE ALL THE GIRLS' DRESSES AND LISTEN IN ON WHAT EVERYONE IS TALKING ABOUT.
LOOK— HE'S A BEAUTY.
AH! HE IS IMPRESSIVE...
AND BOYS DON'T HAVE A TASTE FOR THESE KINDS OF AMAZING DESSERTS!

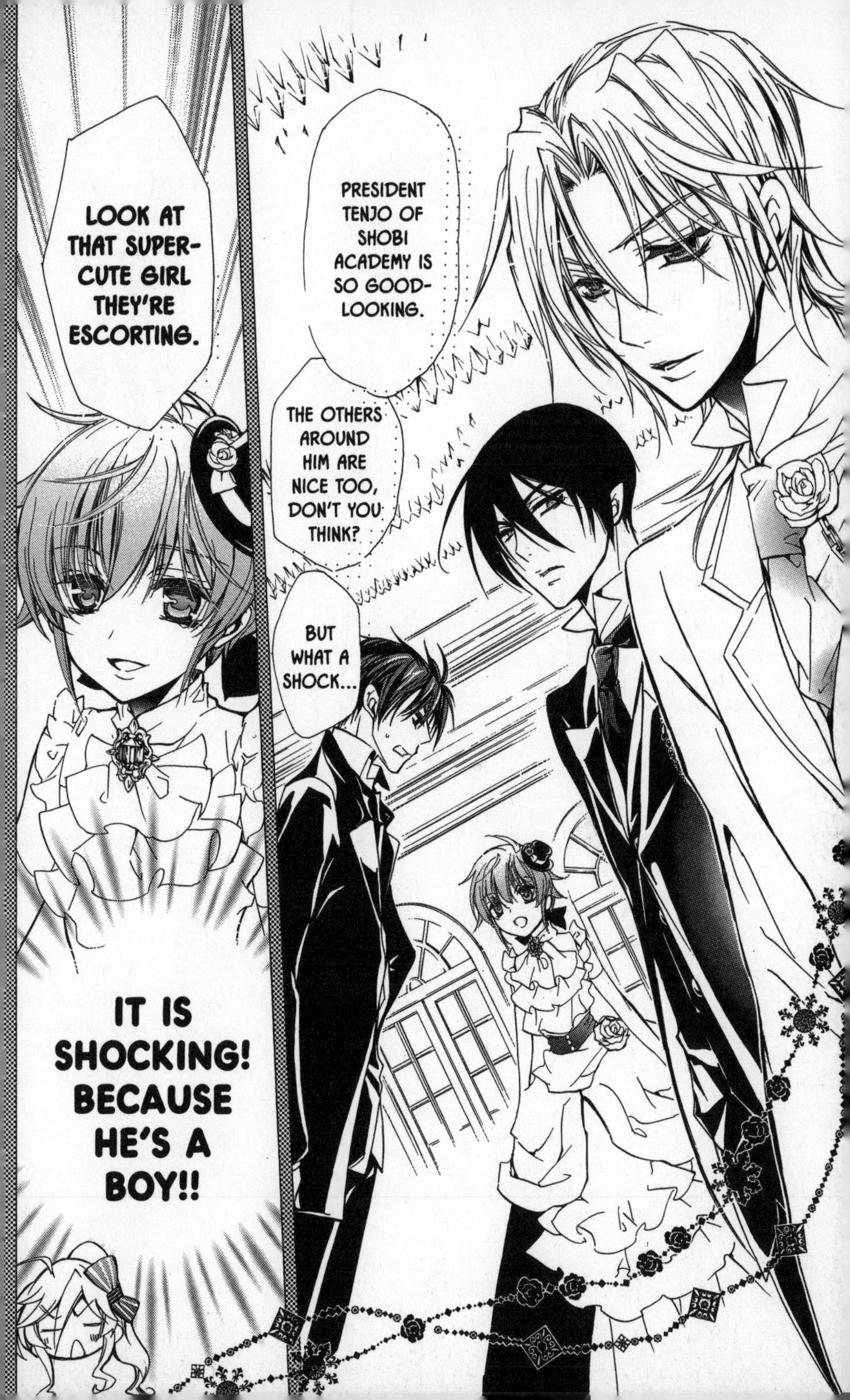
PRESIDENT TENJO OF SHOBI ACADEMY IS SO GOOD-LOOKING.
THE OTHERS AROUND HIM ARE NICE TOO, DON'T YOU THINK?
BUT WHAT A SHOCK...
LOOK AT THAT SUPER-CUTE GIRL THEY'RE ESCORTING.
IT IS SHOCKING! BECAUSE HE'S A BOY!!

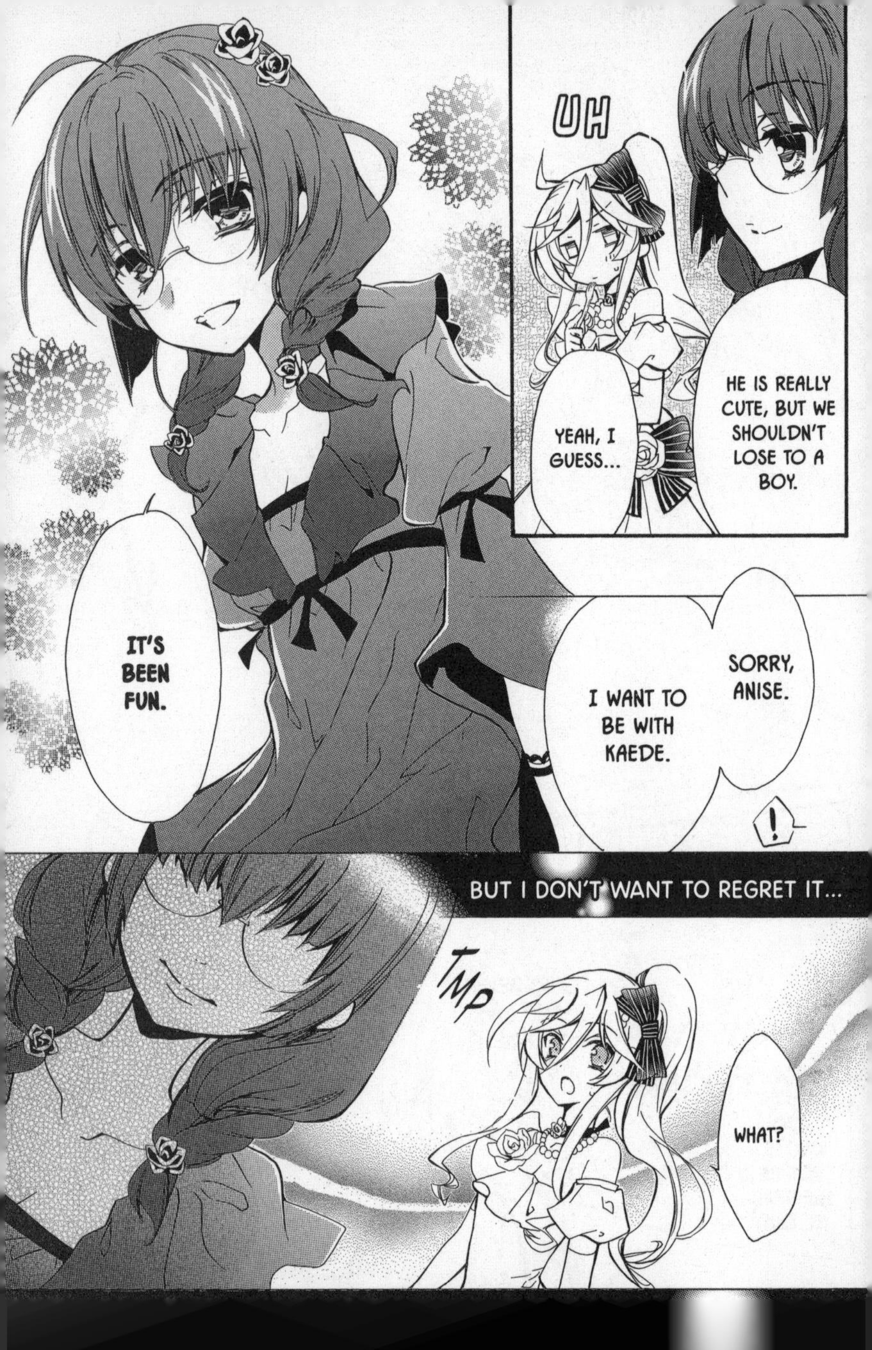
UH
HE IS REALLY CUTE, BUT WE SHOULDN'T LOSE TO A BOY.
YEAH, I GUESS...
SORRY, ANISE.
I WANT TO BE WITH KAEDE.
!
IT'S BEEN FUN.
BUT I DON'T WANT TO REGRET IT...
TMP
WHAT?

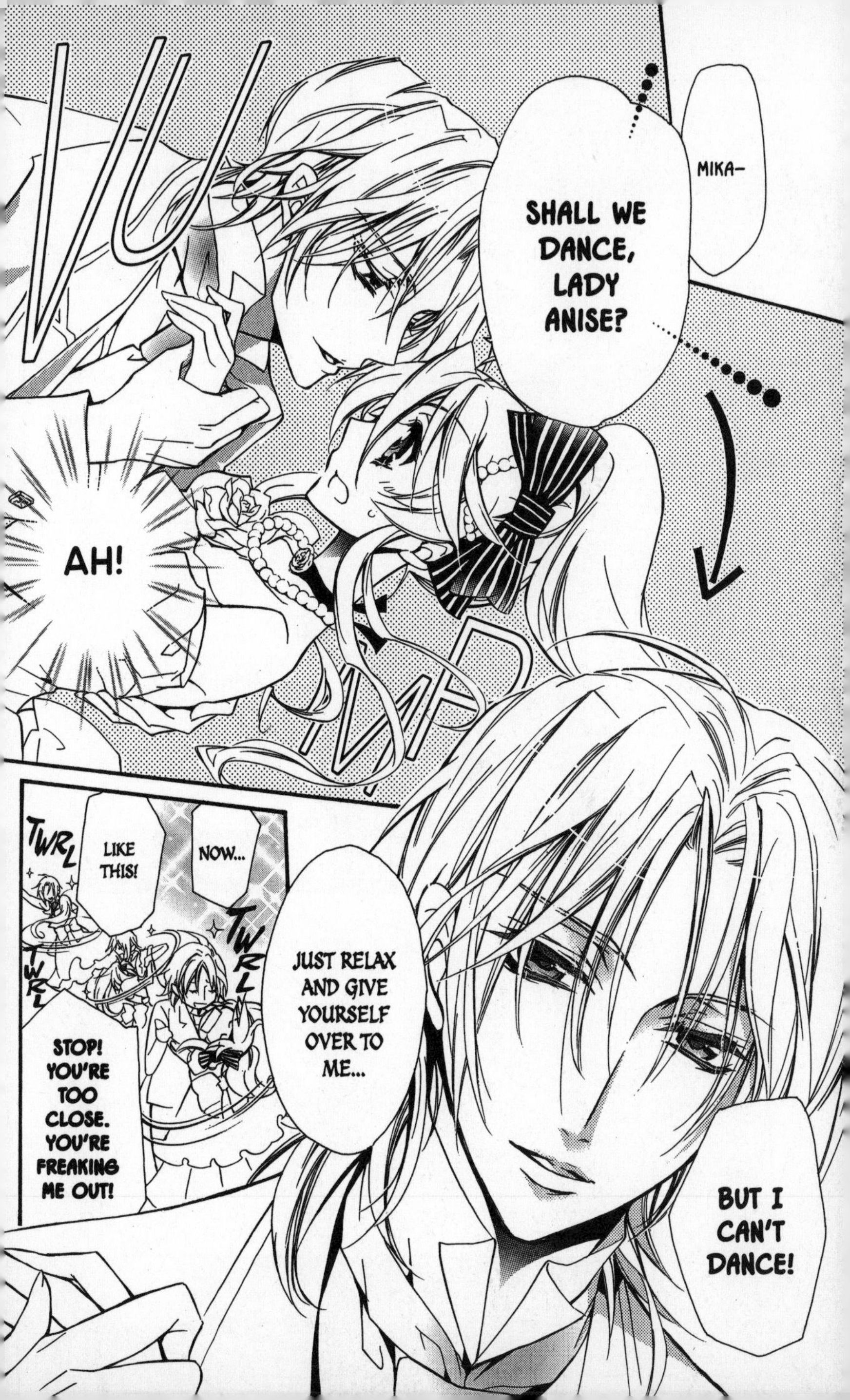
MIKA—
SHALL WE DANCE, LADY ANISE?
AH!
BUT I CAN'T DANCE!
JUST RELAX AND GIVE YOURSELF OVER TO ME...
NOW...
LIKE THIS!
TWRL
TWRL
TWRL
STOP! YOU'RE TOO CLOSE. YOU'RE FREAKING ME OUT!

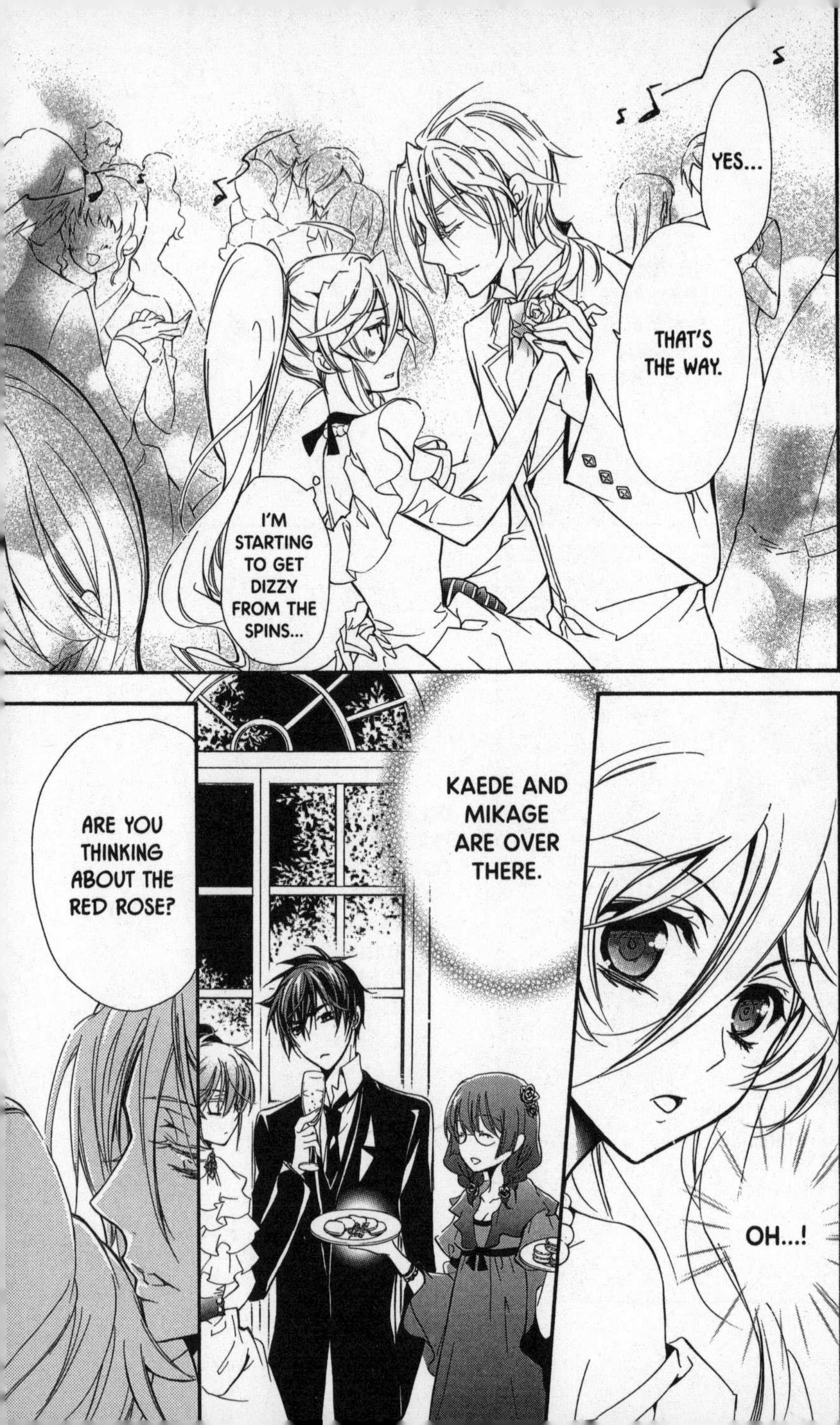
YES...
THAT'S THE WAY.
I'M STARTING TO GET DIZZY FROM THE SPINS...
OH...!
KAEDE AND MIKAGE ARE OVER THERE.
ARE YOU THINKING ABOUT THE RED ROSE?

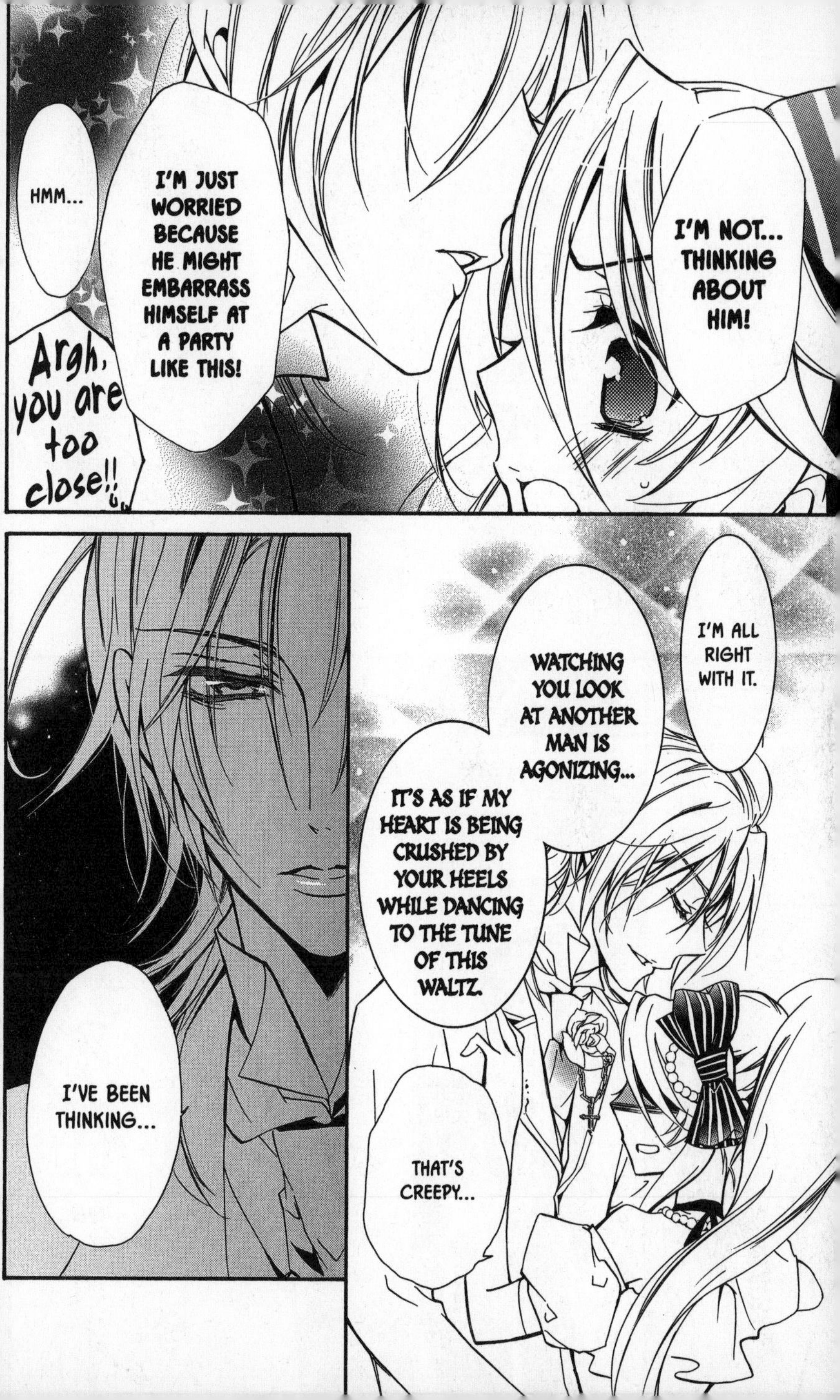
I'M NOT... THINKING ABOUT HIM!
I'M JUST WORRIED BECAUSE HE MIGHT EMBARRASS HIMSELF AT A PARTY LIKE THIS!
HMM...
Argh, you are too close!!
I'M ALL RIGHT WITH IT.
WATCHING YOU LOOK AT ANOTHER MAN IS AGONIZING...
IT'S AS IF MY HEART IS BEING CRUSHED BY YOUR HEELS WHILE DANCING TO THE TUNE OF THIS WALTZ.
THAT'S CREEPY...
I'VE BEEN THINKING...

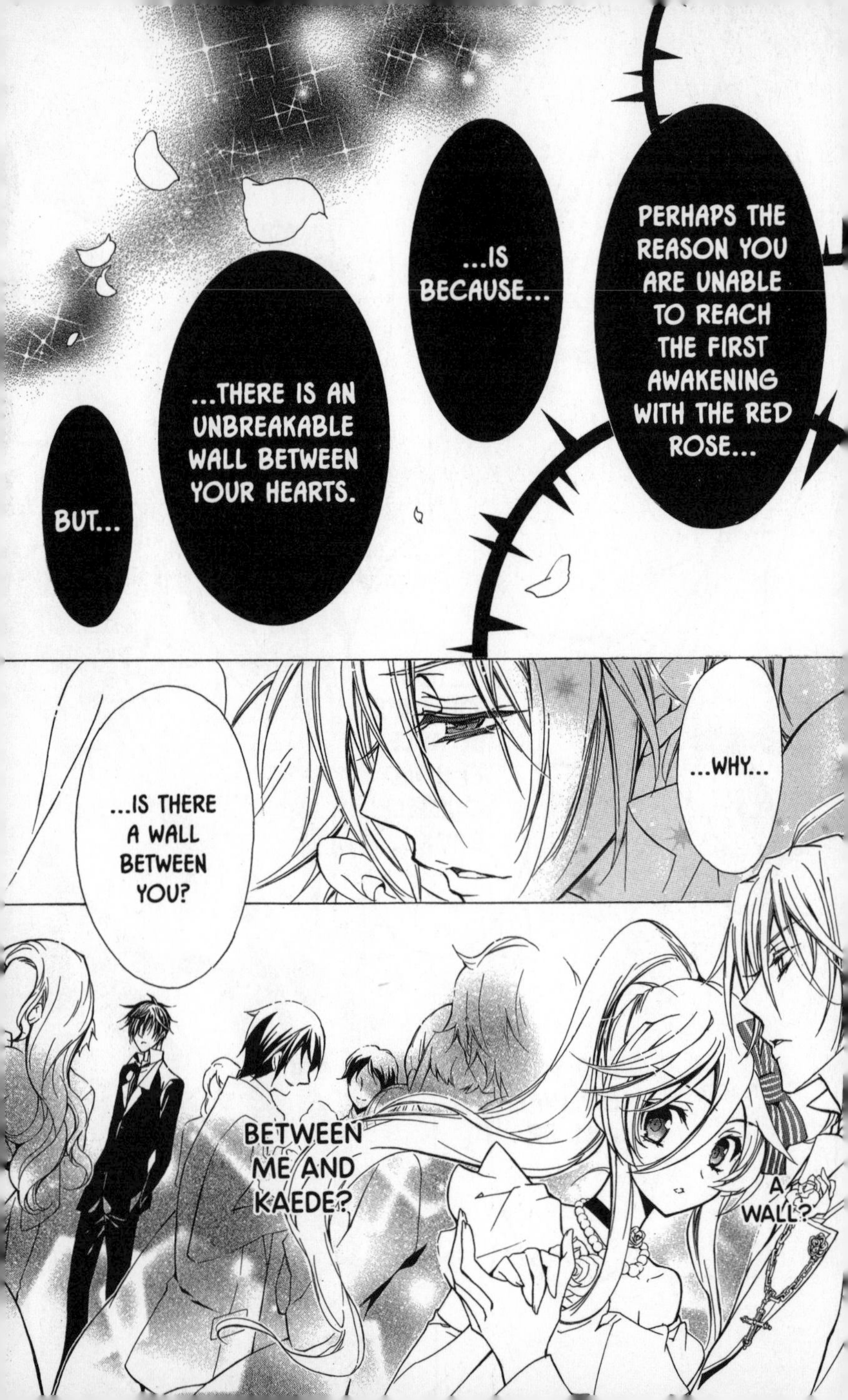
PERHAPS THE REASON YOU ARE UNABLE TO REACH THE FIRST AWAKENING WITH THE RED ROSE...
...IS BECAUSE...
...THERE IS AN UNBREAKABLE WALL BETWEEN YOUR HEARTS.
BUT...
...WHY...
...IS THERE A WALL BETWEEN YOU?
A WALL?
BETWEEN ME AND KAEDE?

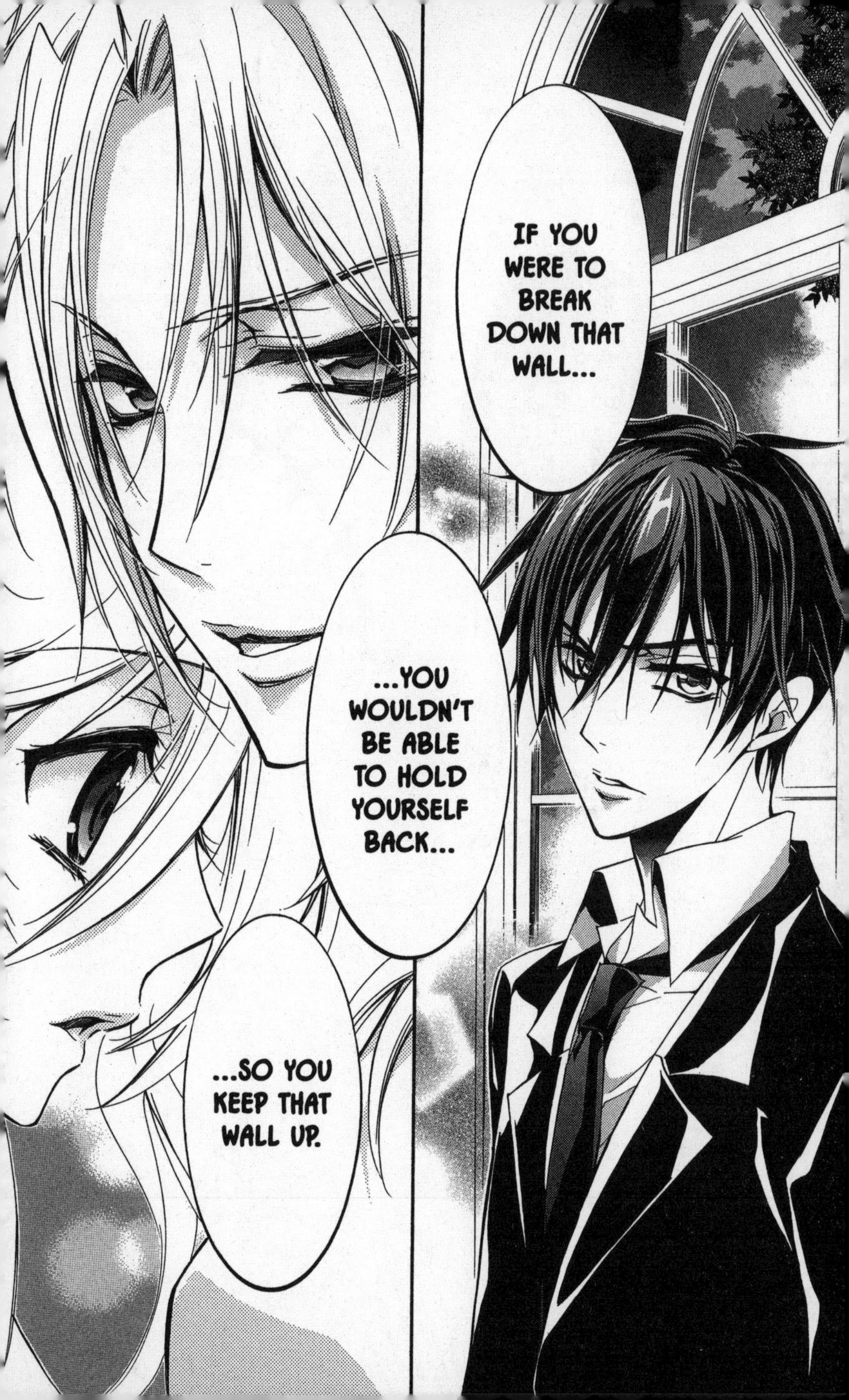
IF YOU WERE TO BREAK DOWN THAT WALL...
...YOU WOULDN'T BE ABLE TO HOLD YOURSELF BACK...
...SO YOU KEEP THAT WALL UP.

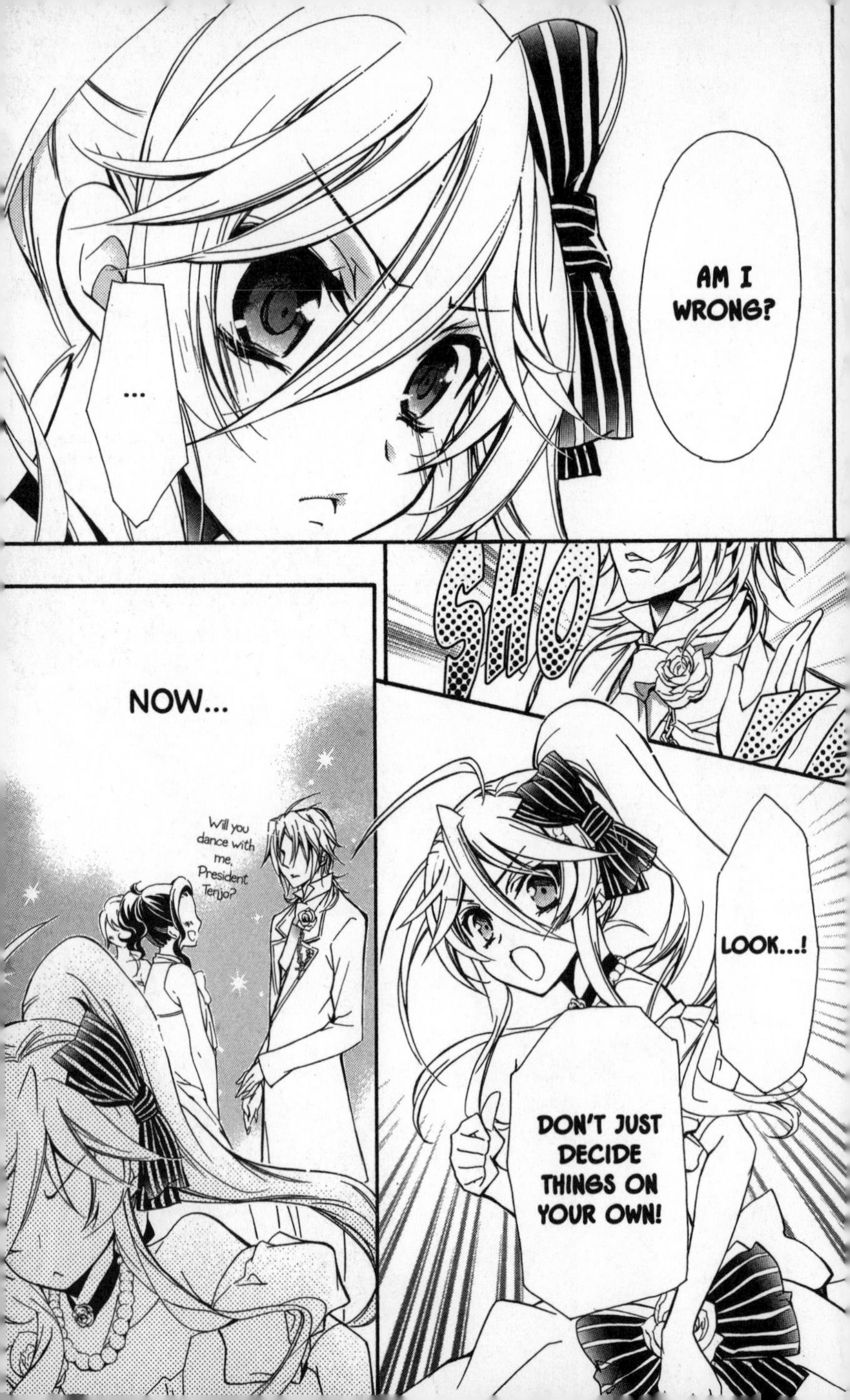
AM I WRONG?
...
SHO
LOOK...!
DON'T JUST DECIDE THINGS ON YOUR OWN!
NOW...
Will you dance with me, President Tenjo?

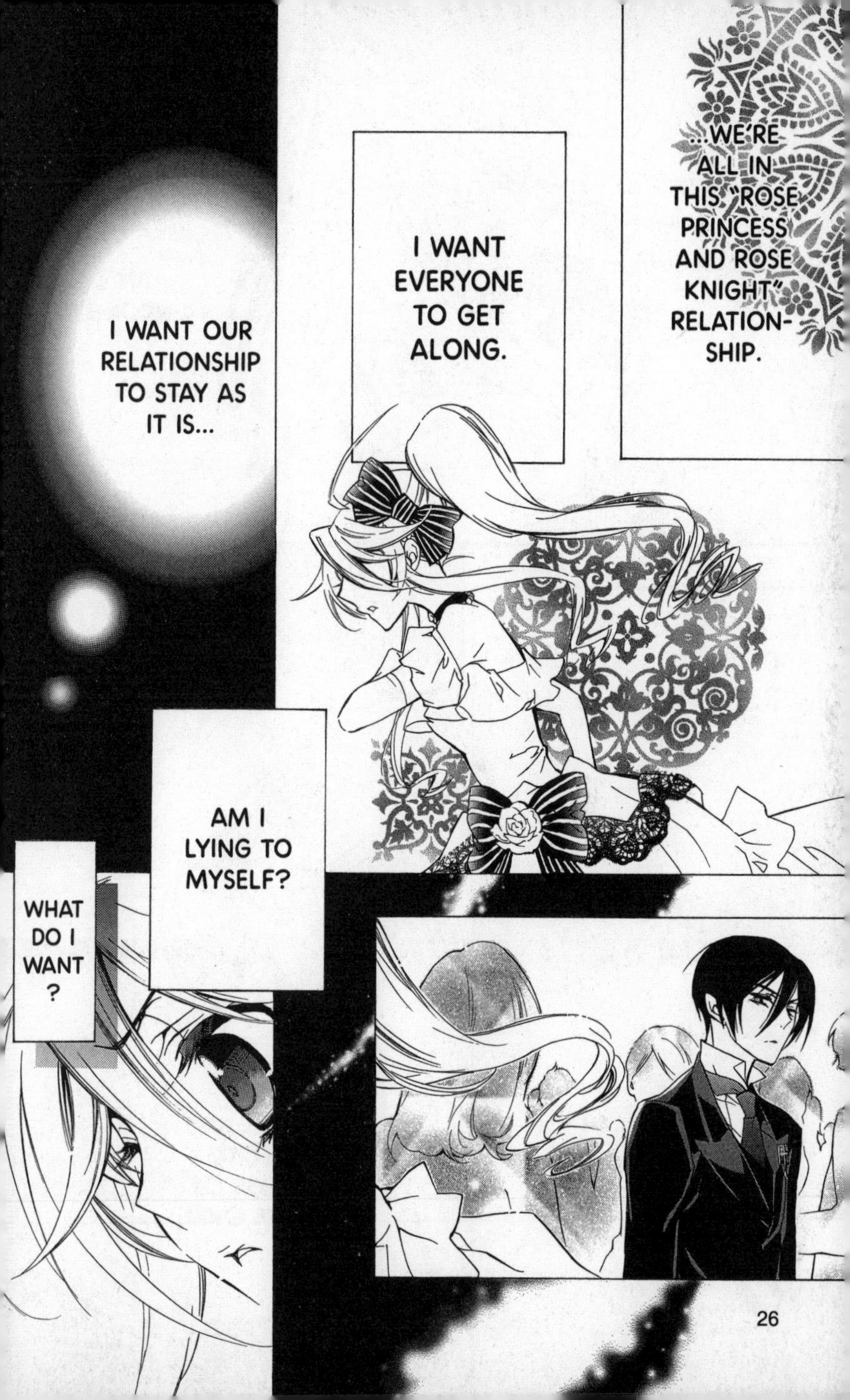
...WE'RE ALL IN THIS "ROSE PRINCESS AND ROSE KNIGHT" RELATION-SHIP.
I WANT EVERYONE TO GET ALONG.
I WANT OUR RELATIONSHIP TO STAY AS IT IS...
AM I LYING TO MYSELF?
WHAT DO I WANT?

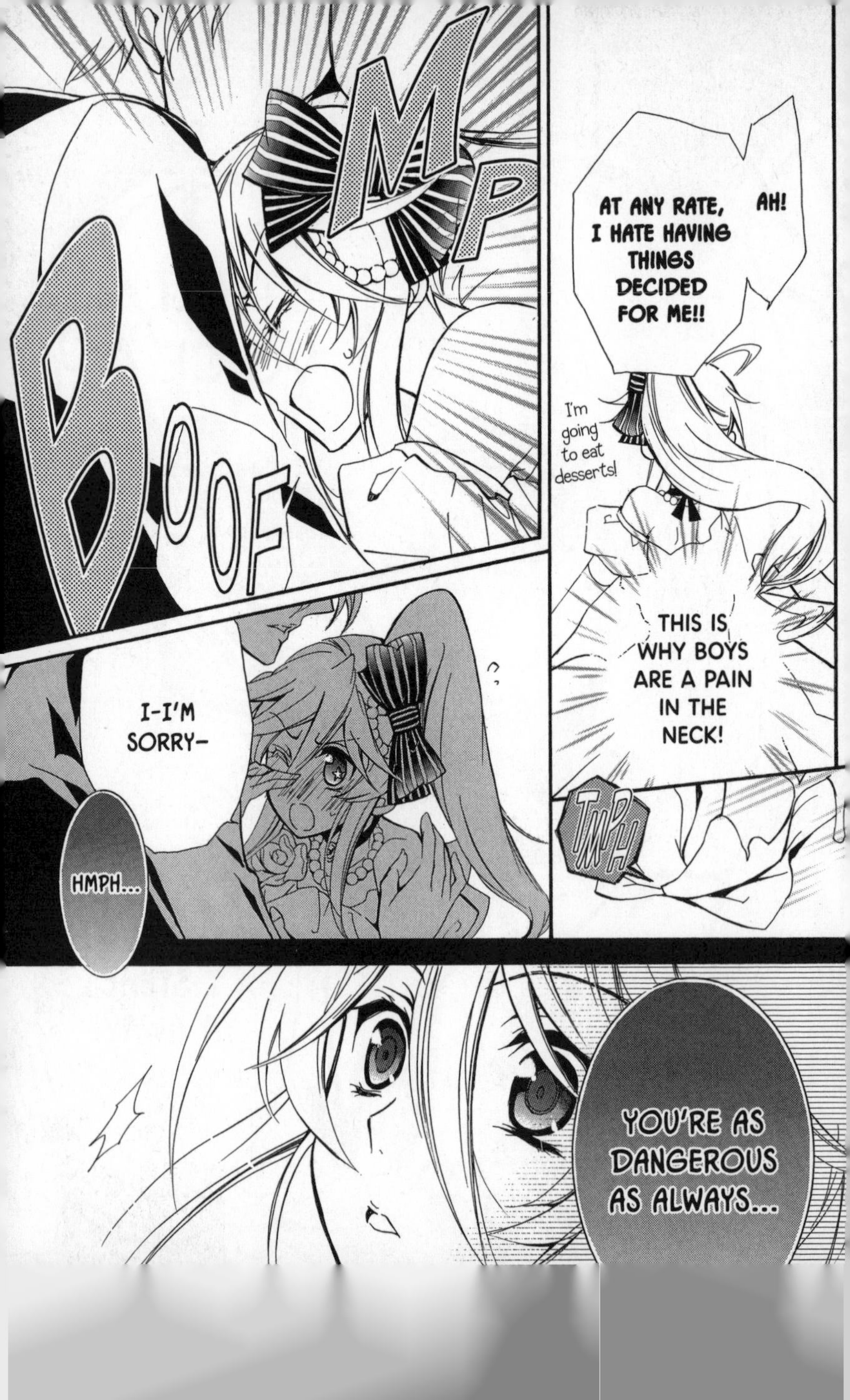
AH!
AT ANY RATE, I HATE HAVING THINGS DECIDED FOR ME!!
I'm going to eat desserts!
THIS IS WHY BOYS ARE A PAIN IN THE NECK!
TMPH
MP
BOOF
I-I'M SORRY-
HMPH...
YOU'RE AS DANGEROUS AS ALWAYS...

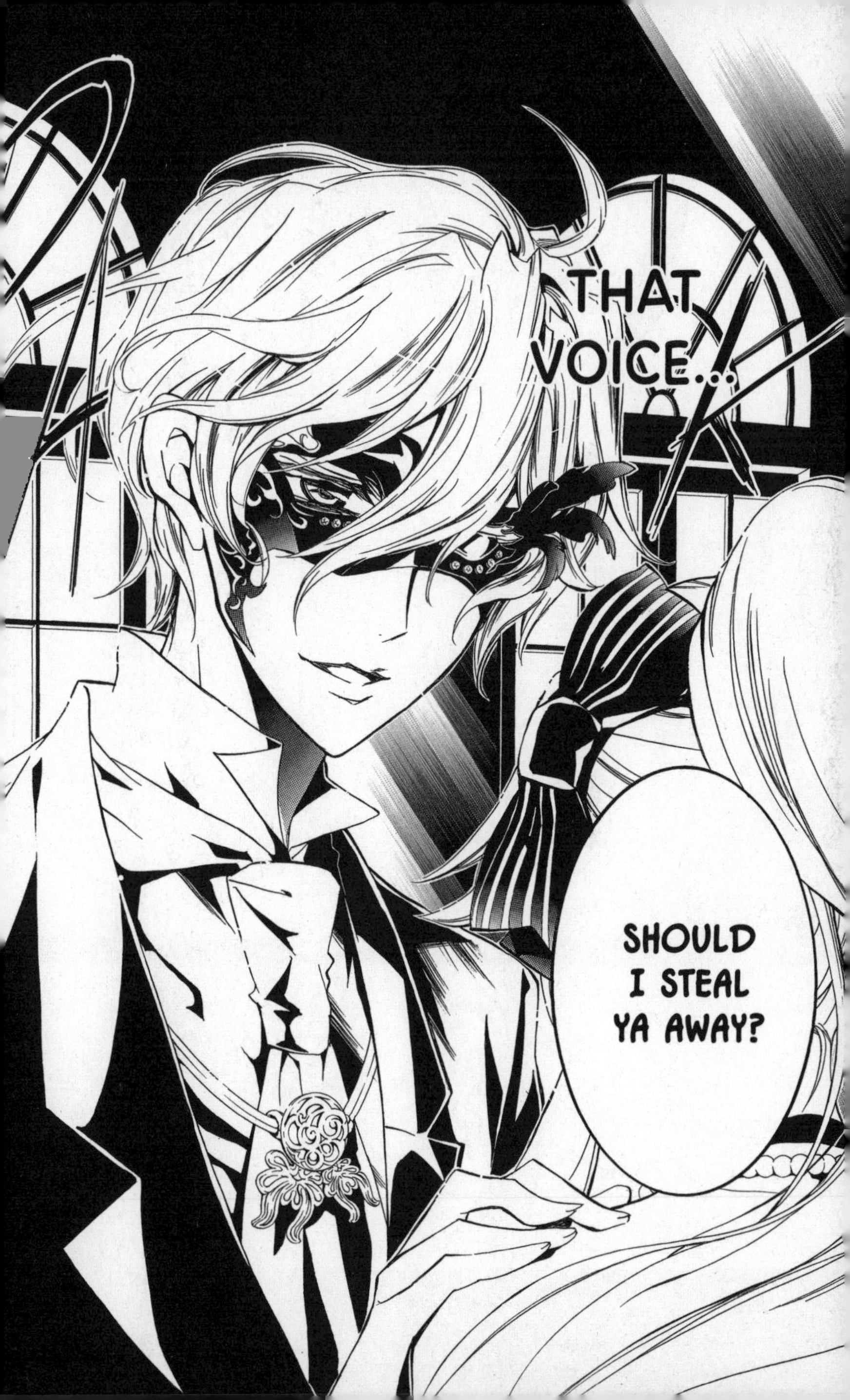
THAT VOICE...
SHOULD I STEAL YA AWAY?

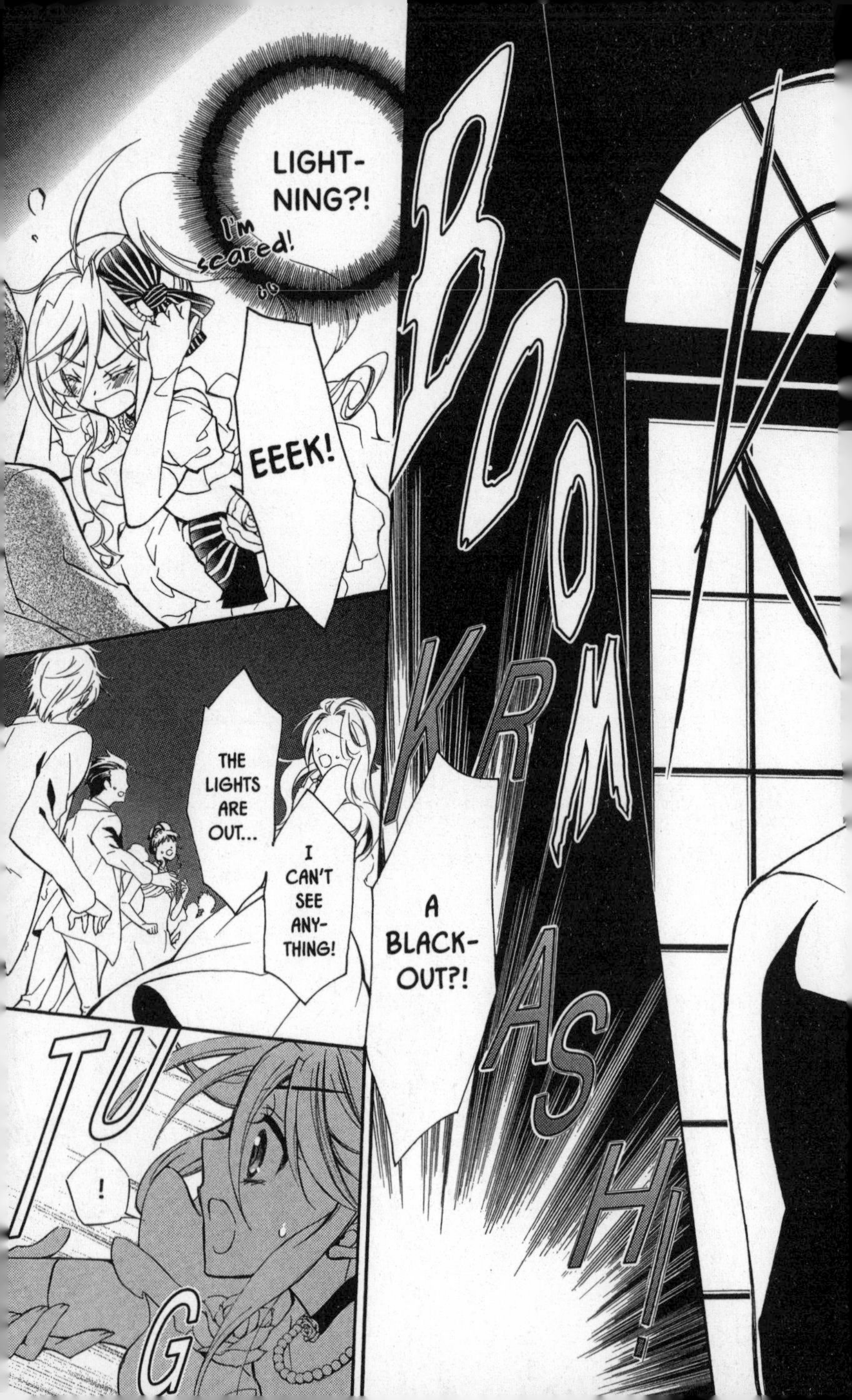
BOOM
KRASH!
LIGHT-NING?!
I'm scared!
EEEK!
A BLACK-OUT?!
I CAN'T SEE ANY-THING!
THE LIGHTS ARE OUT...
TUG
!

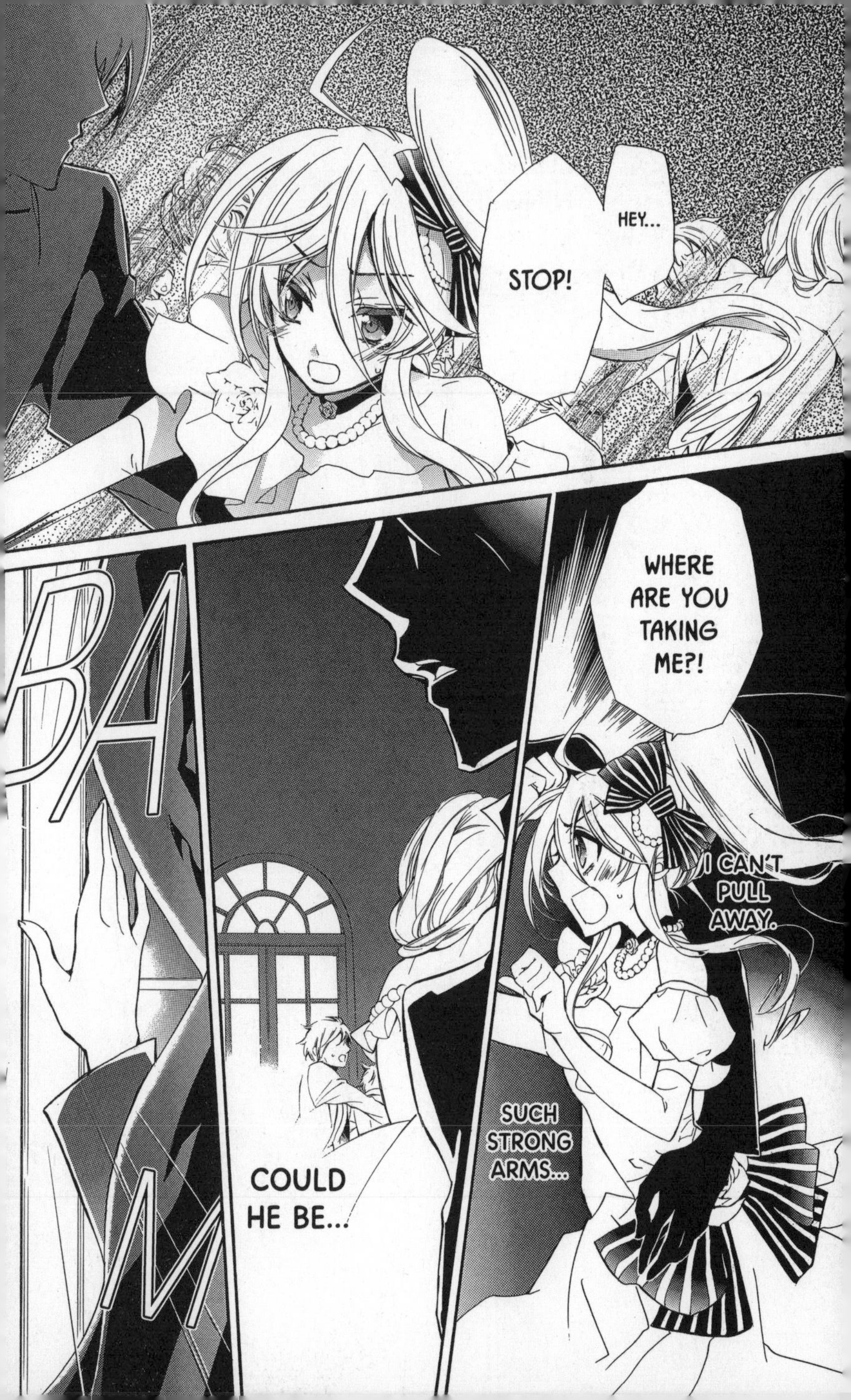
HEY...
STOP!
WHERE ARE YOU TAKING ME?!
I CAN'T PULL AWAY.
SUCH STRONG ARMS...
COULD HE BE...
BAM

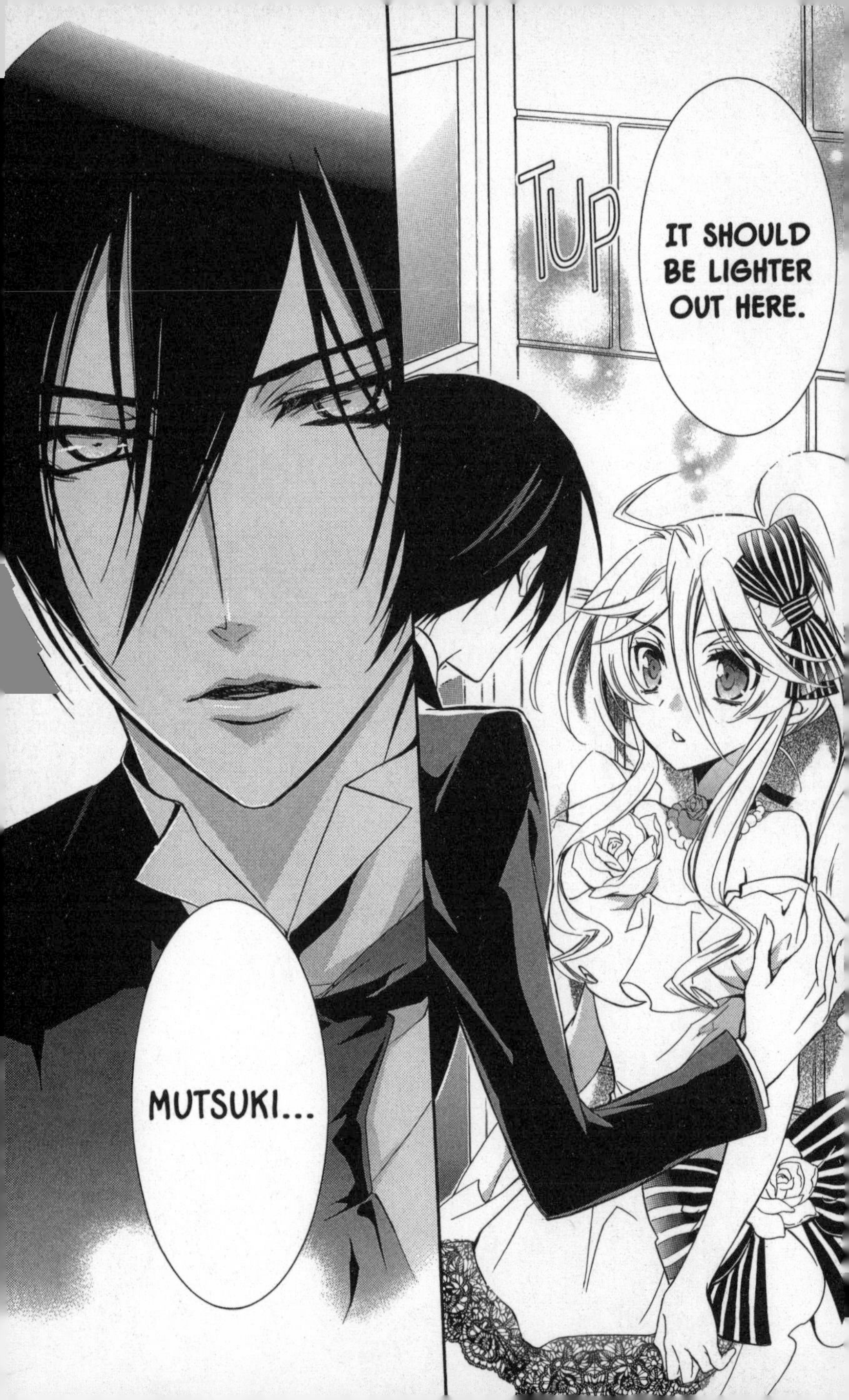
TUP
IT SHOULD BE LIGHTER OUT HERE.
MUTSUKI...

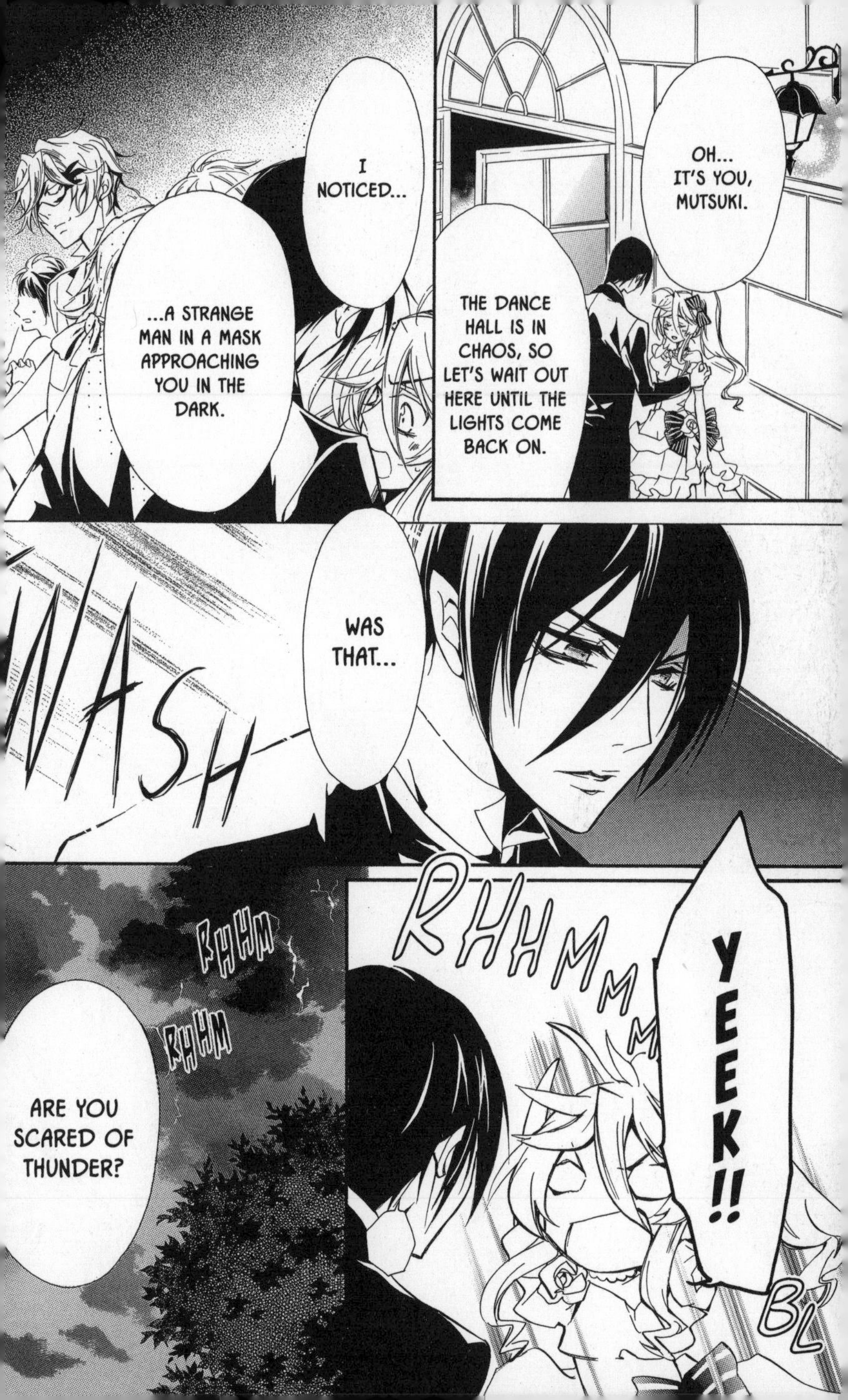
OH... IT'S YOU, MUTSUKI.
THE DANCE HALL IS IN CHAOS, SO LET'S WAIT OUT HERE UNTIL THE LIGHTS COME BACK ON.
I NOTICED...
...A STRANGE MAN IN A MASK APPROACHING YOU IN THE DARK.
WAS THAT...
RHHMMMM
YEEK!!
BL
RHHM
RHHM
ARE YOU SCARED OF THUNDER?

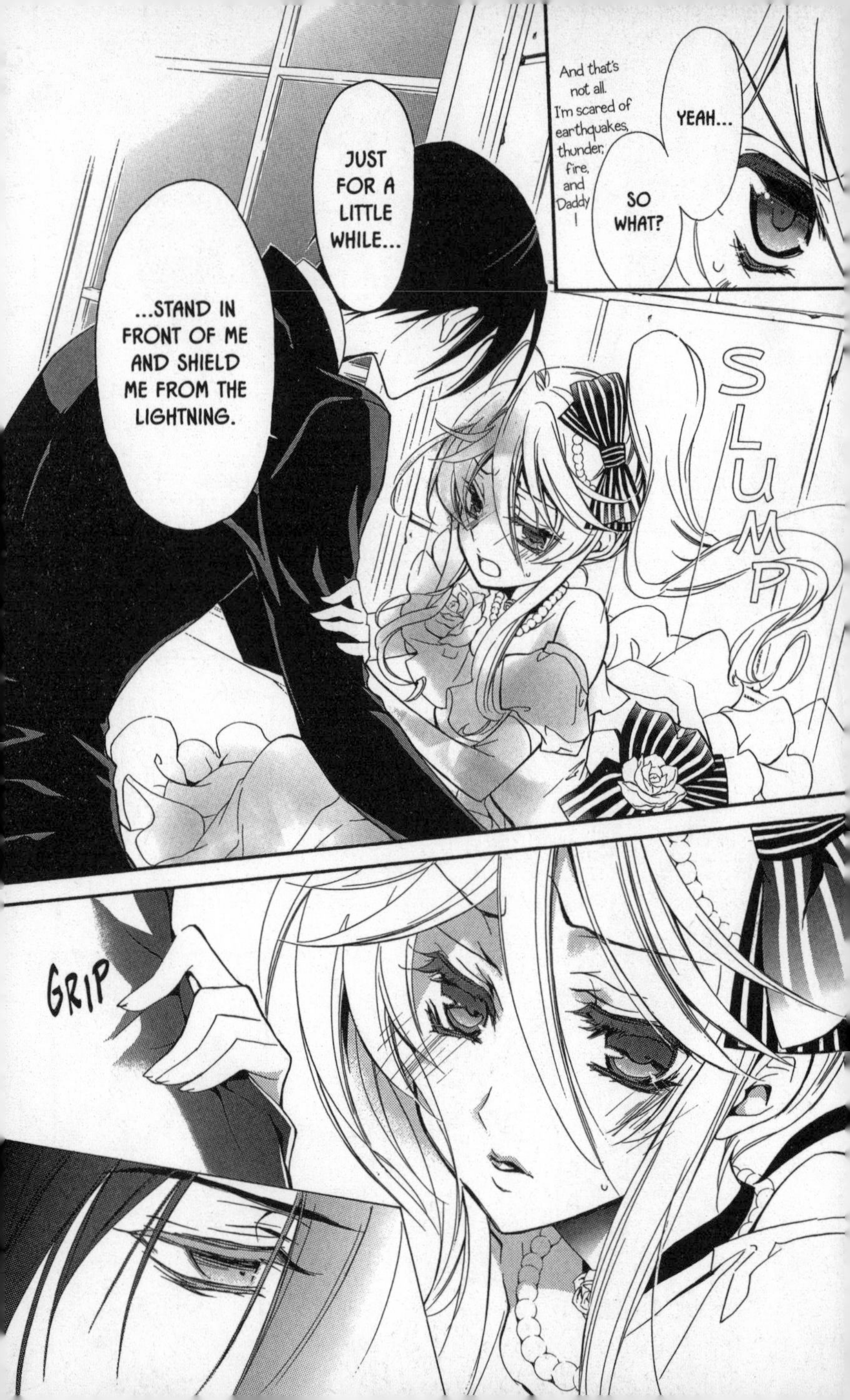
YEAH...
SO WHAT?
And that's not all. I'm scared of earthquakes, thunder, fire, and Daddy!
SLUMP
JUST FOR A LITTLE WHILE...
...STAND IN FRONT OF ME AND SHIELD ME FROM THE LIGHTNING.
GRIP

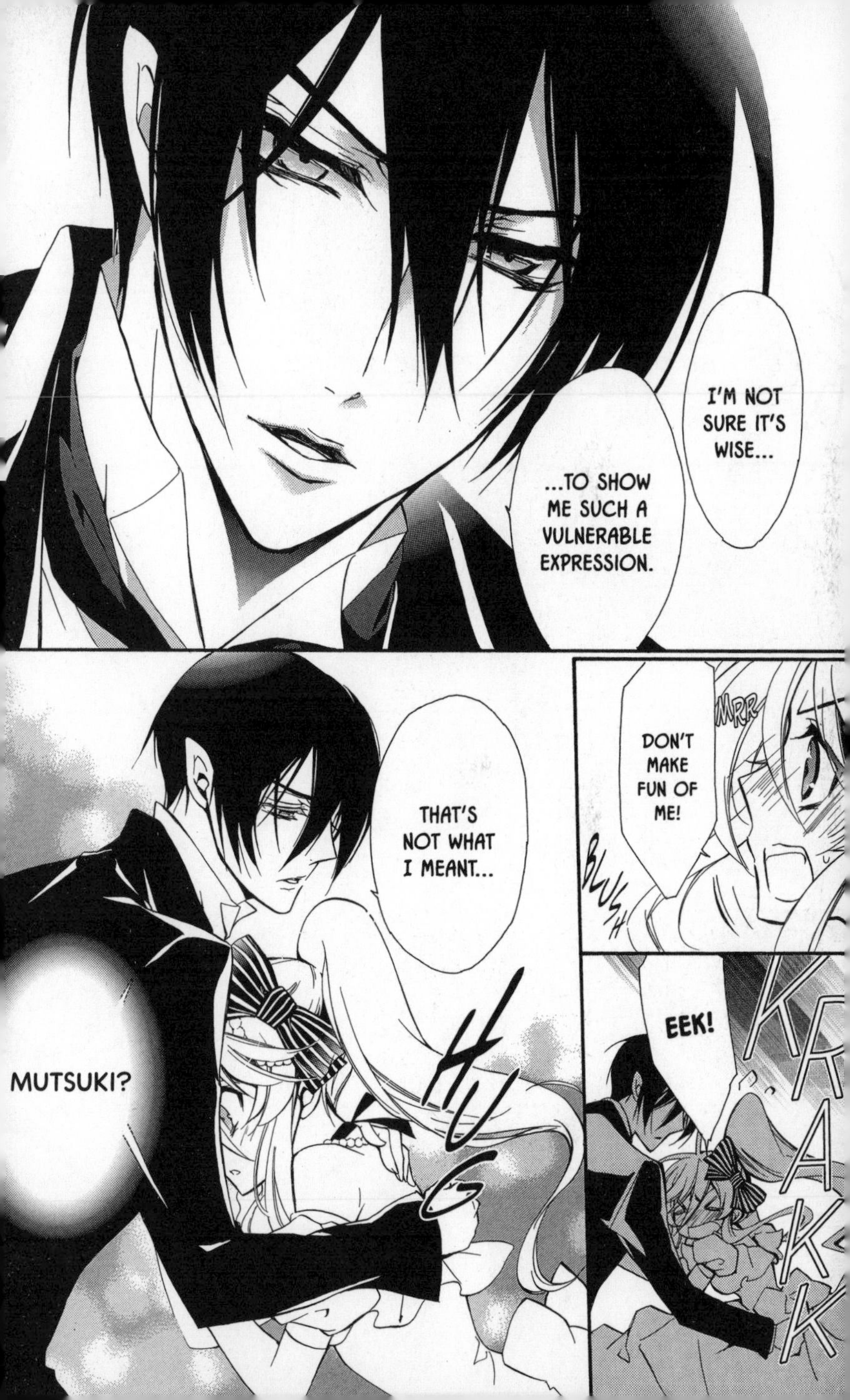
I'M NOT SURE IT'S WISE...
...TO SHOW ME SUCH A VULNERABLE EXPRESSION.
MRR
DON'T MAKE FUN OF ME!
BLUSH
EEK!
KRAKK
THAT'S NOT WHAT I MEANT...
HUG
MUTSUKI?

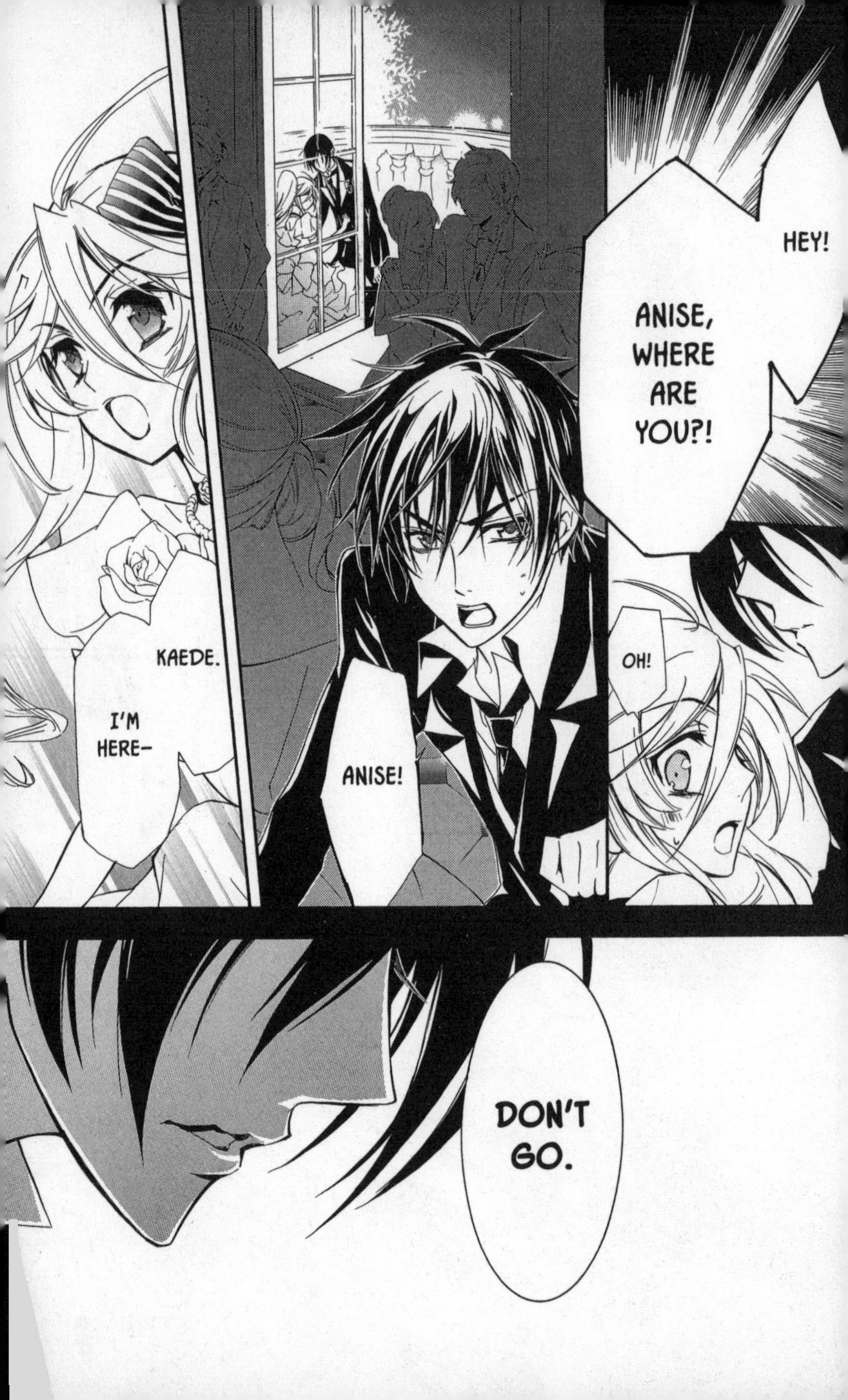
HEY!
ANISE, WHERE ARE YOU?!
OH!
ANISE!
KAEDE.
I'M HERE–
DON'T GO.

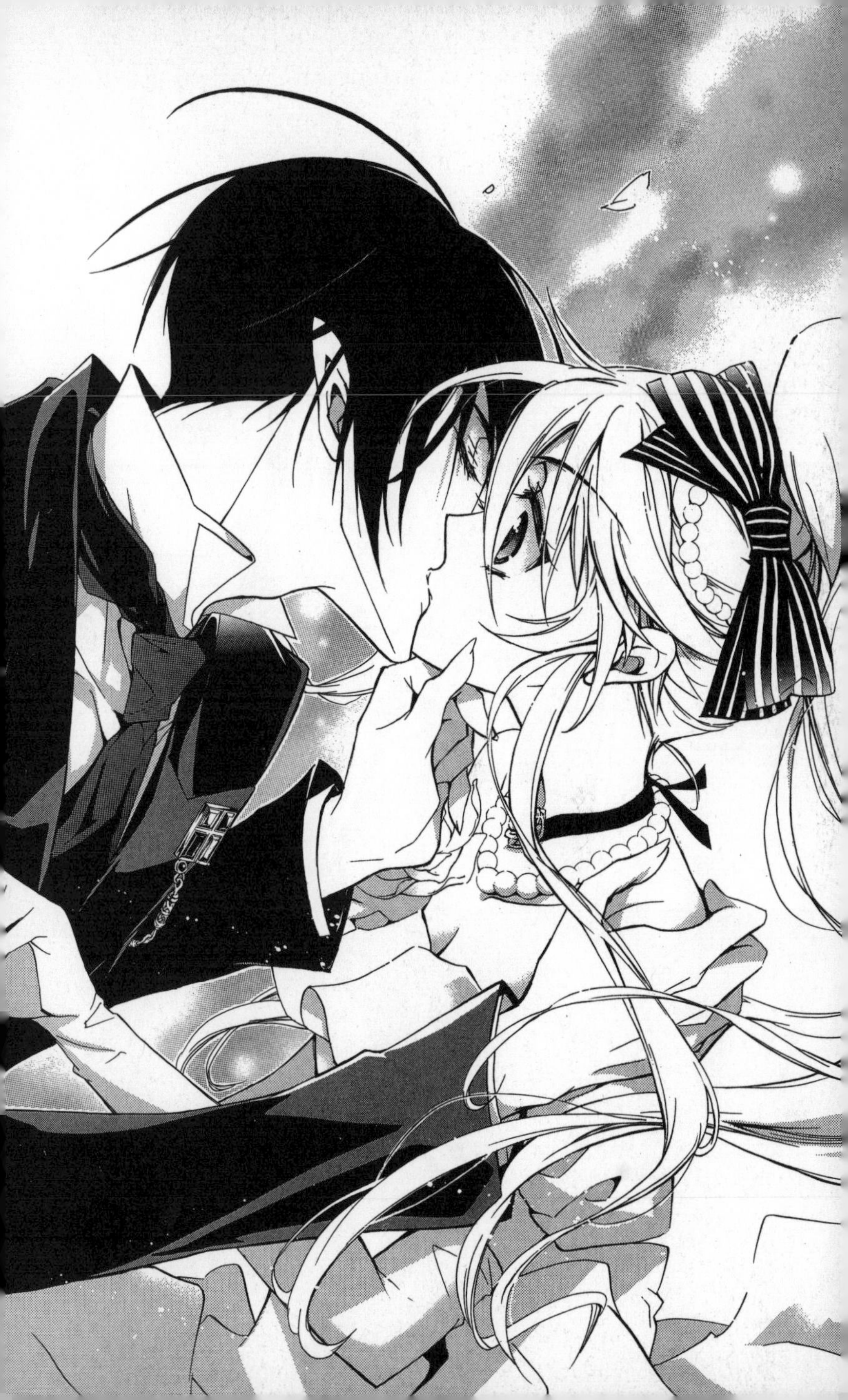

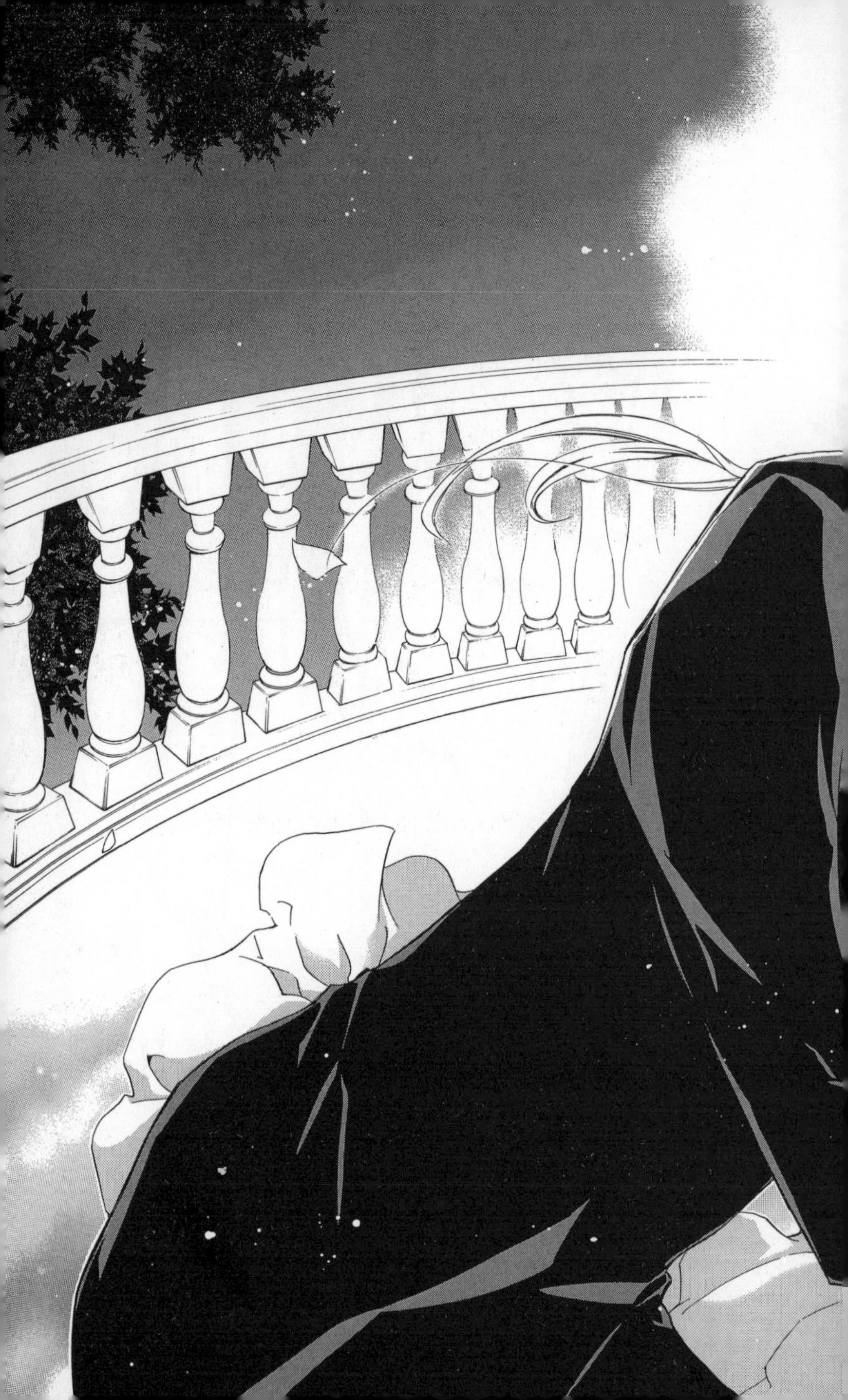

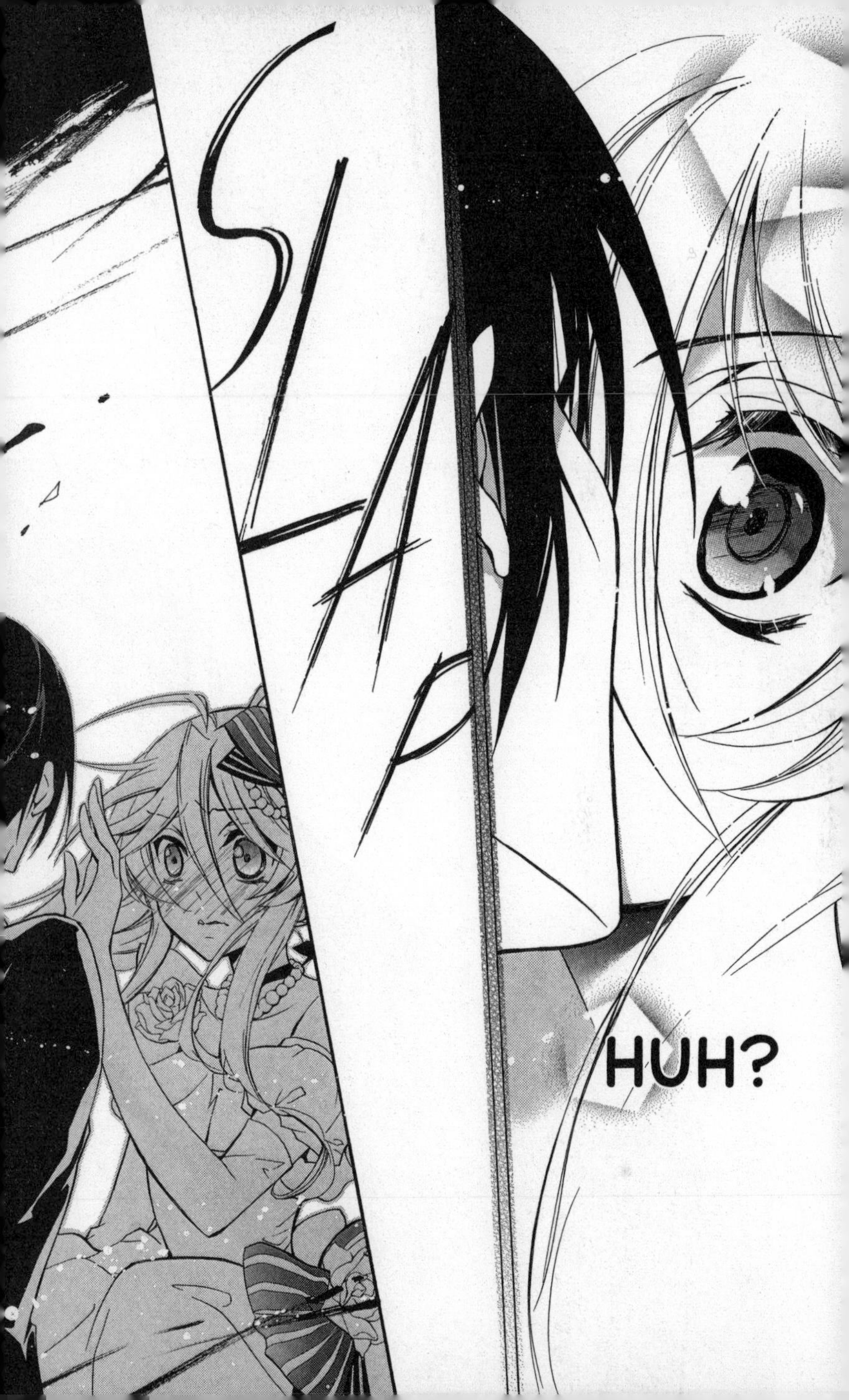
HUH?

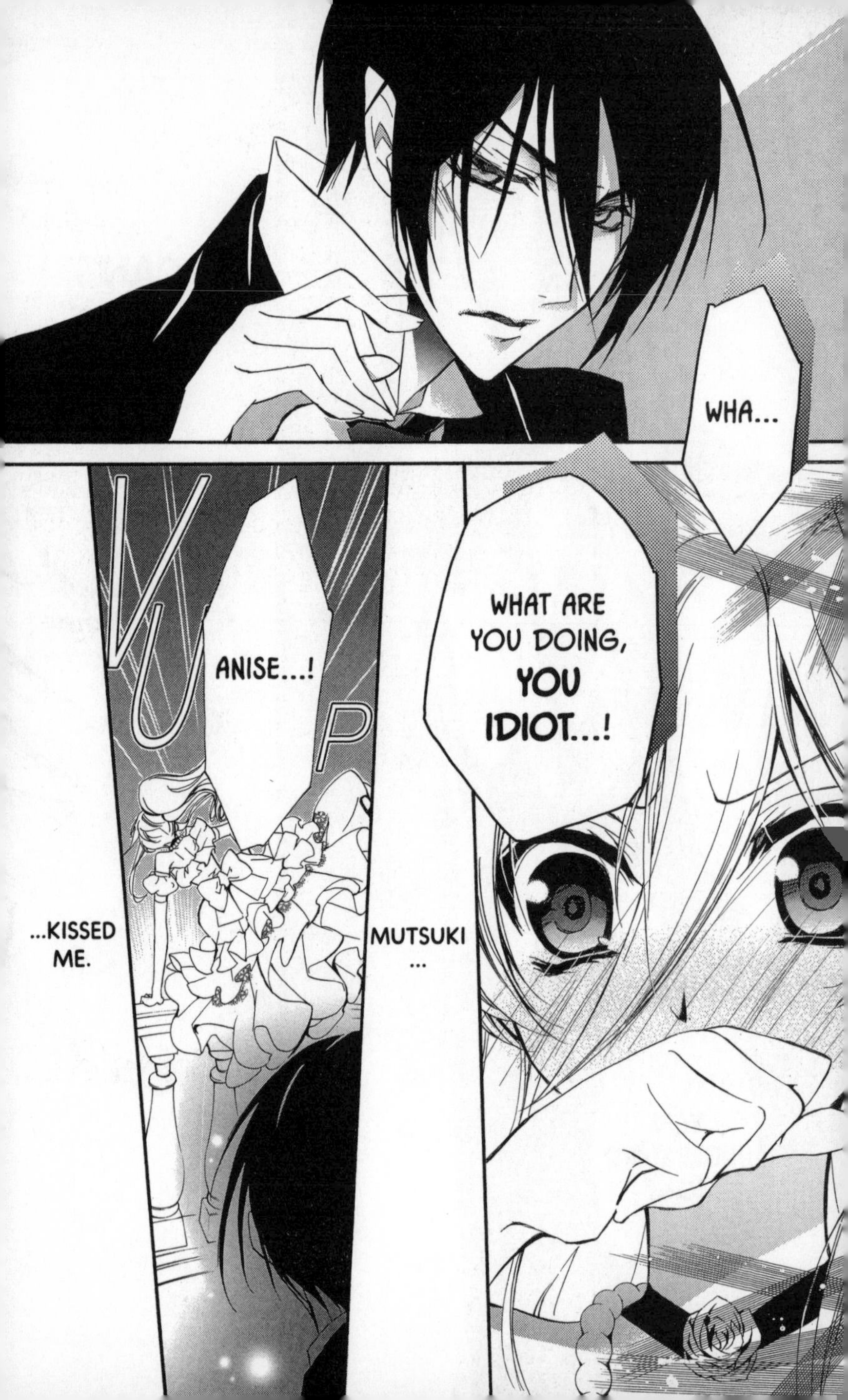
WHA...
WHAT ARE YOU DOING, YOU IDIOT...!
ANISE...!
VUP
MUTSUKI ...
...KISSED ME.

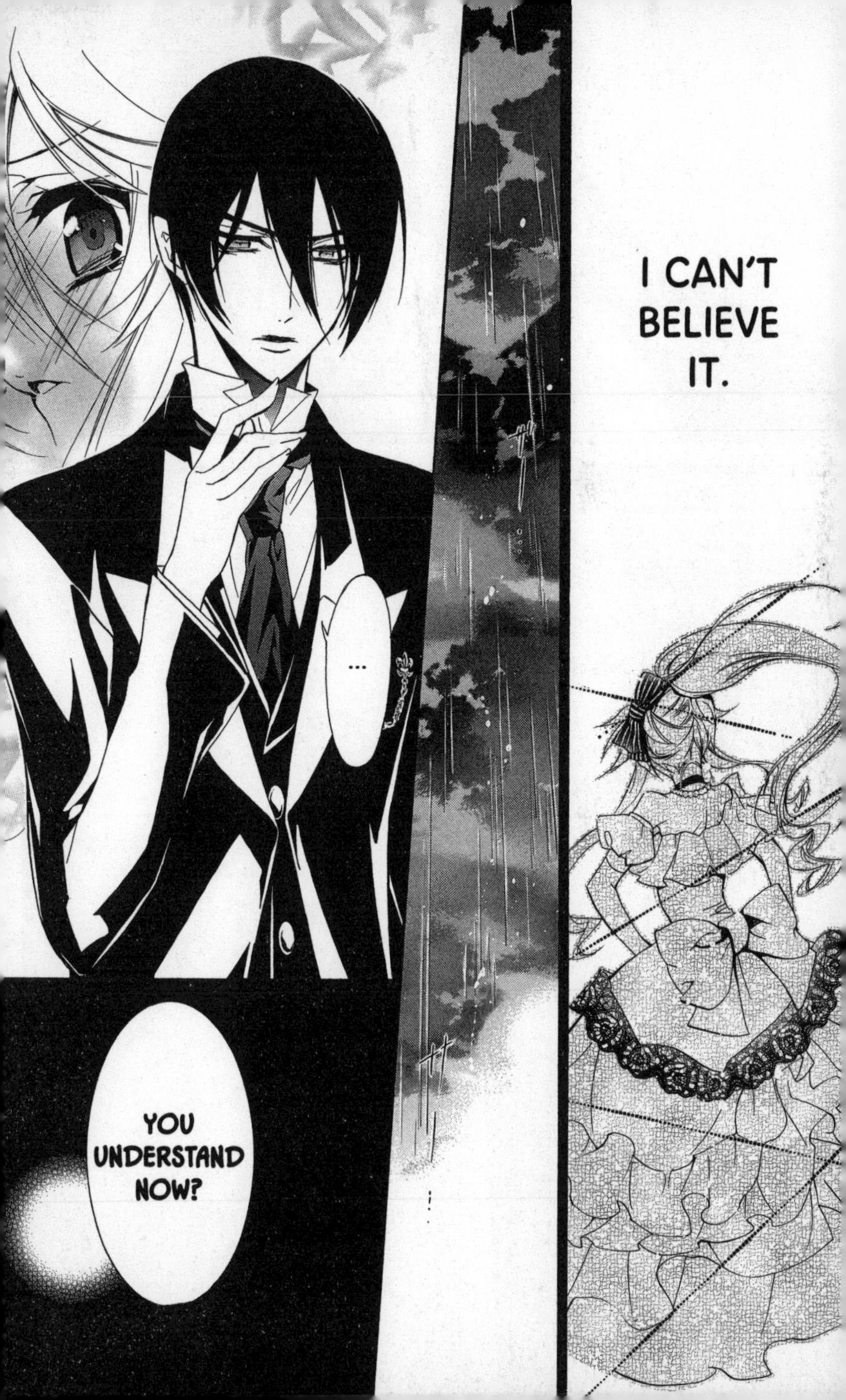
I CAN'T BELIEVE IT.
...
YOU UNDERSTAND NOW?

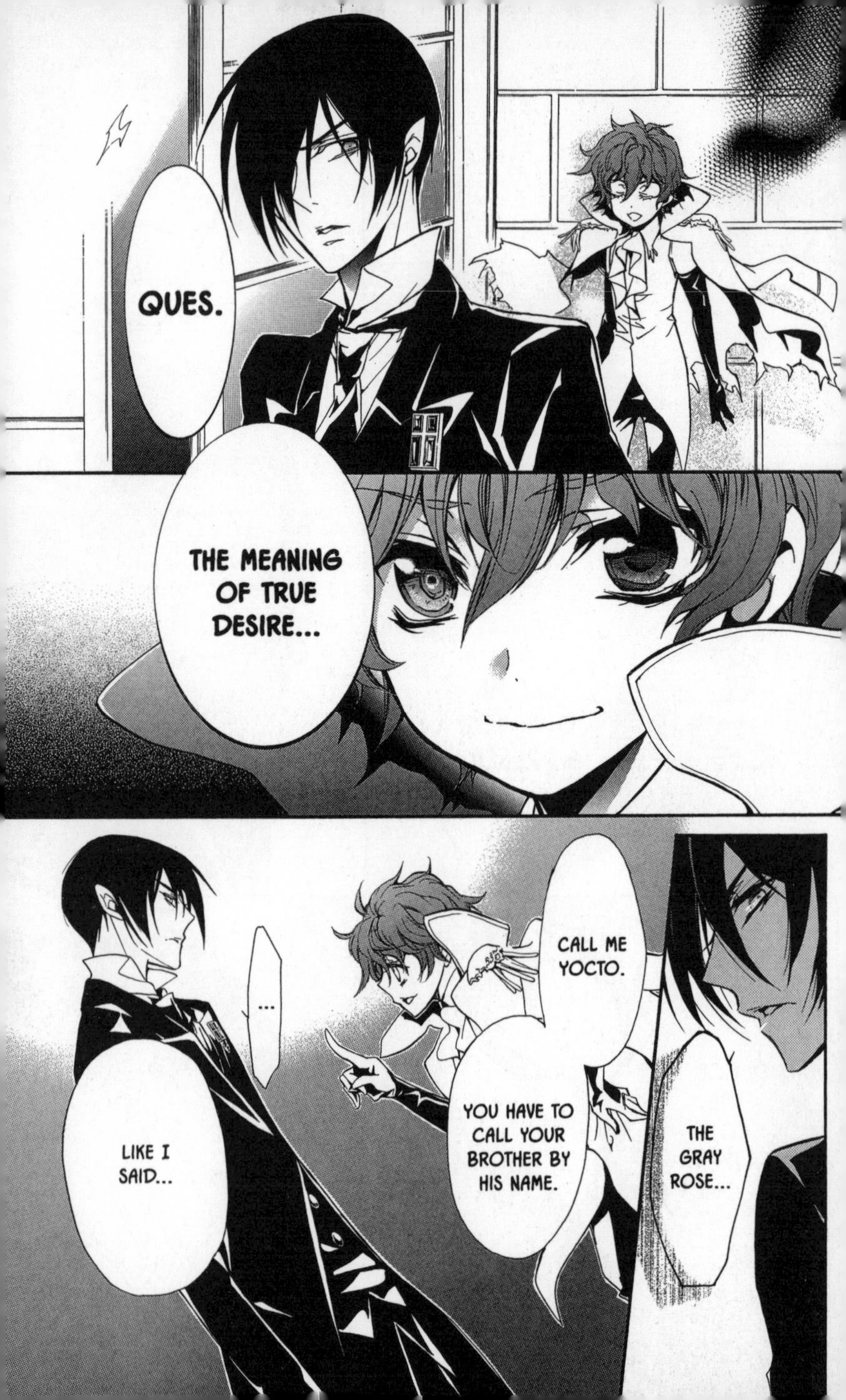
QUES.
THE MEANING OF TRUE DESIRE...
THE GRAY ROSE...
CALL ME YOCTO.
YOU HAVE TO CALL YOUR BROTHER BY HIS NAME.
...
LIKE I SAID...

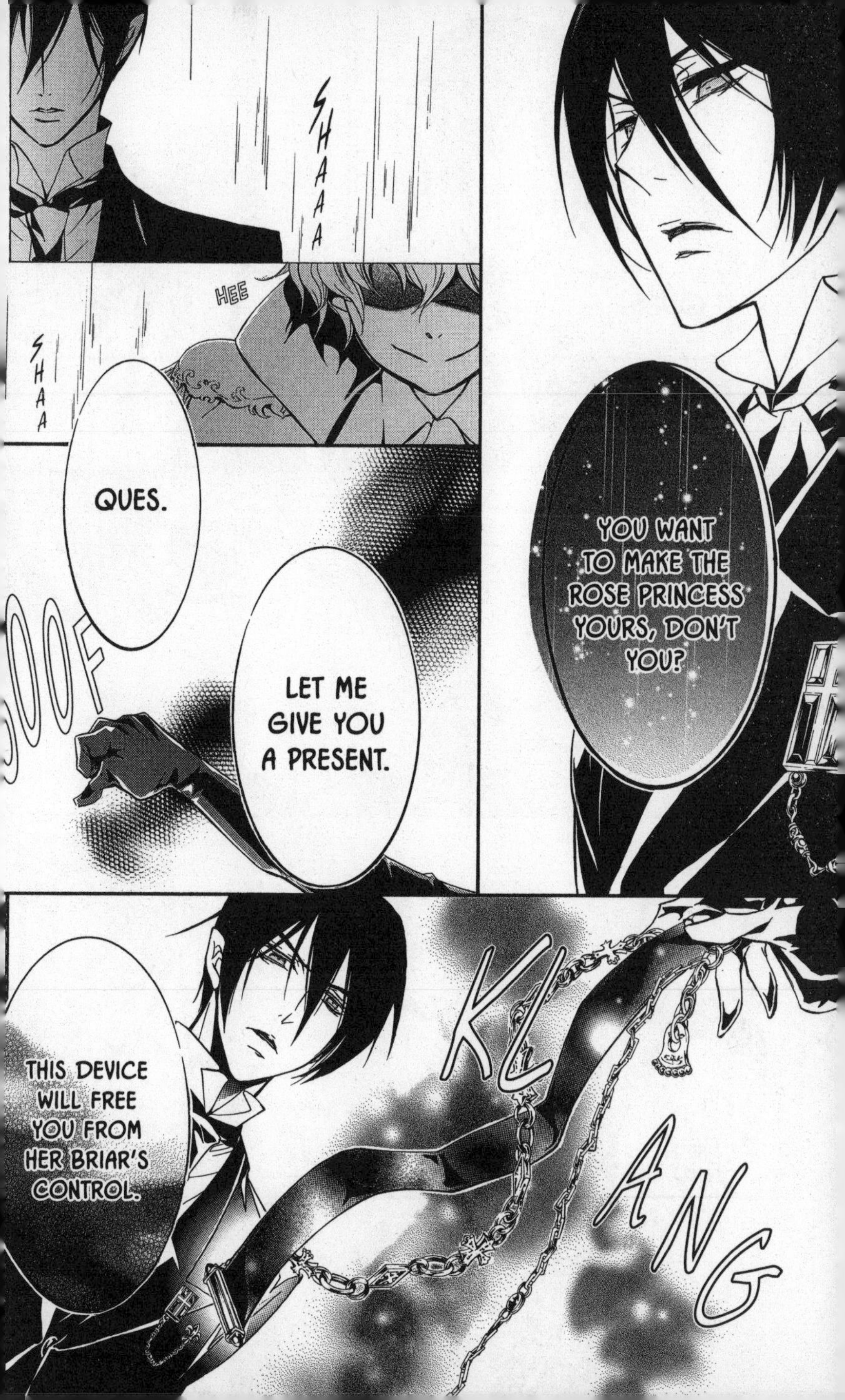
YOU WANT TO MAKE THE ROSE PRINCESS YOURS, DON'T YOU?
SHAAAA
HEE
SHAAA
QUES.
OOF
LET ME GIVE YOU A PRESENT.
KLANG
THIS DEVICE WILL FREE YOU FROM HER BRIAR'S CONTROL.

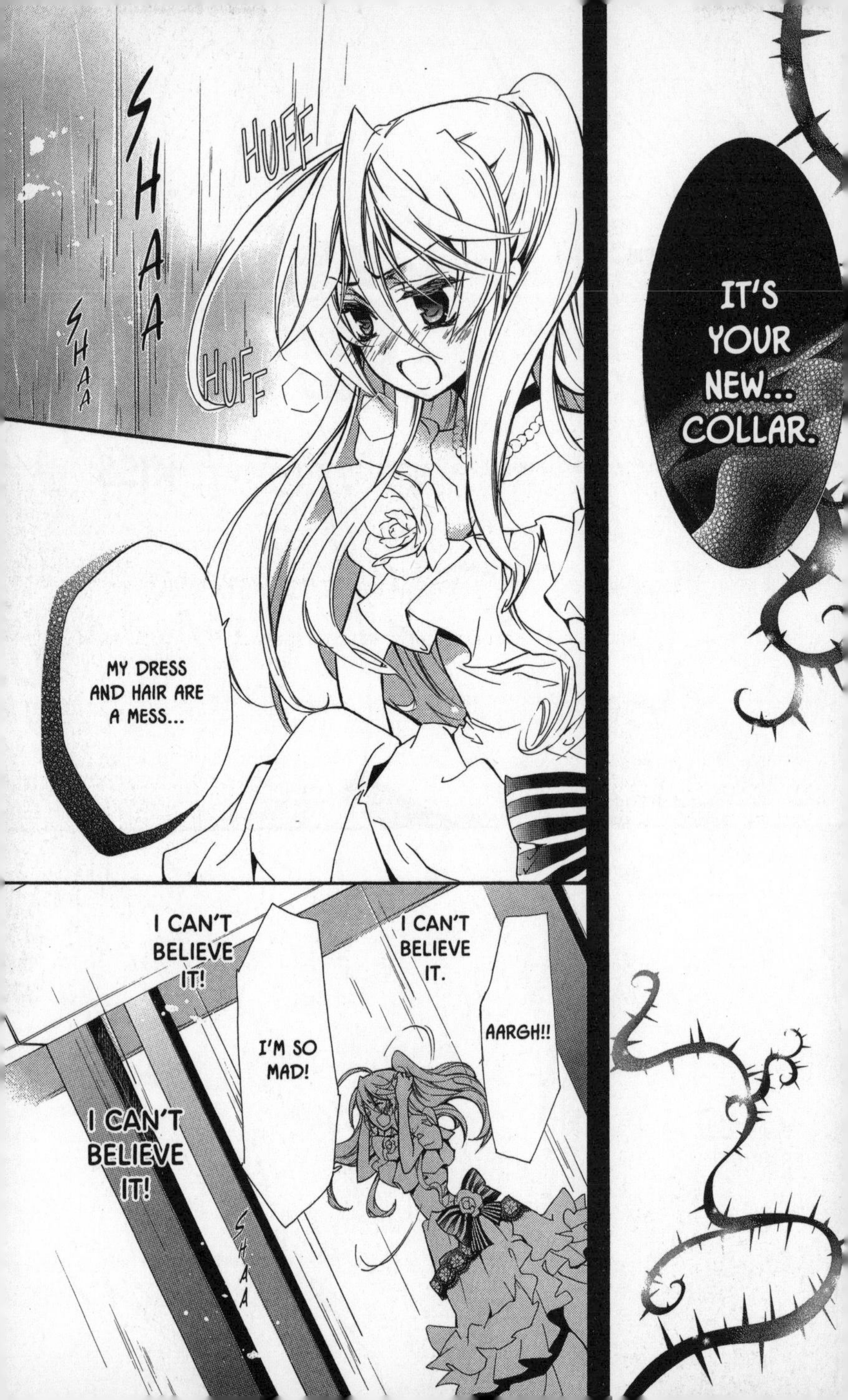
IT'S YOUR NEW... COLLAR.
HUFF
SHAAA
HUFF
SHAA
MY DRESS AND HAIR ARE A MESS...
I CAN'T BELIEVE IT.
AARGH!!
I CAN'T BELIEVE IT!
I'M SO MAD!
I CAN'T BELIEVE IT!
SHAA

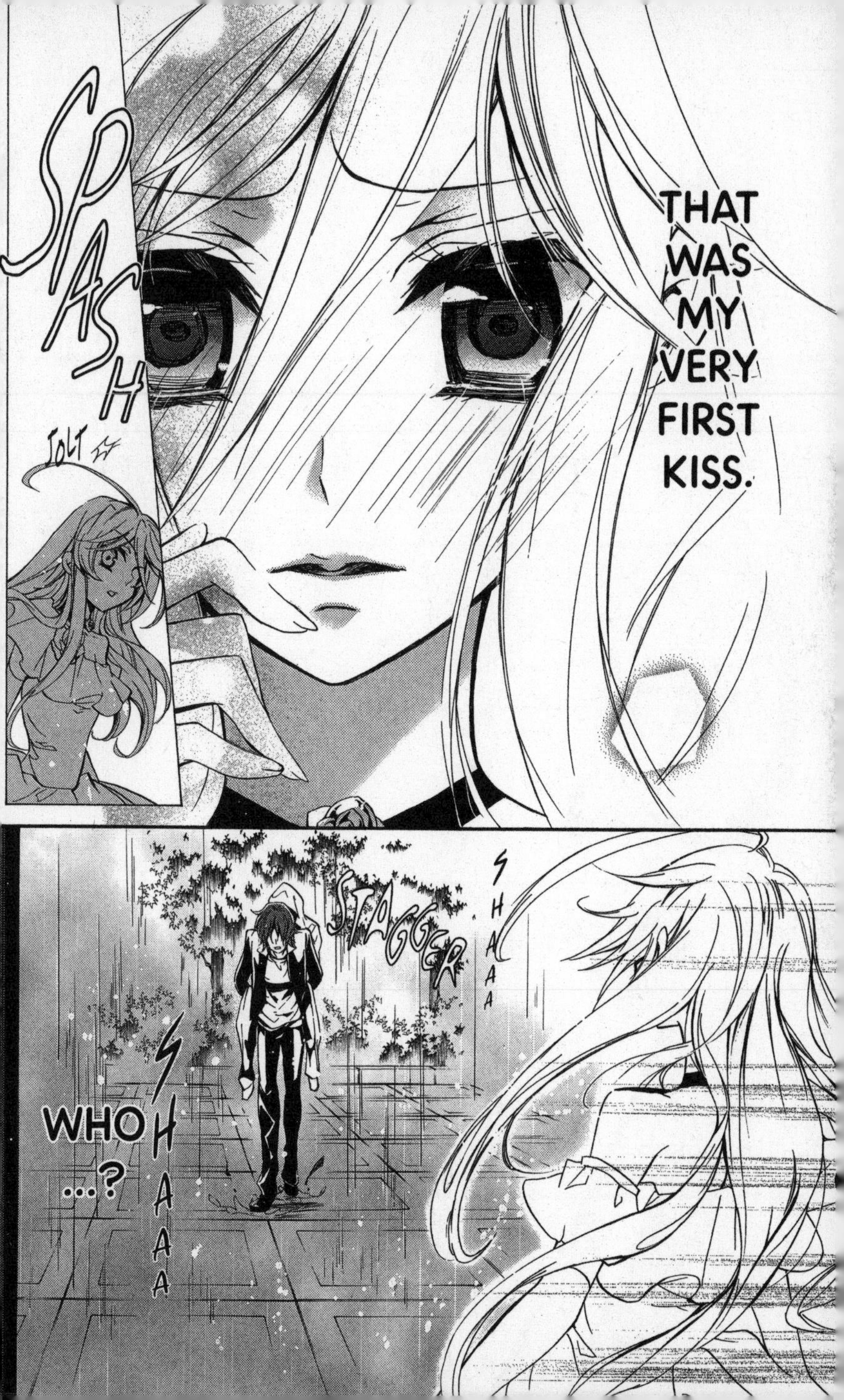
THAT WAS MY VERY FIRST KISS.
SPASH
JOLT
SHHAAAA
STAGGER
SHHAAAA
WHO ...?

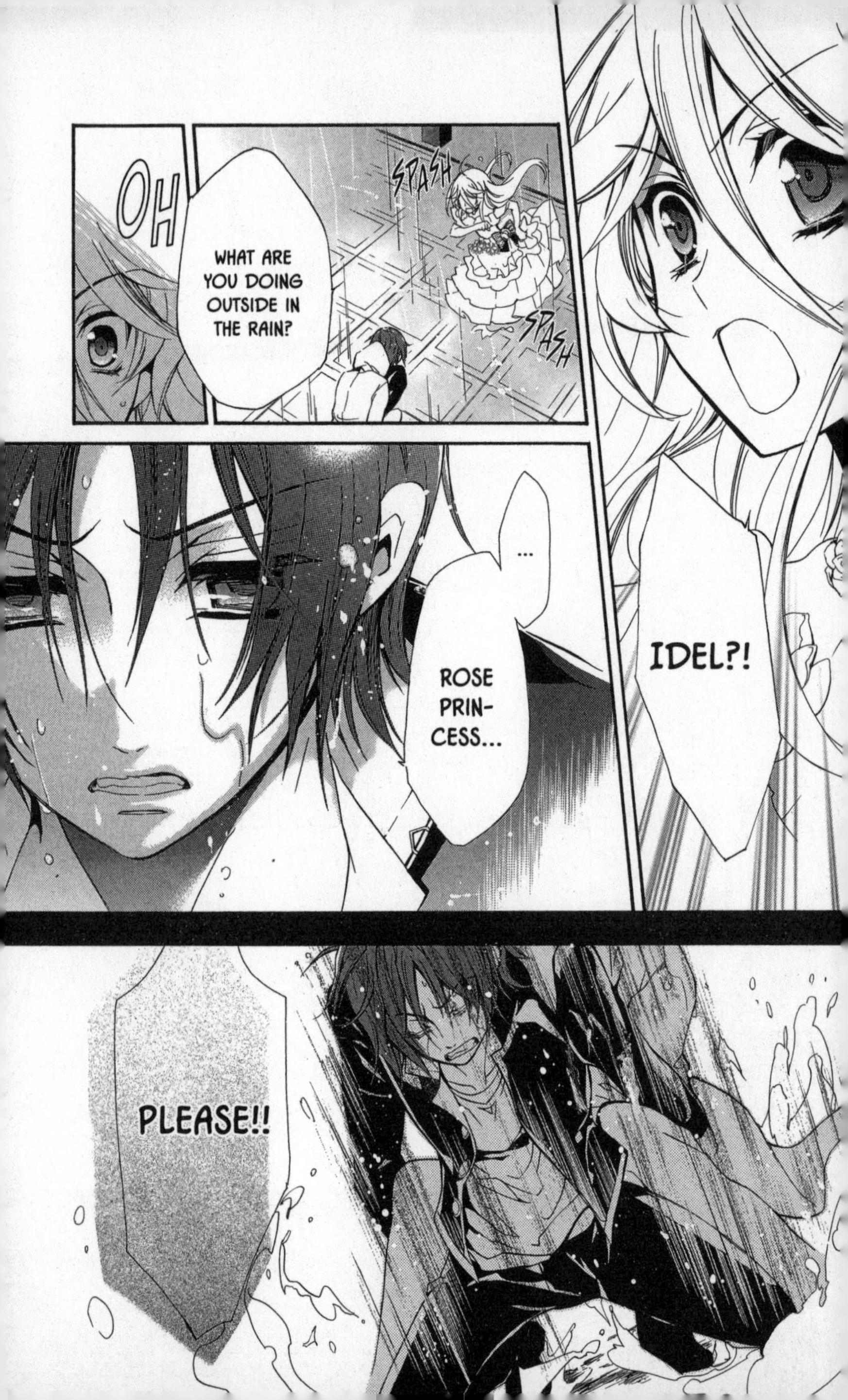
IDEL?!
SPASH
SPASH
WHAT ARE YOU DOING OUTSIDE IN THE RAIN?
OH
...
ROSE PRIN- CESS...
PLEASE!!

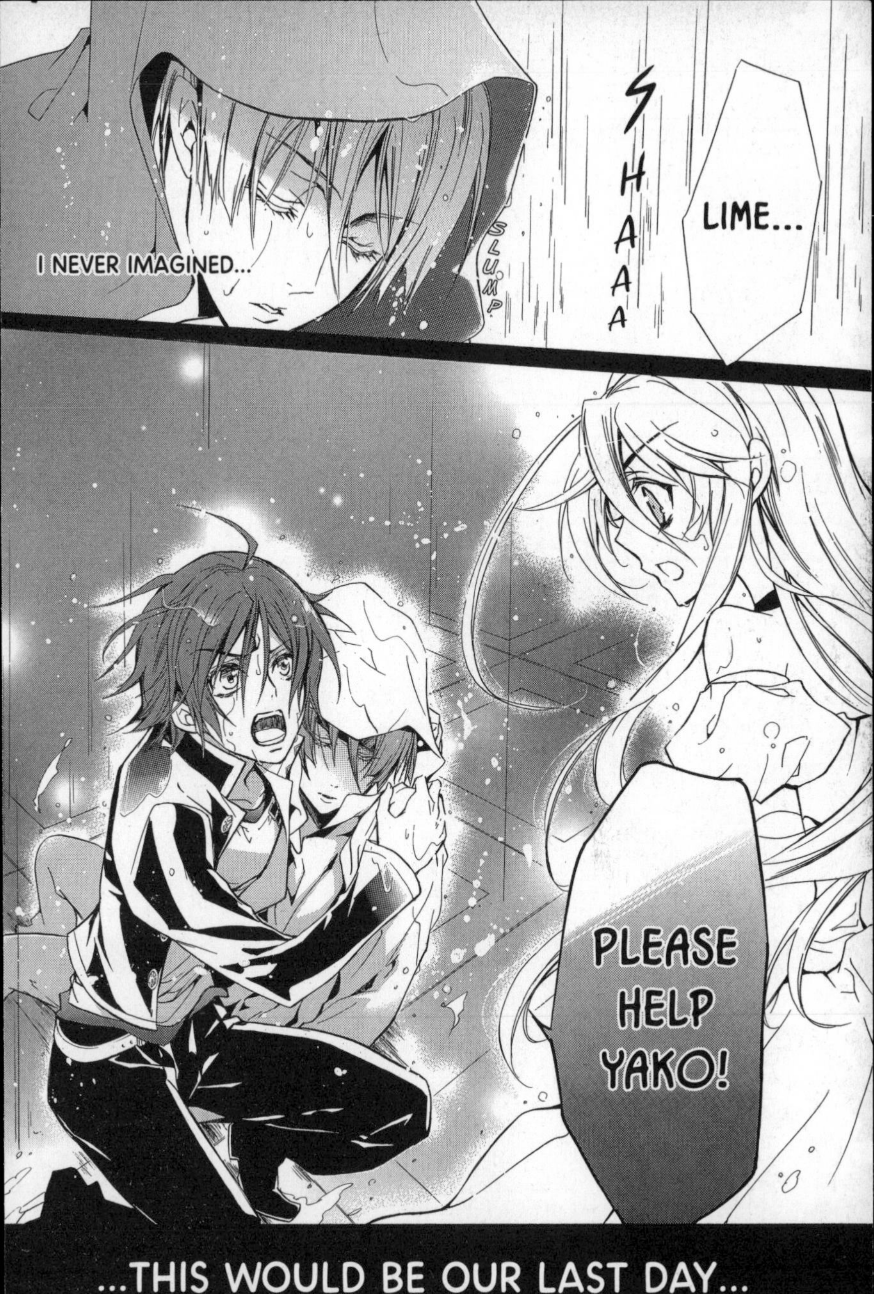
LIME...
SHAAAA
SLUMP
I NEVER IMAGINED...
PLEASE HELP YAKO!
...THIS WOULD BE OUR LAST DAY...

Kiss of the Rose Princess

Kiss of the Rose Princess

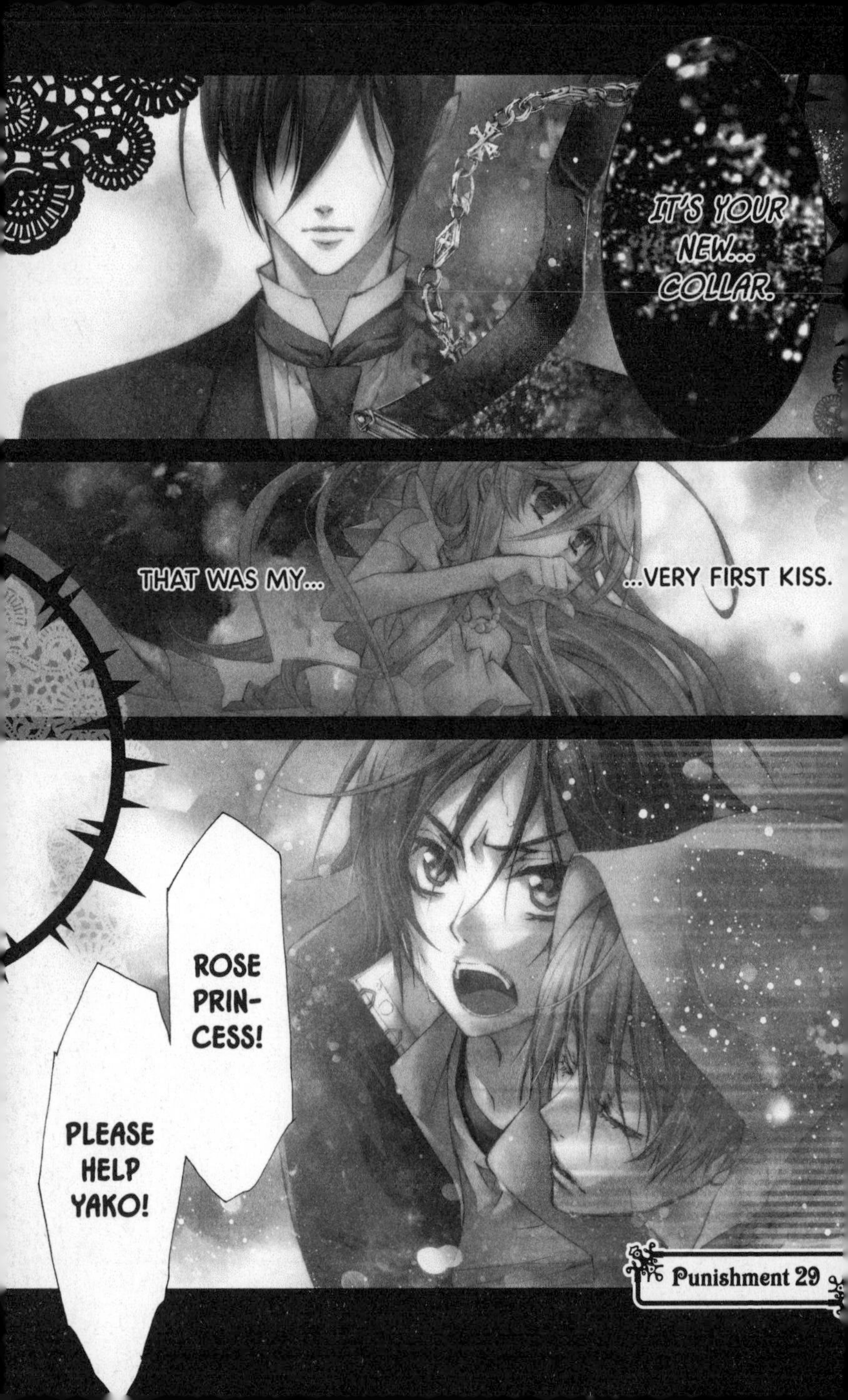
IT'S YOUR NEW... COLLAR.
THAT WAS MY...
...VERY FIRST KISS.
ROSE PRIN-CESS!
PLEASE HELP YAKO!
Punishment 29

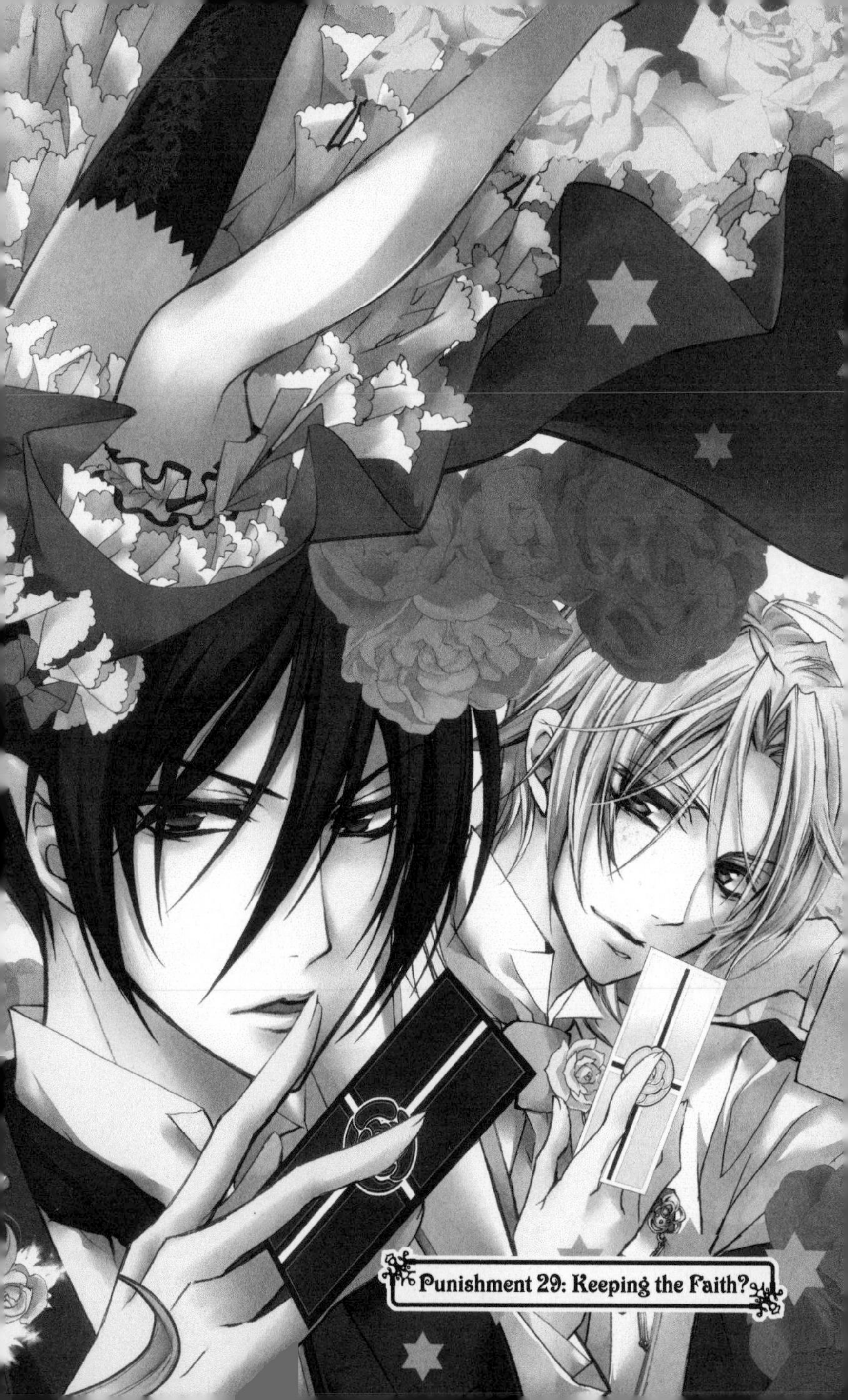
Punishment 29: Keeping the Faith?

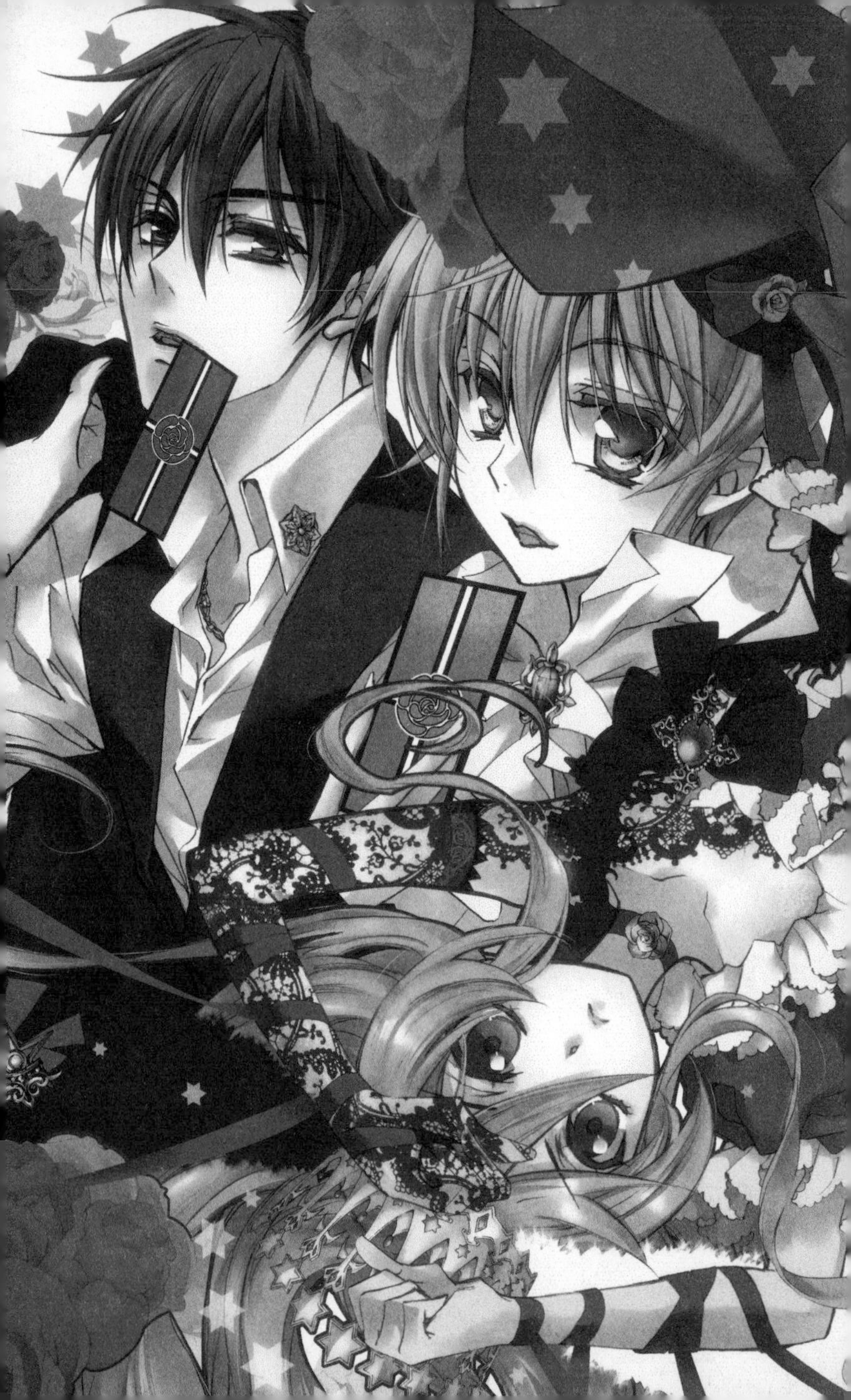

Kiss
of the
Rose
Princess

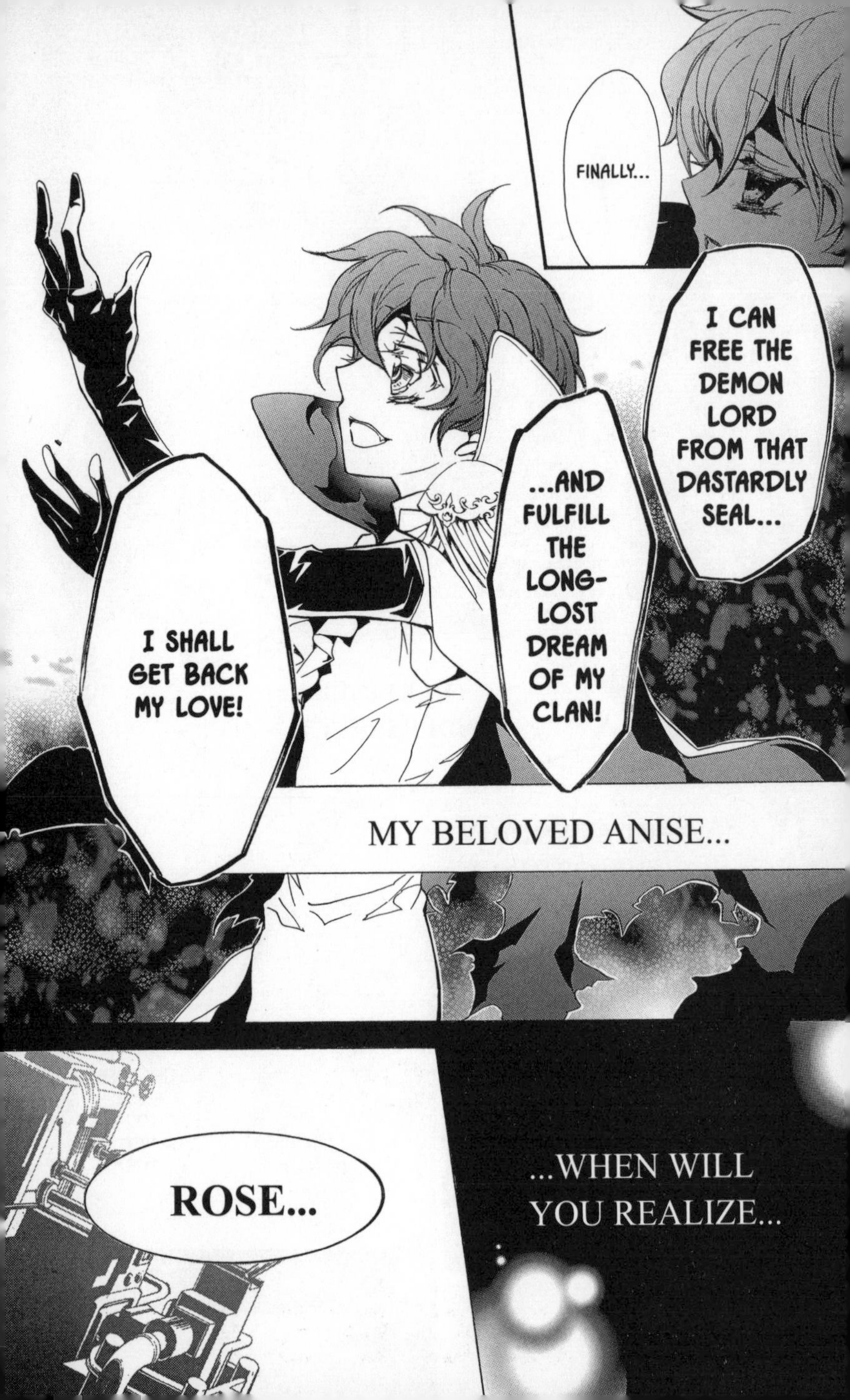
FINALLY...
I CAN FREE THE DEMON LORD FROM THAT DASTARDLY SEAL...
...AND FULFILL THE LONG-LOST DREAM OF MY CLAN!
I SHALL GET BACK MY LOVE!
MY BELOVED ANISE...
...WHEN WILL YOU REALIZE...
ROSE...

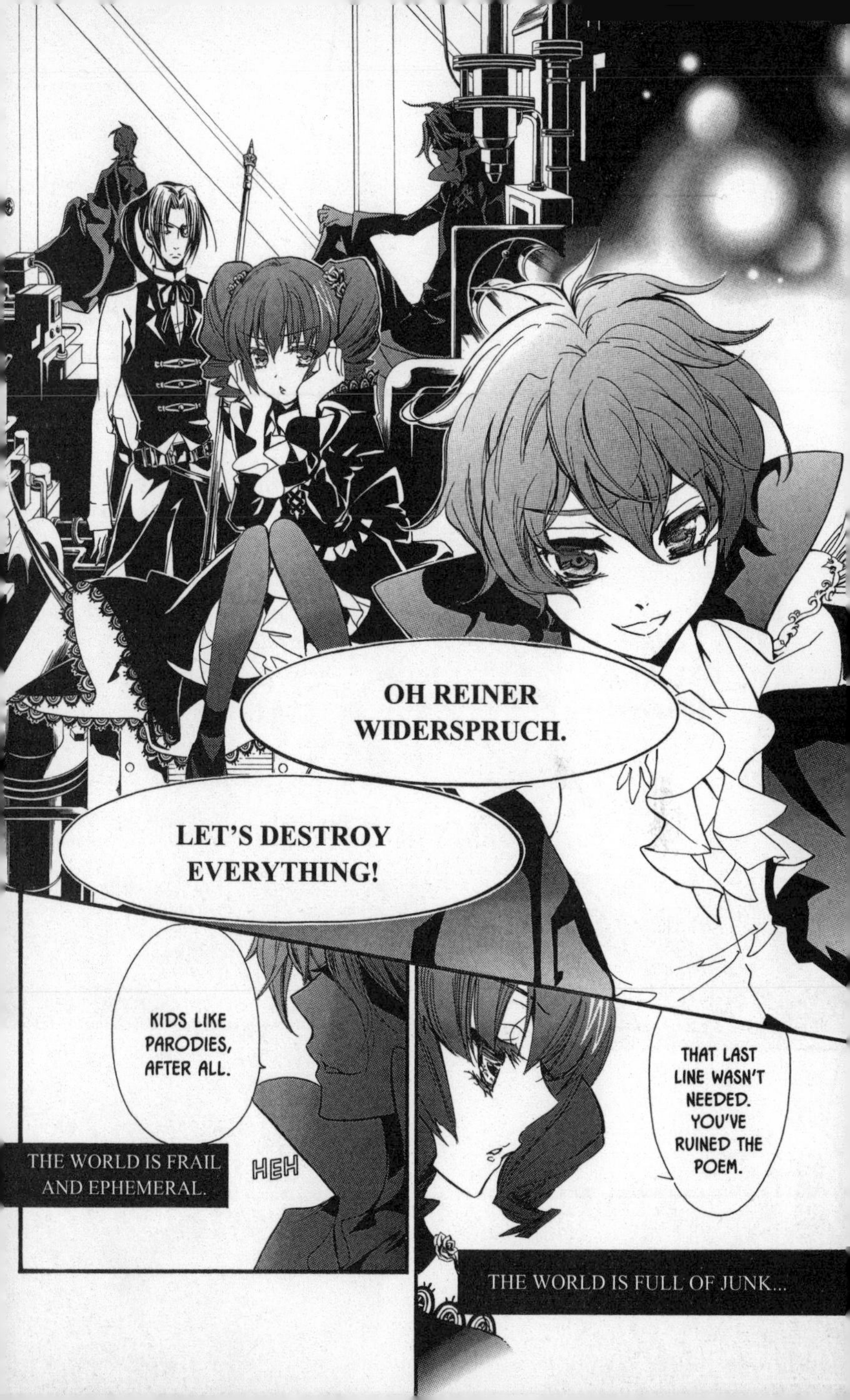
OH REINER WIDERSPRUCH.
LET'S DESTROY EVERYTHING!
THAT LAST LINE WASN'T NEEDED. YOU'VE RUINED THE POEM.
THE WORLD IS FULL OF JUNK...
KIDS LIKE PARODIES, AFTER ALL.
HEH
THE WORLD IS FRAIL AND EPHEMERAL.

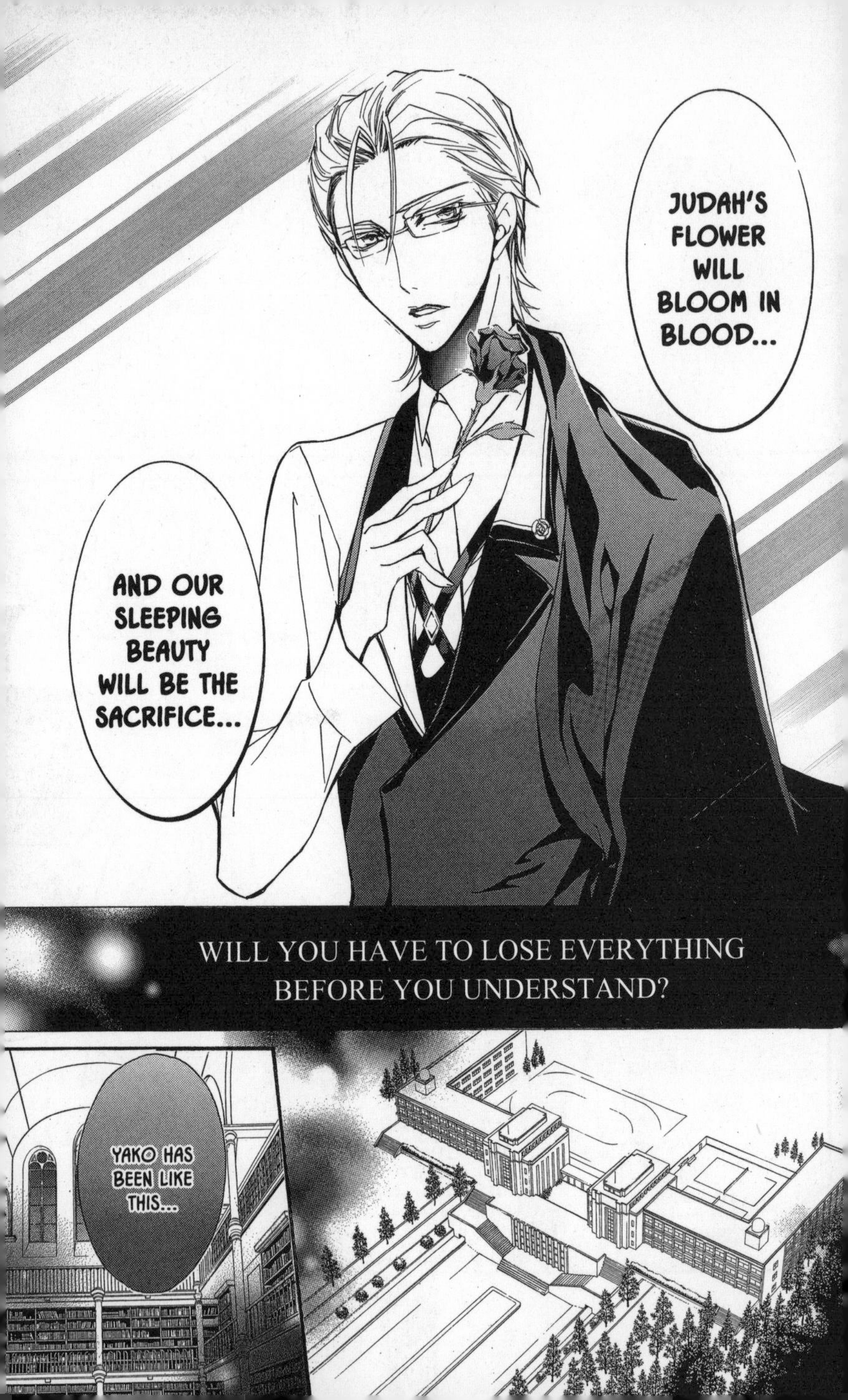
JUDAH'S FLOWER WILL BLOOM IN BLOOD...
AND OUR SLEEPING BEAUTY WILL BE THE SACRIFICE...
WILL YOU HAVE TO LOSE EVERYTHING BEFORE YOU UNDERSTAND?
YAKO HAS BEEN LIKE THIS...

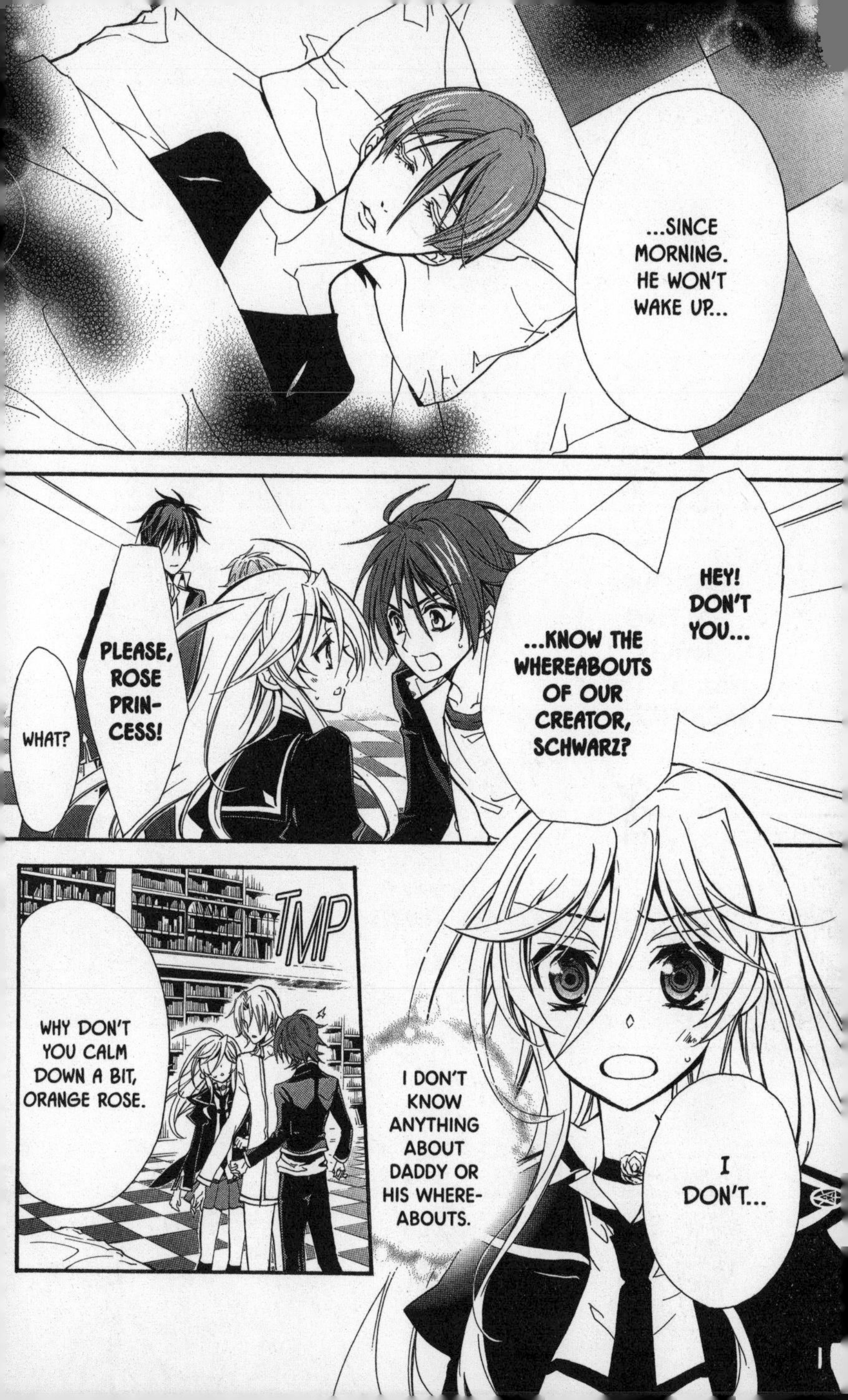
...SINCE MORNING. HE WON'T WAKE UP...
HEY! DON'T YOU...
...KNOW THE WHEREABOUTS OF OUR CREATOR, SCHWARZ?
PLEASE, ROSE PRINCESS!
WHAT?
I DON'T...
I DON'T KNOW ANYTHING ABOUT DADDY OR HIS WHERE-ABOUTS.
TMP
WHY DON'T YOU CALM DOWN A BIT, ORANGE ROSE.

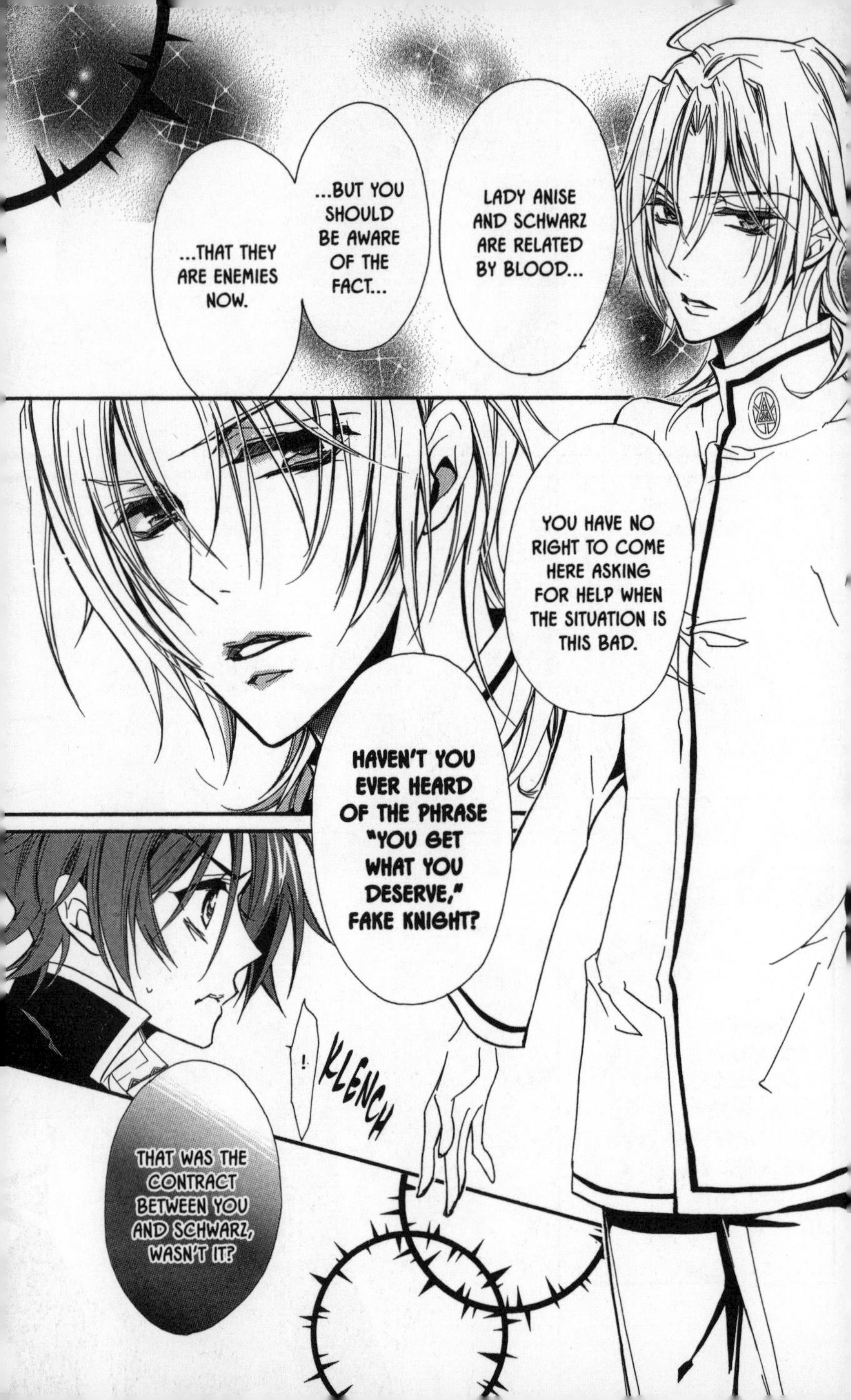
LADY ANISE AND SCHWARZ ARE RELATED BY BLOOD...
...BUT YOU SHOULD BE AWARE OF THE FACT...
...THAT THEY ARE ENEMIES NOW.
YOU HAVE NO RIGHT TO COME HERE ASKING FOR HELP WHEN THE SITUATION IS THIS BAD.
HAVEN'T YOU EVER HEARD OF THE PHRASE "YOU GET WHAT YOU DESERVE," FAKE KNIGHT?
!
KLENCH
THAT WAS THE CONTRACT BETWEEN YOU AND SCHWARZ, WASN'T IT?

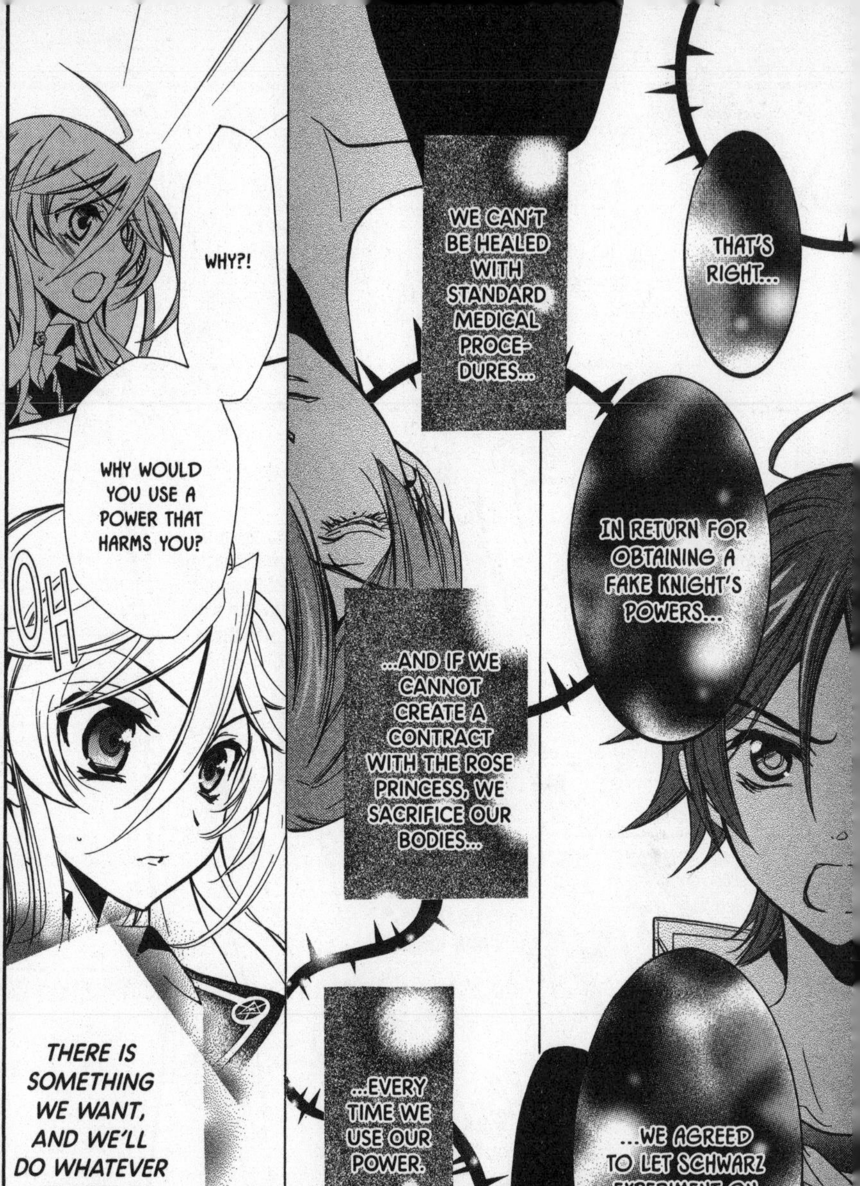
THAT'S RIGHT...
IN RETURN FOR OBTAINING A FAKE KNIGHT'S POWERS...
...WE AGREED TO LET SCHWARZ EXPERIMENT ON US.
WE CAN'T BE HEALED WITH STANDARD MEDICAL PROCE-DURES...
...AND IF WE CANNOT CREATE A CONTRACT WITH THE ROSE PRINCESS, WE SACRIFICE OUR BODIES...
...EVERY TIME WE USE OUR POWER.
WHY?!
WHY WOULD YOU USE A POWER THAT HARMS YOU?
THERE IS SOMETHING WE WANT, AND WE'LL DO WHATEVER WE NEED TO GET IT.

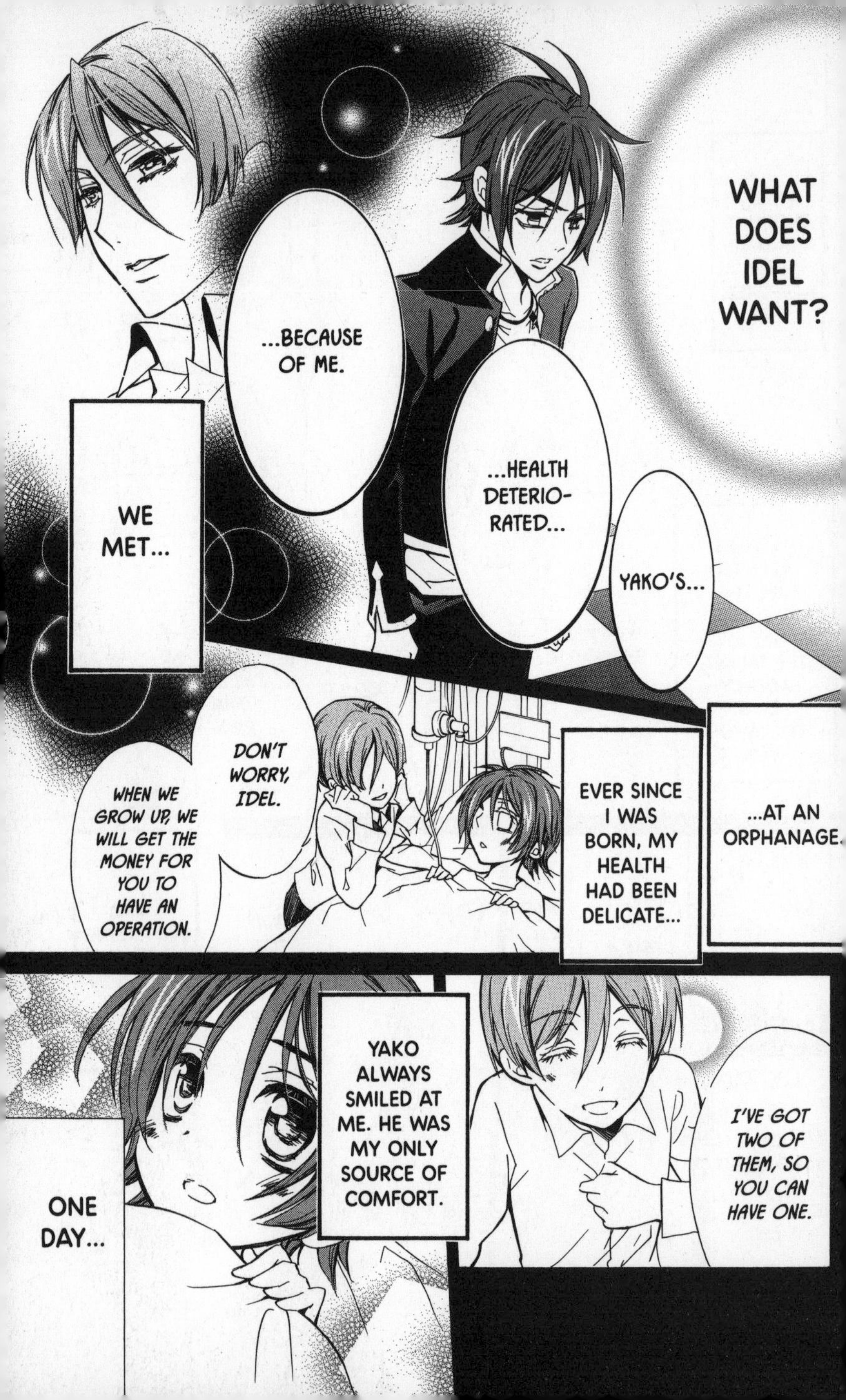
WHAT DOES IDEL WANT?
YAKO'S...
...HEALTH DETERIO-RATED...
...BECAUSE OF ME.
WE MET...
...AT AN ORPHANAGE.
EVER SINCE I WAS BORN, MY HEALTH HAD BEEN DELICATE...
DON'T WORRY, IDEL.
WHEN WE GROW UP, WE WILL GET THE MONEY FOR YOU TO HAVE AN OPERATION.
I'VE GOT TWO OF THEM, SO YOU CAN HAVE ONE.
YAKO ALWAYS SMILED AT ME. HE WAS MY ONLY SOURCE OF COMFORT.
ONE DAY...

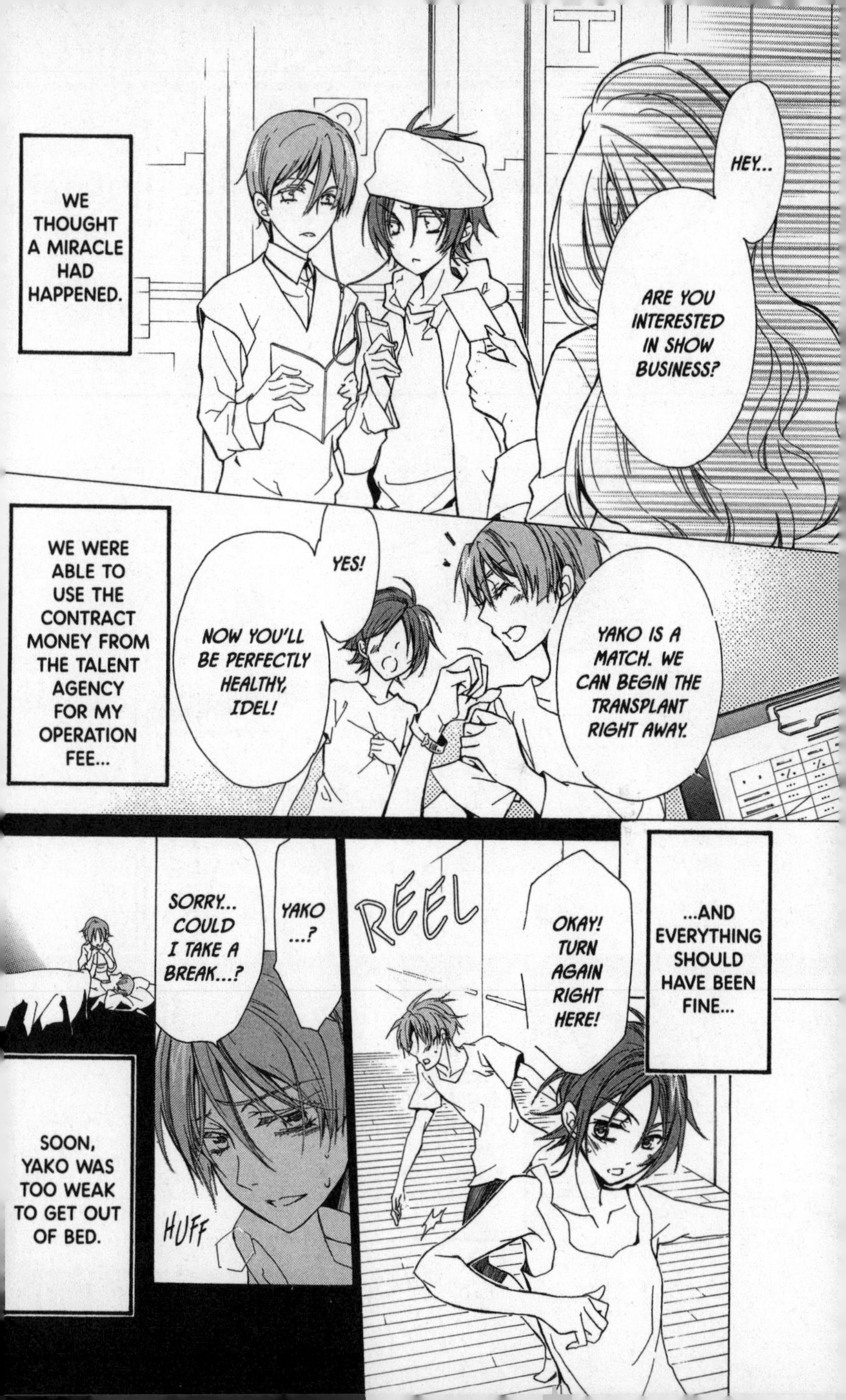
HEY...
ARE YOU INTERESTED IN SHOW BUSINESS?
WE THOUGHT A MIRACLE HAD HAPPENED.
YAKO IS A MATCH. WE CAN BEGIN THE TRANSPLANT RIGHT AWAY.
YES!
NOW YOU'LL BE PERFECTLY HEALTHY, IDEL!
WE WERE ABLE TO USE THE CONTRACT MONEY FROM THE TALENT AGENCY FOR MY OPERATION FEE...
...AND EVERYTHING SHOULD HAVE BEEN FINE...
OKAY! TURN AGAIN RIGHT HERE!
REEL
YAKO ...?
SORRY... COULD I TAKE A BREAK...?
HUFF
SOON, YAKO WAS TOO WEAK TO GET OUT OF BED.

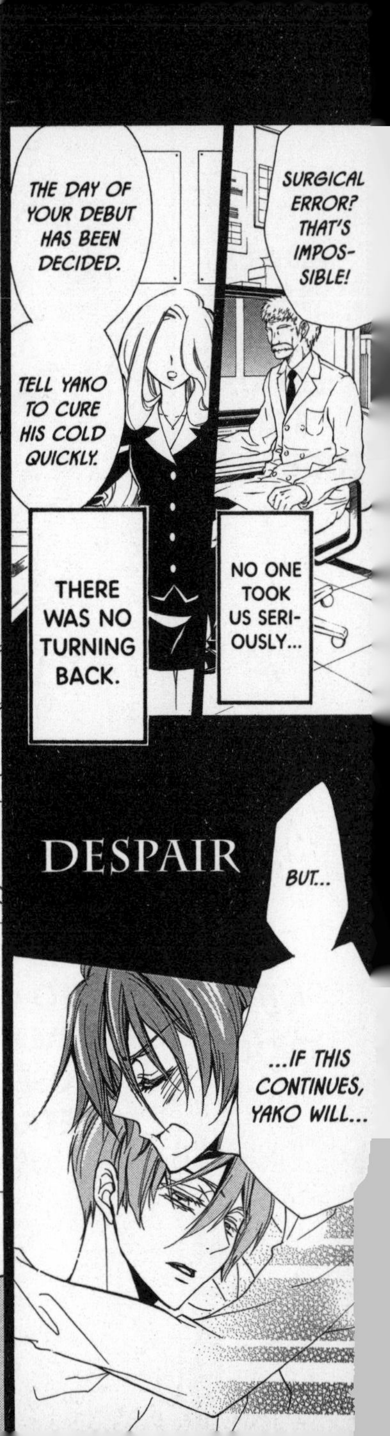
SURGICAL ERROR? THAT'S IMPOSSIBLE!
NO ONE TOOK US SERIOUSLY...
THE DAY OF YOUR DEBUT HAS BEEN DECIDED.
TELL YAKO TO CURE HIS COLD QUICKLY.
THERE WAS NO TURNING BACK.
DESPAIR
BUT...
...IF THIS CONTINUES, YAKO WILL...
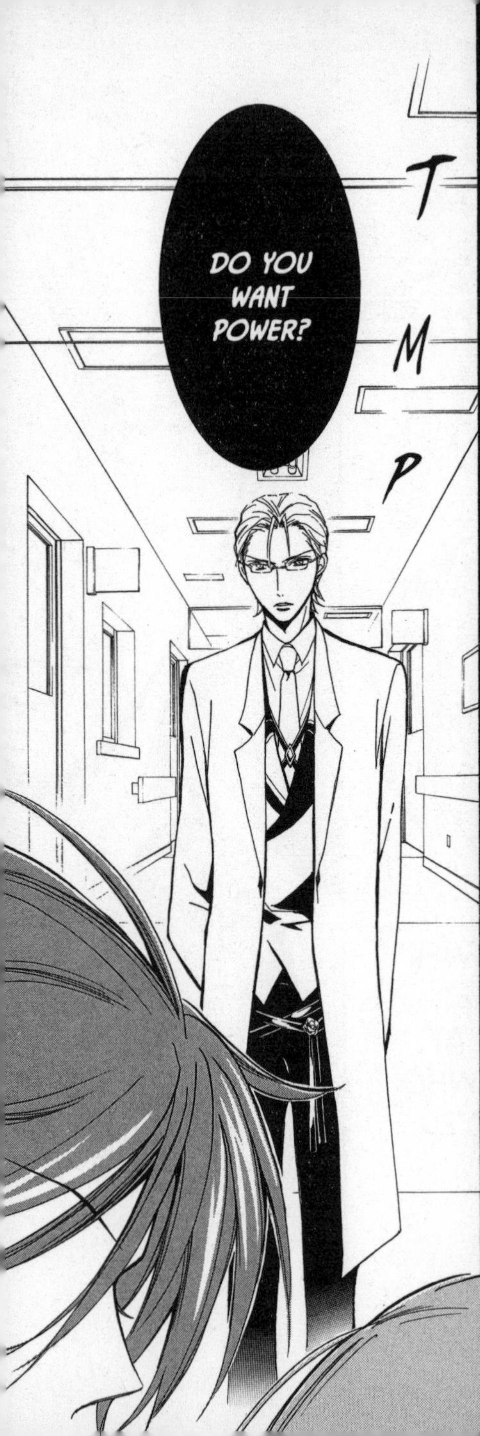
DO YOU WANT POWER?
TMP

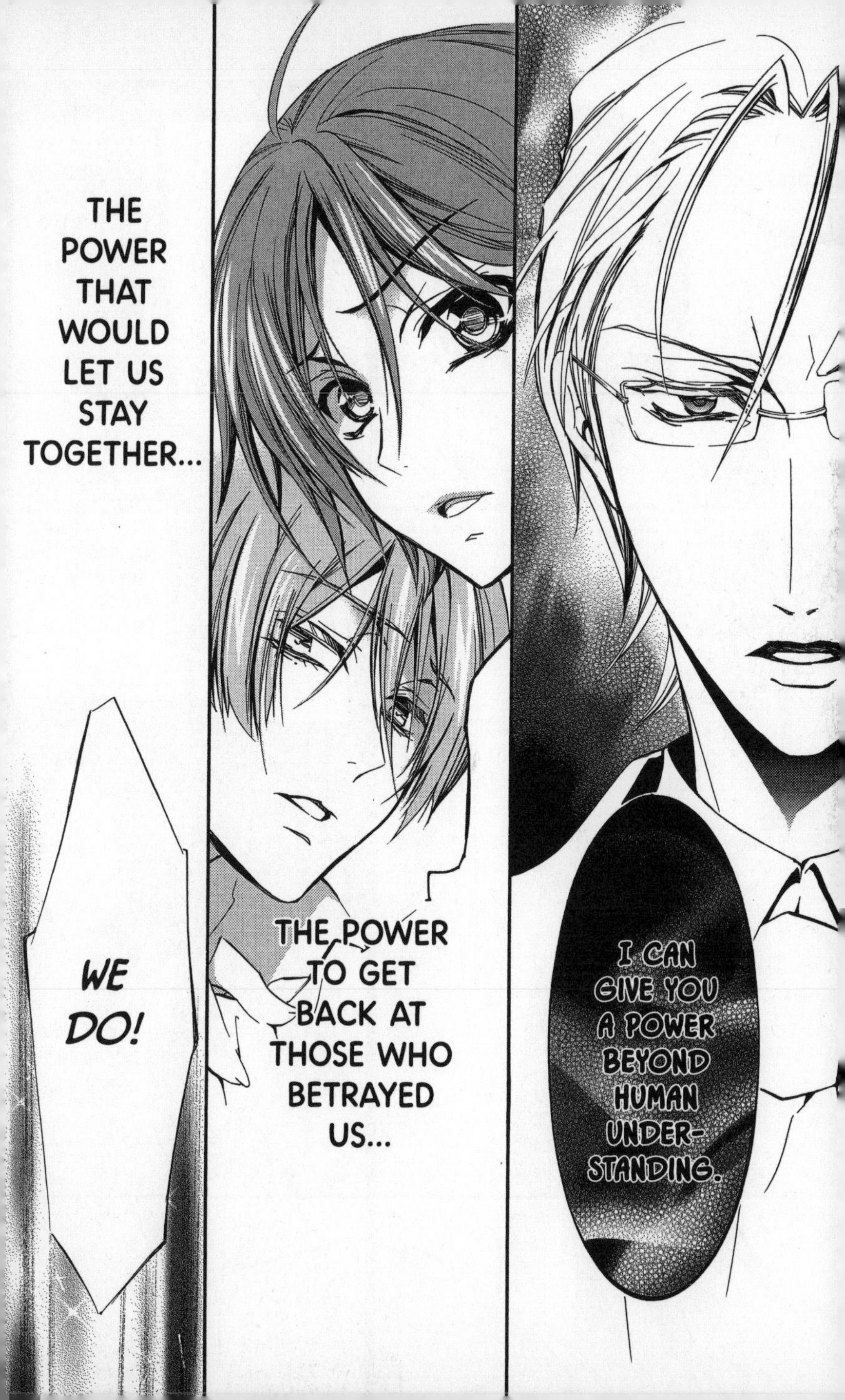
I CAN GIVE YOU A POWER BEYOND HUMAN UNDER-STANDING.
THE POWER TO GET BACK AT THOSE WHO BETRAYED US...
THE POWER THAT WOULD LET US STAY TOGETHER...
WE DO!

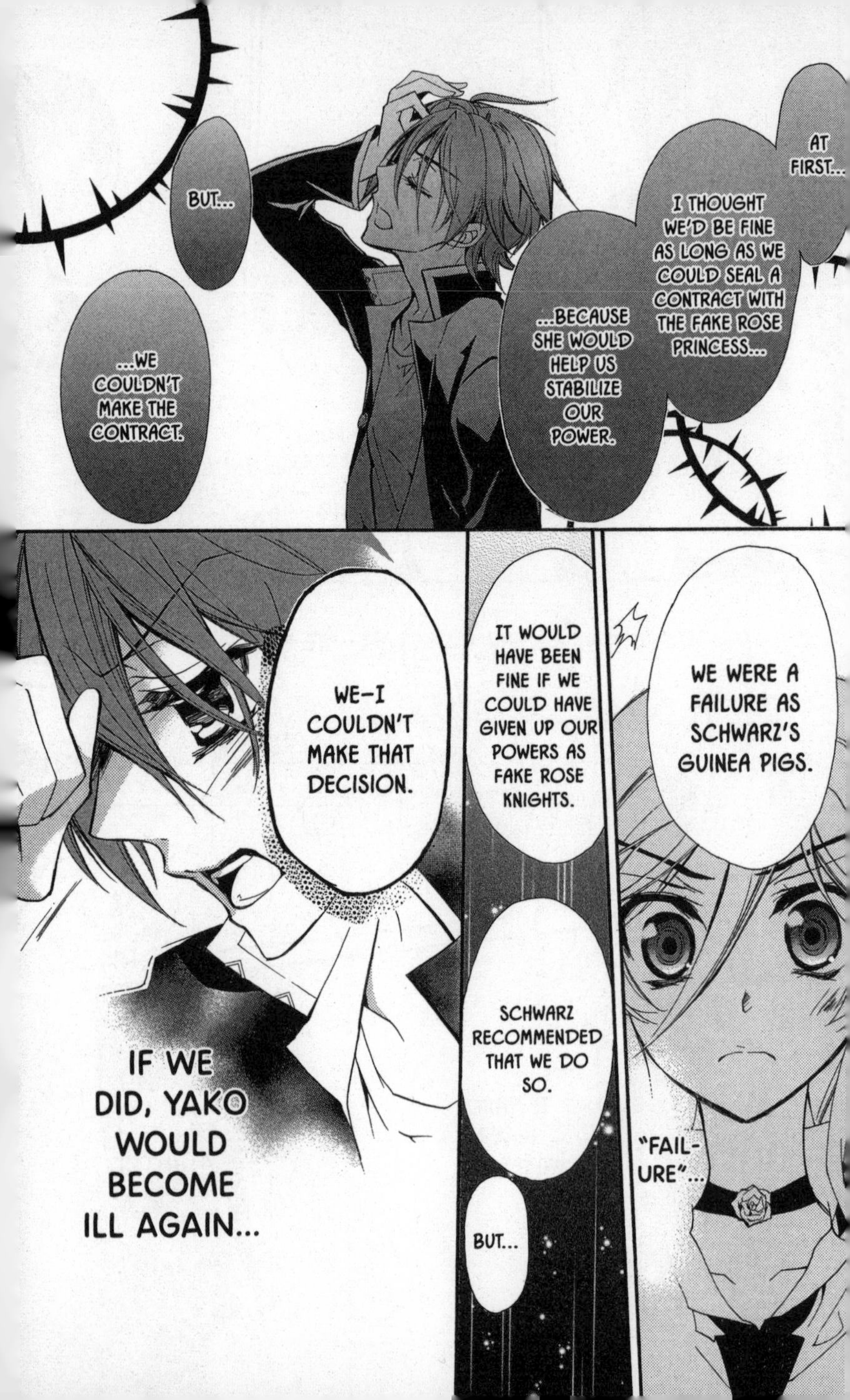
AT FIRST...
I THOUGHT WE'D BE FINE AS LONG AS WE COULD SEAL A CONTRACT WITH THE FAKE ROSE PRINCESS...
...BECAUSE SHE WOULD HELP US STABILIZE OUR POWER.
BUT...
...WE COULDN'T MAKE THE CONTRACT.
WE WERE A FAILURE AS SCHWARZ'S GUINEA PIGS.
"FAIL-URE"...
IT WOULD HAVE BEEN FINE IF WE COULD HAVE GIVEN UP OUR POWERS AS FAKE ROSE KNIGHTS.
SCHWARZ RECOMMENDED THAT WE DO SO.
BUT...
WE—I COULDN'T MAKE THAT DECISION.
IF WE DID, YAKO WOULD BECOME ILL AGAIN...

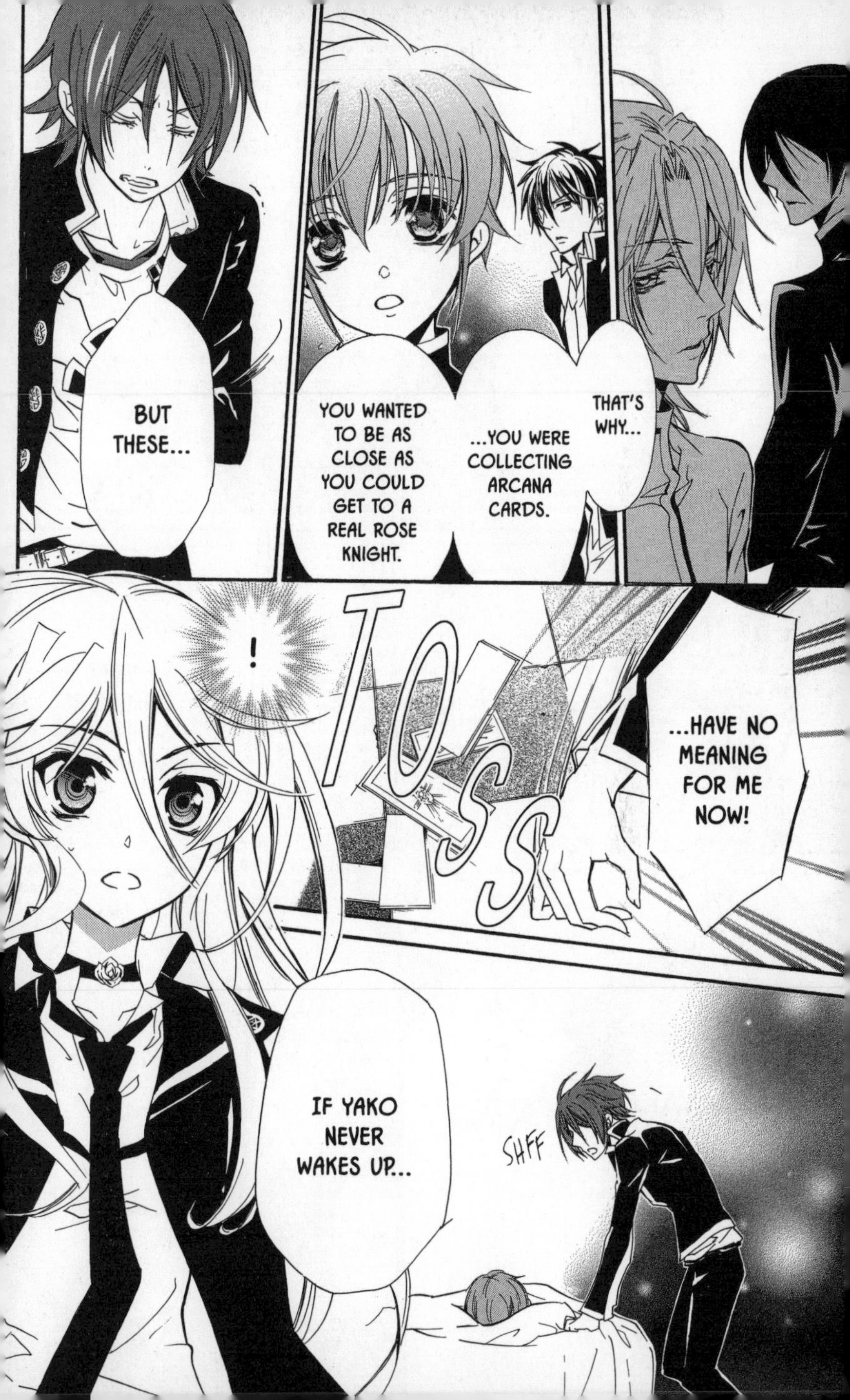
THAT'S WHY...
...YOU WERE COLLECTING ARCANA CARDS.
YOU WANTED TO BE AS CLOSE AS YOU COULD GET TO A REAL ROSE KNIGHT.
BUT THESE...
...HAVE NO MEANING FOR ME NOW!
TOSS
!
SHFF
IF YAKO NEVER WAKES UP...

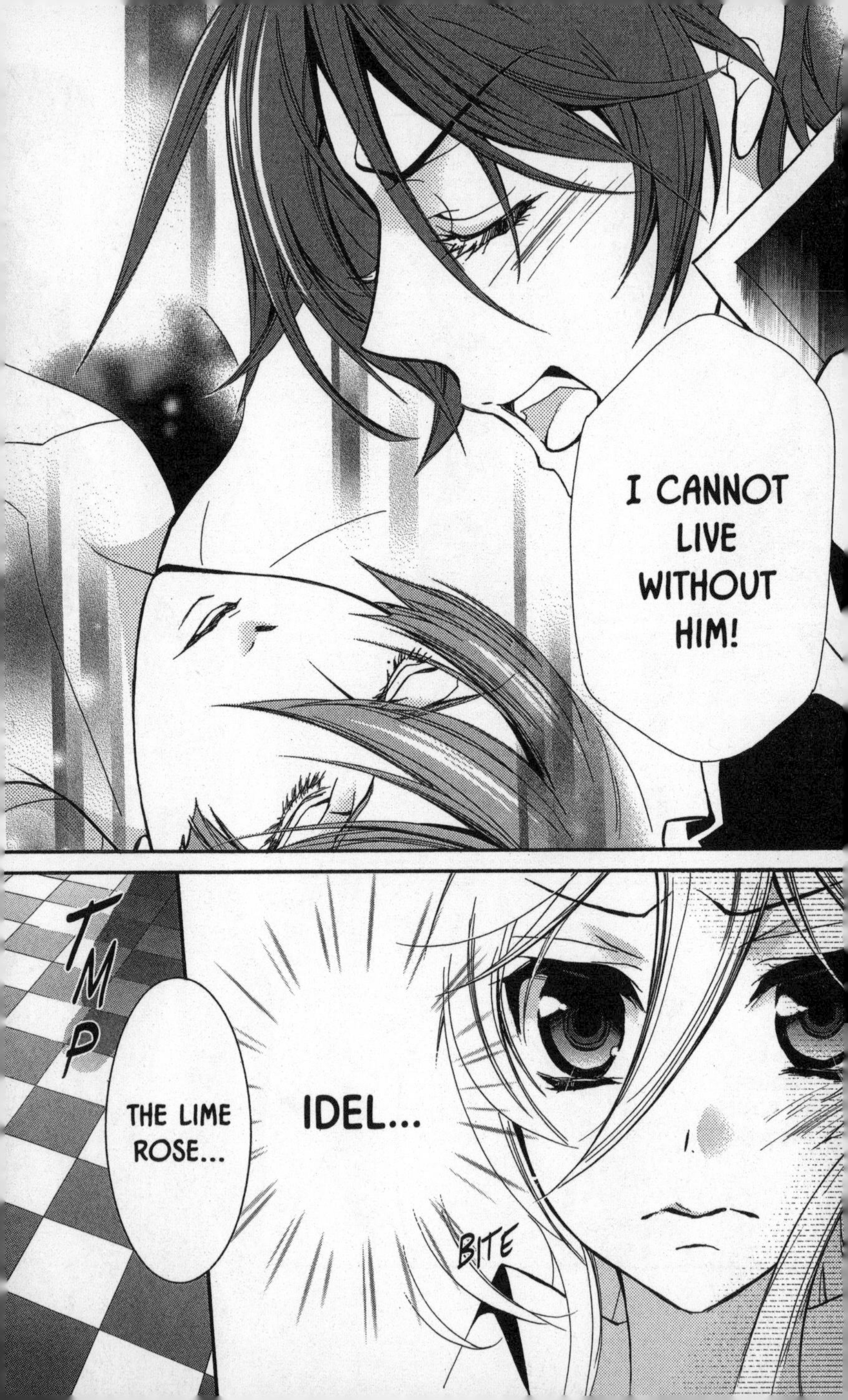
I CANNOT LIVE WITHOUT HIM!
TMP
IDEL...
THE LIME ROSE...
BITE

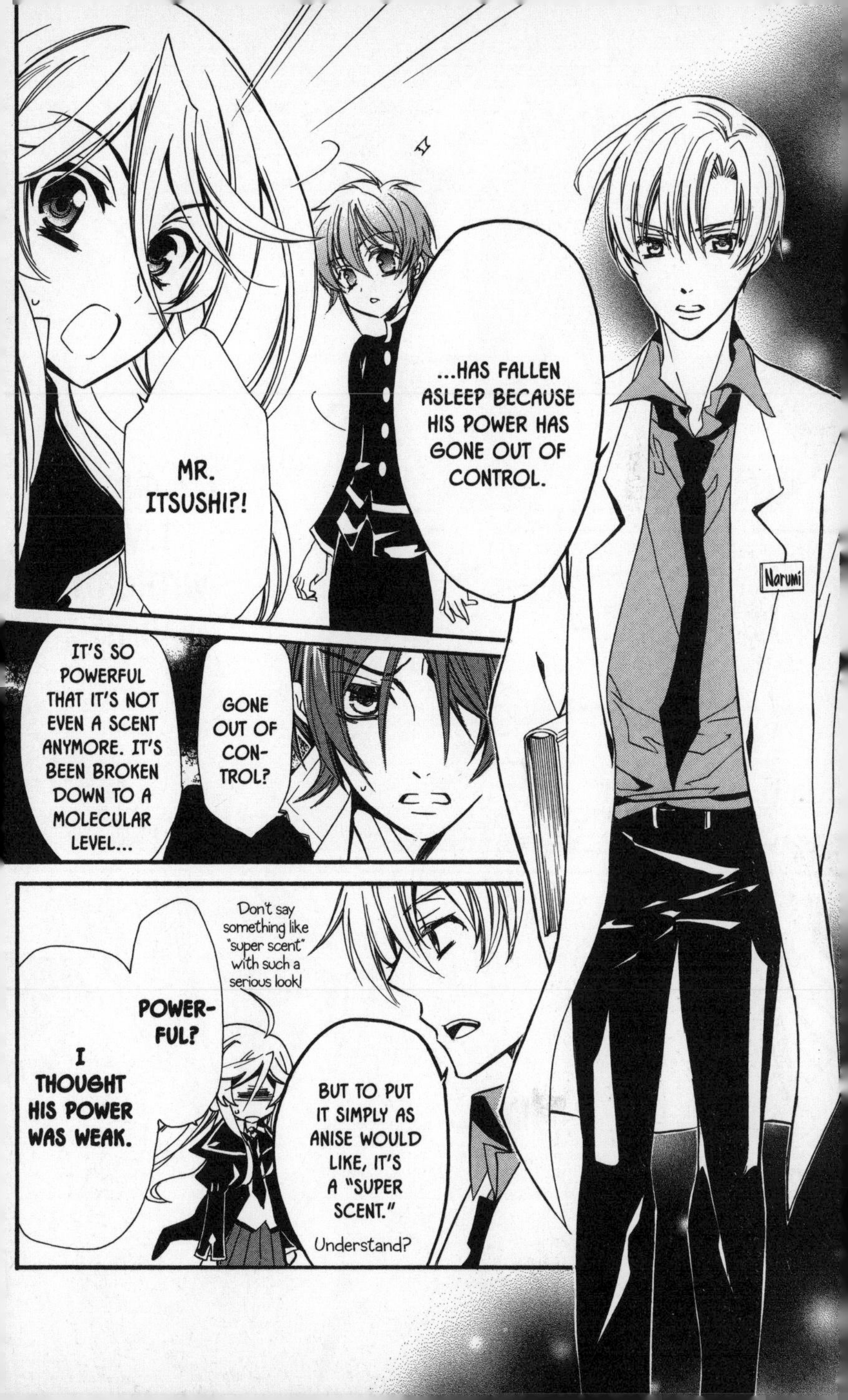
Narumi
...HAS FALLEN ASLEEP BECAUSE HIS POWER HAS GONE OUT OF CONTROL.
MR. ITSUSHI?!
GONE OUT OF CON-TROL?
IT'S SO POWERFUL THAT IT'S NOT EVEN A SCENT ANYMORE. IT'S BEEN BROKEN DOWN TO A MOLECULAR LEVEL...
BUT TO PUT IT SIMPLY AS ANISE WOULD LIKE, IT'S A "SUPER SCENT."
Understand?
Don't say something like "super scent" with such a serious look!
POWER-FUL?
I THOUGHT HIS POWER WAS WEAK.

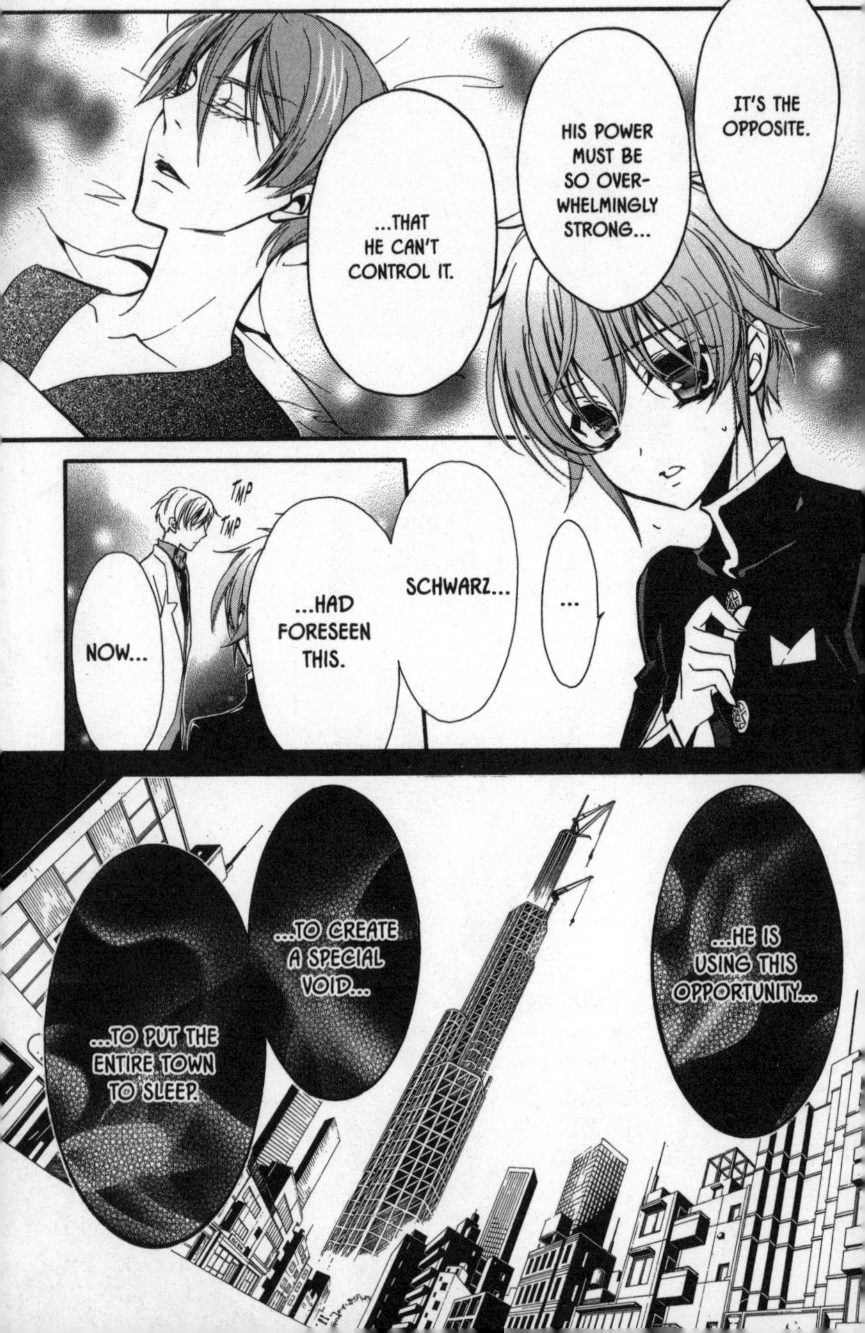
IT'S THE OPPOSITE.
HIS POWER MUST BE SO OVER-WHELMINGLY STRONG...
...THAT HE CAN'T CONTROL IT.
...
SCHWARZ...
...HAD FORESEEN THIS.
TMP TMP
NOW...
...HE IS USING THIS OPPORTUNITY...
...TO CREATE A SPECIAL VOID...
...TO PUT THE ENTIRE TOWN TO SLEEP.

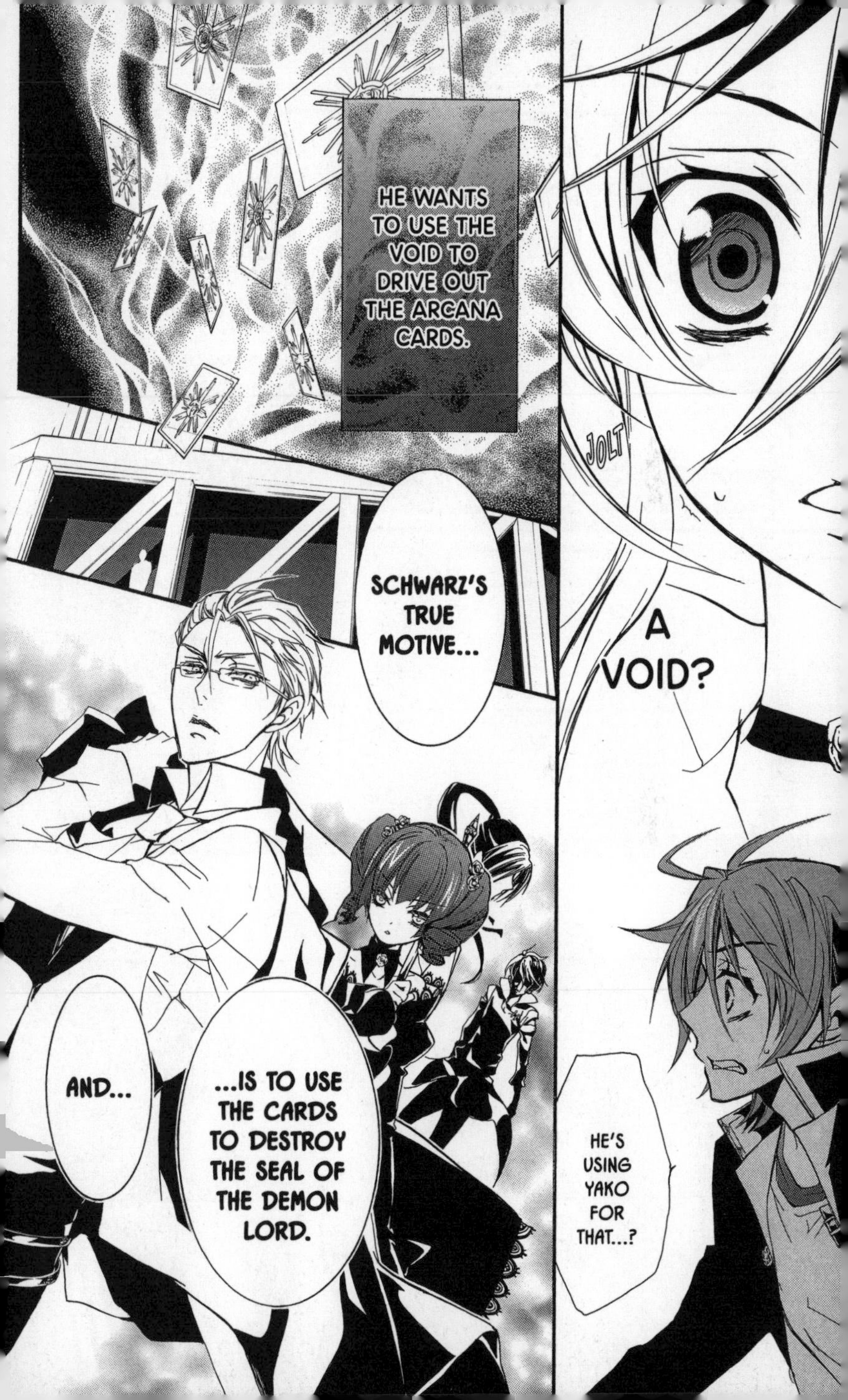
JOLT
A VOID?
HE'S USING YAKO FOR THAT...?
HE WANTS TO USE THE VOID TO DRIVE OUT THE ARCANA CARDS.
SCHWARZ'S TRUE MOTIVE...
...IS TO USE THE CARDS TO DESTROY THE SEAL OF THE DEMON LORD.
AND...

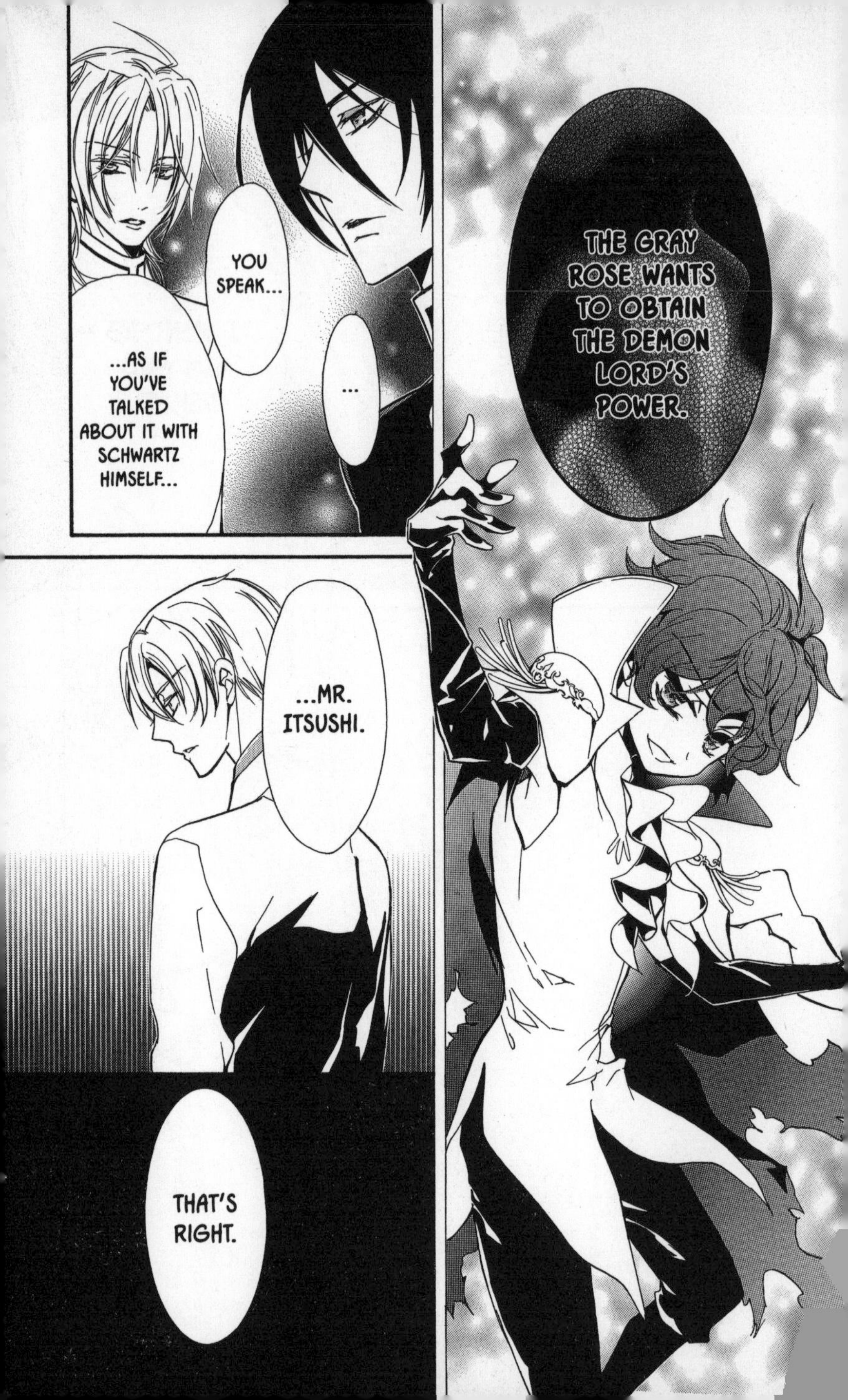
THE GRAY ROSE WANTS TO OBTAIN THE DEMON LORD'S POWER.
YOU SPEAK...
...AS IF YOU'VE TALKED ABOUT IT WITH SCHWARTZ HIMSELF...
...
...MR. ITSUSHI.
THAT'S RIGHT.

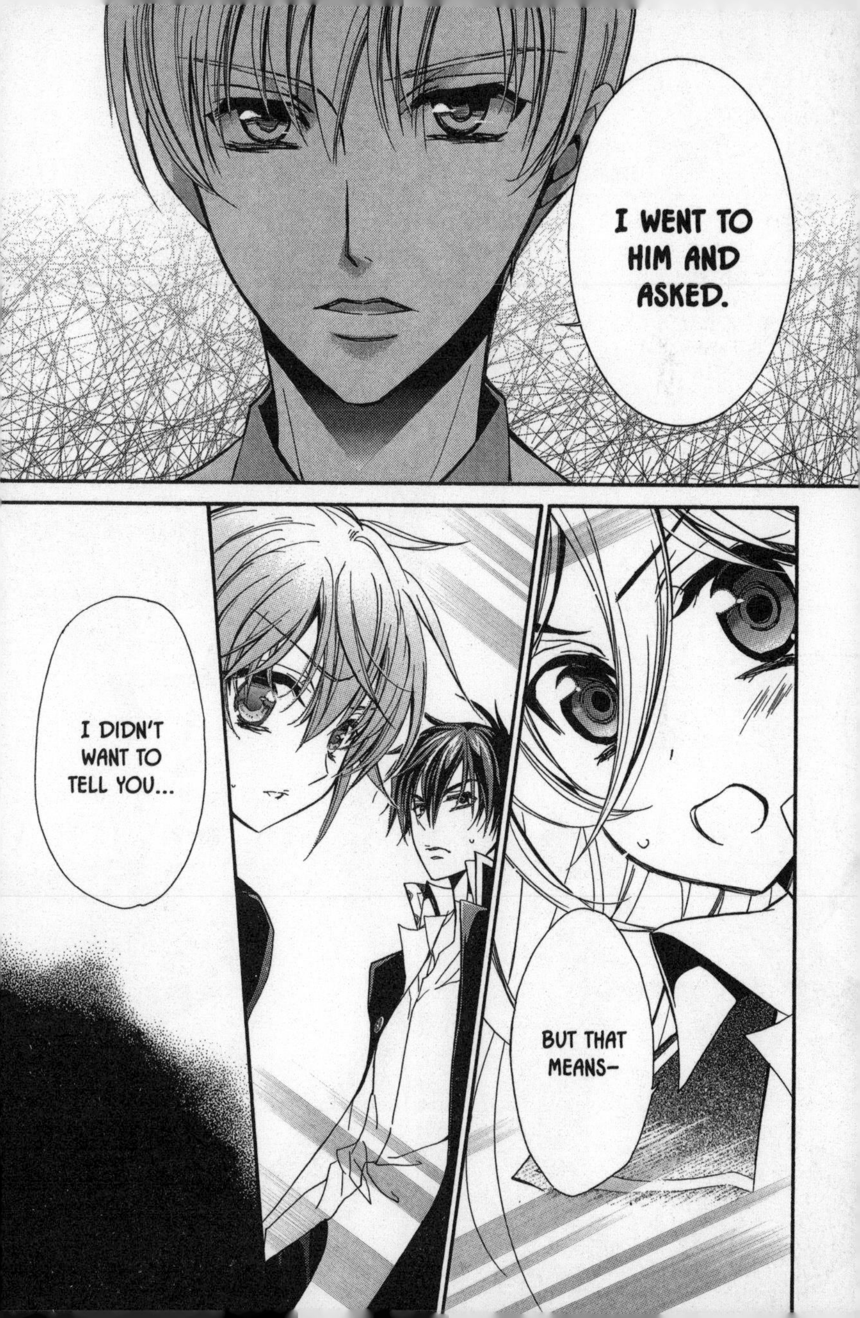
I WENT TO HIM AND ASKED.
BUT THAT MEANS—
I DIDN'T WANT TO TELL YOU...

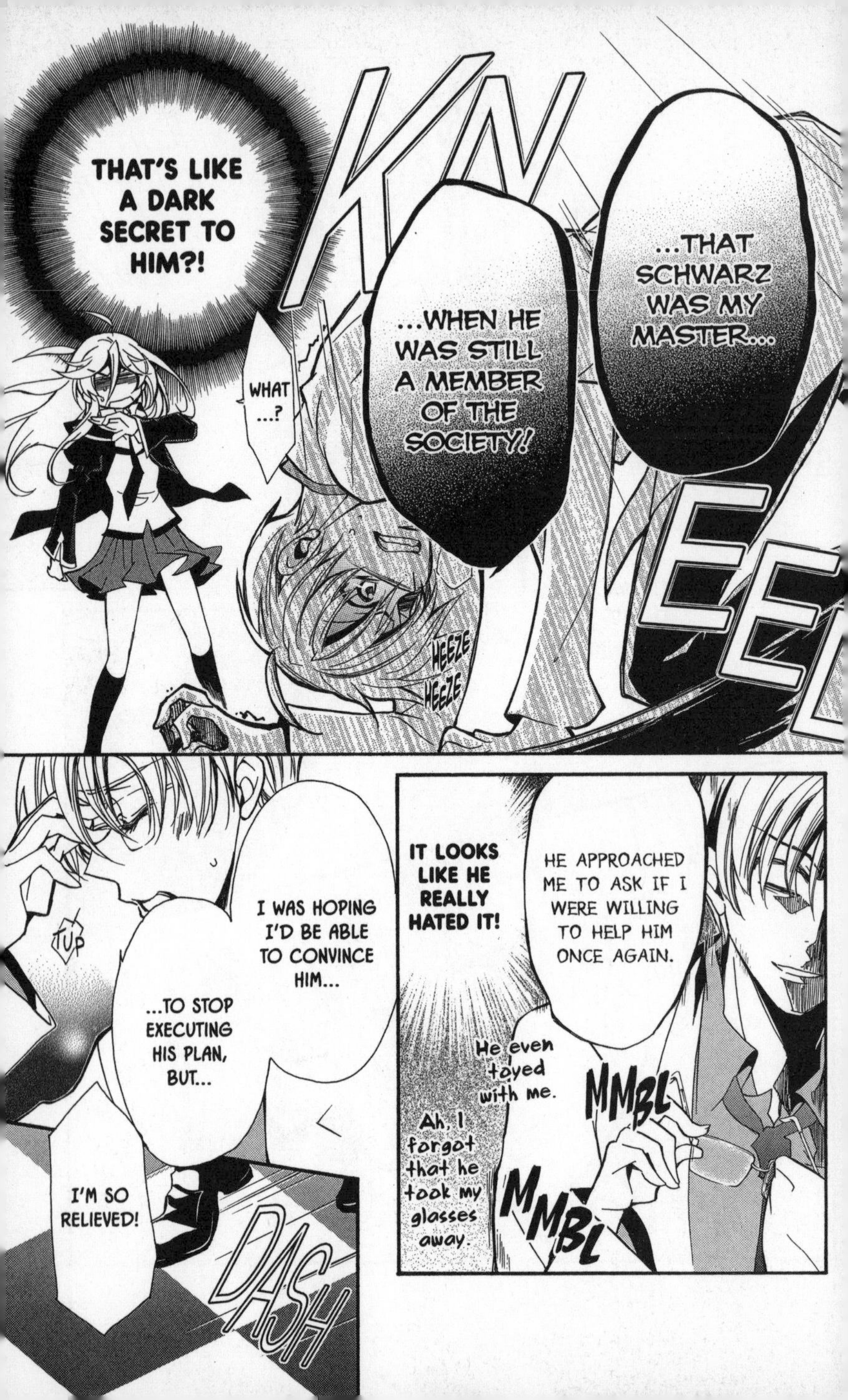
KN
...THAT SCHWARZ WAS MY MASTER...
...WHEN HE WAS STILL A MEMBER OF THE SOCIETY!
EEE
WHAT ...?
THAT'S LIKE A DARK SECRET TO HIM?!
HEEZE HEEZE
HE APPROACHED ME TO ASK IF I WERE WILLING TO HELP HIM ONCE AGAIN.
IT LOOKS LIKE HE REALLY HATED IT!
He even toyed with me.
MMBL
MMBL
Ah, I forgot that he took my glasses away.
I WAS HOPING I'D BE ABLE TO CONVINCE HIM...
...TO STOP EXECUTING HIS PLAN, BUT...
TUP
I'M SO RELIEVED!
DASH

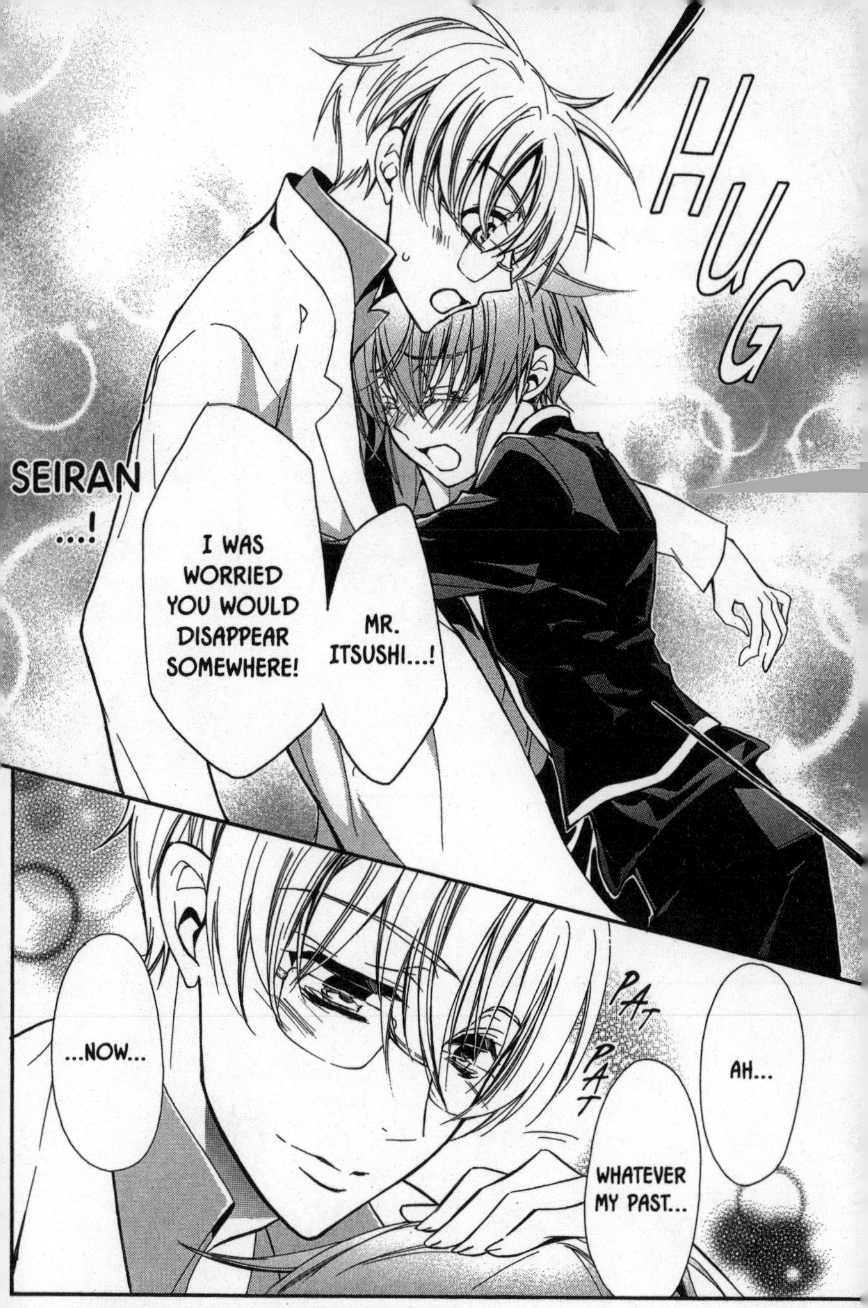
HUG
MR. ITSUSHI...!
I WAS WORRIED YOU WOULD DISAPPEAR SOMEWHERE!
SEIRAN ...!
AH...
PAT PAT
WHATEVER MY PAST...
...NOW...

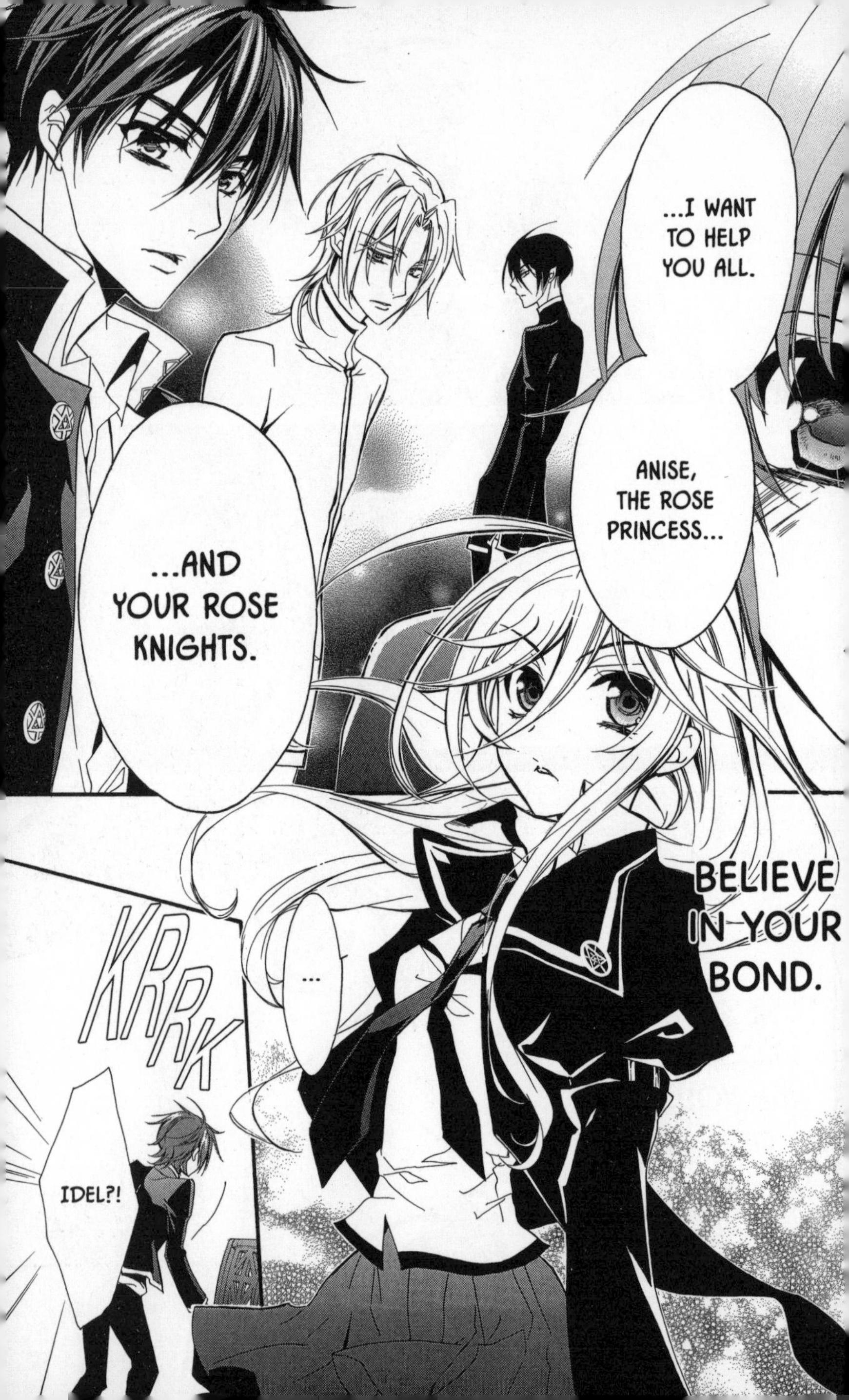
...I WANT TO HELP YOU ALL.
ANISE, THE ROSE PRINCESS...
...AND YOUR ROSE KNIGHTS.
BELIEVE IN YOUR BOND.
...
KRRK
IDEL?!

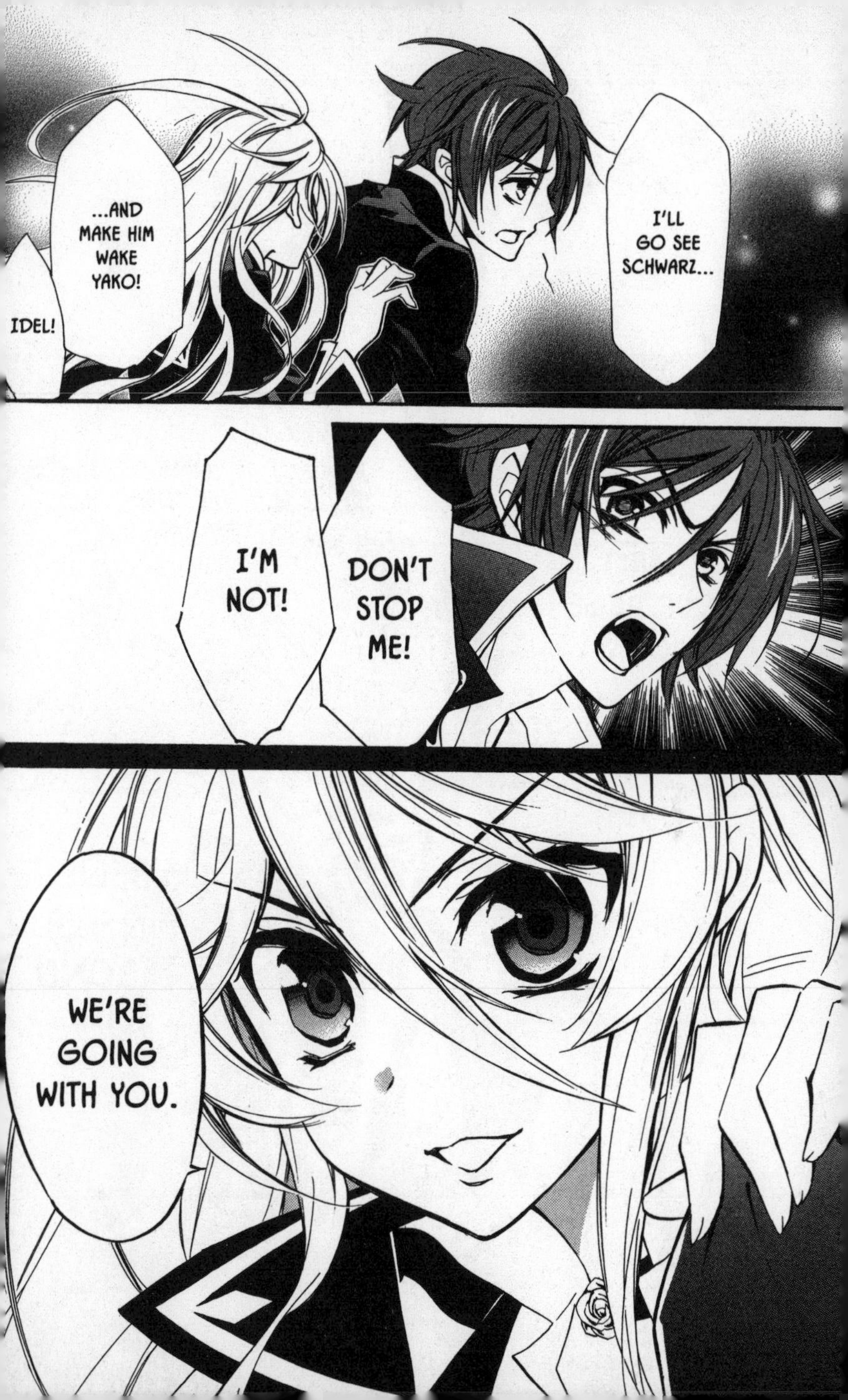
I'LL GO SEE SCHWARZ...
...AND MAKE HIM WAKE YAKO!
IDEL!
DON'T STOP ME!
I'M NOT!
WE'RE GOING WITH YOU.

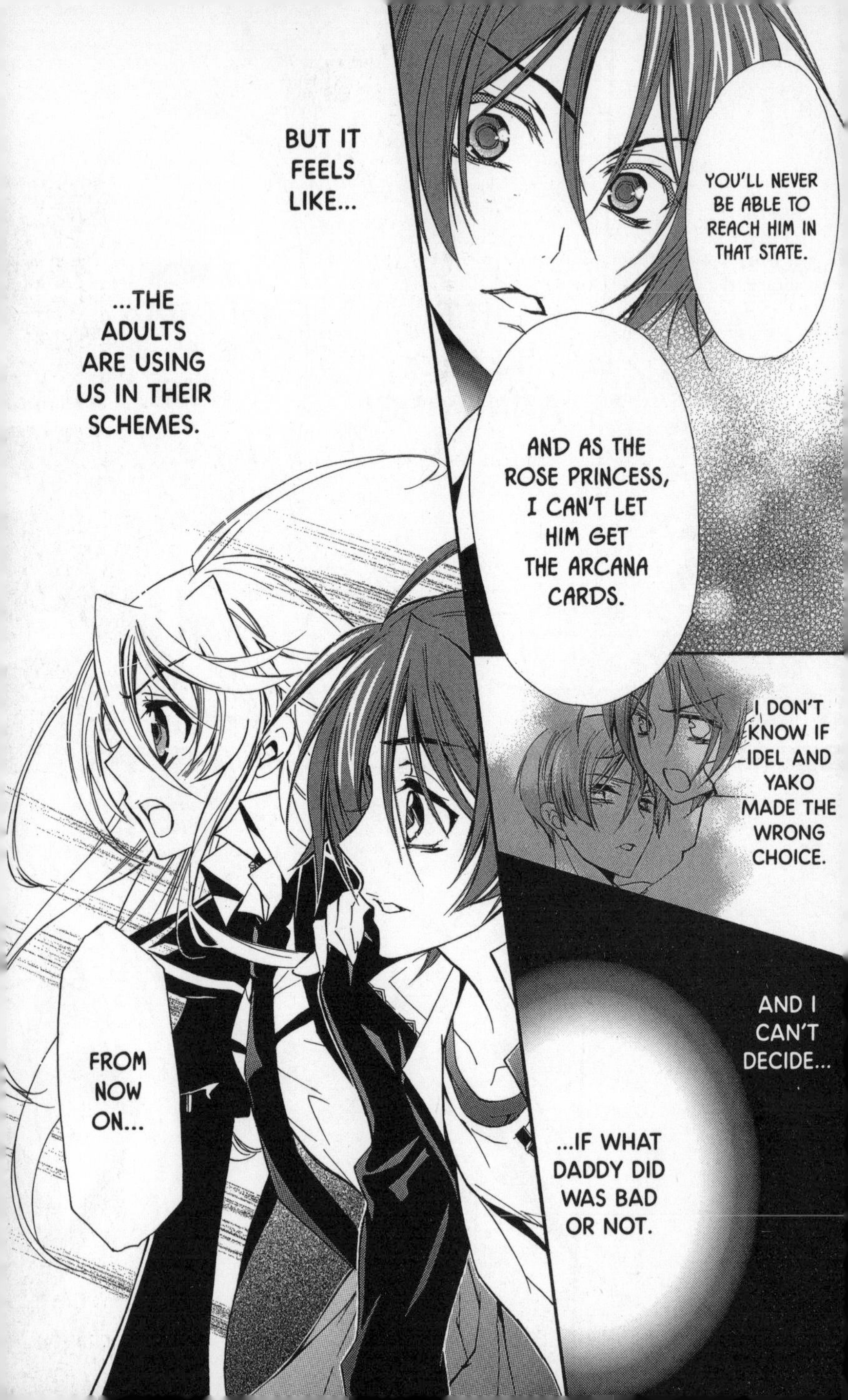
YOU'LL NEVER BE ABLE TO REACH HIM IN THAT STATE.
AND AS THE ROSE PRINCESS, I CAN'T LET HIM GET THE ARCANA CARDS.
I DON'T KNOW IF IDEL AND YAKO MADE THE WRONG CHOICE.
AND I CAN'T DECIDE...
...IF WHAT DADDY DID WAS BAD OR NOT.
BUT IT FEELS LIKE...
...THE ADULTS ARE USING US IN THEIR SCHEMES.
FROM NOW ON...

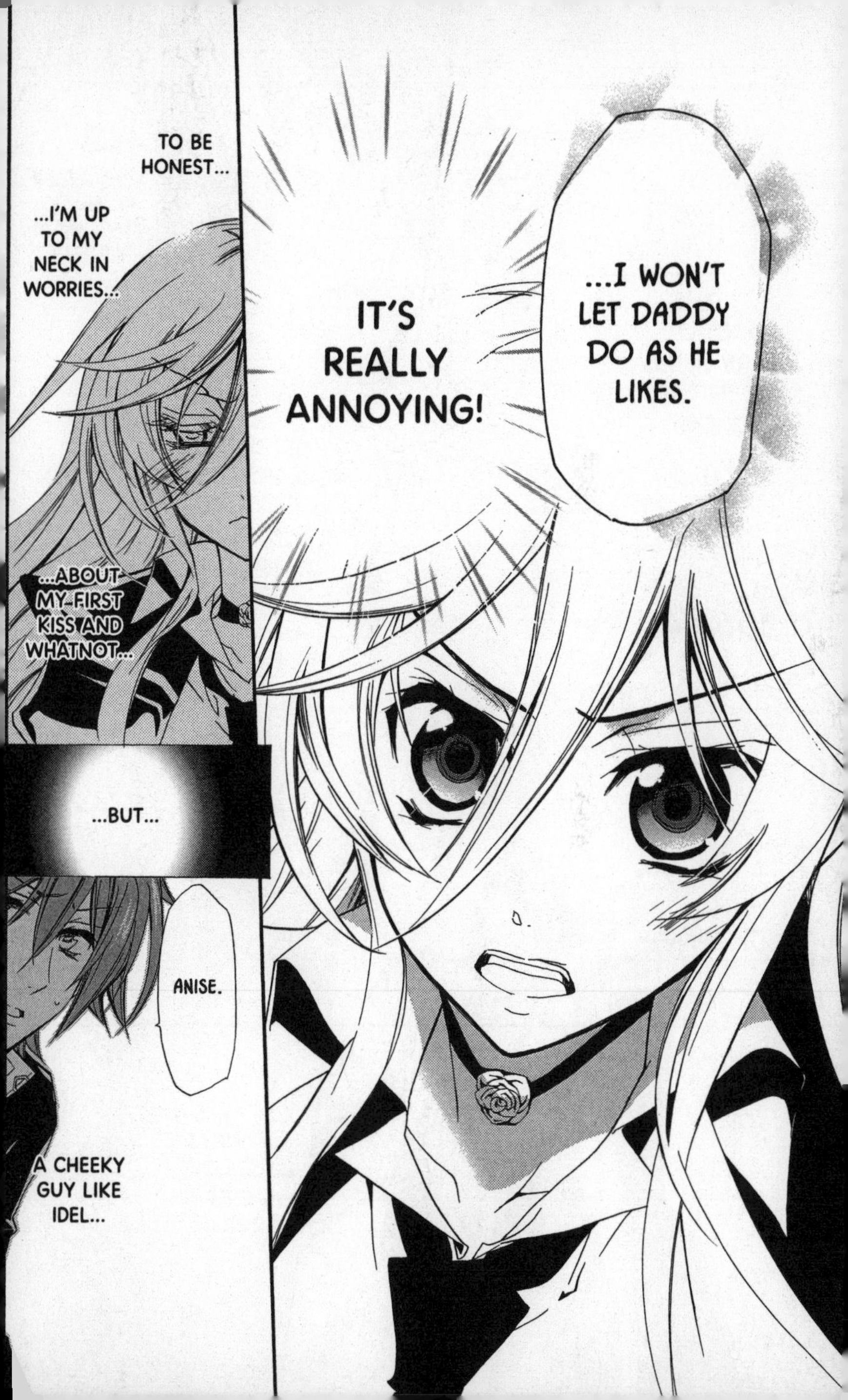
...I WON'T LET DADDY DO AS HE LIKES.
IT'S REALLY ANNOYING!
TO BE HONEST...
...I'M UP TO MY NECK IN WORRIES...
...ABOUT MY FIRST KISS AND WHATNOT...
...BUT...
ANISE.
A CHEEKY GUY LIKE IDEL...

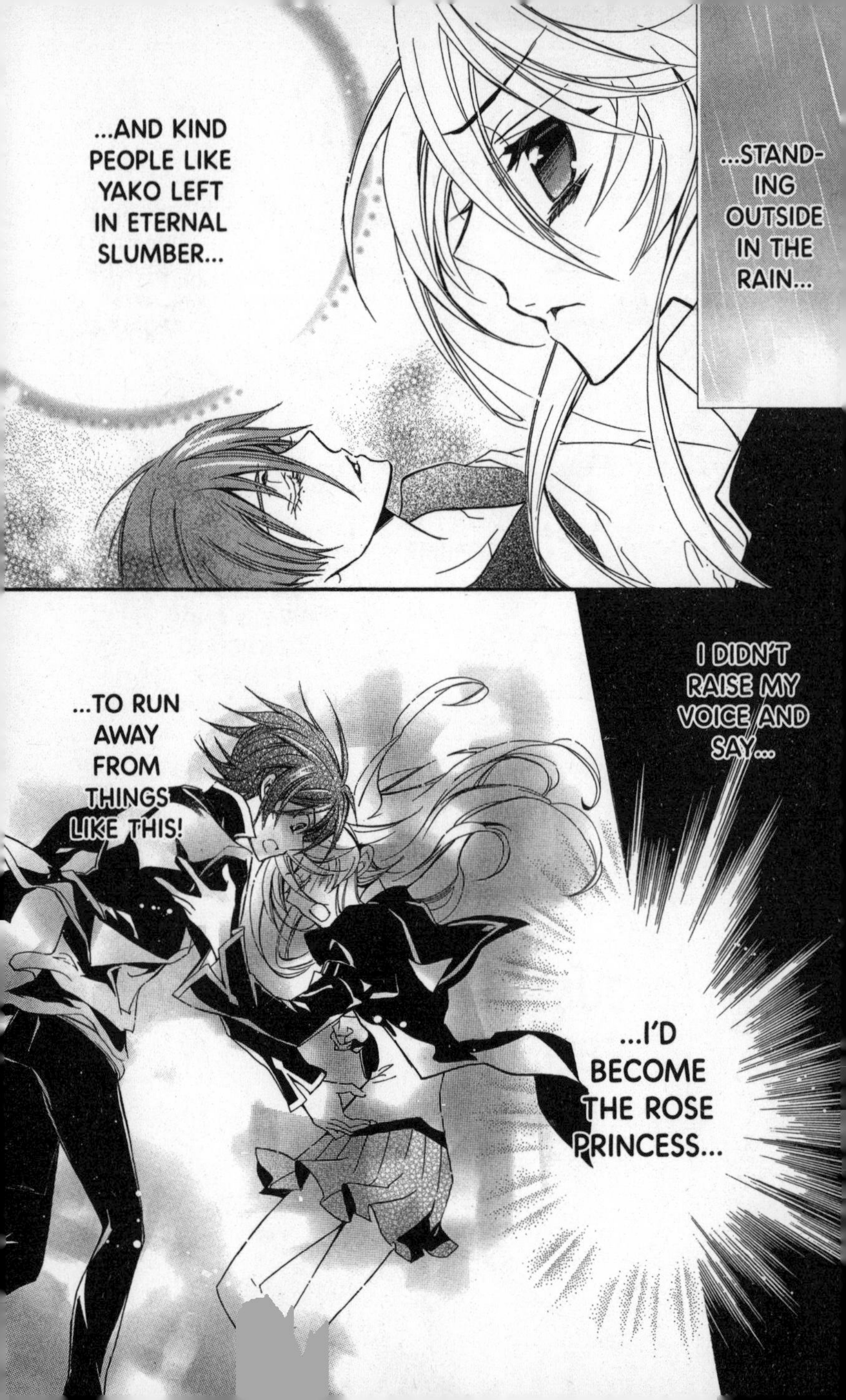
...STAND-ING OUTSIDE IN THE RAIN...
...AND KIND PEOPLE LIKE YAKO LEFT IN ETERNAL SLUMBER...
I DIDN'T RAISE MY VOICE AND SAY...
...TO RUN AWAY FROM THINGS LIKE THIS!
...I'D BECOME THE ROSE PRINCESS...

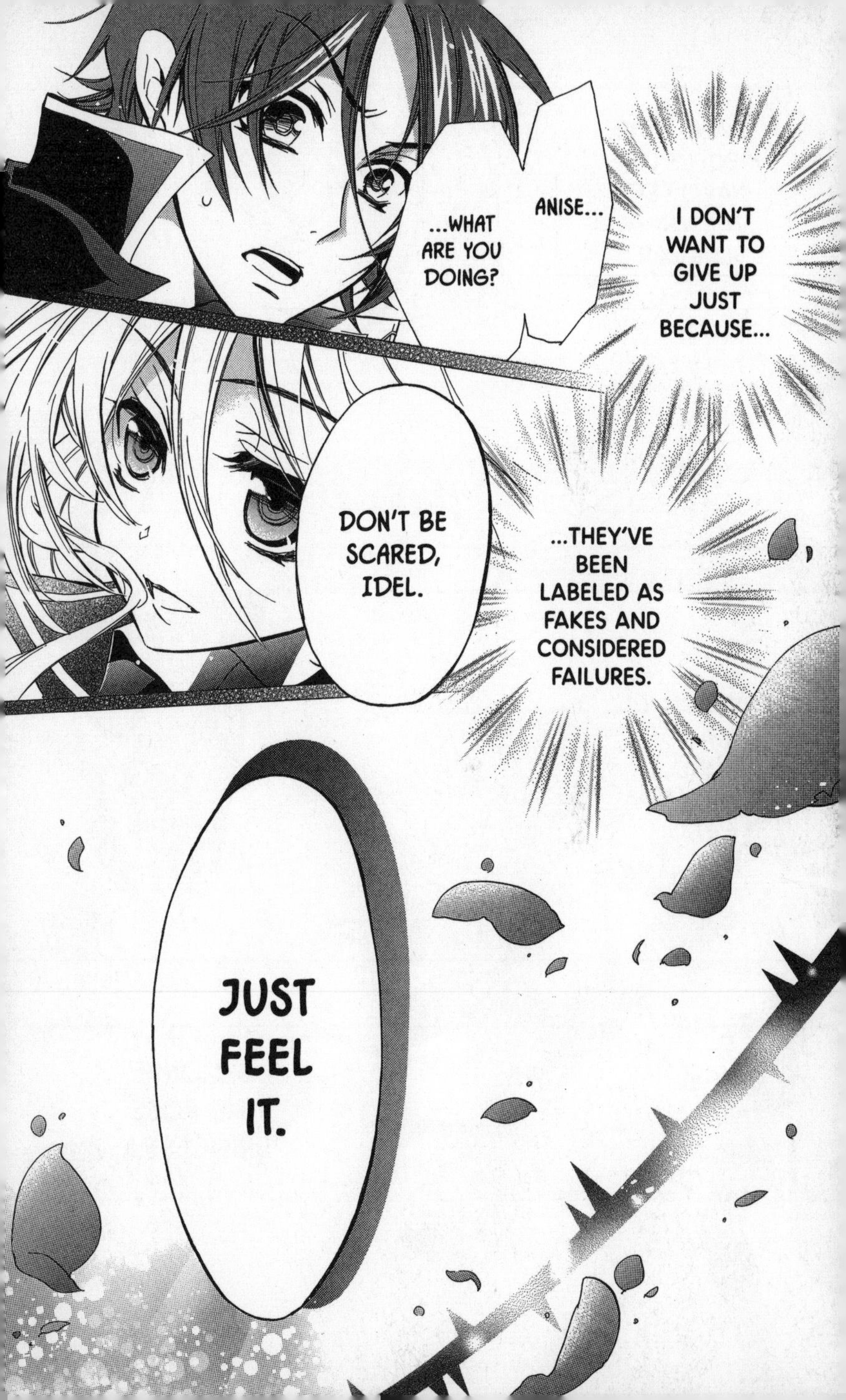
I DON'T WANT TO GIVE UP JUST BECAUSE...
ANISE...
...WHAT ARE YOU DOING?
...THEY'VE BEEN LABELED AS FAKES AND CONSIDERED FAILURES.
DON'T BE SCARED, IDEL.
JUST FEEL IT.

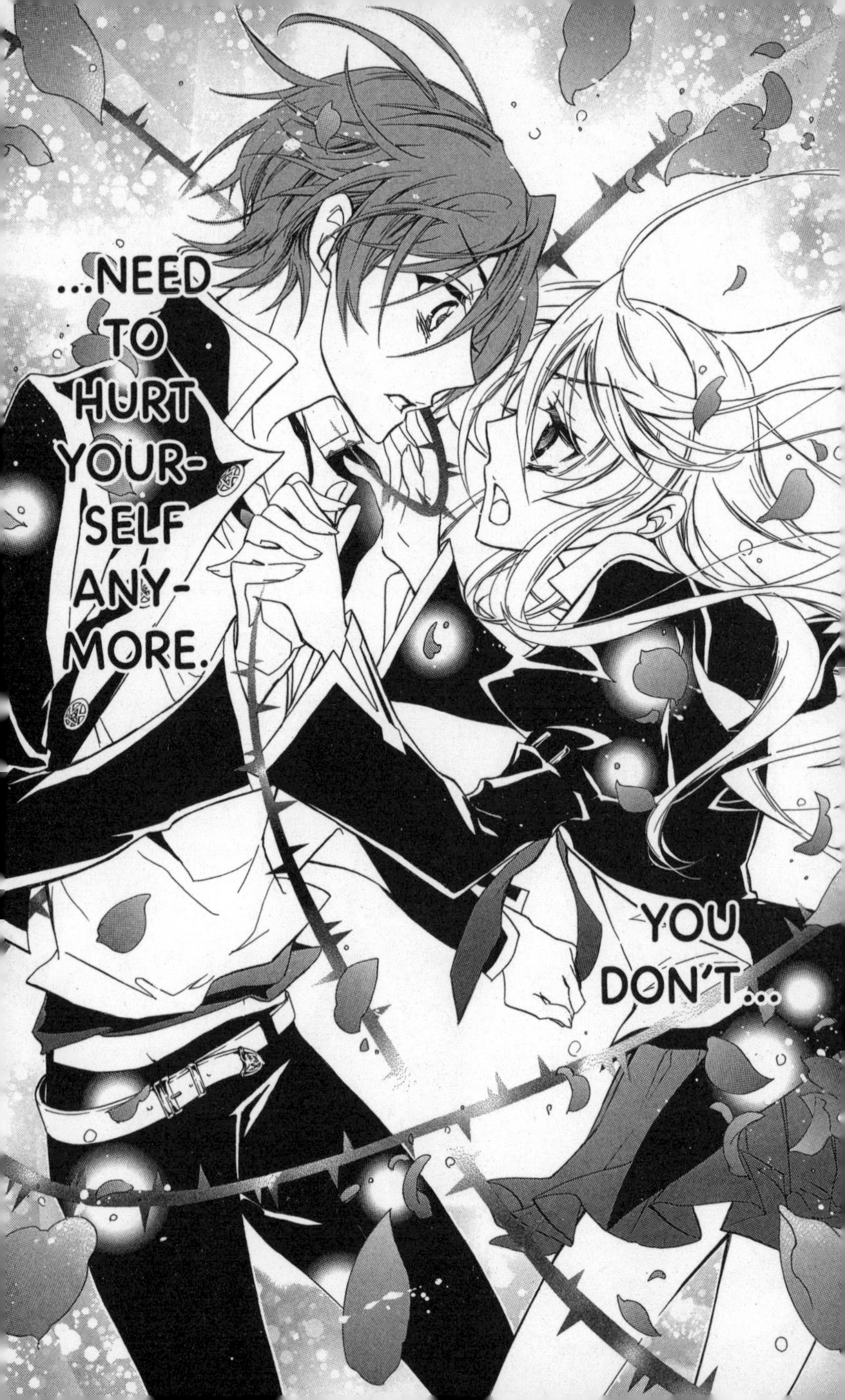
...NEED TO HURT YOUR-SELF ANY-MORE.
YOU DON'T...

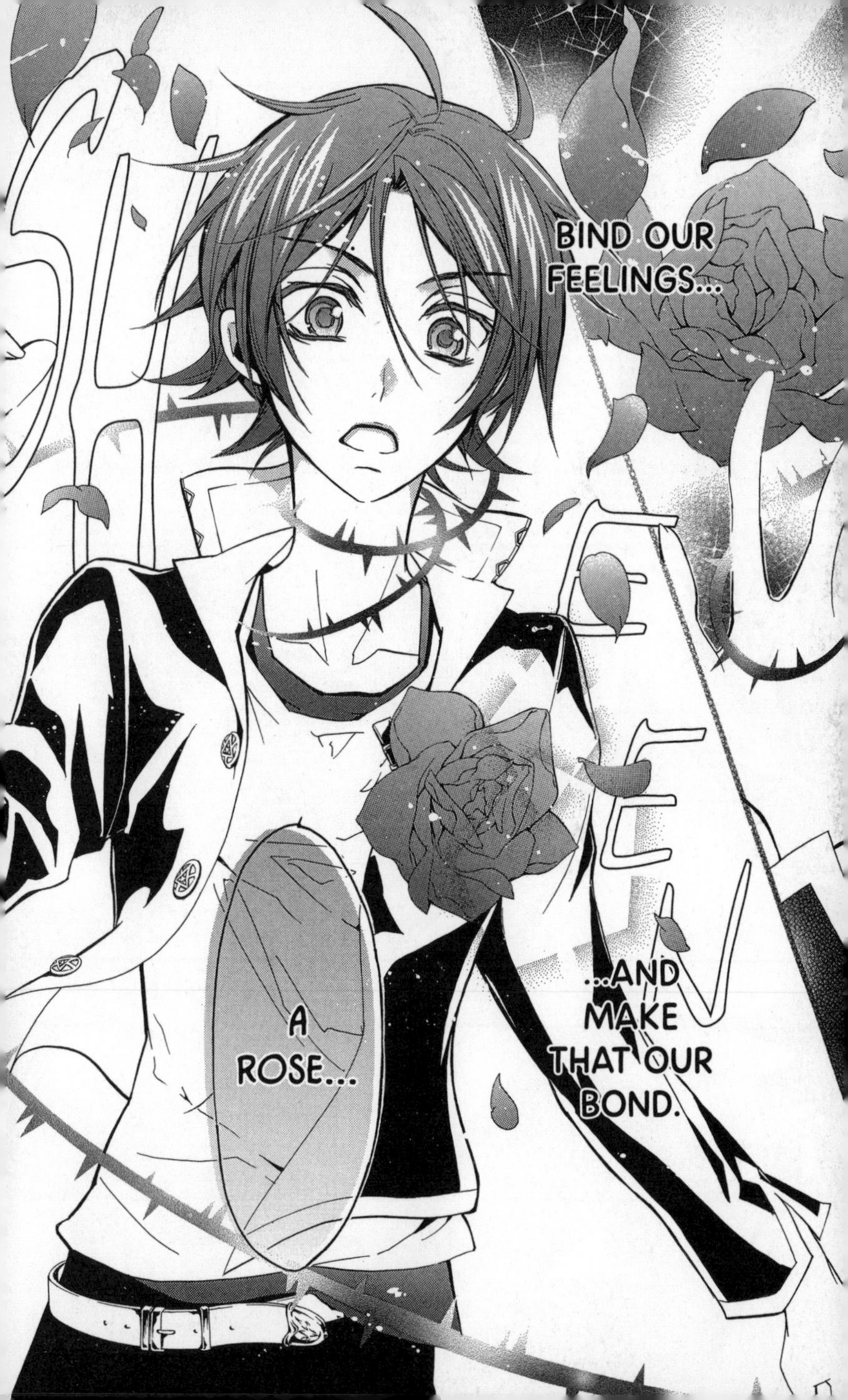
BIND OUR FEELINGS...
...AND MAKE THAT OUR BOND.
A ROSE...

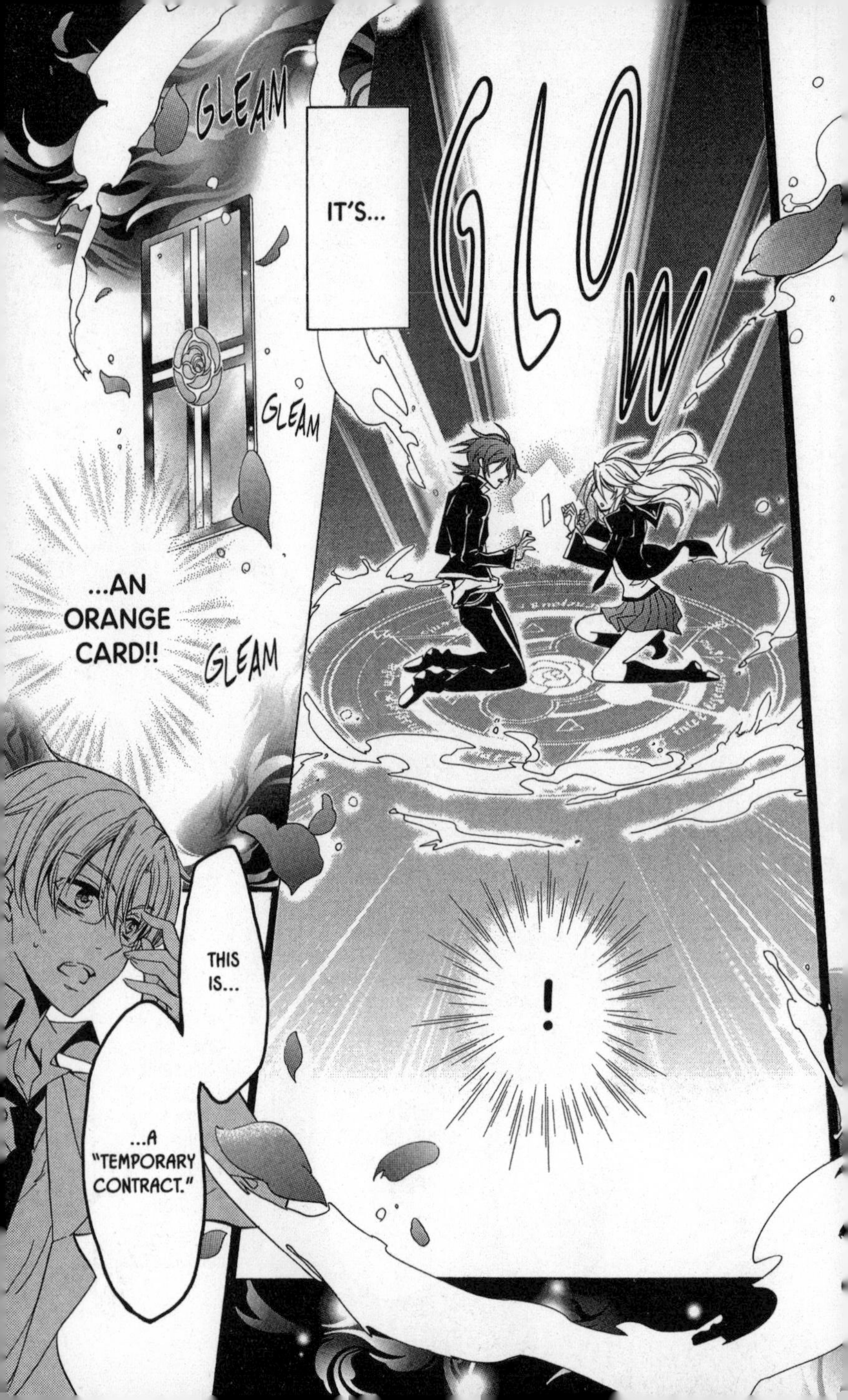
GLOW
IT'S...
GLEAM
GLEAM
...AN ORANGE CARD!!
GLEAM
!
THIS IS...
...A "TEMPORARY CONTRACT."

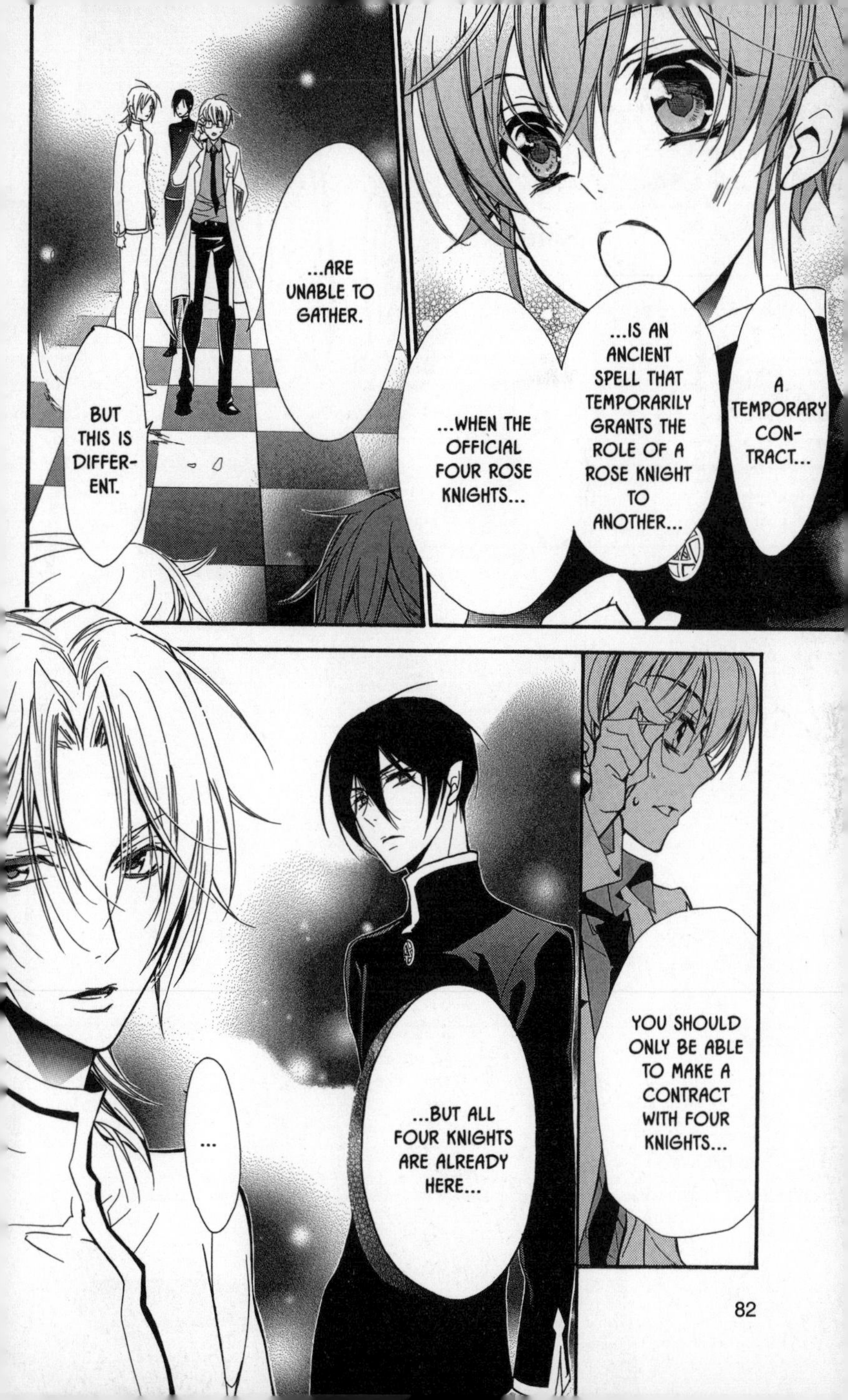
A TEMPORARY CONTRACT...
...IS AN ANCIENT SPELL THAT TEMPORARILY GRANTS THE ROLE OF A ROSE KNIGHT TO ANOTHER...
...WHEN THE OFFICIAL FOUR ROSE KNIGHTS...
...ARE UNABLE TO GATHER.
BUT THIS IS DIFFERENT.
YOU SHOULD ONLY BE ABLE TO MAKE A CONTRACT WITH FOUR KNIGHTS...
...BUT ALL FOUR KNIGHTS ARE ALREADY HERE...
...

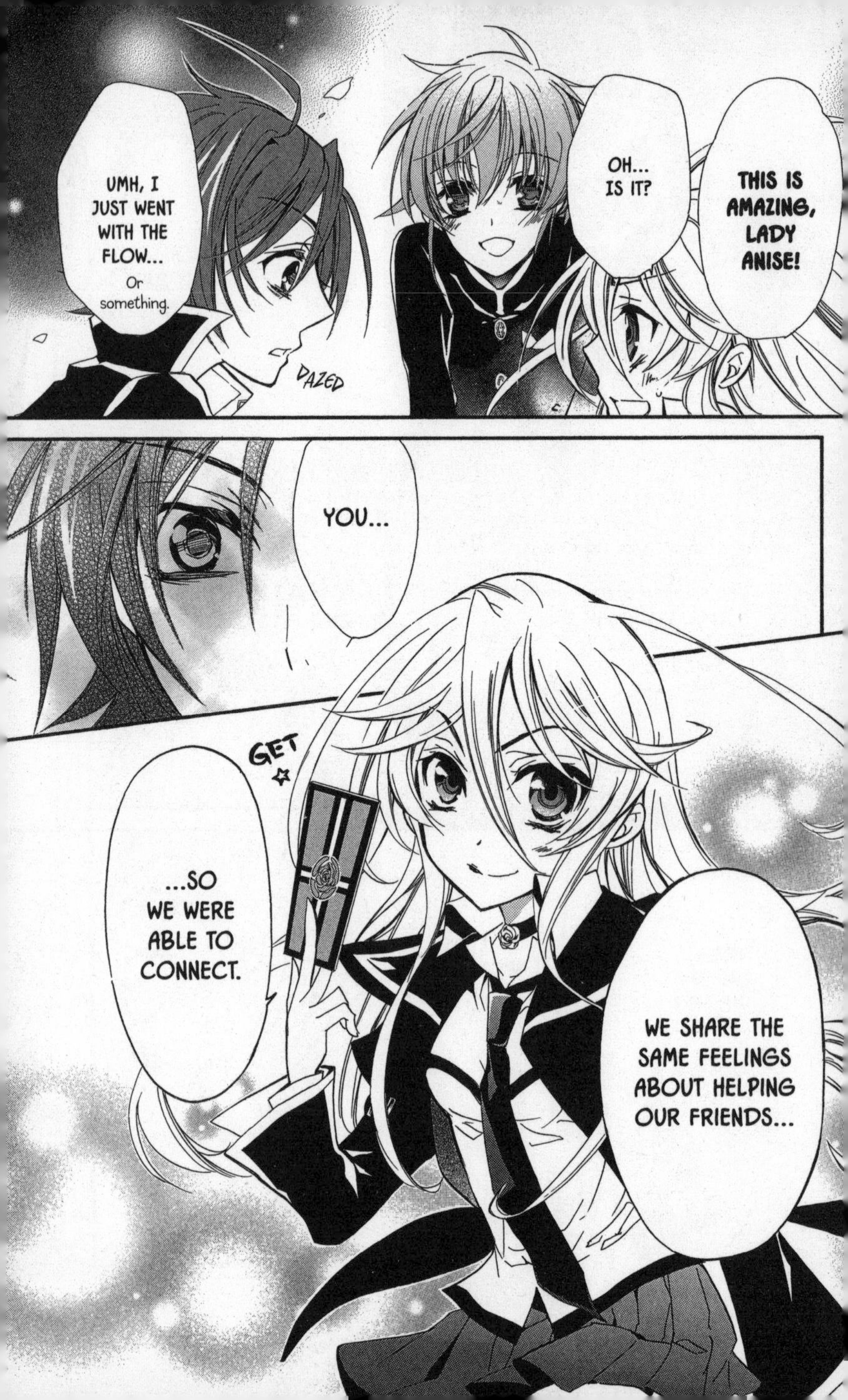
THIS IS AMAZING, LADY ANISE!
OH... IS IT?
UMH, I JUST WENT WITH THE FLOW...
Or something.
DAZED
YOU...
WE SHARE THE SAME FEELINGS ABOUT HELPING OUR FRIENDS...
GET ☆
...SO WE WERE ABLE TO CONNECT.

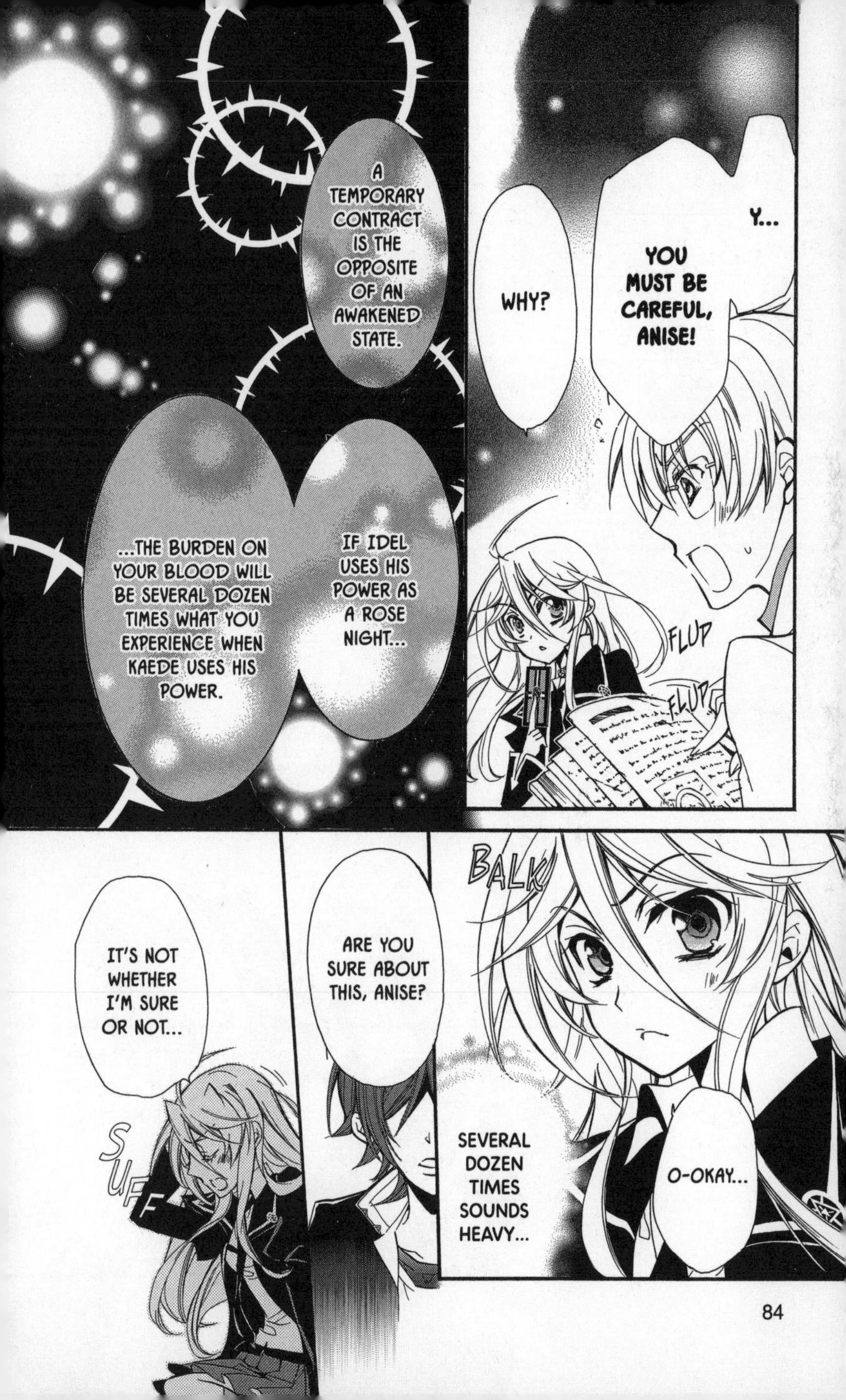
Y...
YOU MUST BE CAREFUL, ANISE!
WHY?
FLUP
FLUP
A TEMPORARY CONTRACT IS THE OPPOSITE OF AN AWAKENED STATE.
IF IDEL USES HIS POWER AS A ROSE NIGHT...
...THE BURDEN ON YOUR BLOOD WILL BE SEVERAL DOZEN TIMES WHAT YOU EXPERIENCE WHEN KAEDE USES HIS POWER.
BALK
O-OKAY...
SEVERAL DOZEN TIMES SOUNDS HEAVY...
ARE YOU SURE ABOUT THIS, ANISE?
IT'S NOT WHETHER I'M SURE OR NOT...
SUFF

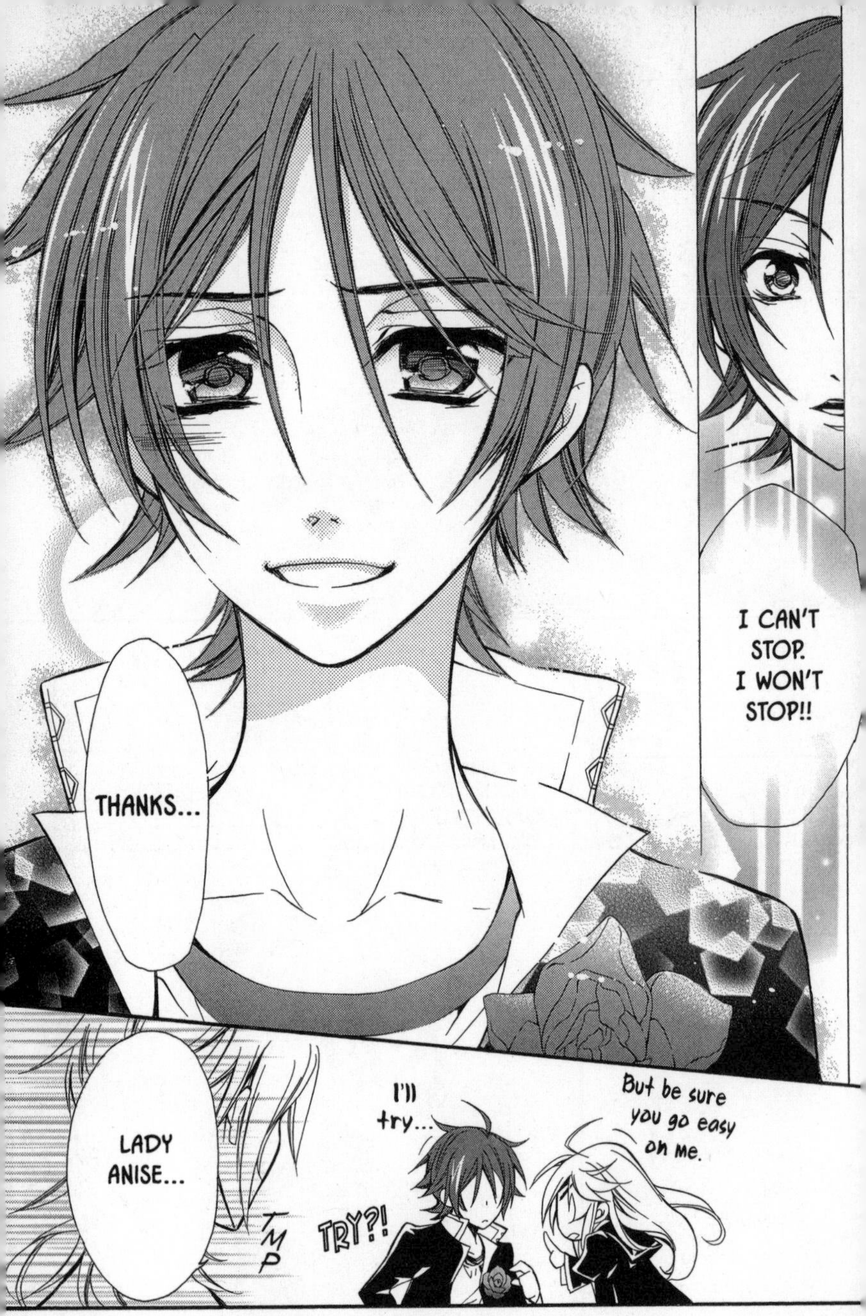

I CAN'T STOP. I WON'T STOP!!
THANKS...
But be sure you go easy on me.
I'll try...
TRY?!
TMP
LADY ANISE...

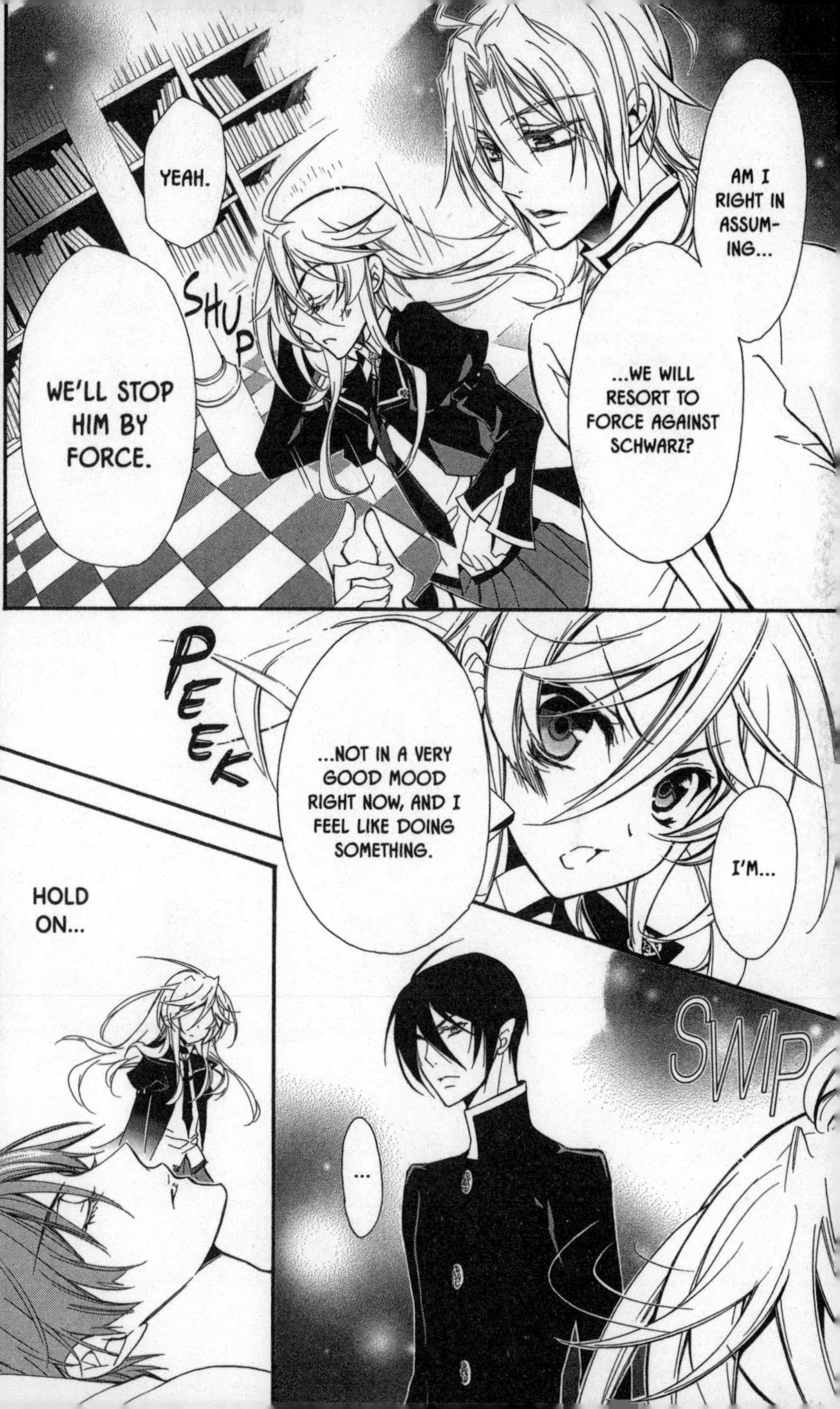
AM I RIGHT IN ASSUMING...
...WE WILL RESORT TO FORCE AGAINST SCHWARZ?
YEAH.
SHUP
WE'LL STOP HIM BY FORCE.
I'M...
...NOT IN A VERY GOOD MOOD RIGHT NOW, AND I FEEL LIKE DOING SOMETHING.
PEEK
SWIP
...
HOLD ON...

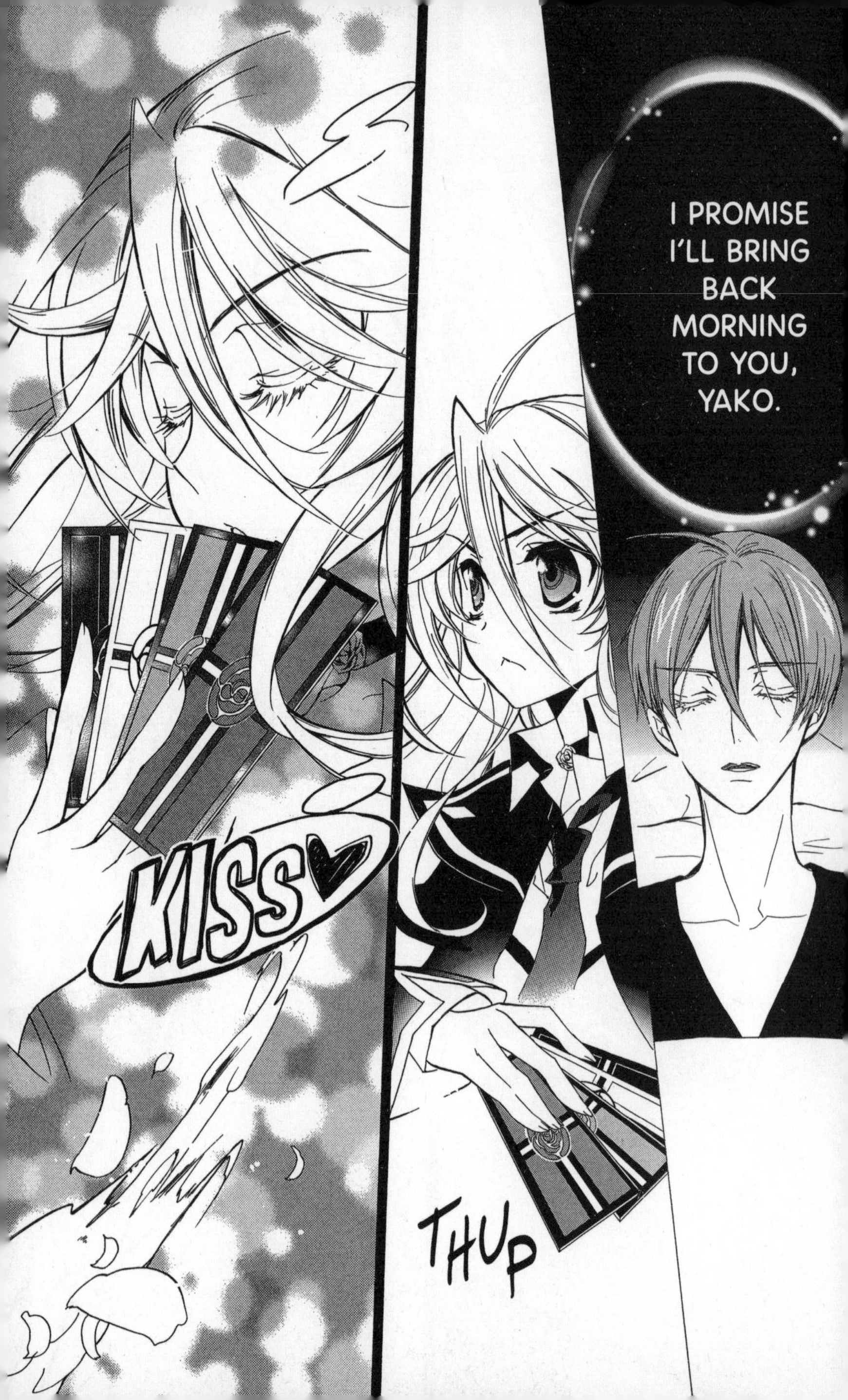
I PROMISE I'LL BRING BACK MORNING TO YOU, YAKO.
THUP
KISS

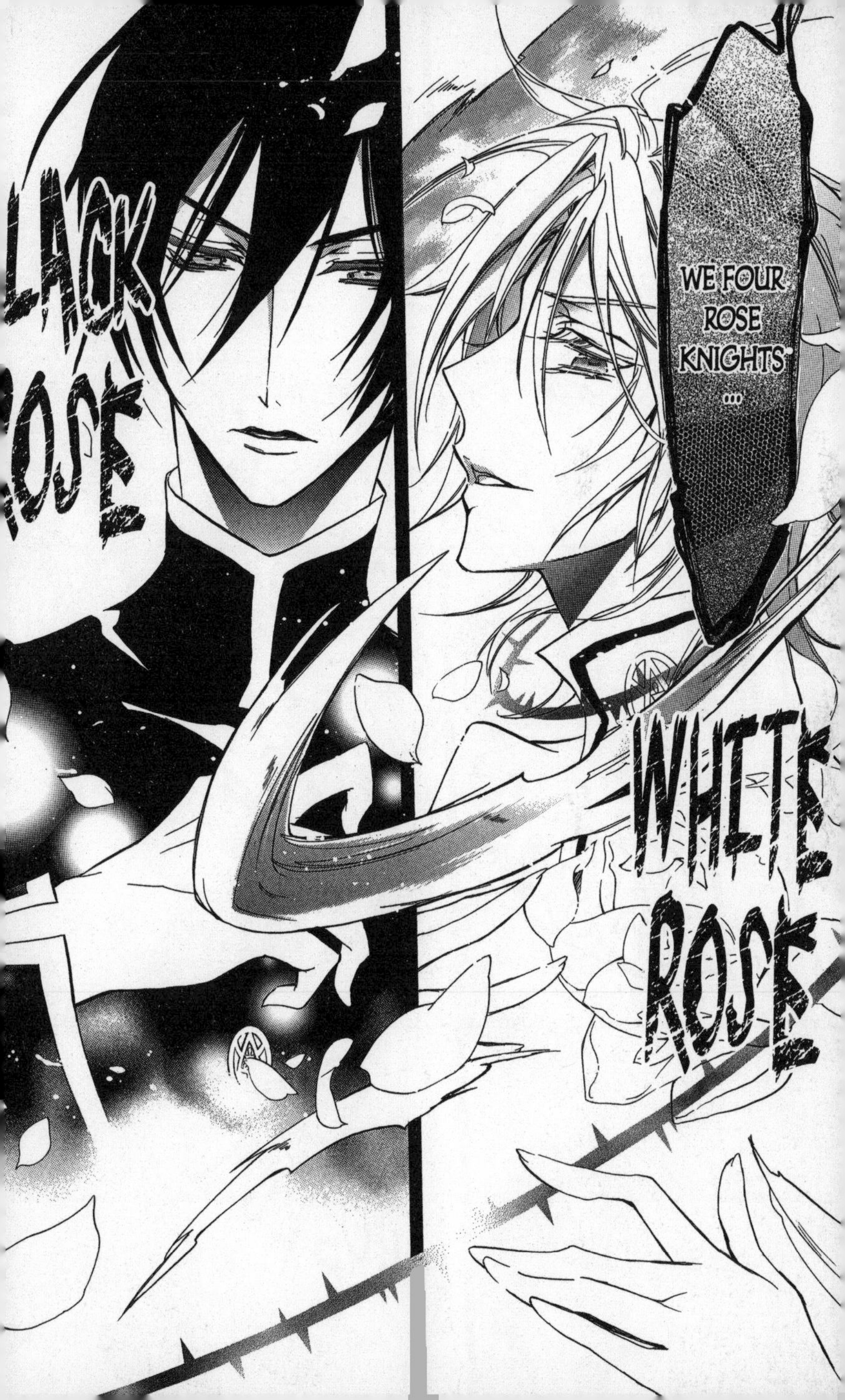
WE FOUR ROSE KNIGHTS ...
WHITE ROSE
LACK ROSE

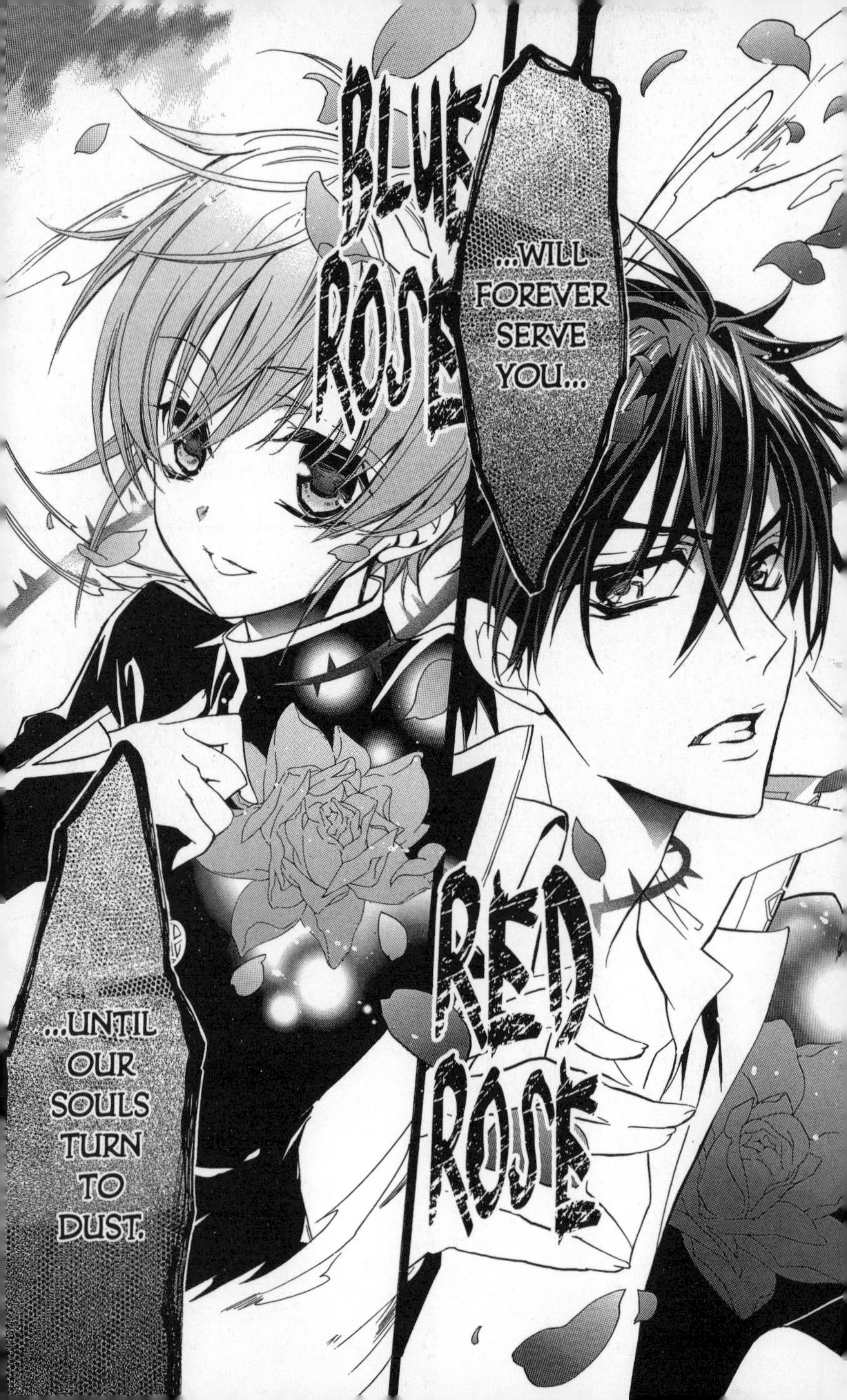
BLUE ROSE
...WILL FOREVER SERVE YOU...
RED ROSE
...UNTIL OUR SOULS TURN TO DUST.

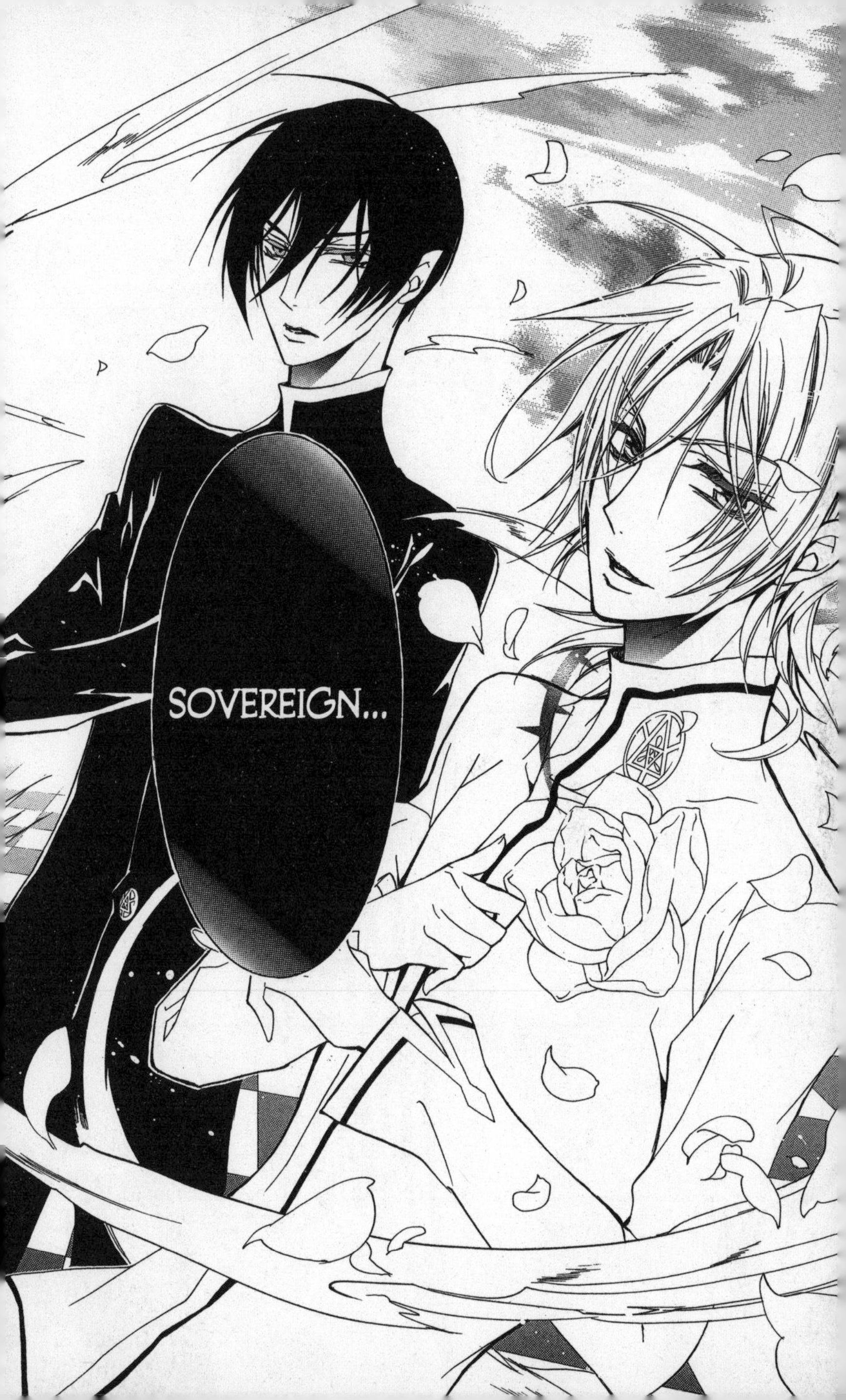
SOVEREIGN...

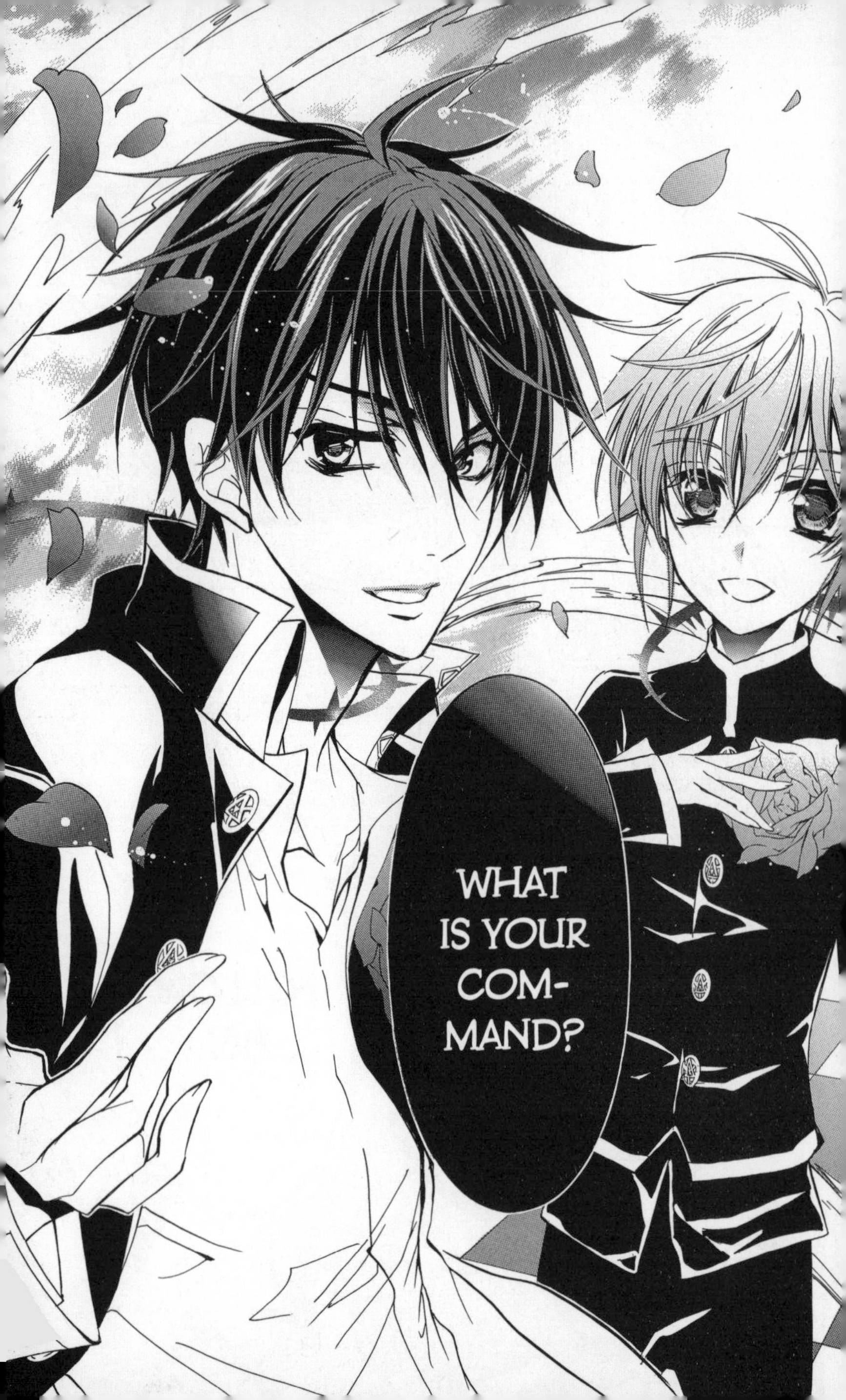
WHAT IS YOUR COM-MAND?

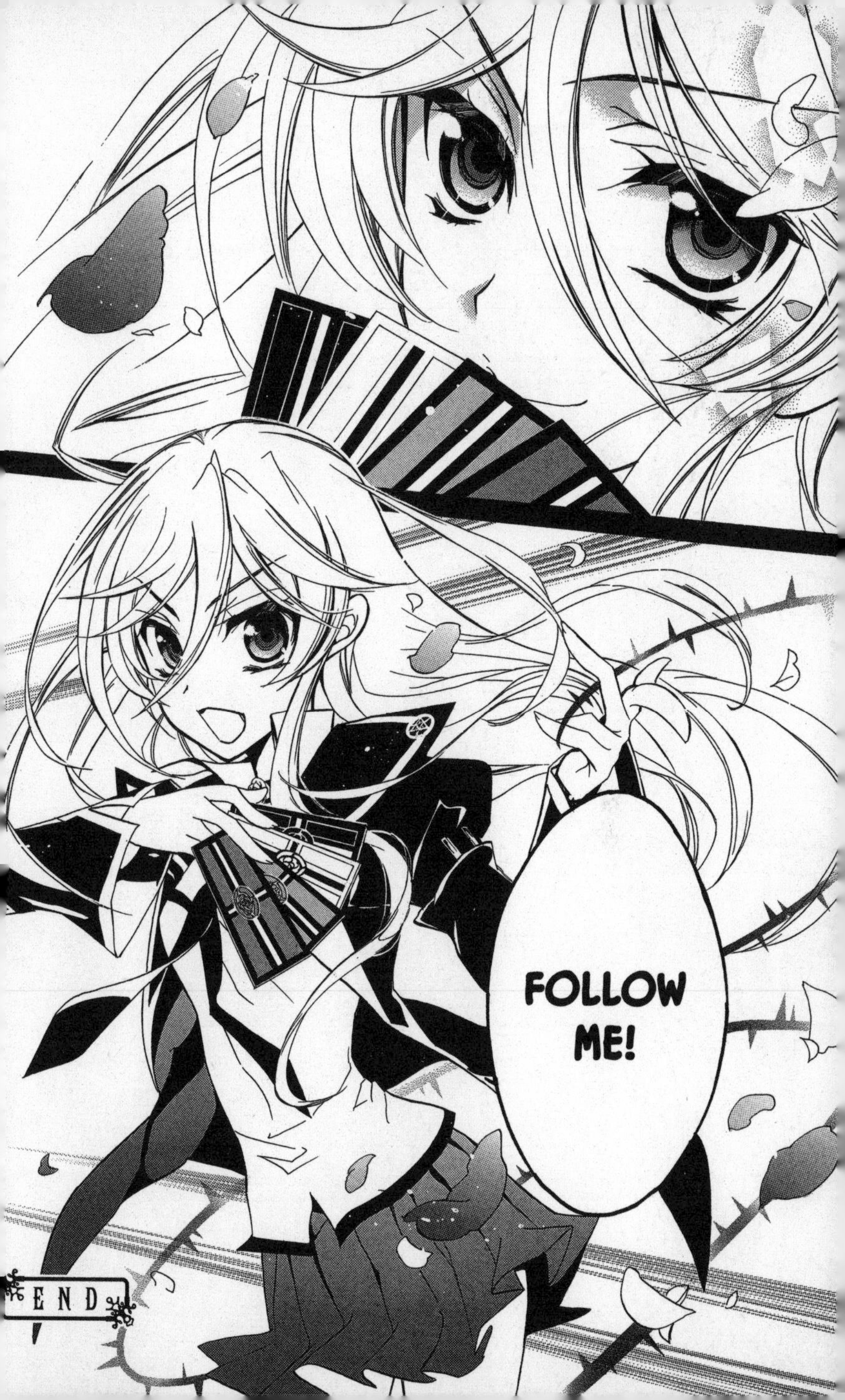
FOLLOW ME!
END

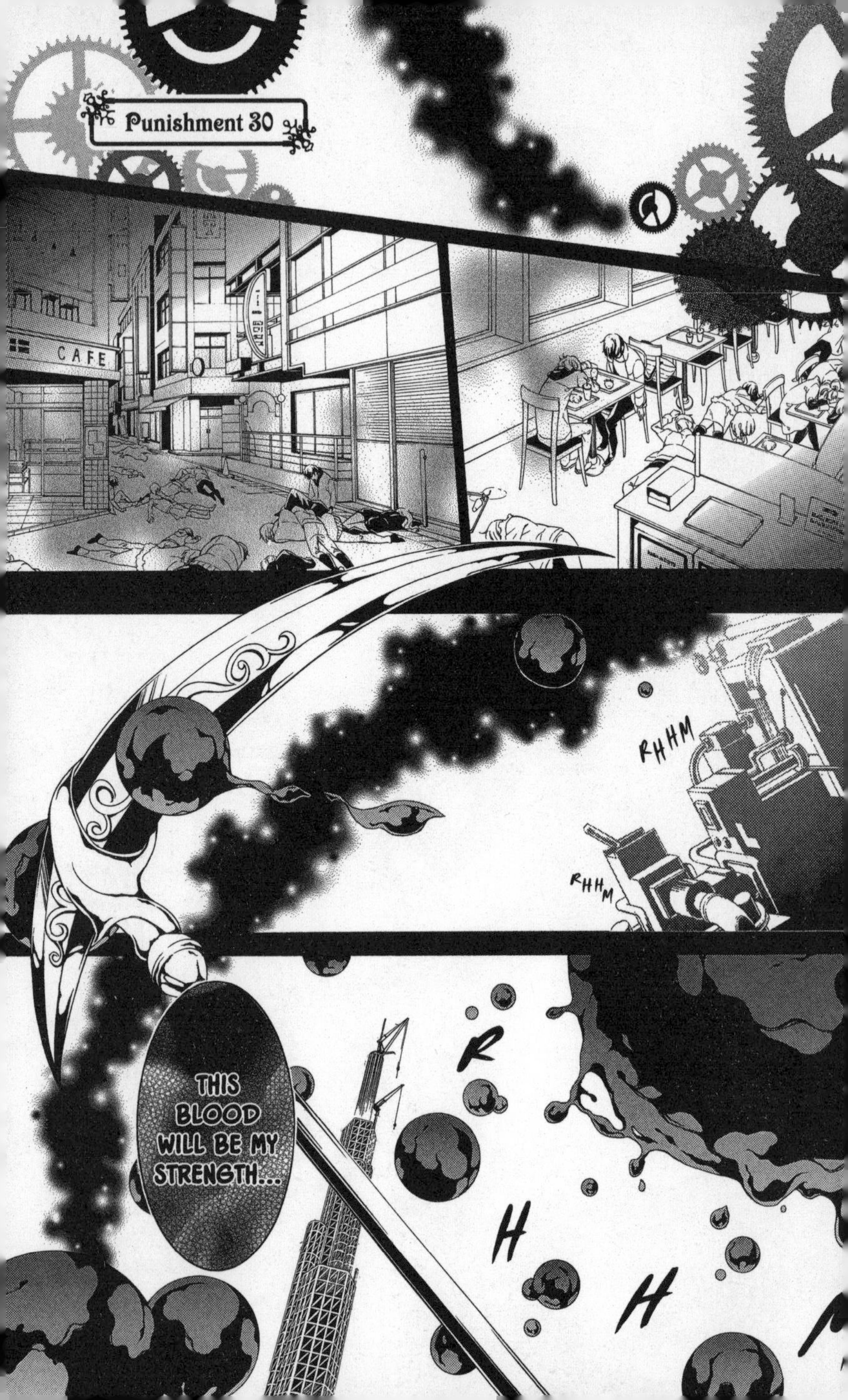
Punishment 30
RHHM
RHHM
RHHM
THIS BLOOD WILL BE MY STRENGTH...

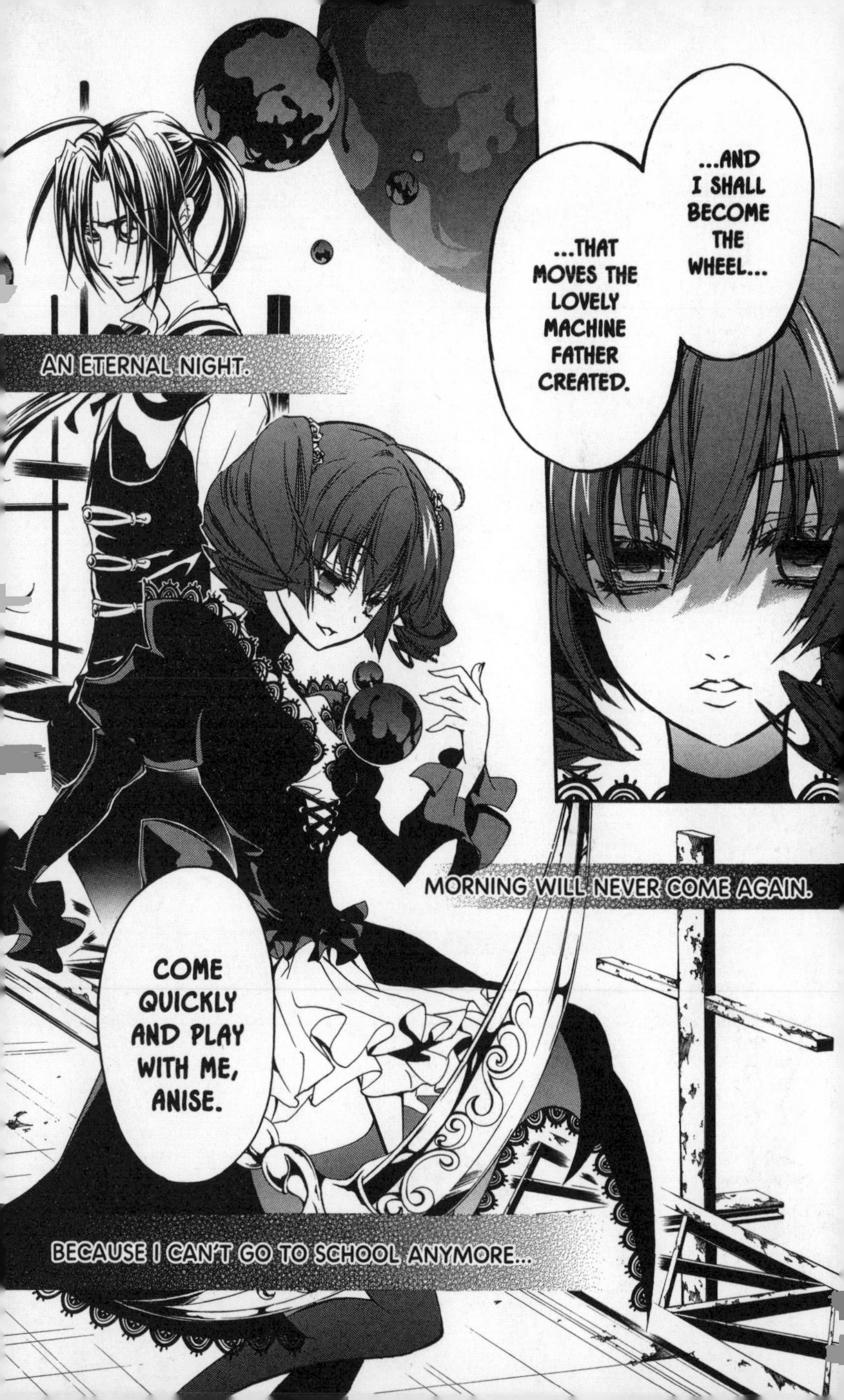
...AND I SHALL BECOME THE WHEEL...
...THAT MOVES THE LOVELY MACHINE FATHER CREATED.
AN ETERNAL NIGHT.
MORNING WILL NEVER COME AGAIN.
COME QUICKLY AND PLAY WITH ME, ANISE.
BECAUSE I CAN'T GO TO SCHOOL ANYMORE...

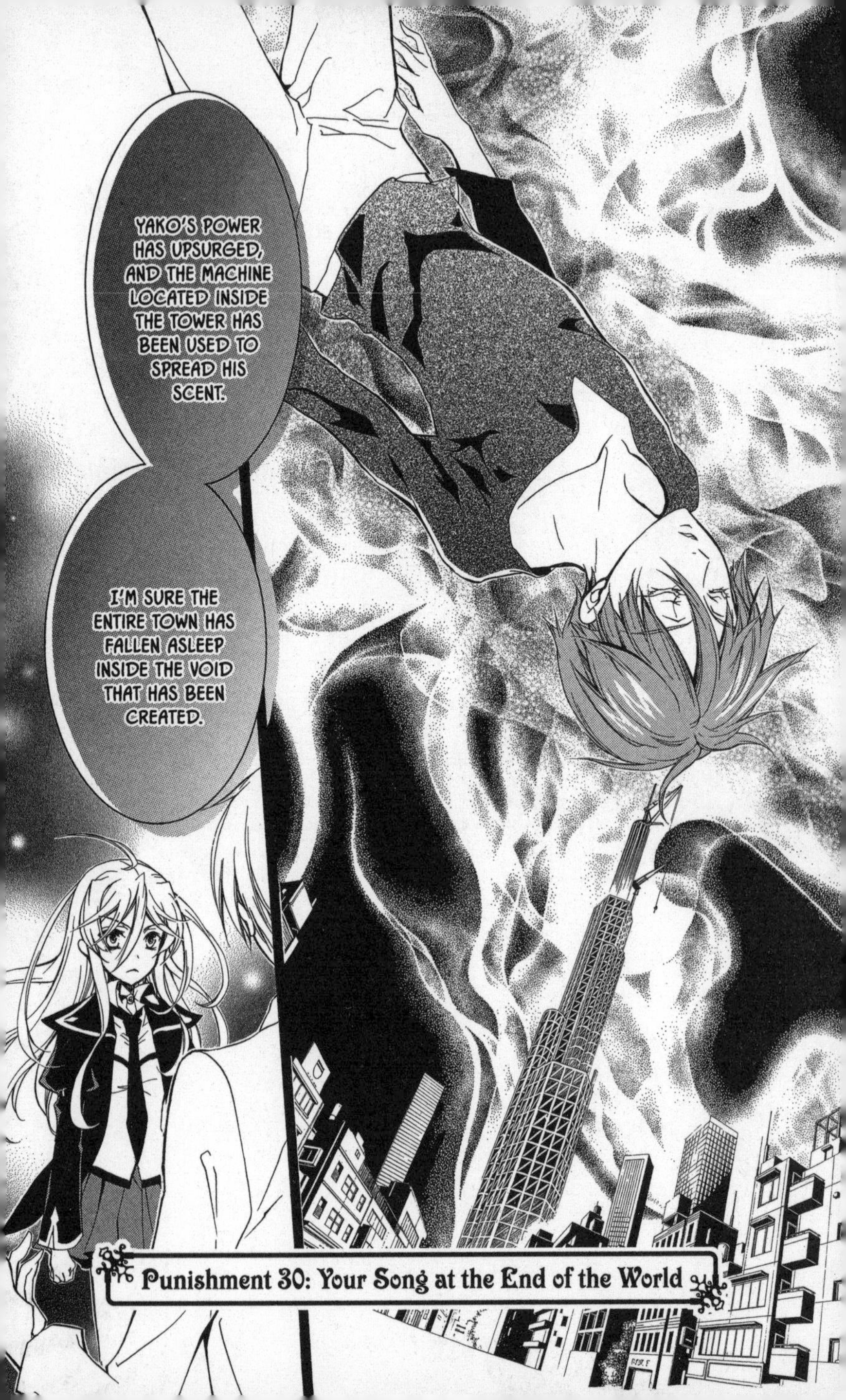
YAKO'S POWER HAS UPSURGED, AND THE MACHINE LOCATED INSIDE THE TOWER HAS BEEN USED TO SPREAD HIS SCENT.
I'M SURE THE ENTIRE TOWN HAS FALLEN ASLEEP INSIDE THE VOID THAT HAS BEEN CREATED.
Punishment 30: Your Song at the End of the World

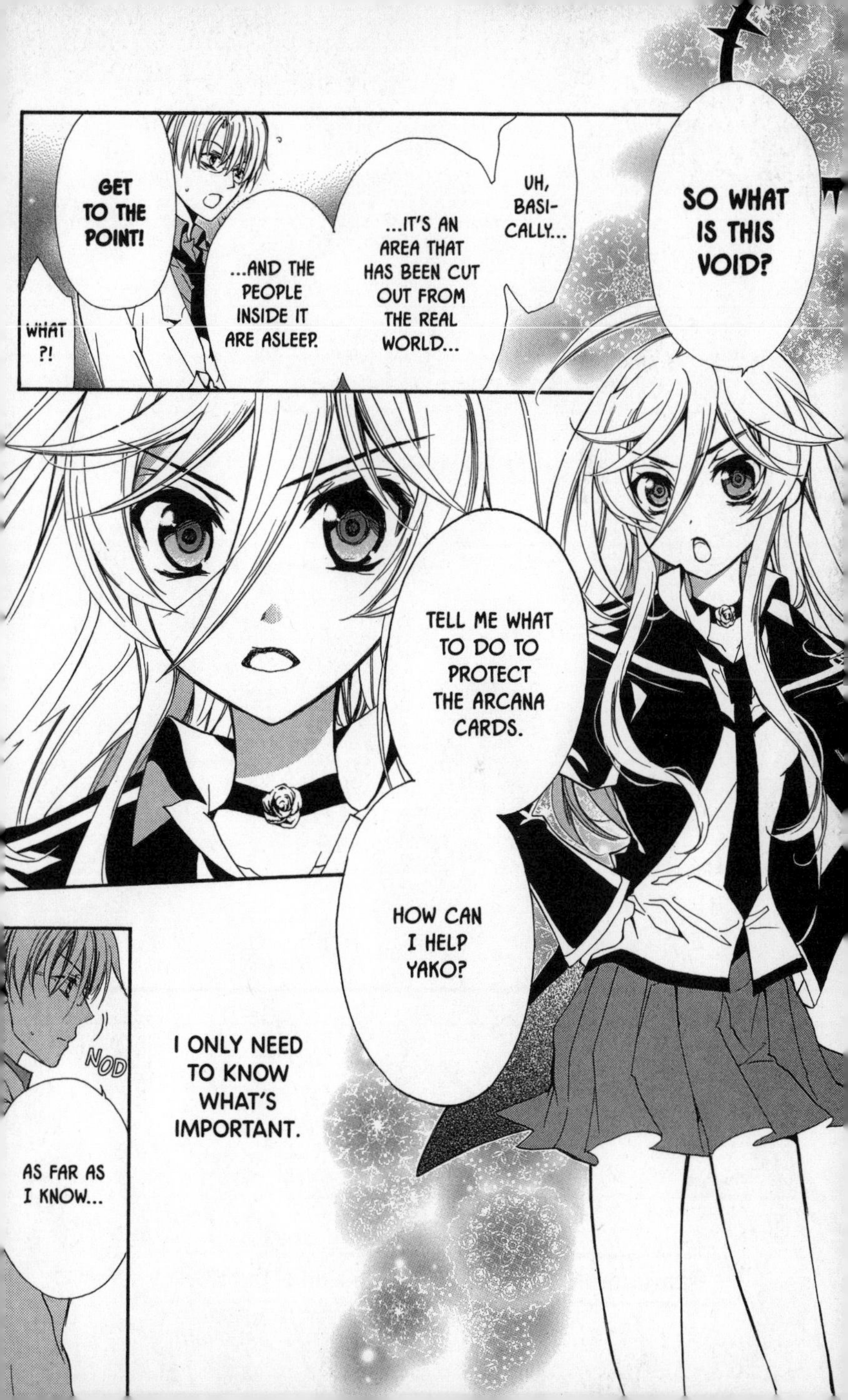
SO WHAT IS THIS VOID?
UH, BASI-CALLY...
...IT'S AN AREA THAT HAS BEEN CUT OUT FROM THE REAL WORLD...
...AND THE PEOPLE INSIDE IT ARE ASLEEP.
GET TO THE POINT!
WHAT ?!
TELL ME WHAT TO DO TO PROTECT THE ARCANA CARDS.
HOW CAN I HELP YAKO?
I ONLY NEED TO KNOW WHAT'S IMPORTANT.
NOD
AS FAR AS I KNOW...

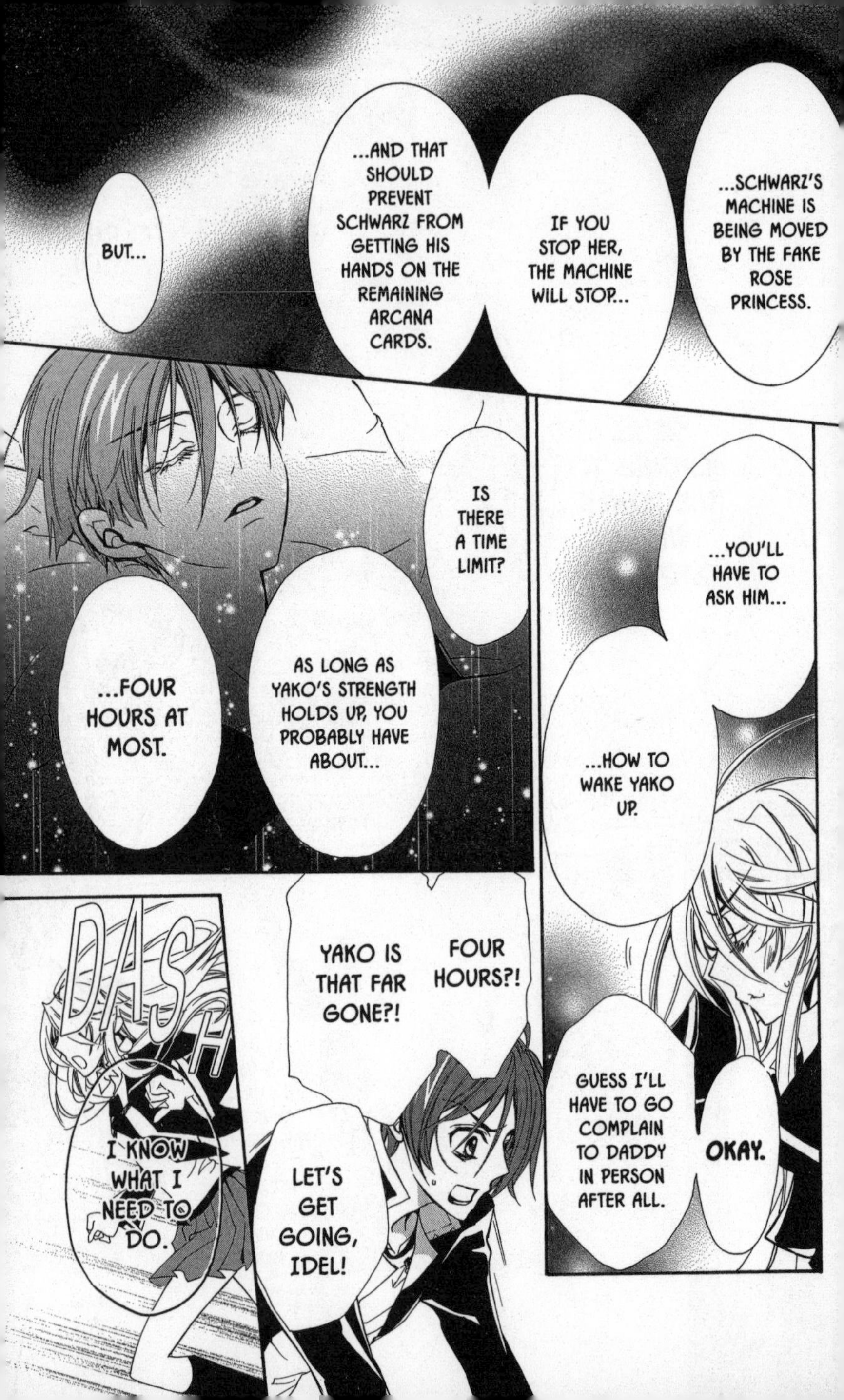
...SCHWARZ'S MACHINE IS BEING MOVED BY THE FAKE ROSE PRINCESS.
IF YOU STOP HER, THE MACHINE WILL STOP...
...AND THAT SHOULD PREVENT SCHWARZ FROM GETTING HIS HANDS ON THE REMAINING ARCANA CARDS.
BUT...
...YOU'LL HAVE TO ASK HIM...
...HOW TO WAKE YAKO UP.
OKAY.
GUESS I'LL HAVE TO GO COMPLAIN TO DADDY IN PERSON AFTER ALL.
IS THERE A TIME LIMIT?
AS LONG AS YAKO'S STRENGTH HOLDS UP, YOU PROBABLY HAVE ABOUT...
...FOUR HOURS AT MOST.
FOUR HOURS?!
YAKO IS THAT FAR GONE?!
DASH
LET'S GET GOING, IDEL!
I KNOW WHAT I NEED TO DO.

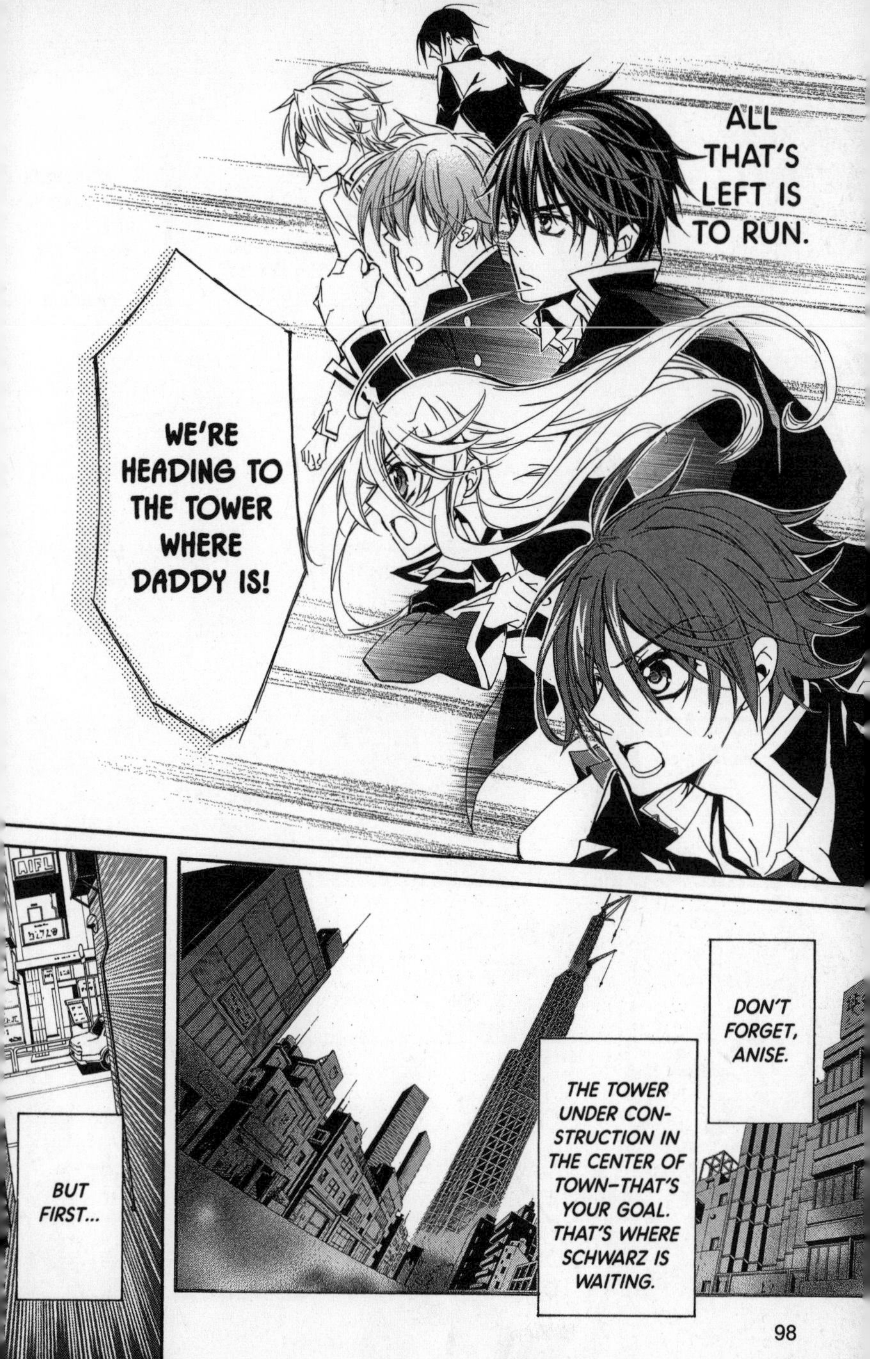
ALL THAT'S LEFT IS TO RUN.
WE'RE HEADING TO THE TOWER WHERE DADDY IS!
DON'T FORGET, ANISE.
THE TOWER UNDER CON-STRUCTION IN THE CENTER OF TOWN—THAT'S YOUR GOAL. THAT'S WHERE SCHWARZ IS WAITING.
BUT FIRST...

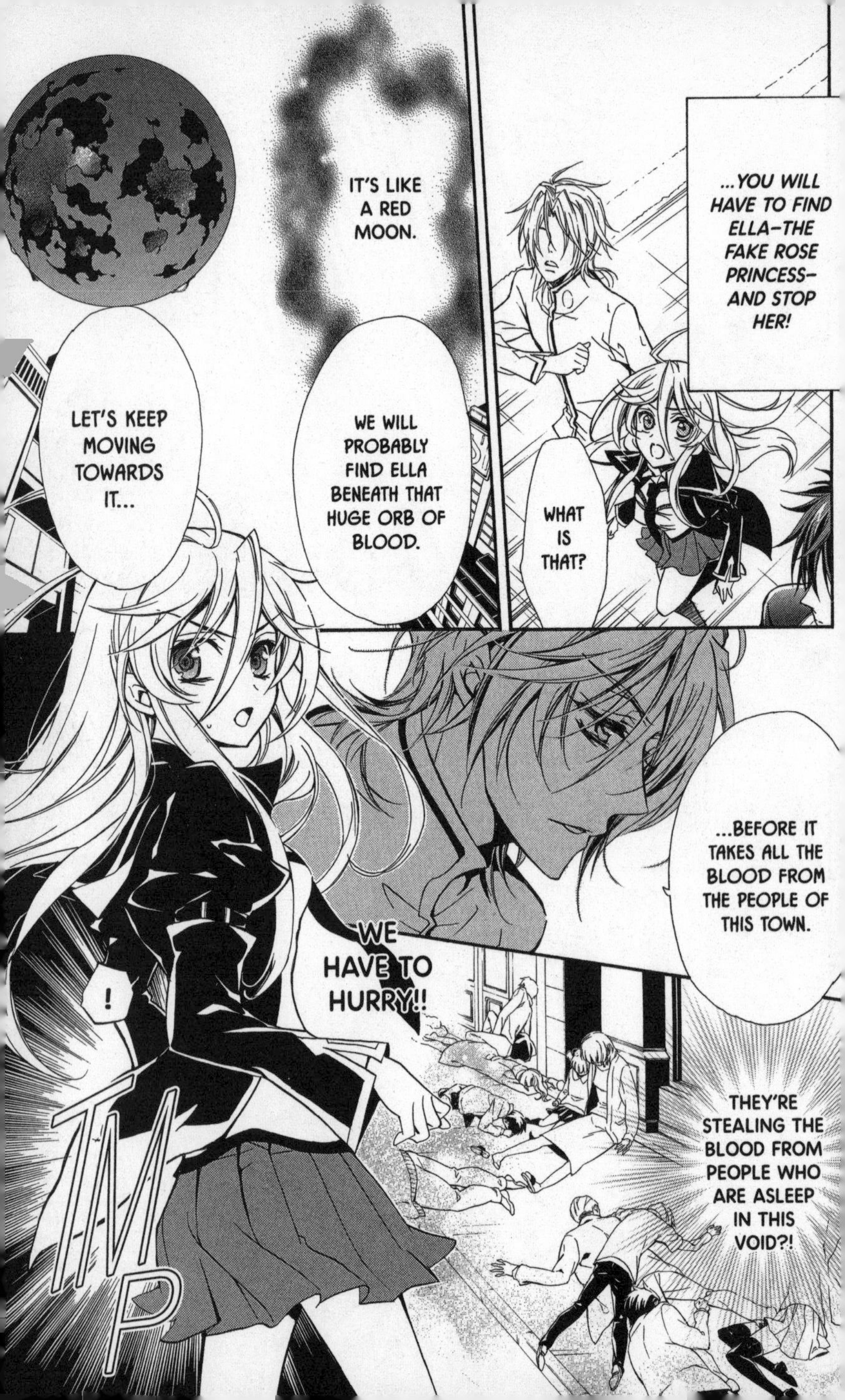
...YOU WILL HAVE TO FIND ELLA—THE FAKE ROSE PRINCESS—AND STOP HER!
WHAT IS THAT?
IT'S LIKE A RED MOON.
WE WILL PROBABLY FIND ELLA BENEATH THAT HUGE ORB OF BLOOD.
LET'S KEEP MOVING TOWARDS IT...
...BEFORE IT TAKES ALL THE BLOOD FROM THE PEOPLE OF THIS TOWN.
WE HAVE TO HURRY!!
THEY'RE STEALING THE BLOOD FROM PEOPLE WHO ARE ASLEEP IN THIS VOID?!
!
TMP

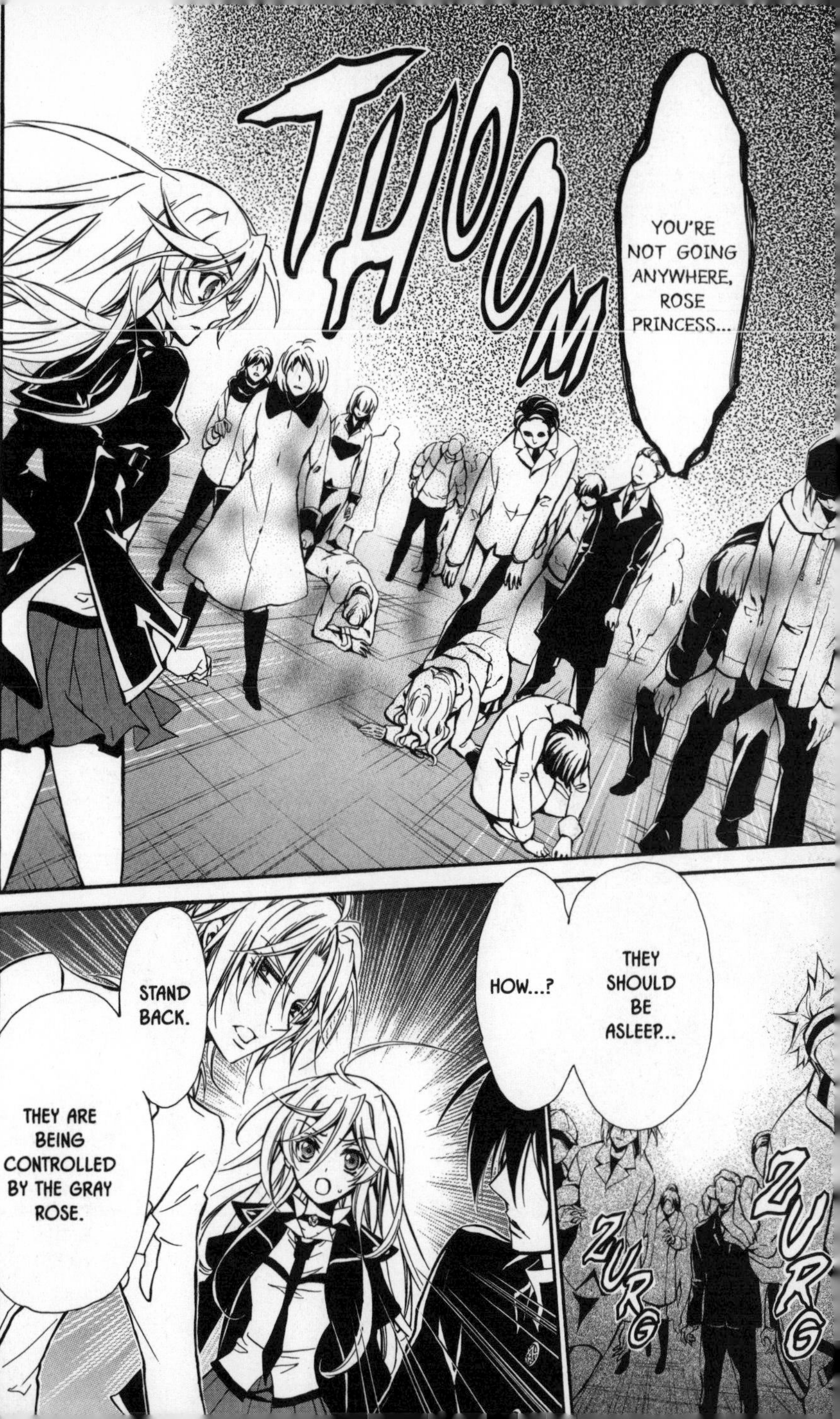
THOOOM
YOU'RE NOT GOING ANYWHERE, ROSE PRINCESS...
THEY SHOULD BE ASLEEP...
HOW...?
STAND BACK.
THEY ARE BEING CONTROLLED BY THE GRAY ROSE.
ZURG
ZURG

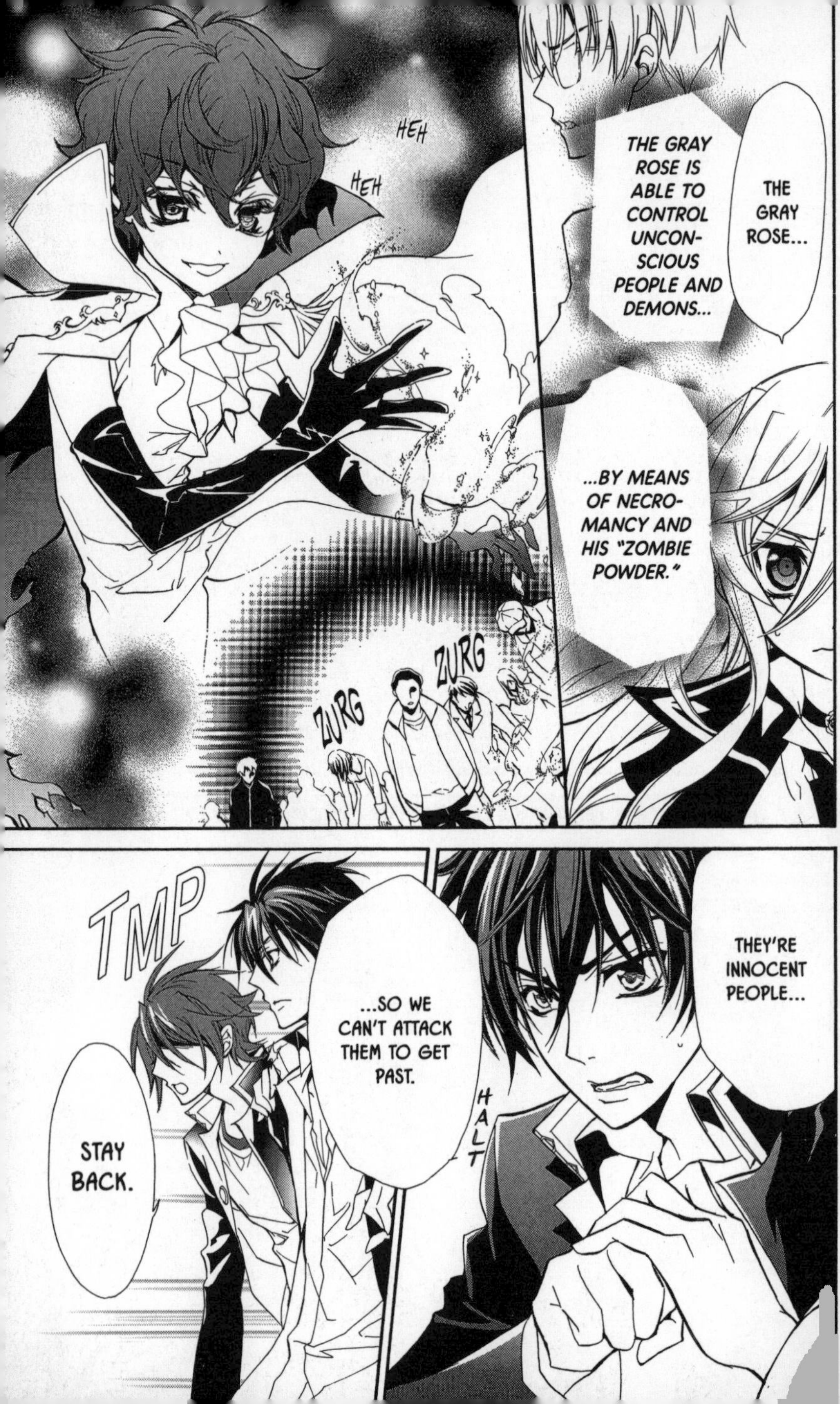
THE GRAY ROSE...
THE GRAY ROSE IS ABLE TO CONTROL UNCONSCIOUS PEOPLE AND DEMONS...
...BY MEANS OF NECROMANCY AND HIS "ZOMBIE POWDER."
HEH
HEH
ZURG
ZURG
THEY'RE INNOCENT PEOPLE...
...SO WE CAN'T ATTACK THEM TO GET PAST.
HALT
TMP
STAY BACK.

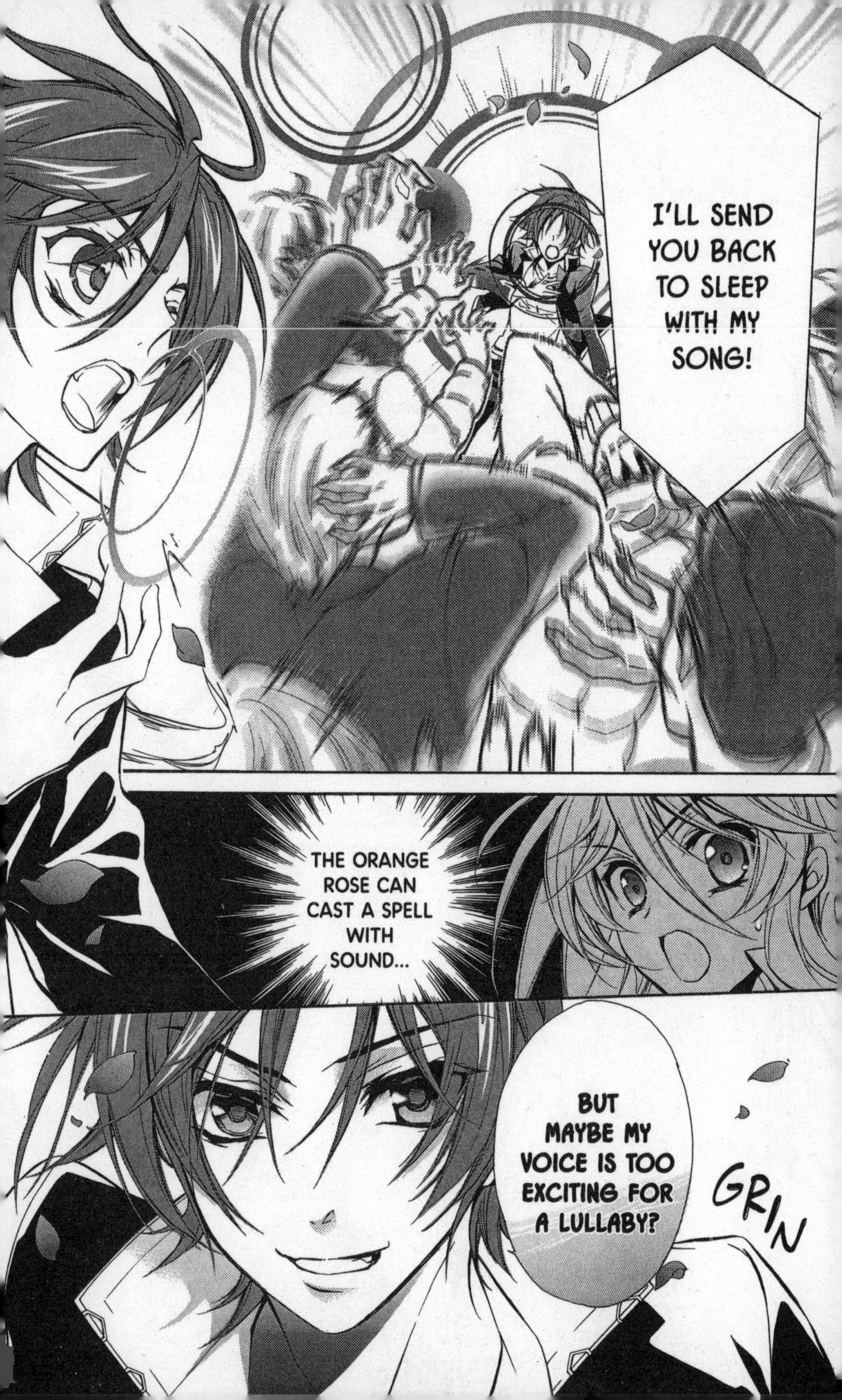
I'LL SEND YOU BACK TO SLEEP WITH MY SONG!
THE ORANGE ROSE CAN CAST A SPELL WITH SOUND...
GRIN
BUT MAYBE MY VOICE IS TOO EXCITING FOR A LULLABY?

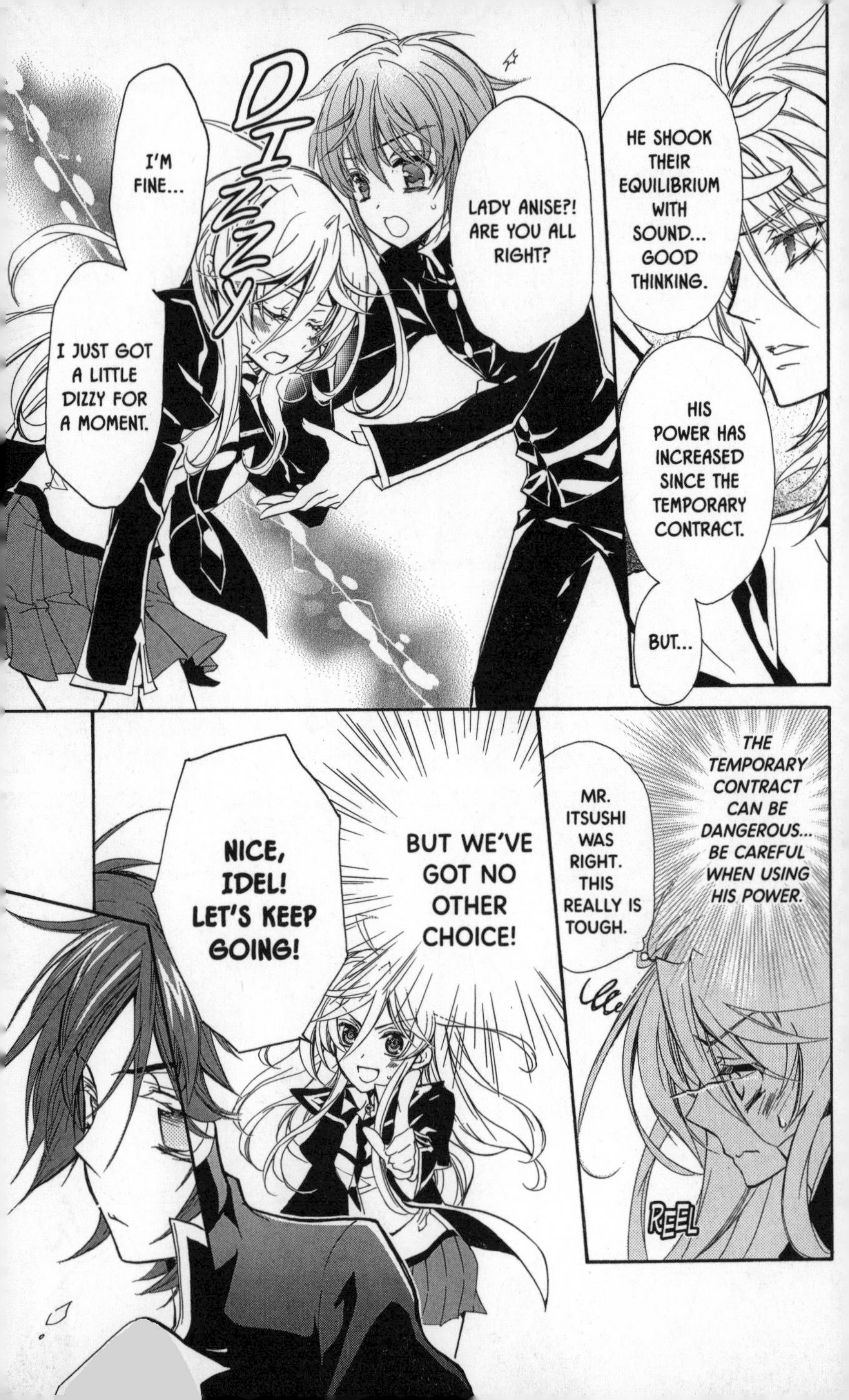
HE SHOOK THEIR EQUILIBRIUM WITH SOUND... GOOD THINKING.
HIS POWER HAS INCREASED SINCE THE TEMPORARY CONTRACT.
BUT...
LADY ANISE?! ARE YOU ALL RIGHT?
DIZZY
I'M FINE...
I JUST GOT A LITTLE DIZZY FOR A MOMENT.
THE TEMPORARY CONTRACT CAN BE DANGEROUS... BE CAREFUL WHEN USING HIS POWER.
MR. ITSUSHI WAS RIGHT. THIS REALLY IS TOUGH.
REEL
BUT WE'VE GOT NO OTHER CHOICE!
NICE, IDEL! LET'S KEEP GOING!

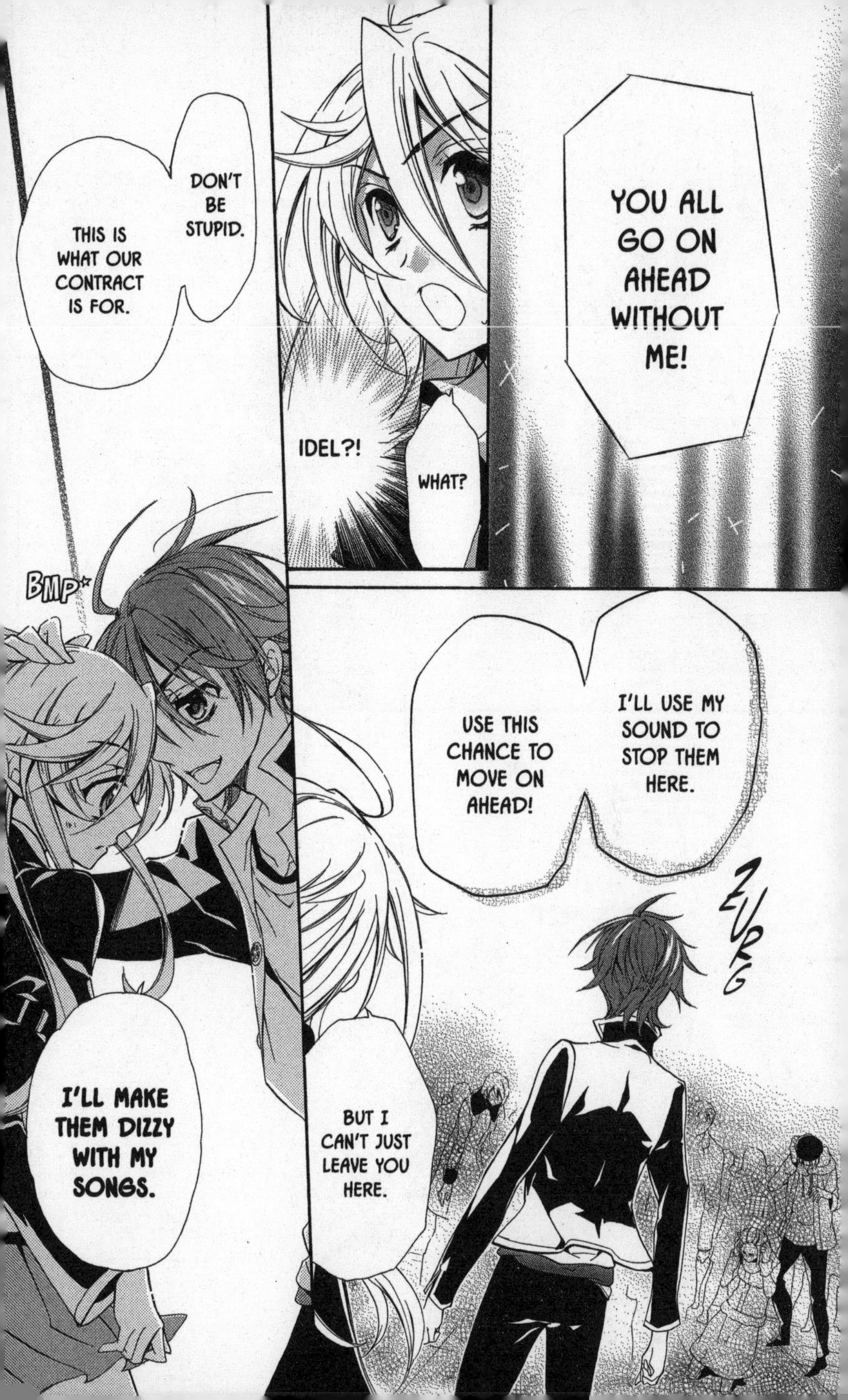
YOU ALL GO ON AHEAD WITHOUT ME!
WHAT?
IDEL?!
I'LL USE MY SOUND TO STOP THEM HERE.
USE THIS CHANCE TO MOVE ON AHEAD!
ZURG
BUT I CAN'T JUST LEAVE YOU HERE.
DON'T BE STUPID.
THIS IS WHAT OUR CONTRACT IS FOR.
BMP
I'LL MAKE THEM DIZZY WITH MY SONGS.

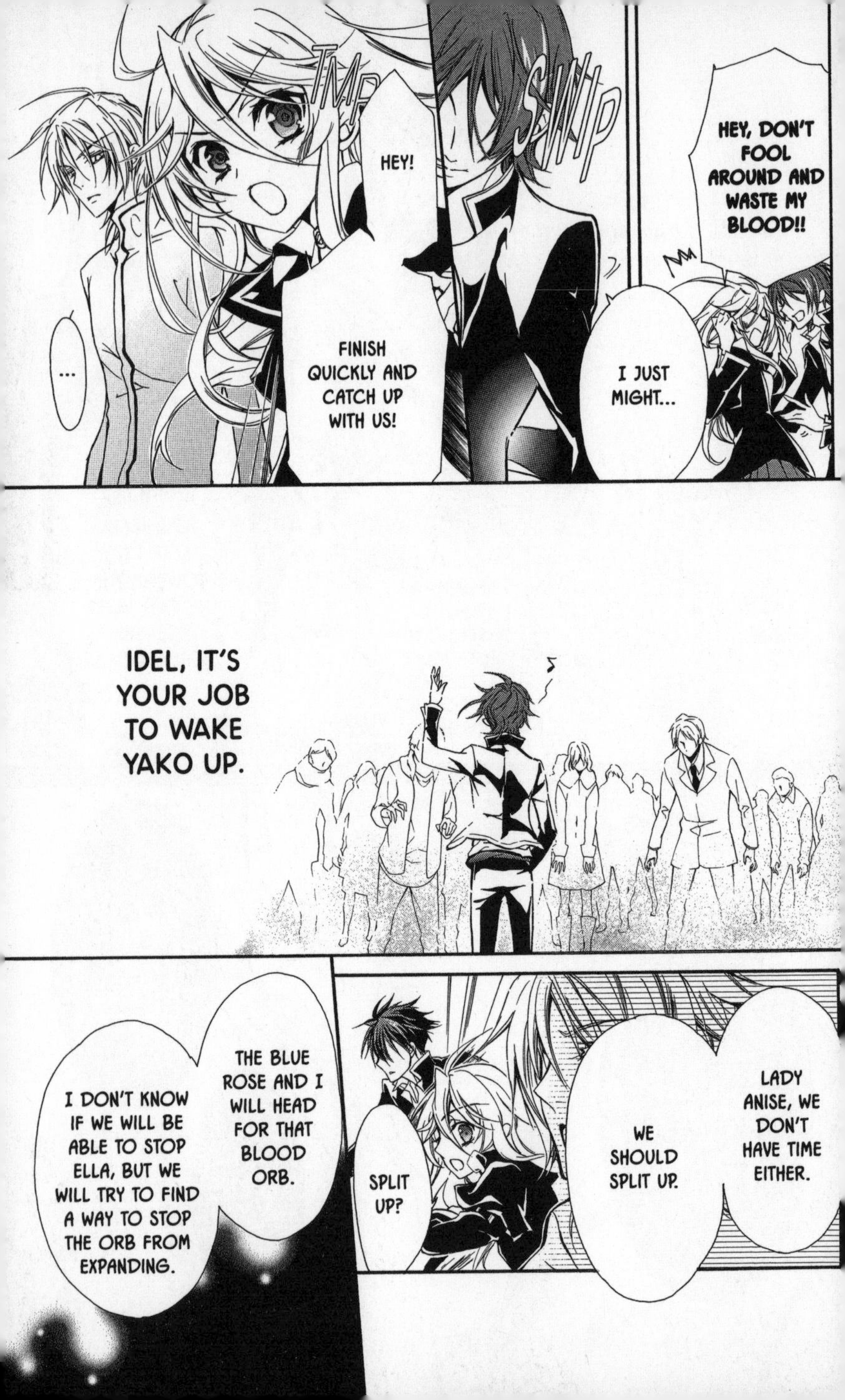
HEY, DON'T FOOL AROUND AND WASTE MY BLOOD!!
I JUST MIGHT...
SWIP
FINISH QUICKLY AND CATCH UP WITH US!
TMP
HEY!
...
IDEL, IT'S YOUR JOB TO WAKE YAKO UP.
LADY ANISE, WE DON'T HAVE TIME EITHER.
WE SHOULD SPLIT UP.
SPLIT UP?
THE BLUE ROSE AND I WILL HEAD FOR THAT BLOOD ORB.
I DON'T KNOW IF WE WILL BE ABLE TO STOP ELLA, BUT WE WILL TRY TO FIND A WAY TO STOP THE ORB FROM EXPANDING.

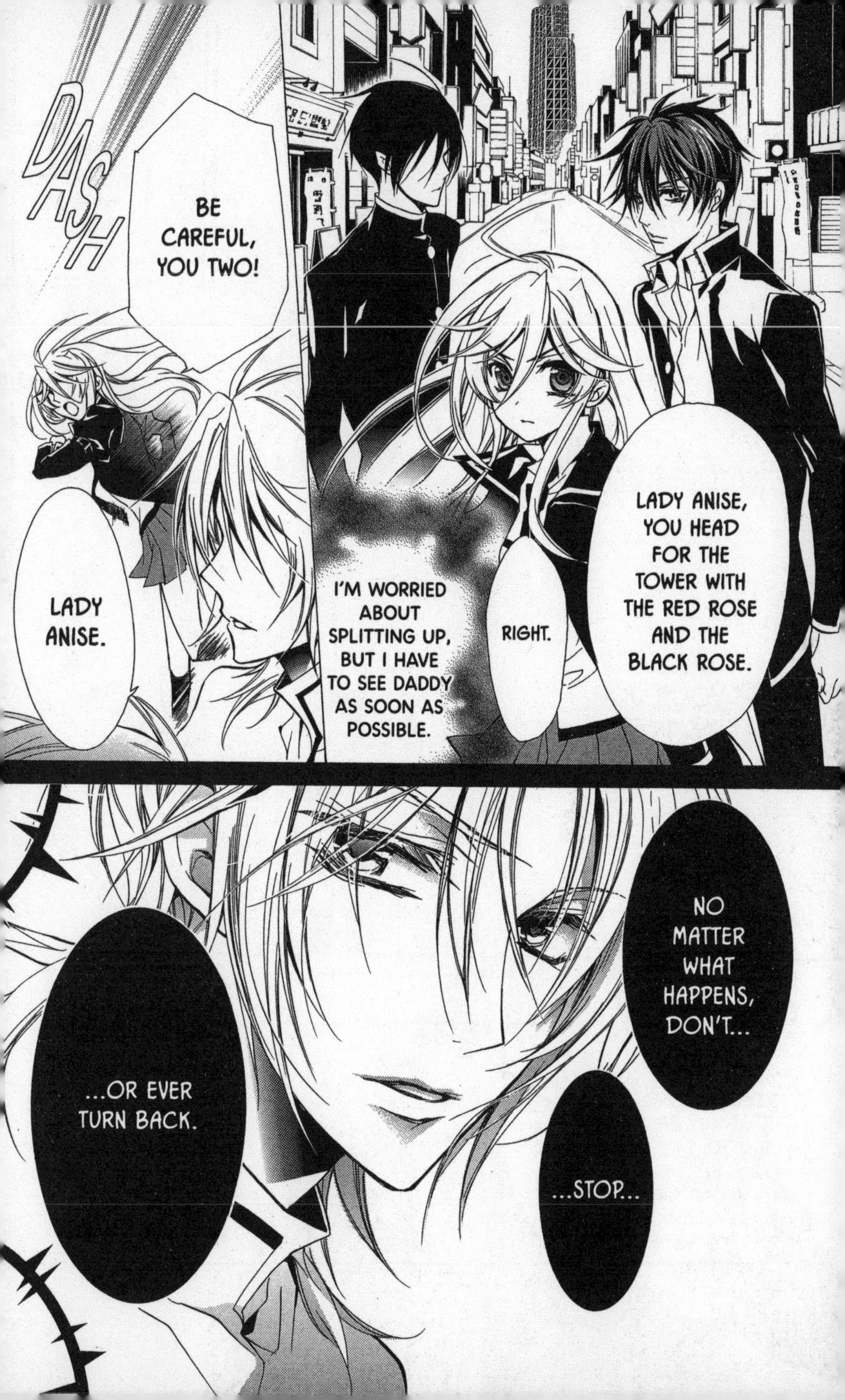
LADY ANISE, YOU HEAD FOR THE TOWER WITH THE RED ROSE AND THE BLACK ROSE.
RIGHT.
I'M WORRIED ABOUT SPLITTING UP, BUT I HAVE TO SEE DADDY AS SOON AS POSSIBLE.
BE CAREFUL, YOU TWO!
DASH
LADY ANISE.
NO MATTER WHAT HAPPENS, DON'T...
...STOP...
...OR EVER TURN BACK.

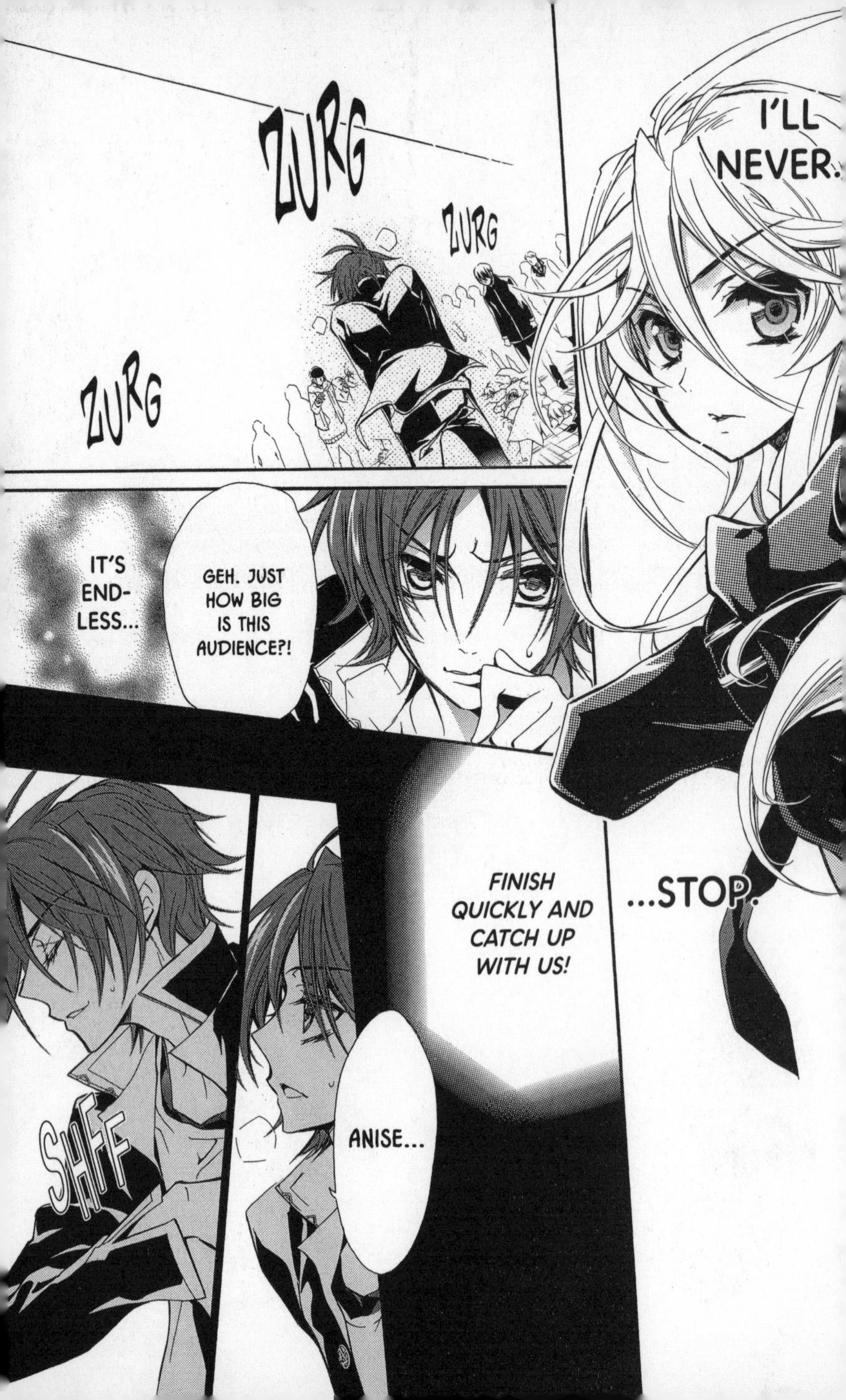
I'LL NEVER...
...STOP.
ZURG
ZURG
ZURG
GEH. JUST HOW BIG IS THIS AUDIENCE?!
IT'S END-LESS...
FINISH QUICKLY AND CATCH UP WITH US!
ANISE...
SHFF

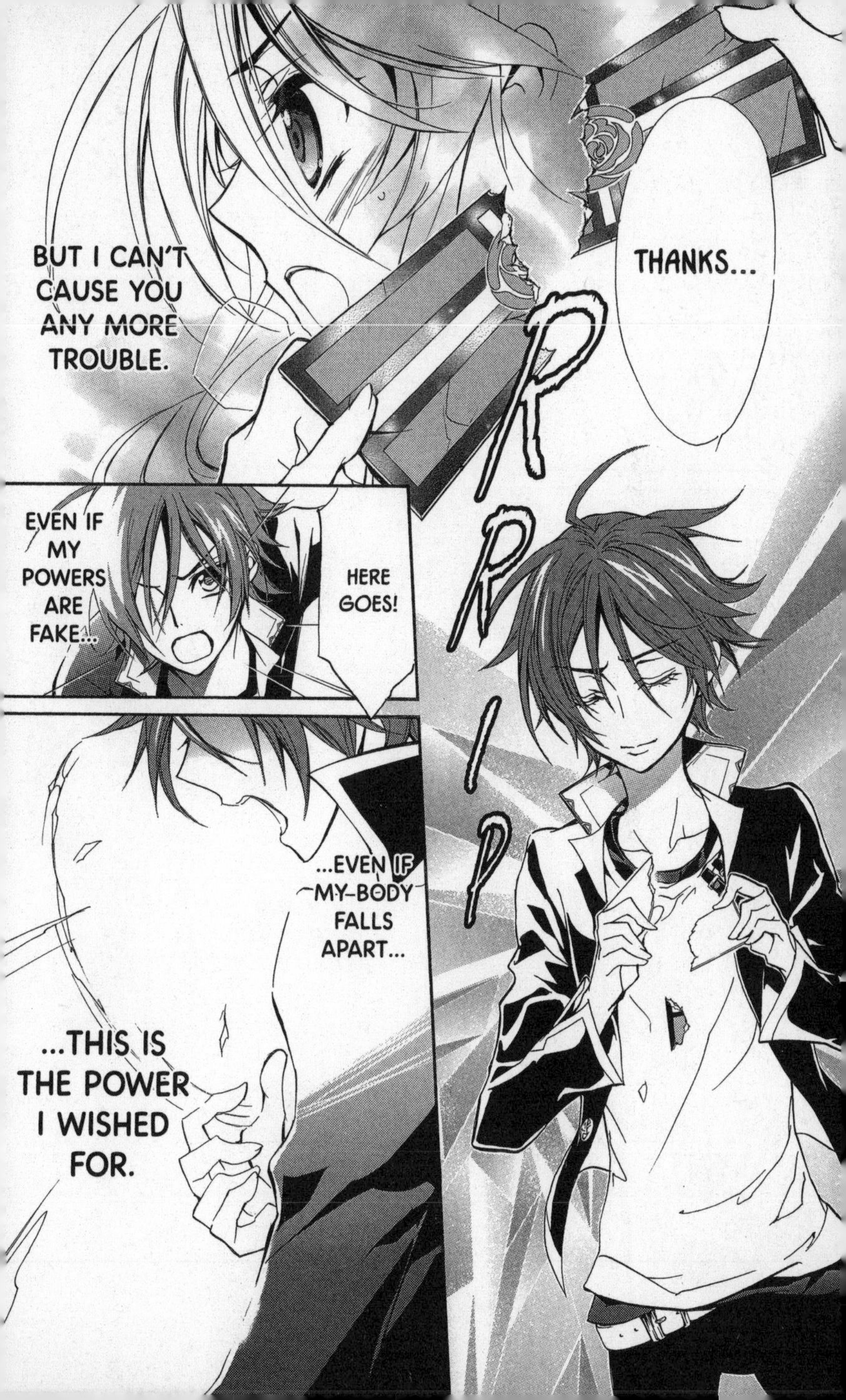
THANKS...
BUT I CAN'T CAUSE YOU ANY MORE TROUBLE.
RRIP
HERE GOES!
EVEN IF MY POWERS ARE FAKE...
...EVEN IF MY BODY FALLS APART...
...THIS IS THE POWER I WISHED FOR.

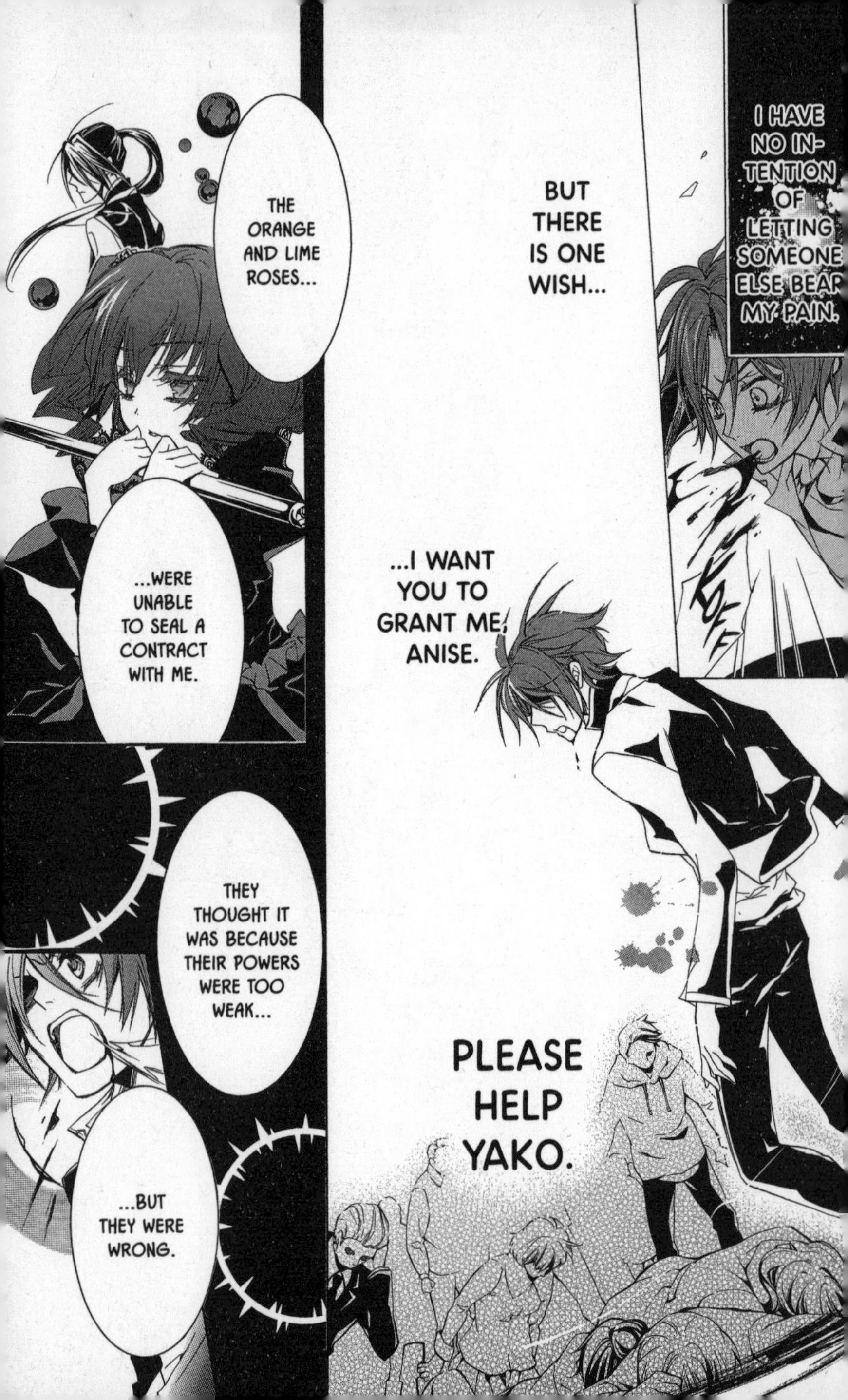

I HAVE NO INTENTION OF LETTING SOMEONE ELSE BEAR MY PAIN.
BUT THERE IS ONE WISH...
...I WANT YOU TO GRANT ME, ANISE.
PLEASE HELP YAKO.
THE ORANGE AND LIME ROSES...
...WERE UNABLE TO SEAL A CONTRACT WITH ME.
THEY THOUGHT IT WAS BECAUSE THEIR POWERS WERE TOO WEAK...
...BUT THEY WERE WRONG.

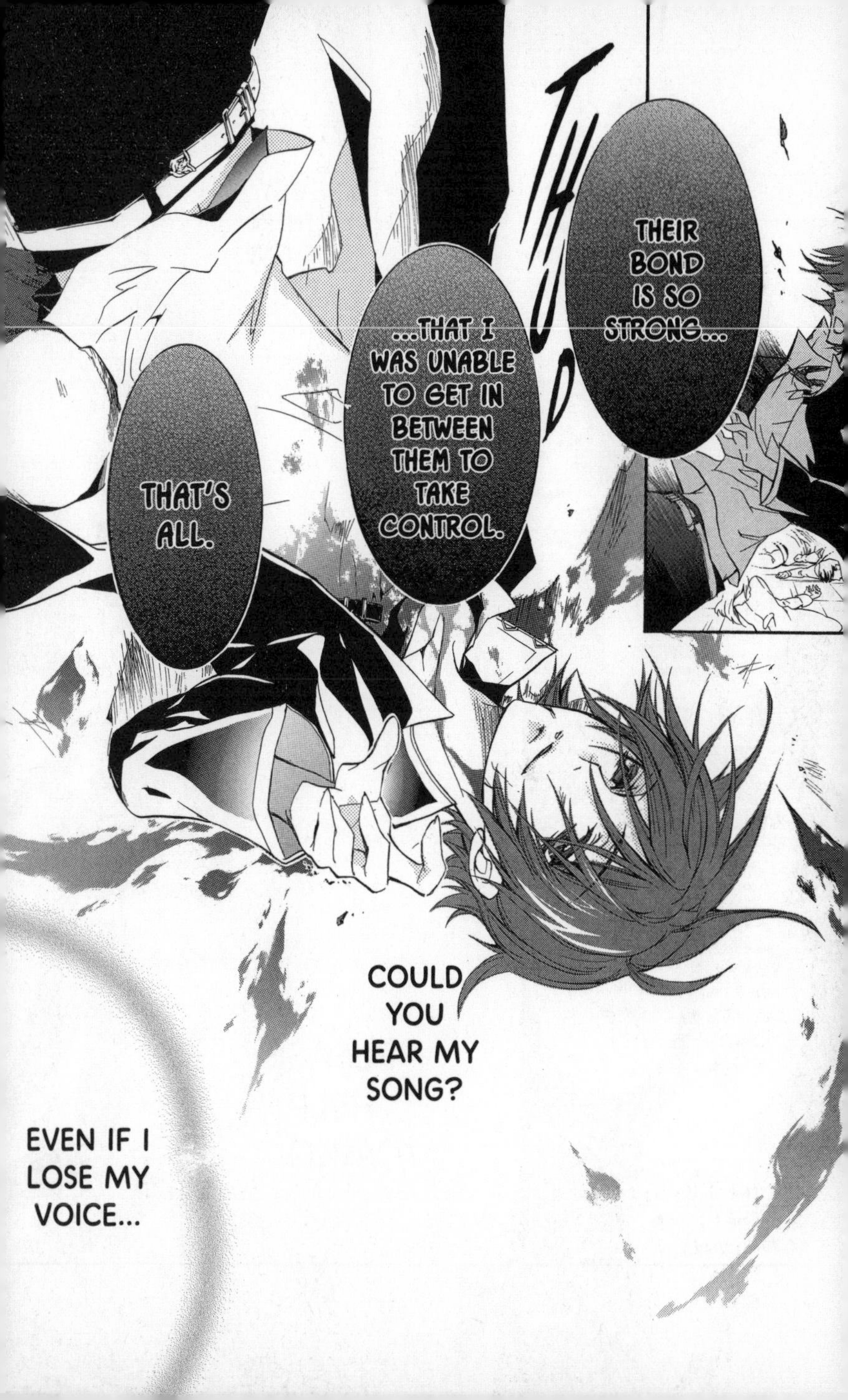
THEIR BOND IS SO STRONG...
THUD
...THAT I WAS UNABLE TO GET IN BETWEEN THEM TO TAKE CONTROL.
THAT'S ALL.
COULD YOU HEAR MY SONG?
EVEN IF I LOSE MY VOICE...

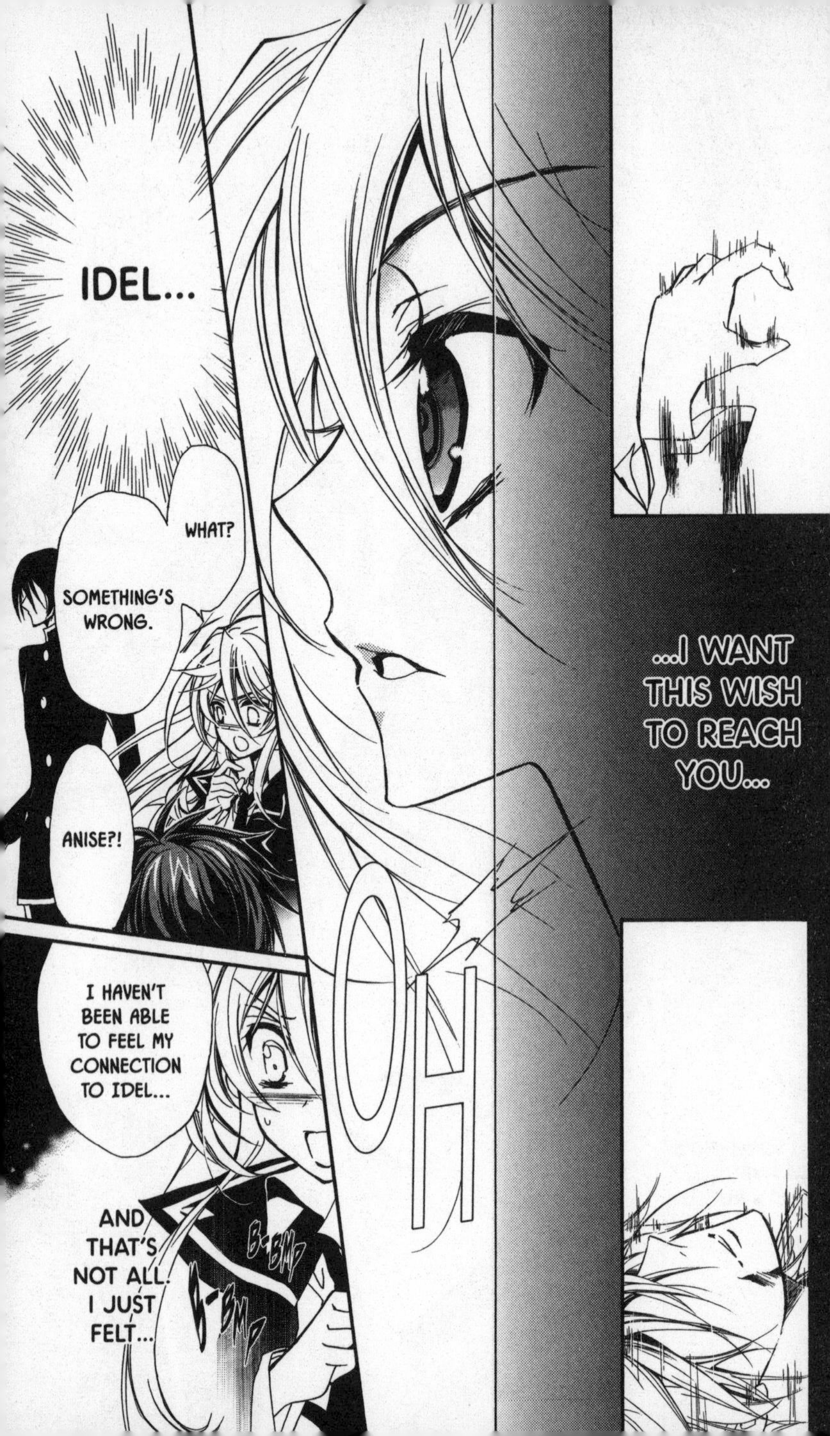
...I WANT THIS WISH TO REACH YOU...
IDEL...
OH
WHAT?
SOMETHING'S WRONG.
ANISE?!
I HAVEN'T BEEN ABLE TO FEEL MY CONNECTION TO IDEL...
AND THAT'S NOT ALL. I JUST FELT...
B-BMP
B-BMP

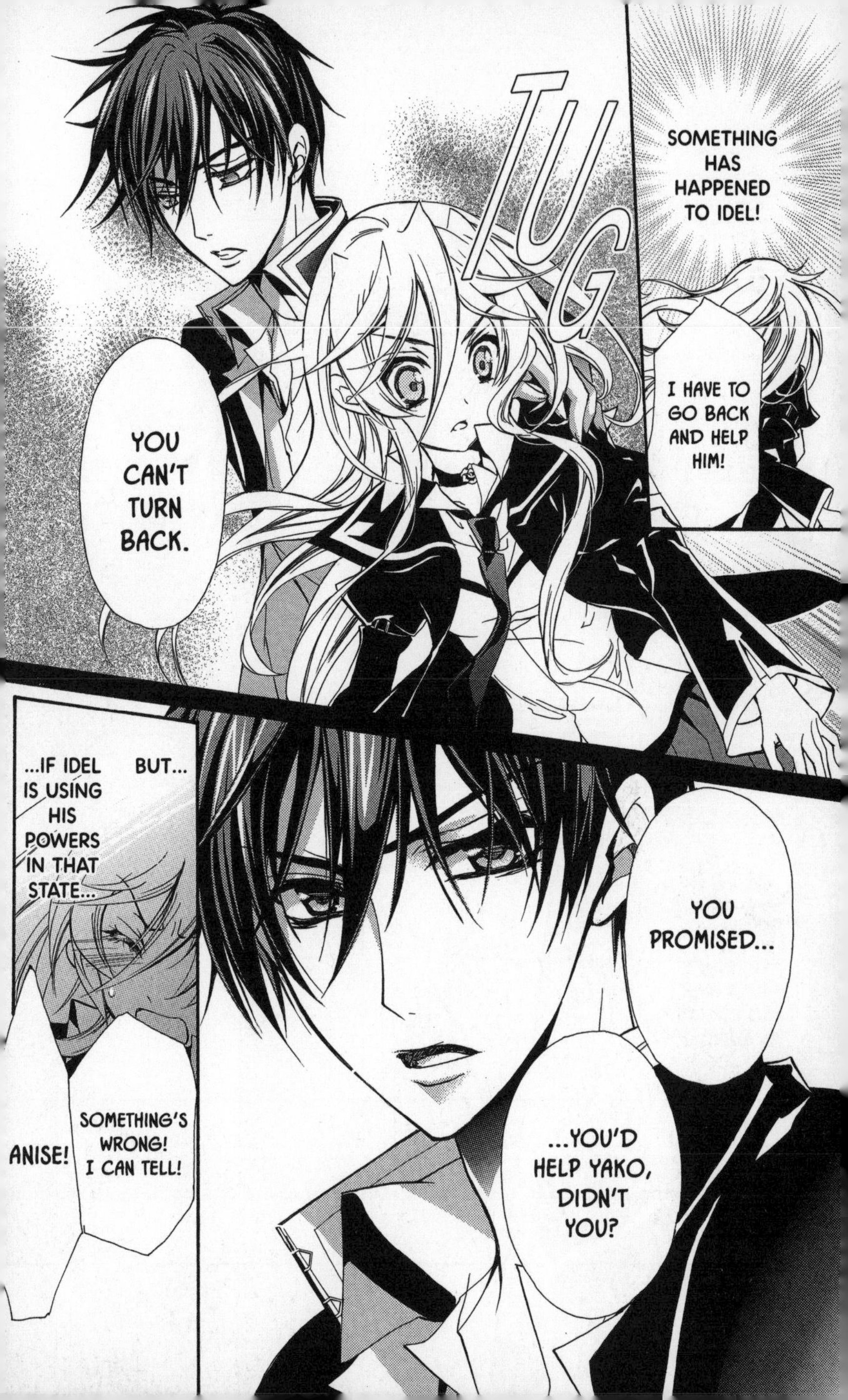
SOMETHING HAS HAPPENED TO IDEL!
I HAVE TO GO BACK AND HELP HIM!
TUG
YOU CAN'T TURN BACK.
YOU PROMISED...
...YOU'D HELP YAKO, DIDN'T YOU?
BUT...
...IF IDEL IS USING HIS POWERS IN THAT STATE...
SOMETHING'S WRONG! I CAN TELL!
ANISE!

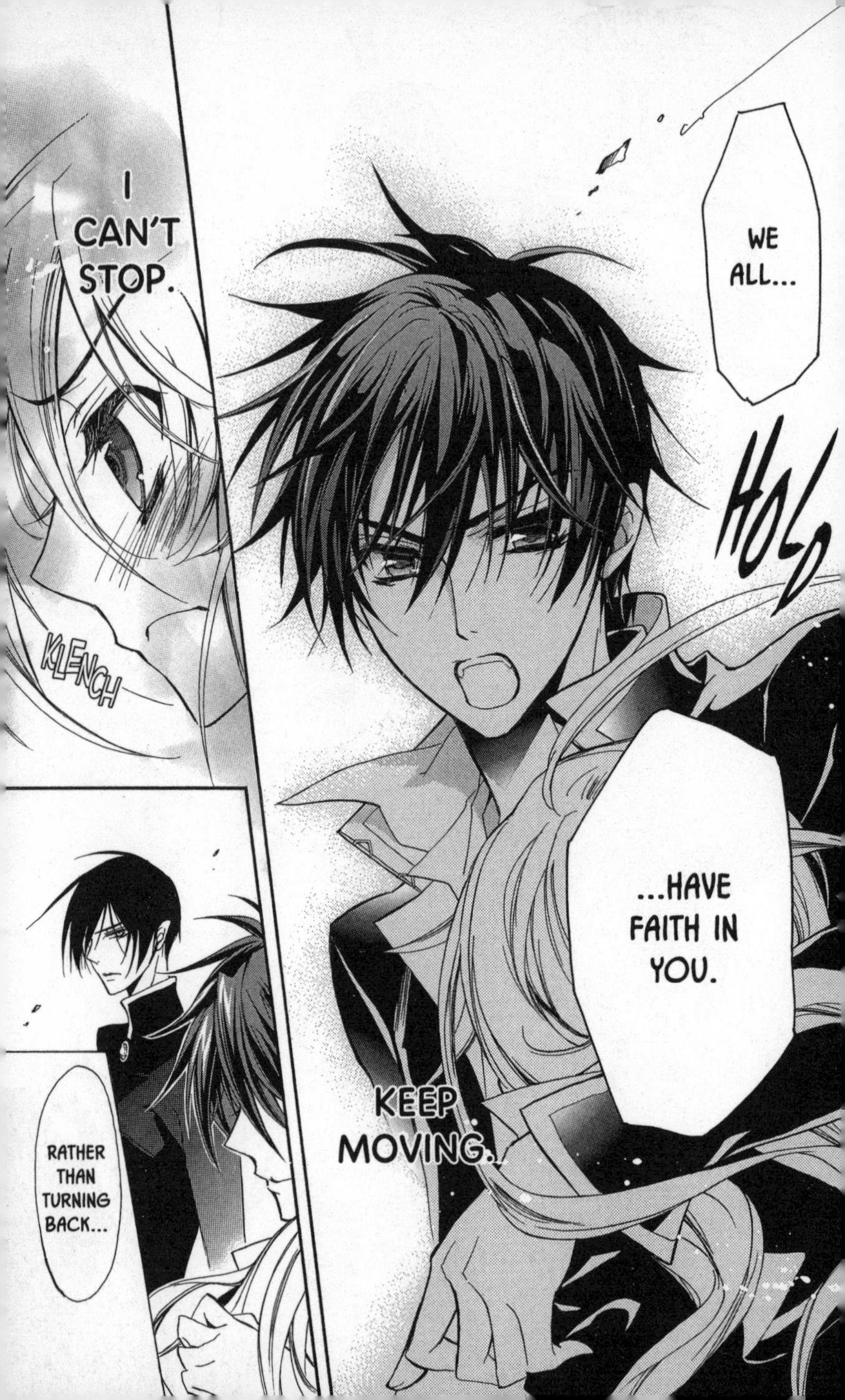
WE ALL...
HOLD
...HAVE FAITH IN YOU.
KEEP MOVING...
I CAN'T STOP.
KLENCH
RATHER THAN TURNING BACK...

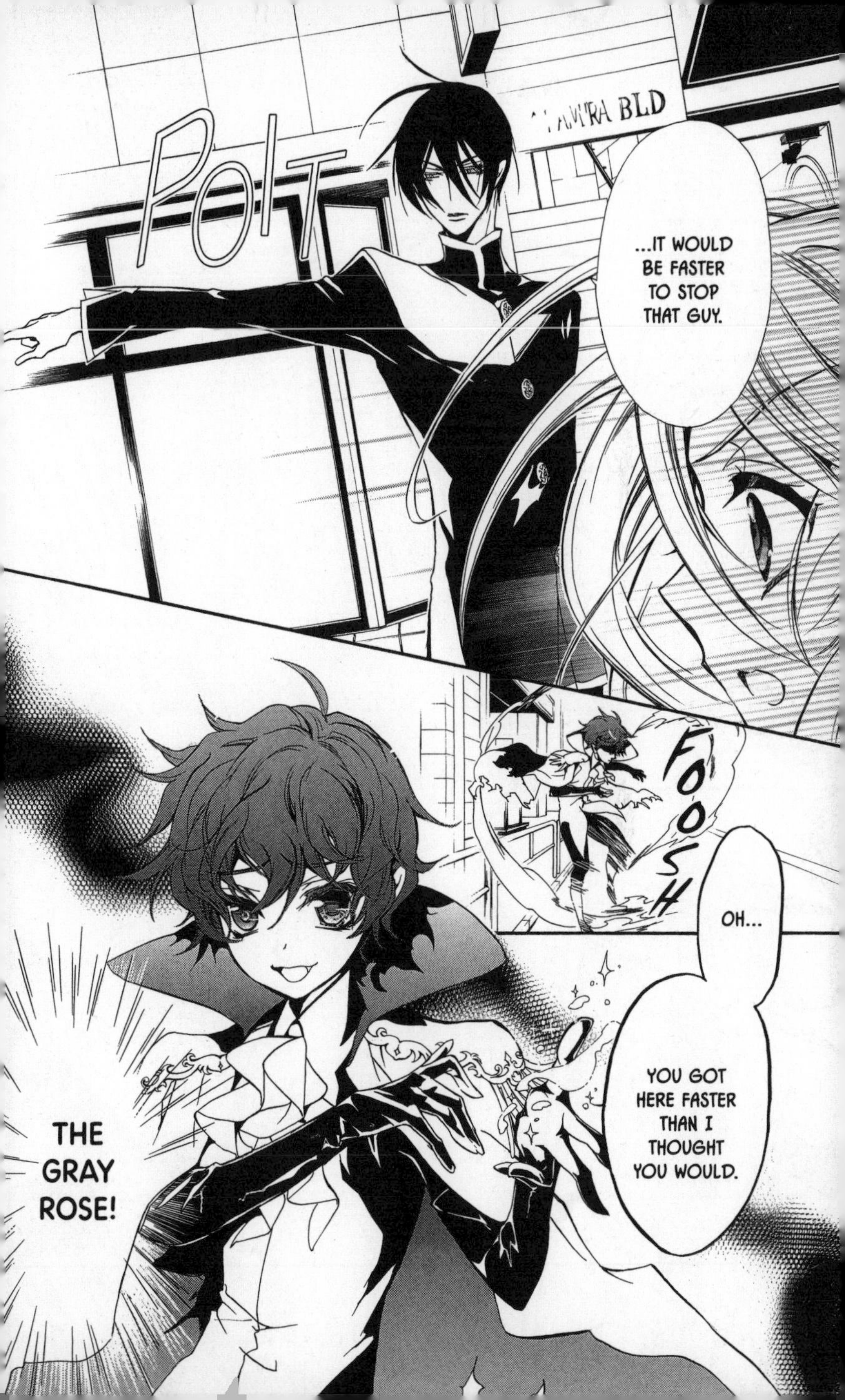
POIT
...IT WOULD BE FASTER TO STOP THAT GUY.
FOOOSH
OH...
YOU GOT HERE FASTER THAN I THOUGHT YOU WOULD.
THE GRAY ROSE!

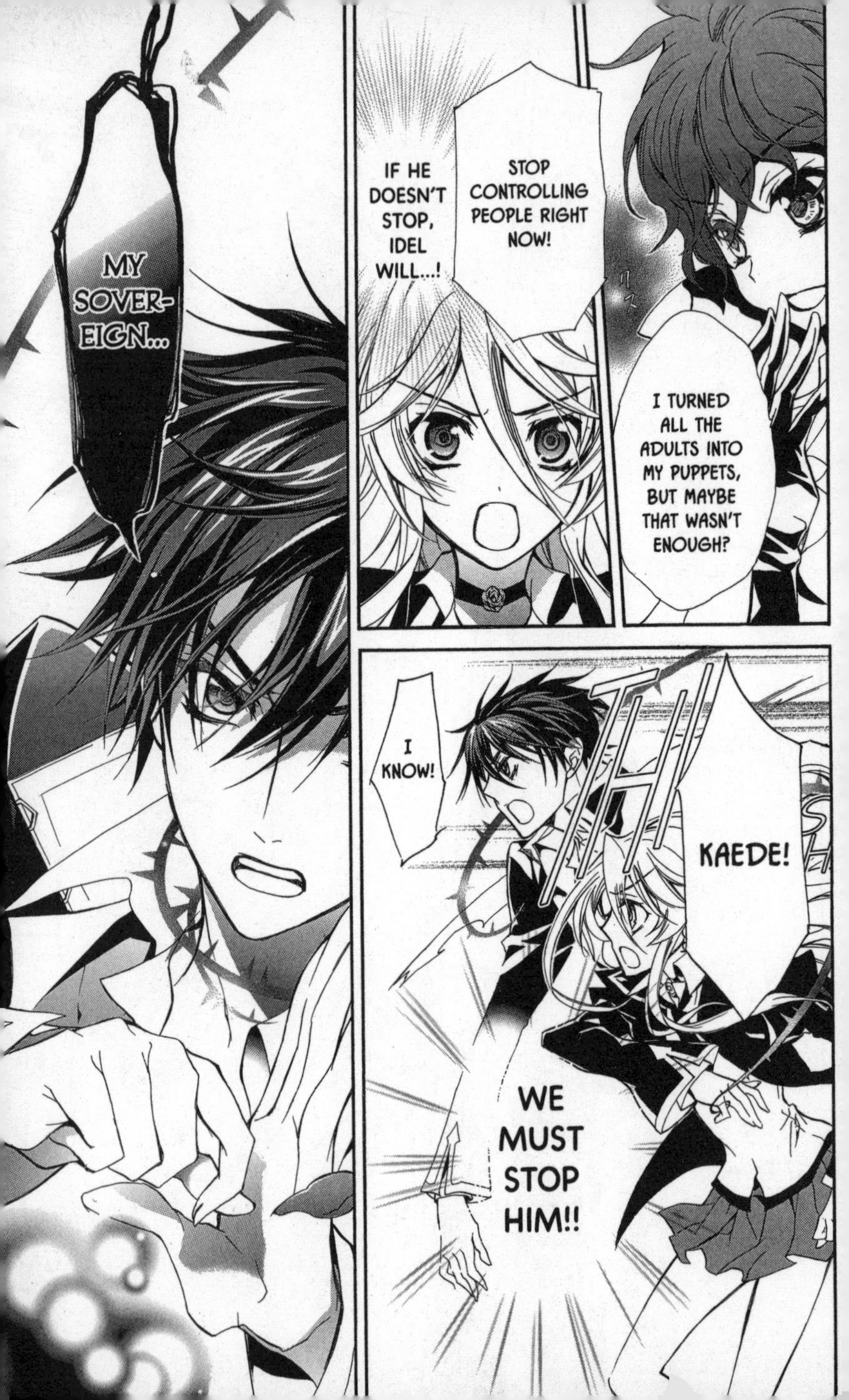
I TURNED ALL THE ADULTS INTO MY PUPPETS, BUT MAYBE THAT WASN'T ENOUGH?
STOP CONTROLLING PEOPLE RIGHT NOW!
IF HE DOESN'T STOP, IDEL WILL...!
KAEDE!
I KNOW!
WE MUST STOP HIM!!
MY SOVER-EIGN...

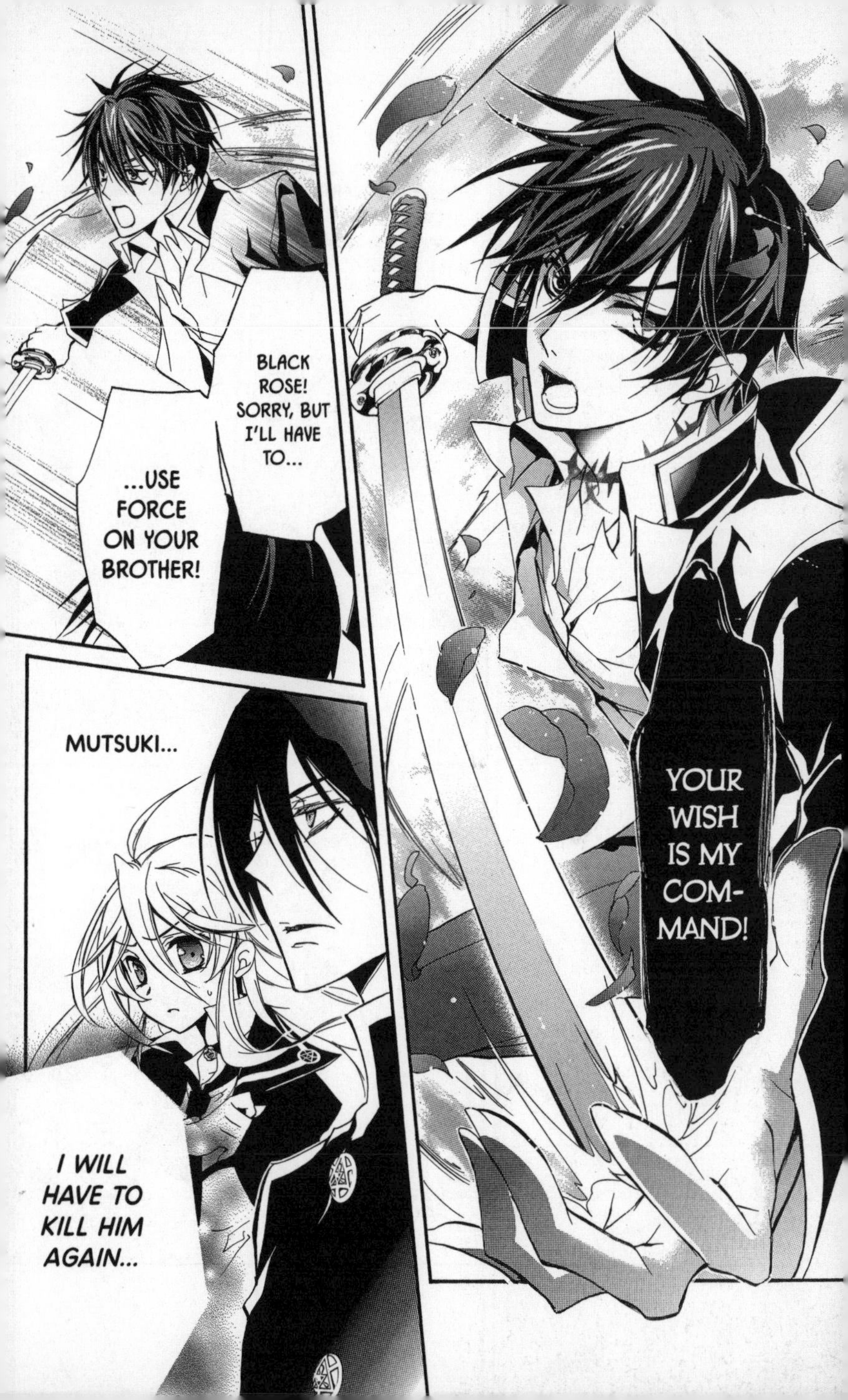
YOUR WISH IS MY COM-MAND!
BLACK ROSE! SORRY, BUT I'LL HAVE TO...
...USE FORCE ON YOUR BROTHER!
MUTSUKI...
I WILL HAVE TO KILL HIM AGAIN...

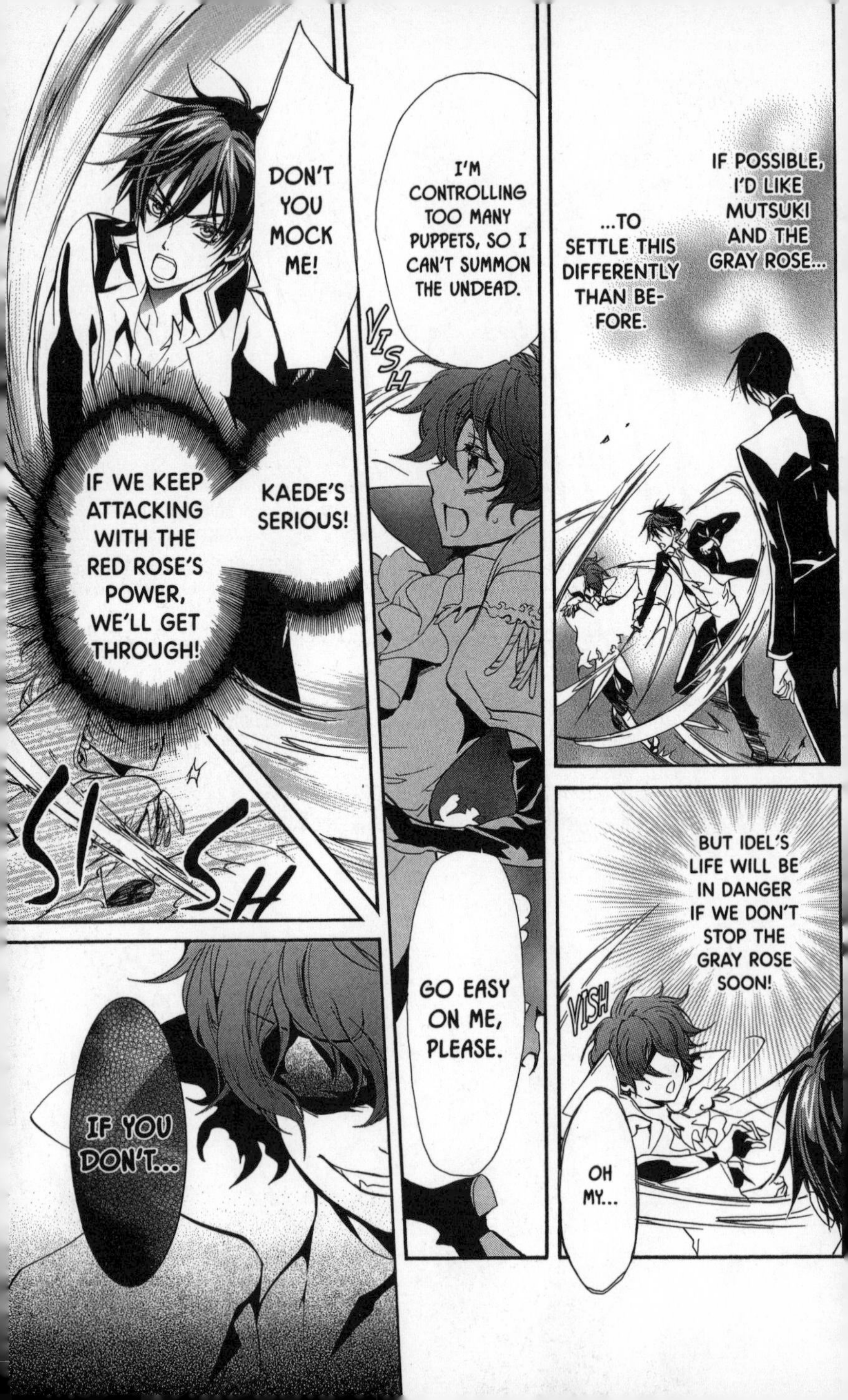
IF POSSIBLE, I'D LIKE MUTSUKI AND THE GRAY ROSE...
...TO SETTLE THIS DIFFERENTLY THAN BE-FORE.
BUT IDEL'S LIFE WILL BE IN DANGER IF WE DON'T STOP THE GRAY ROSE SOON!
VISH
OH MY...
I'M CONTROLLING TOO MANY PUPPETS, SO I CAN'T SUMMON THE UNDEAD.
VISH
GO EASY ON ME, PLEASE.
DON'T YOU MOCK ME!
KAEDE'S SERIOUS!
IF WE KEEP ATTACKING WITH THE RED ROSE'S POWER, WE'LL GET THROUGH!
SISSH
IF YOU DON'T...

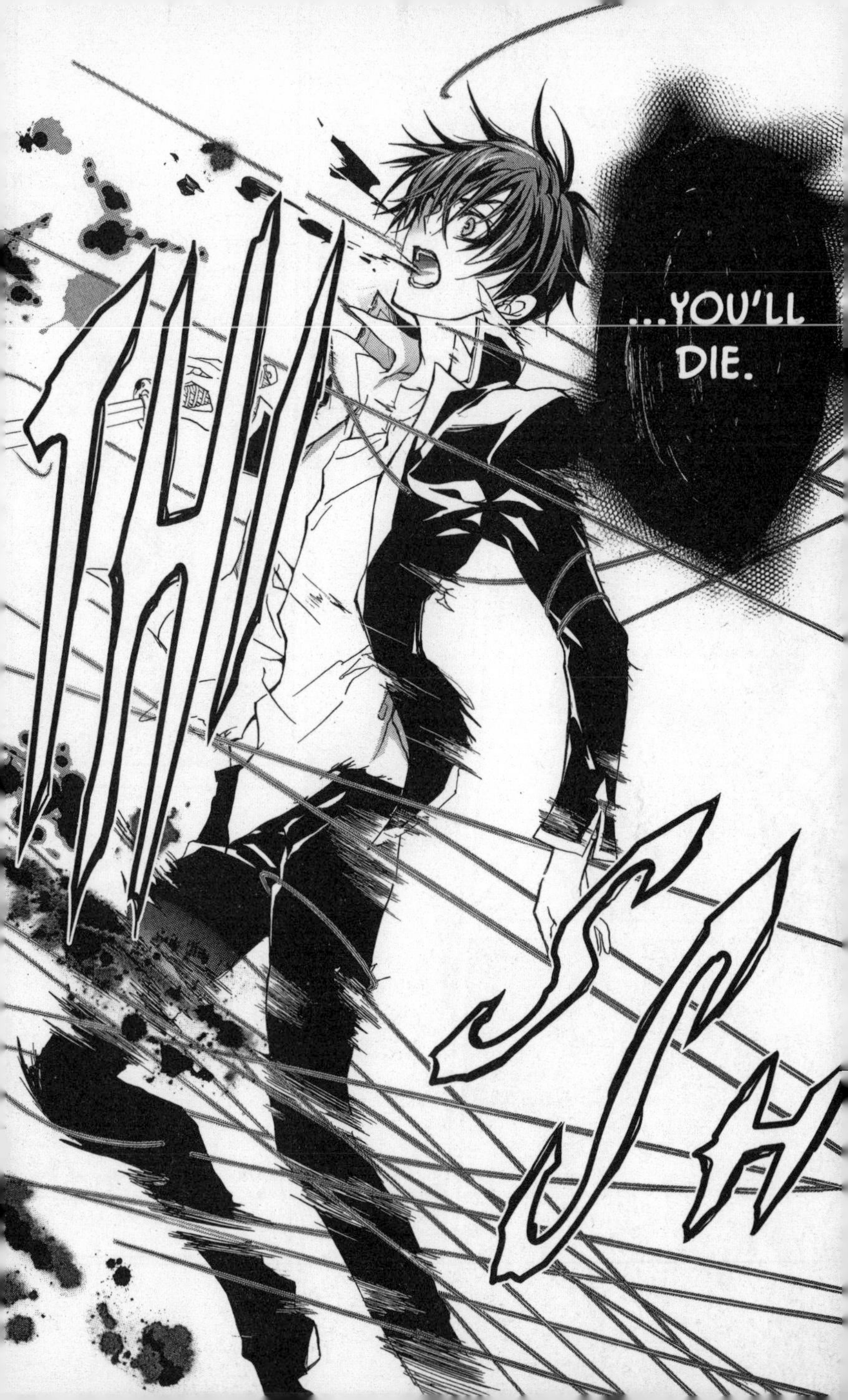
...YOU'LL DIE.
THUD
SSH

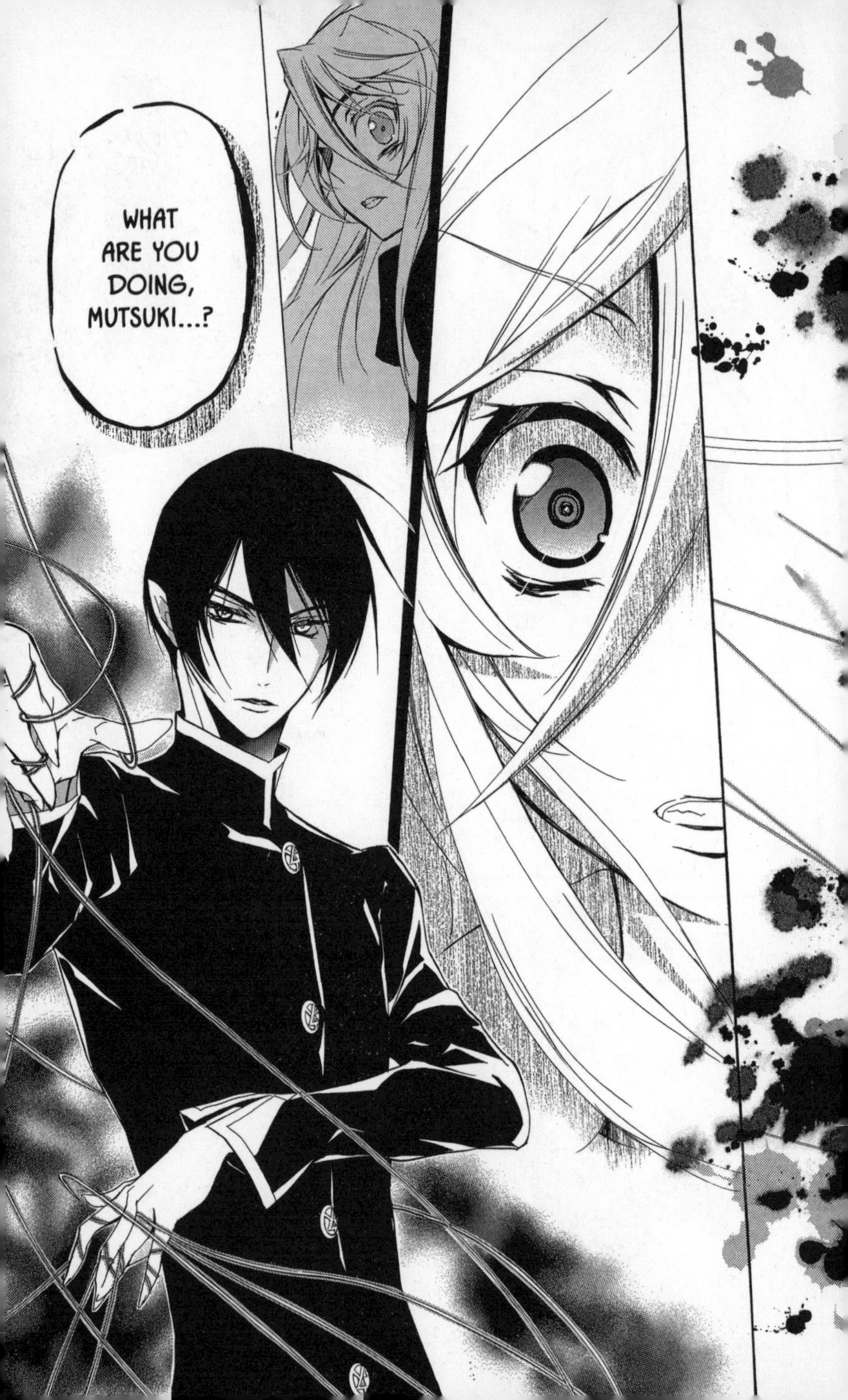
WHAT ARE YOU DOING, MUTSUKI...?

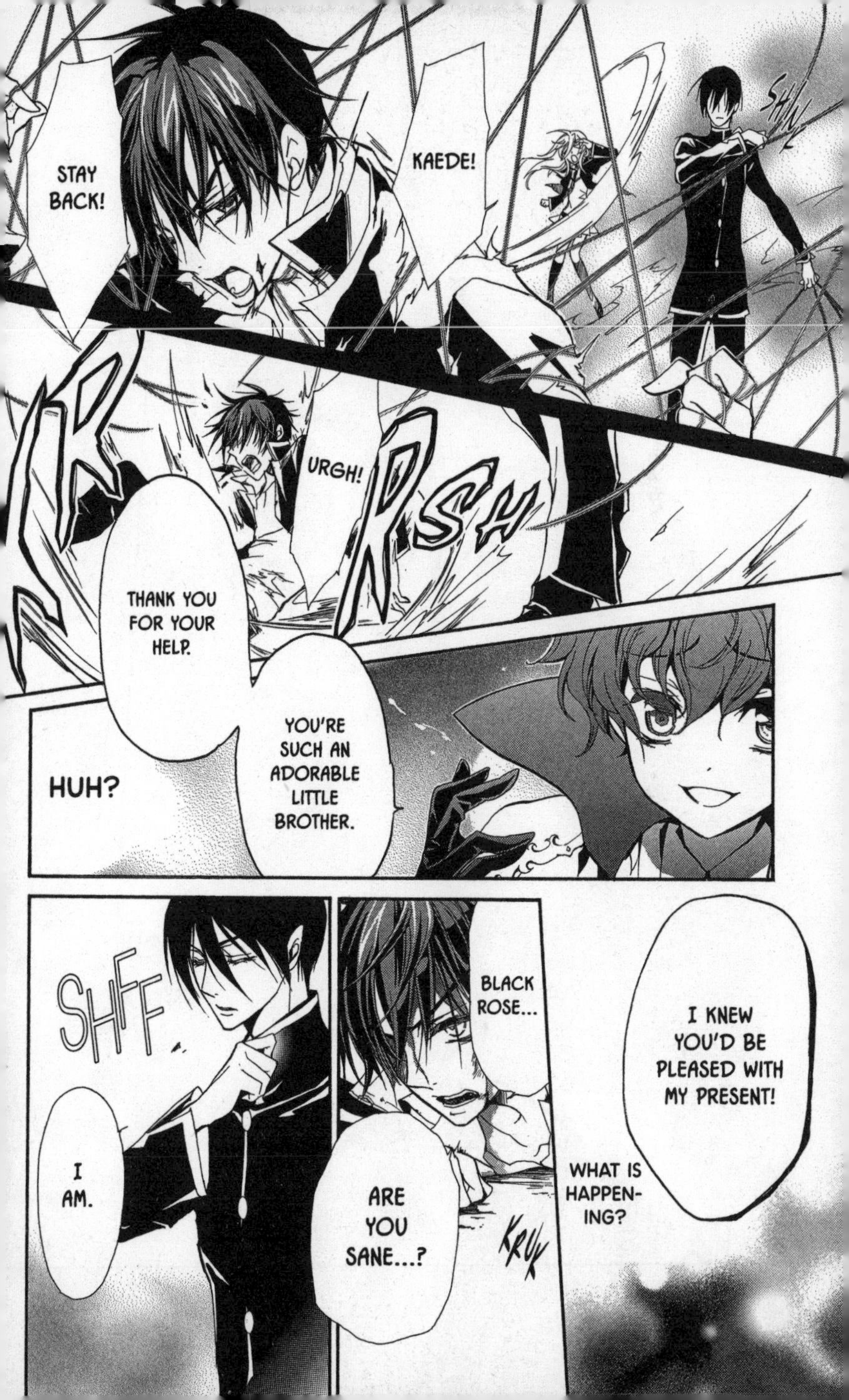
SHN
KAEDE!
STAY BACK!
RSH
URGH!
THANK YOU FOR YOUR HELP.
YOU'RE SUCH AN ADORABLE LITTLE BROTHER.
HUH?
I KNEW YOU'D BE PLEASED WITH MY PRESENT!
BLACK ROSE...
WHAT IS HAPPEN-ING?
ARE YOU SANE...?
KRUK
SHFF
I AM.

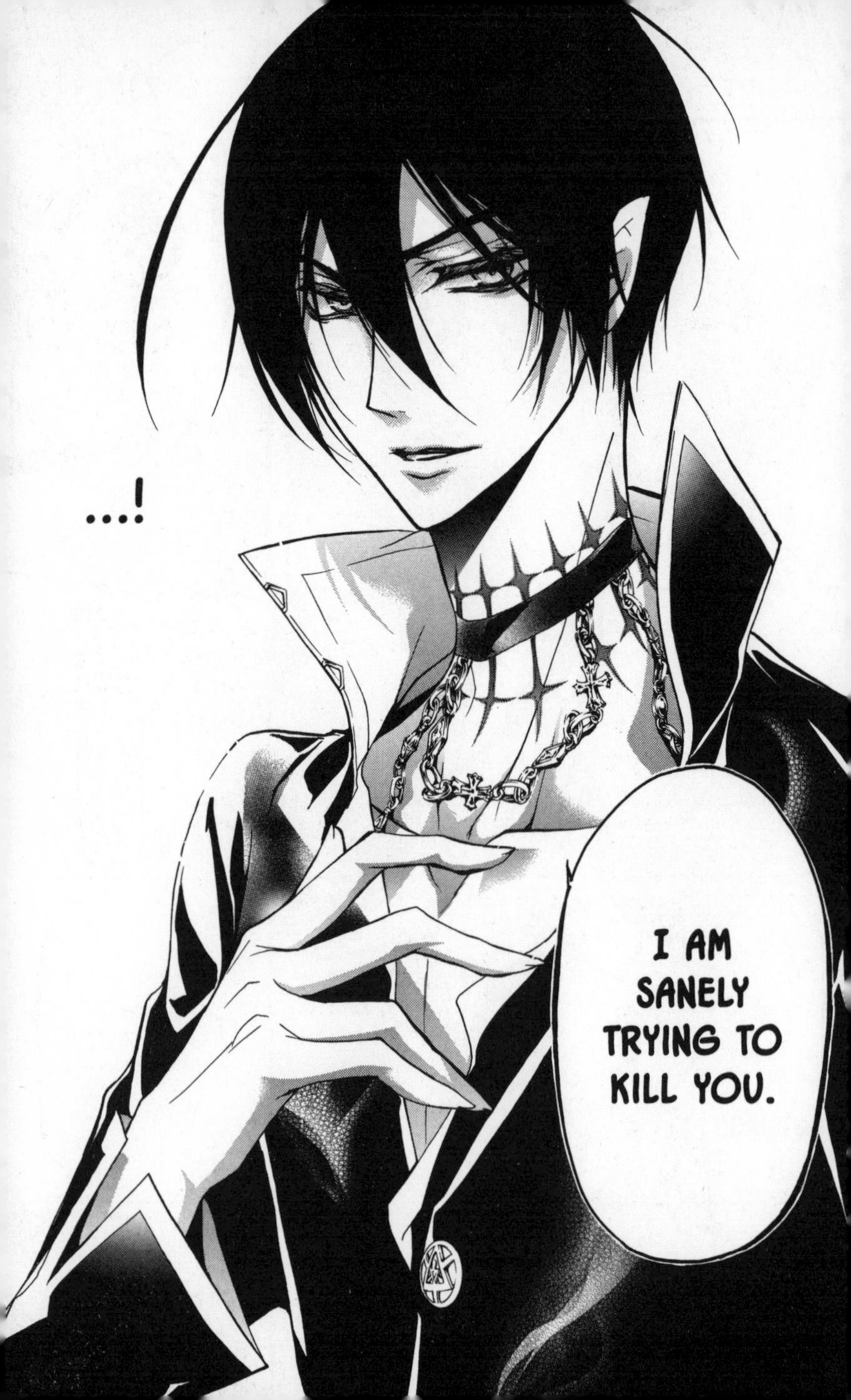
...!
I AM SANELY TRYING TO KILL YOU.

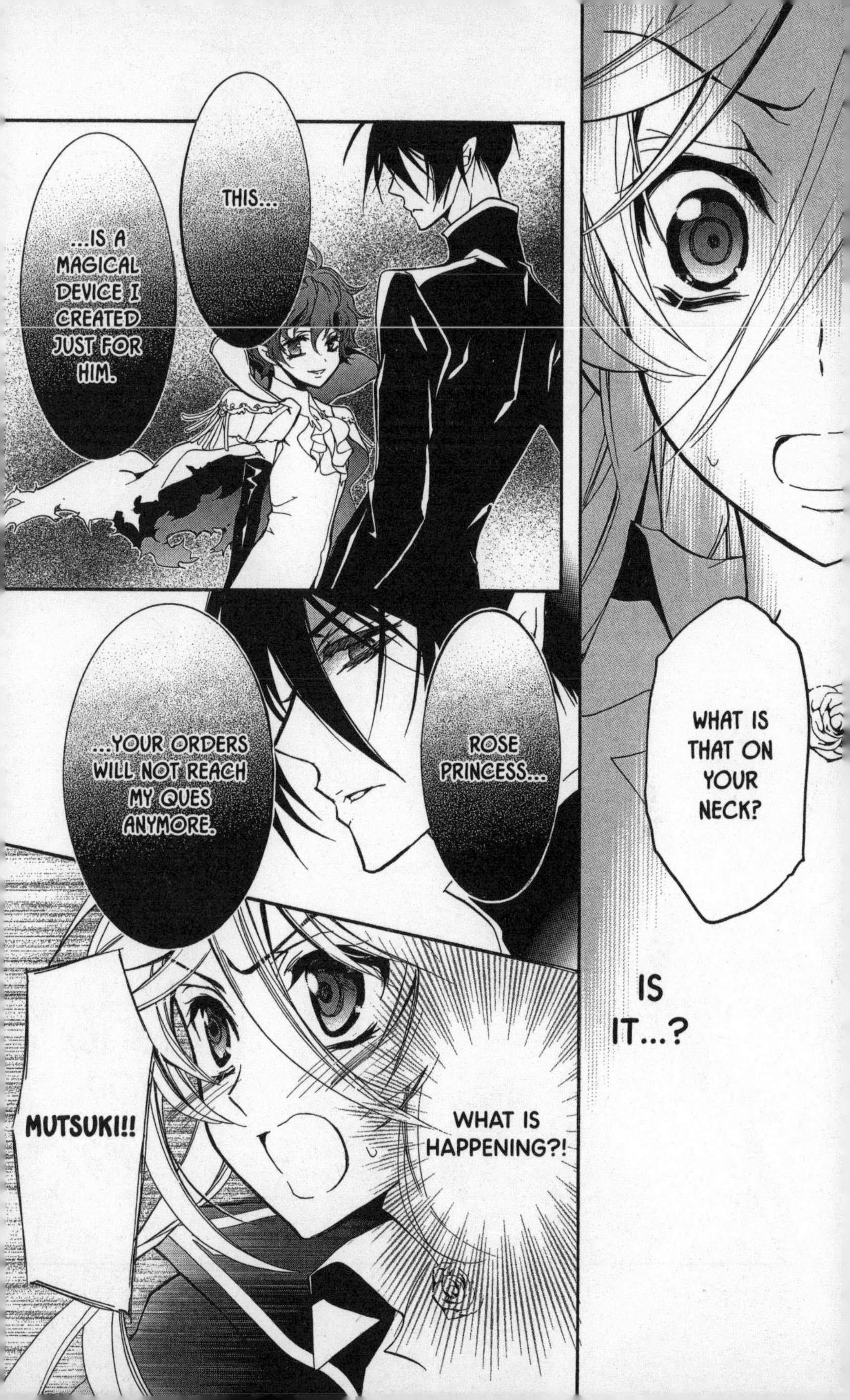
WHAT IS THAT ON YOUR NECK?
IS IT...?
THIS...
...IS A MAGICAL DEVICE I CREATED JUST FOR HIM.
ROSE PRINCESS...
...YOUR ORDERS WILL NOT REACH MY QUES ANYMORE.
WHAT IS HAPPENING?!
MUTSUKI!!

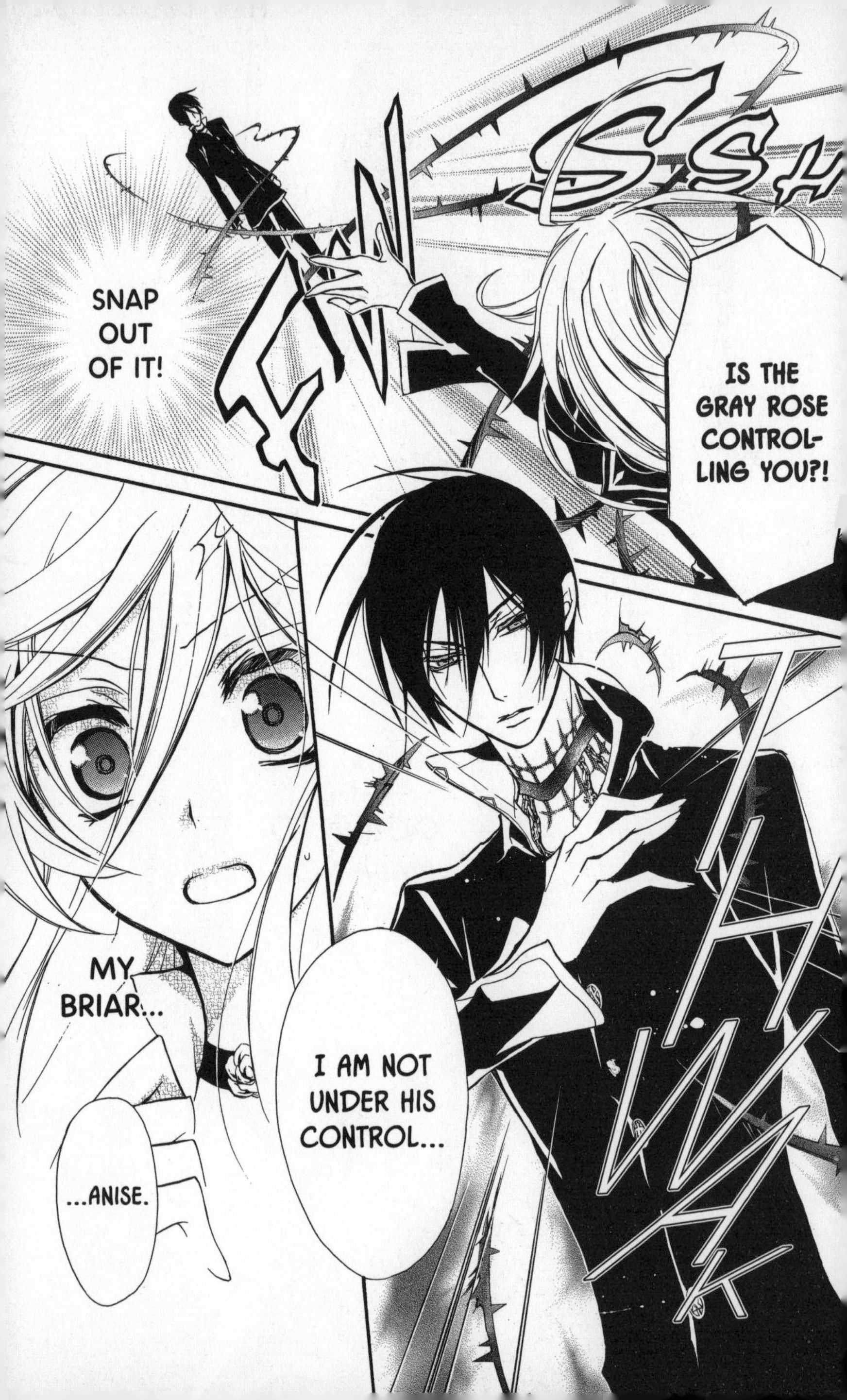
IS THE GRAY ROSE CONTROLLING YOU?!
SNAP OUT OF IT!
MY BRIAR...
I AM NOT UNDER HIS CONTROL...
...ANISE.

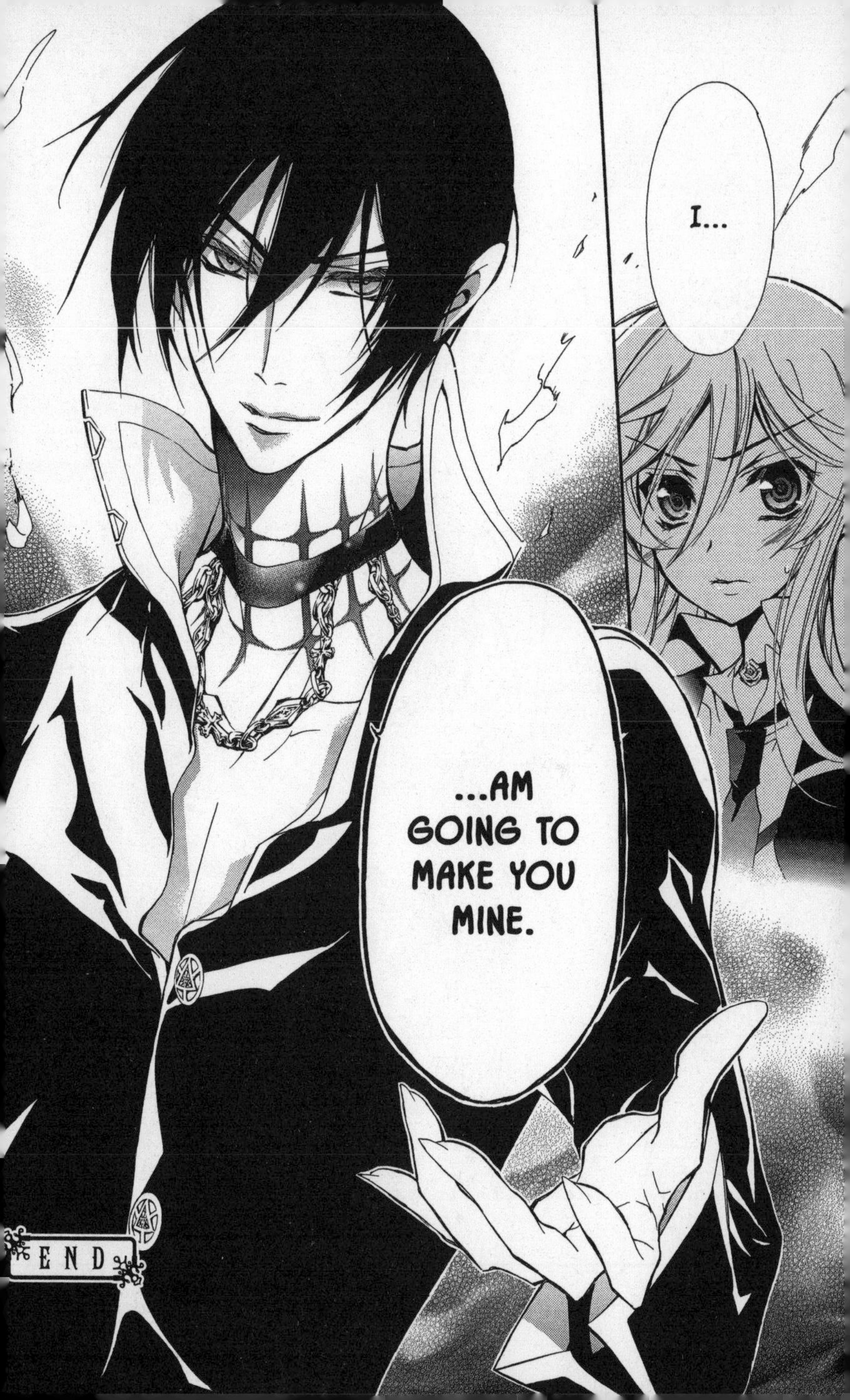
I...
...AM GOING TO MAKE YOU MINE.
END

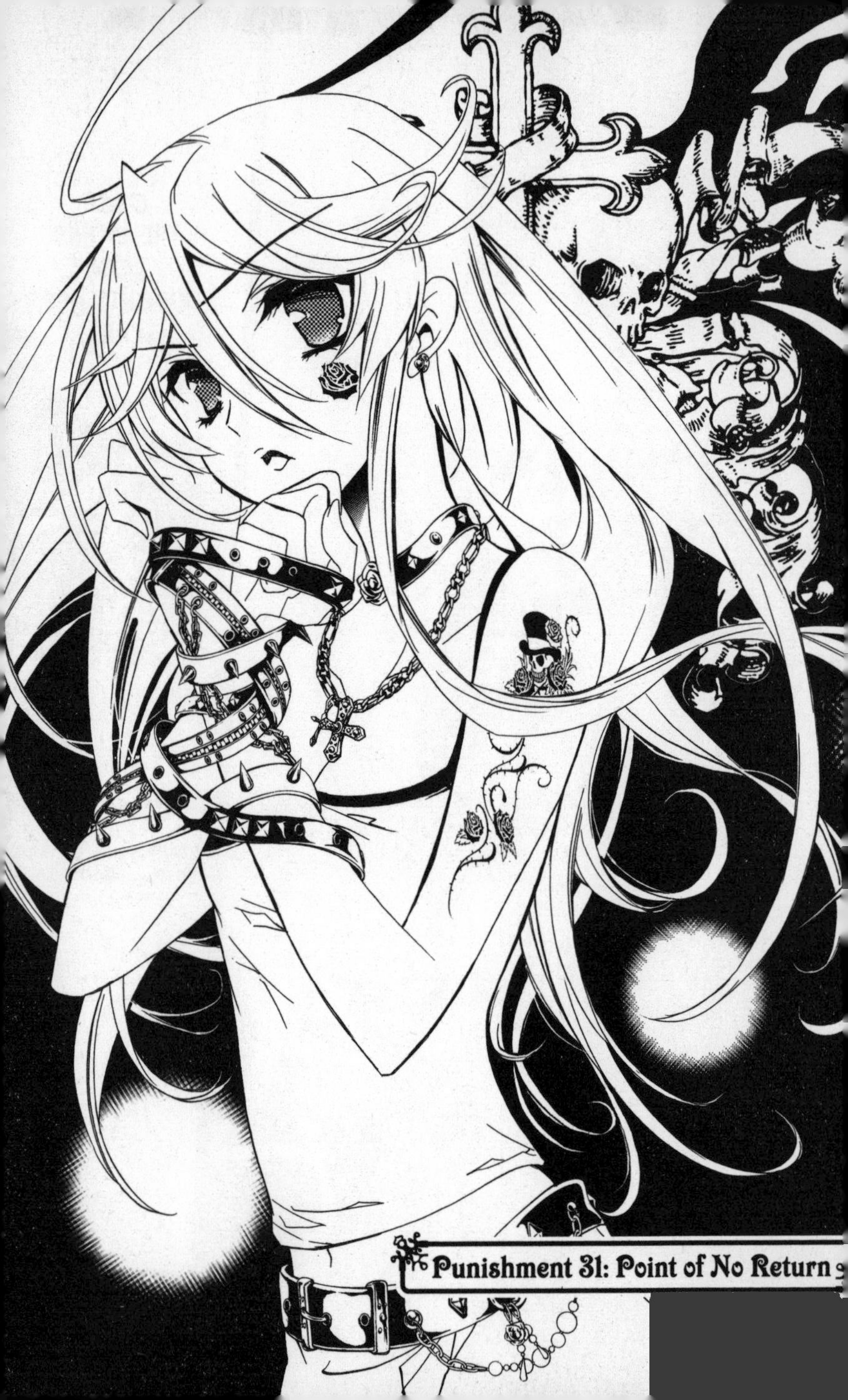
Punishment 31: Point of No Return

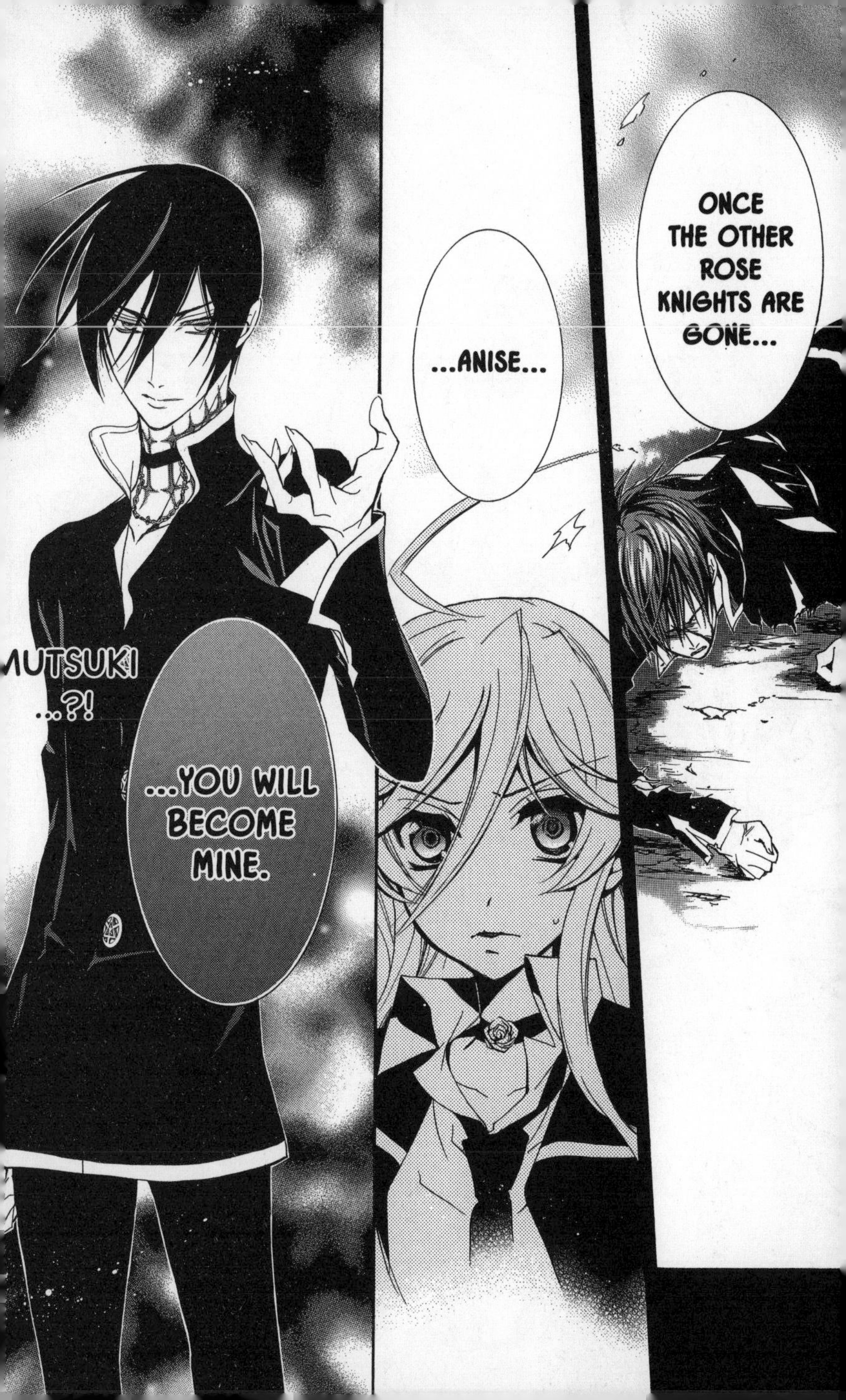
ONCE THE OTHER ROSE KNIGHTS ARE GONE...
...ANISE...
...YOU WILL BECOME MINE.
MUTSUKI ...?!

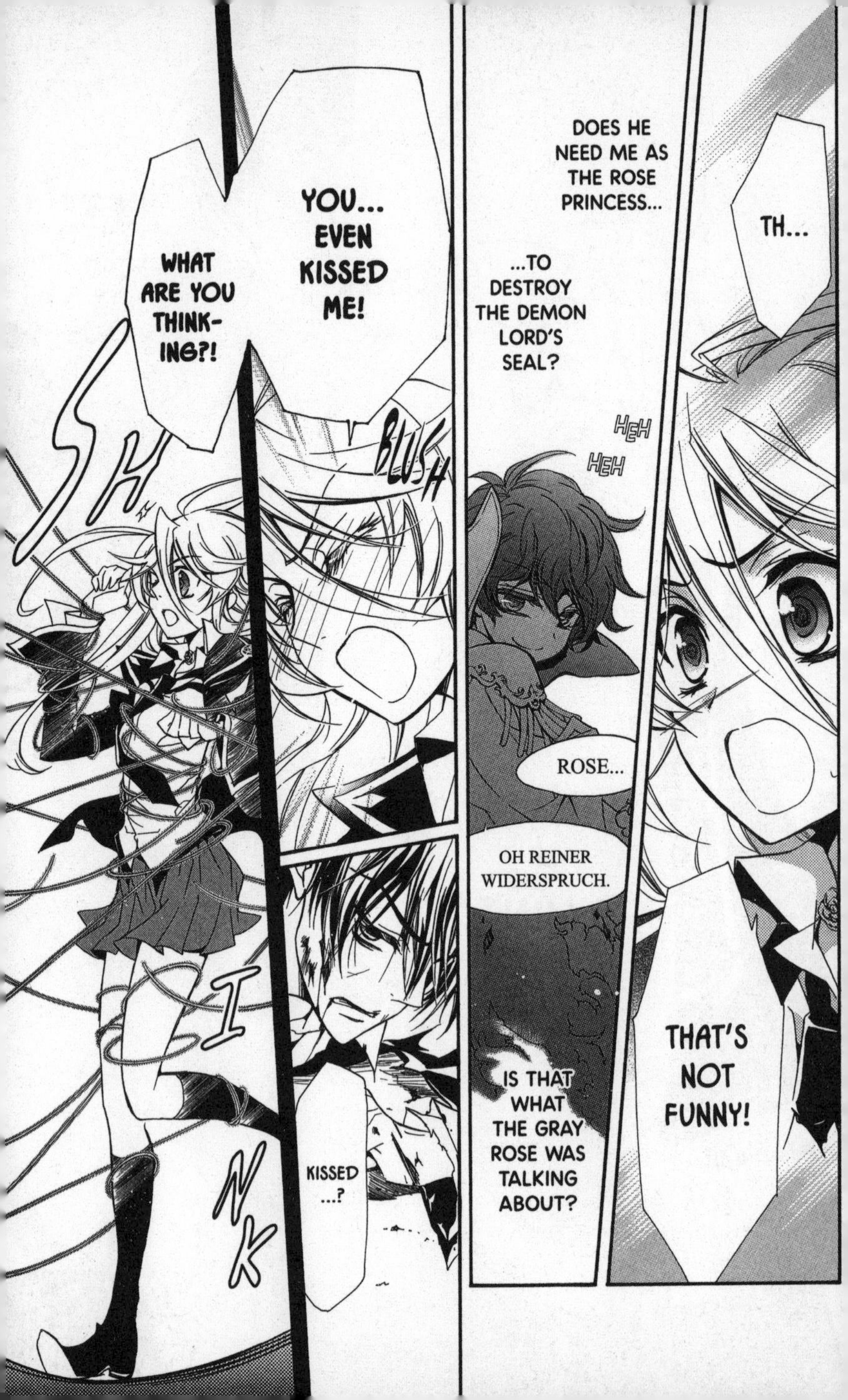
TH...
THAT'S NOT FUNNY!
DOES HE NEED ME AS THE ROSE PRINCESS...
...TO DESTROY THE DEMON LORD'S SEAL?
HEH HEH
ROSE...
OH REINER WIDERSPRUCH.
IS THAT WHAT THE GRAY ROSE WAS TALKING ABOUT?
YOU... EVEN KISSED ME!
WHAT ARE YOU THINKING?!
BLUSH
SHINK
KISSED ...?

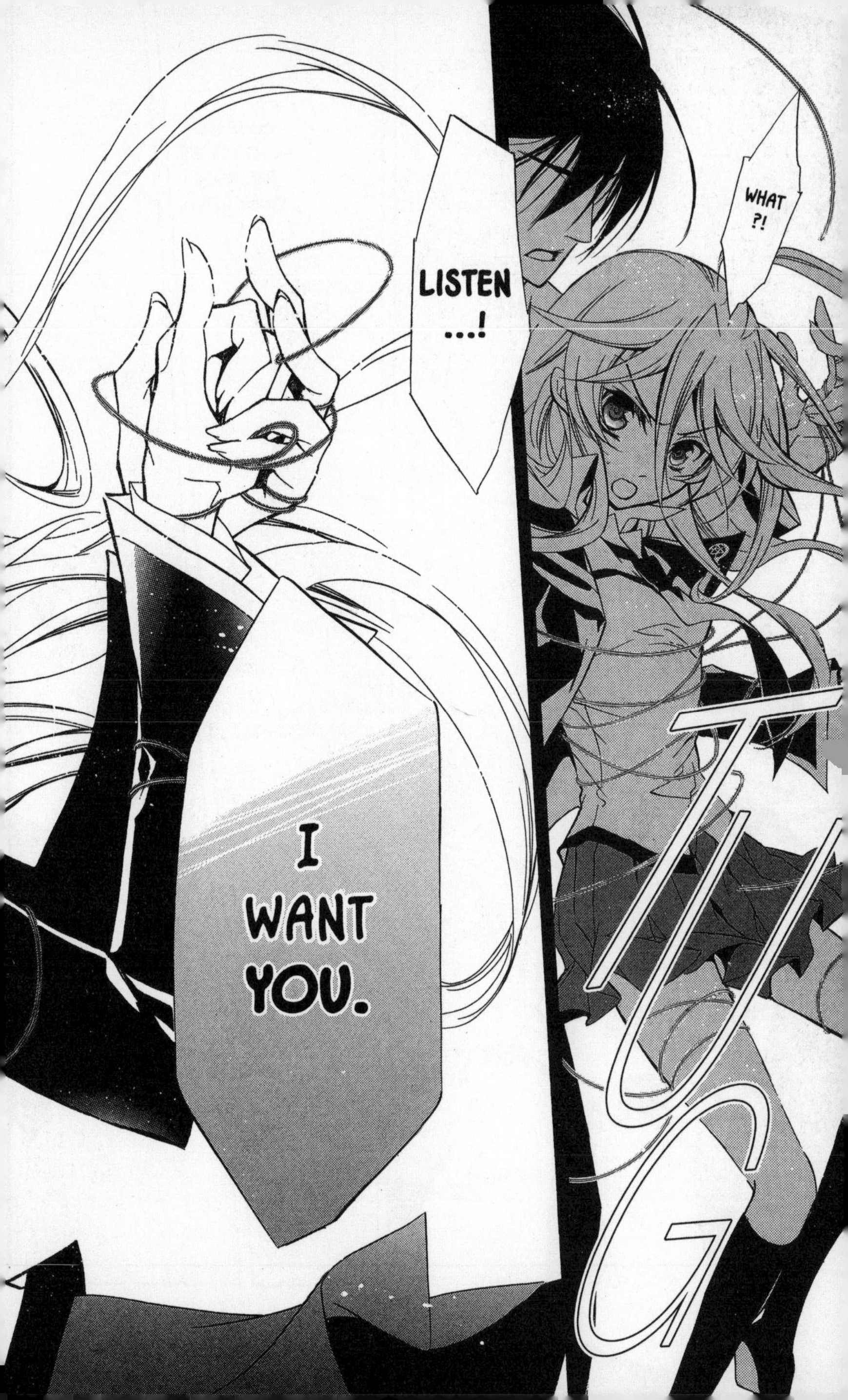
WHAT ?!
LISTEN ...!
I WANT YOU.

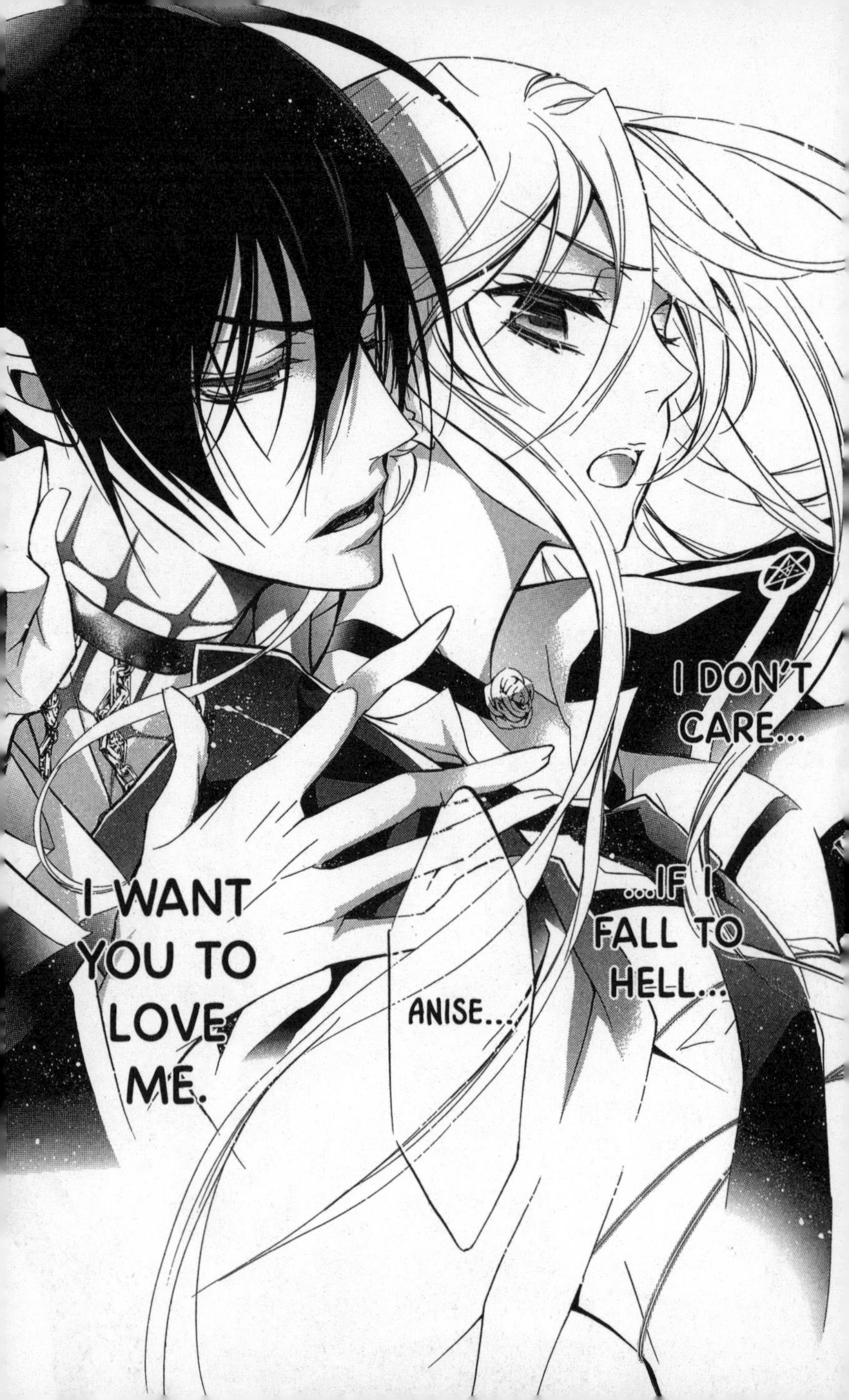
I DON'T CARE...
...IF I FALL TO HELL...
ANISE...
I WANT YOU TO LOVE ME.

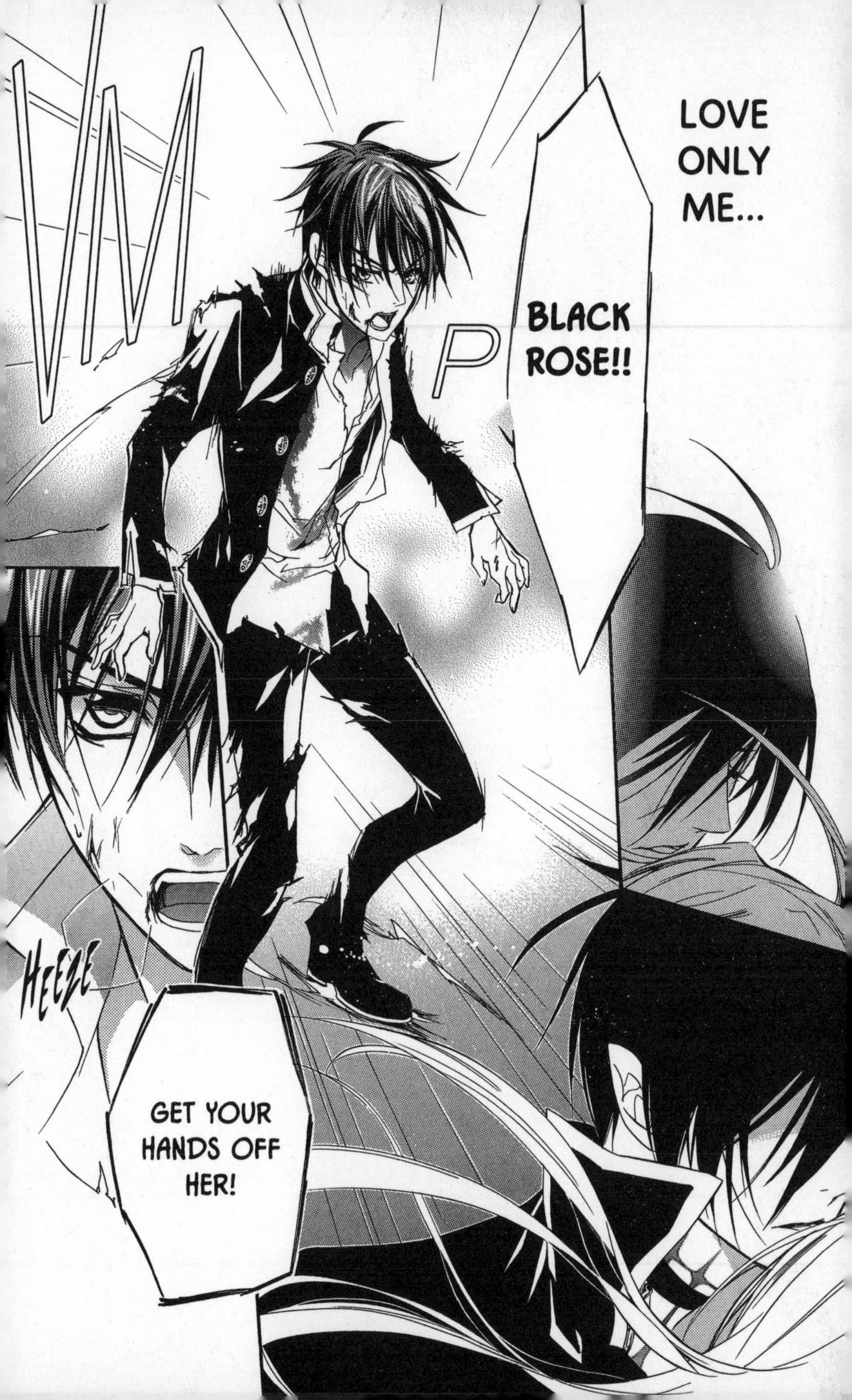
LOVE ONLY ME...
BLACK ROSE!!
VM
P
HEEZE
GET YOUR HANDS OFF HER!

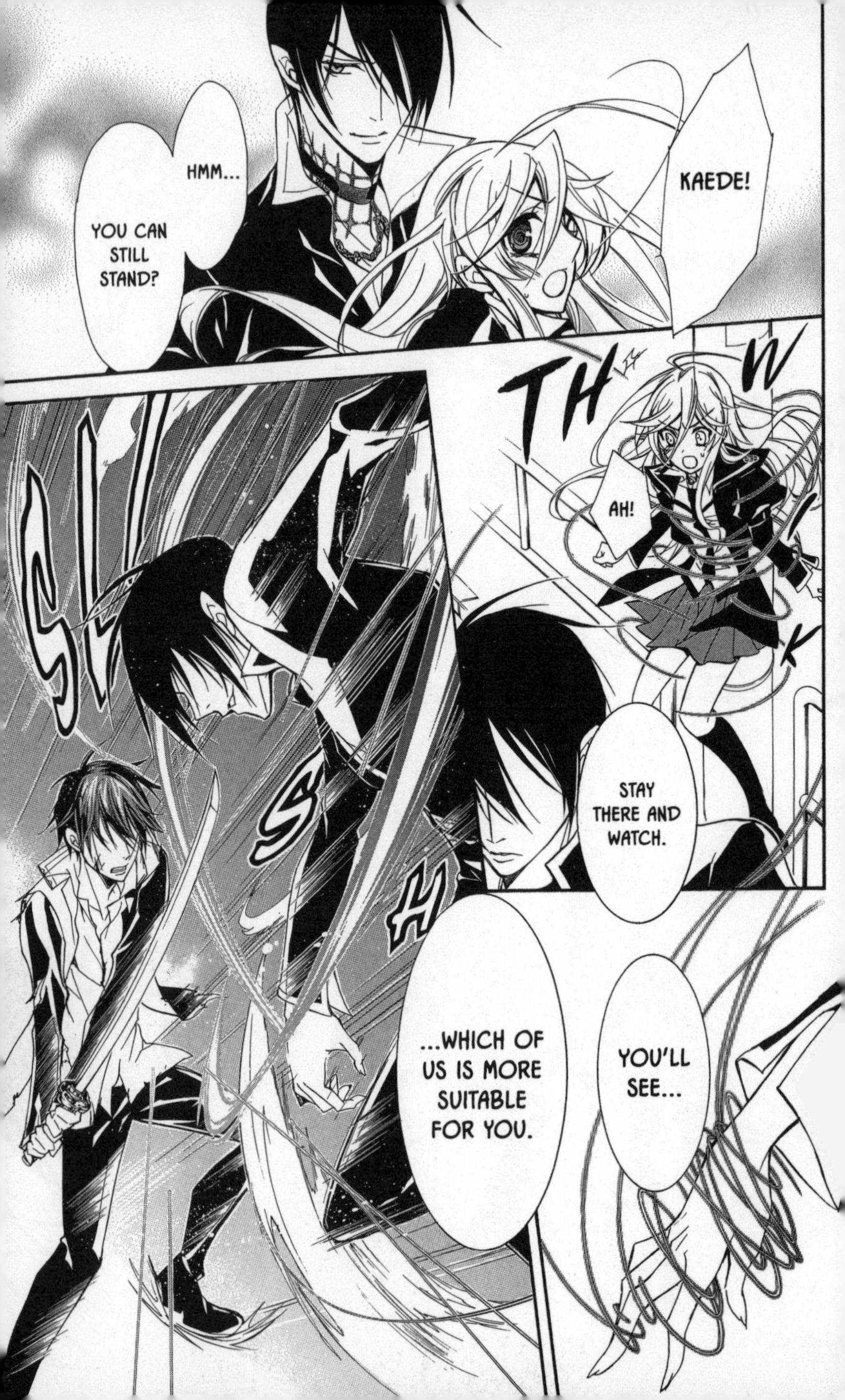
KAEDE!
HMM...
YOU CAN STILL STAND?
AH!
STAY THERE AND WATCH.
YOU'LL SEE...
...WHICH OF US IS MORE SUITABLE FOR YOU.

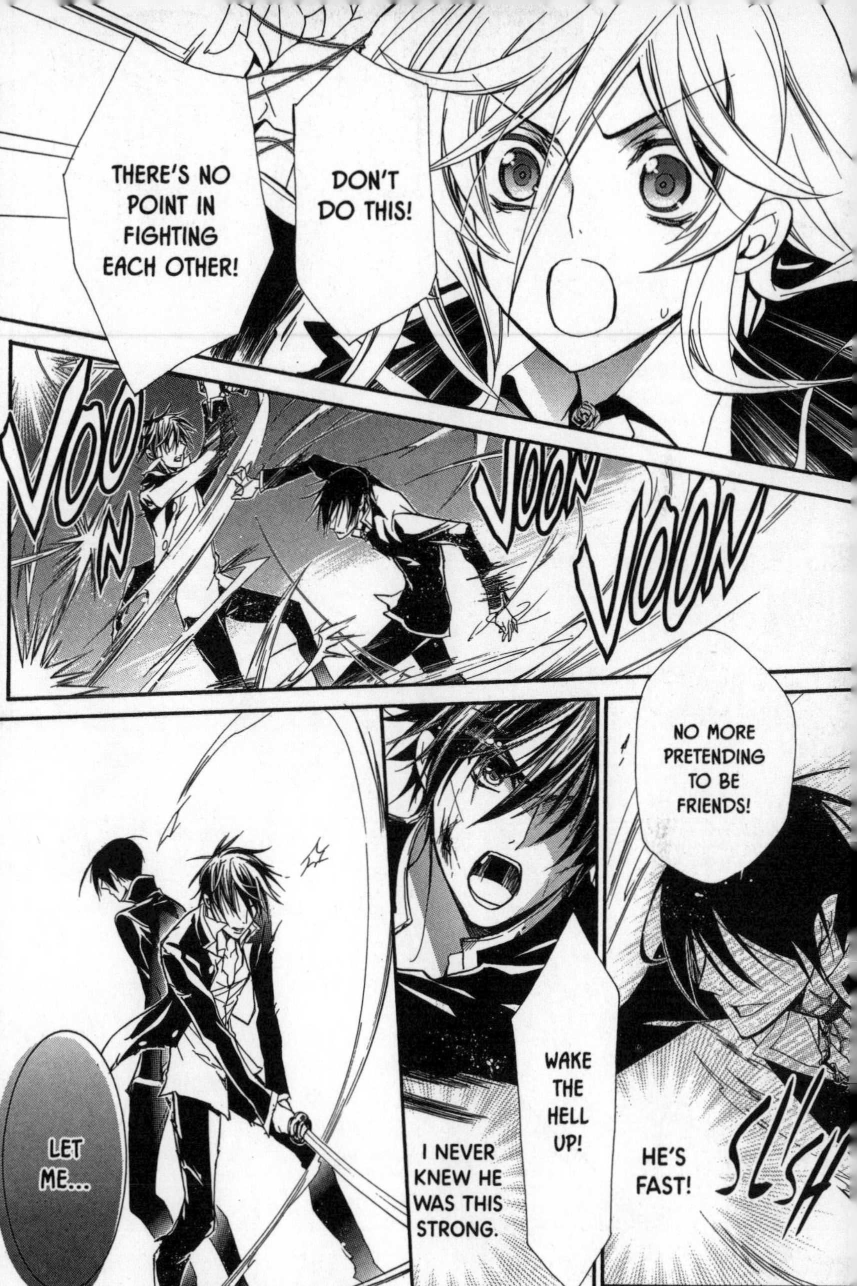
DON'T DO THIS!
THERE'S NO POINT IN FIGHTING EACH OTHER!
VOOM
VOOM
VOOM
NO MORE PRETENDING TO BE FRIENDS!
HE'S FAST!
SLSH
WAKE THE HELL UP!
I NEVER KNEW HE WAS THIS STRONG.
LET ME...

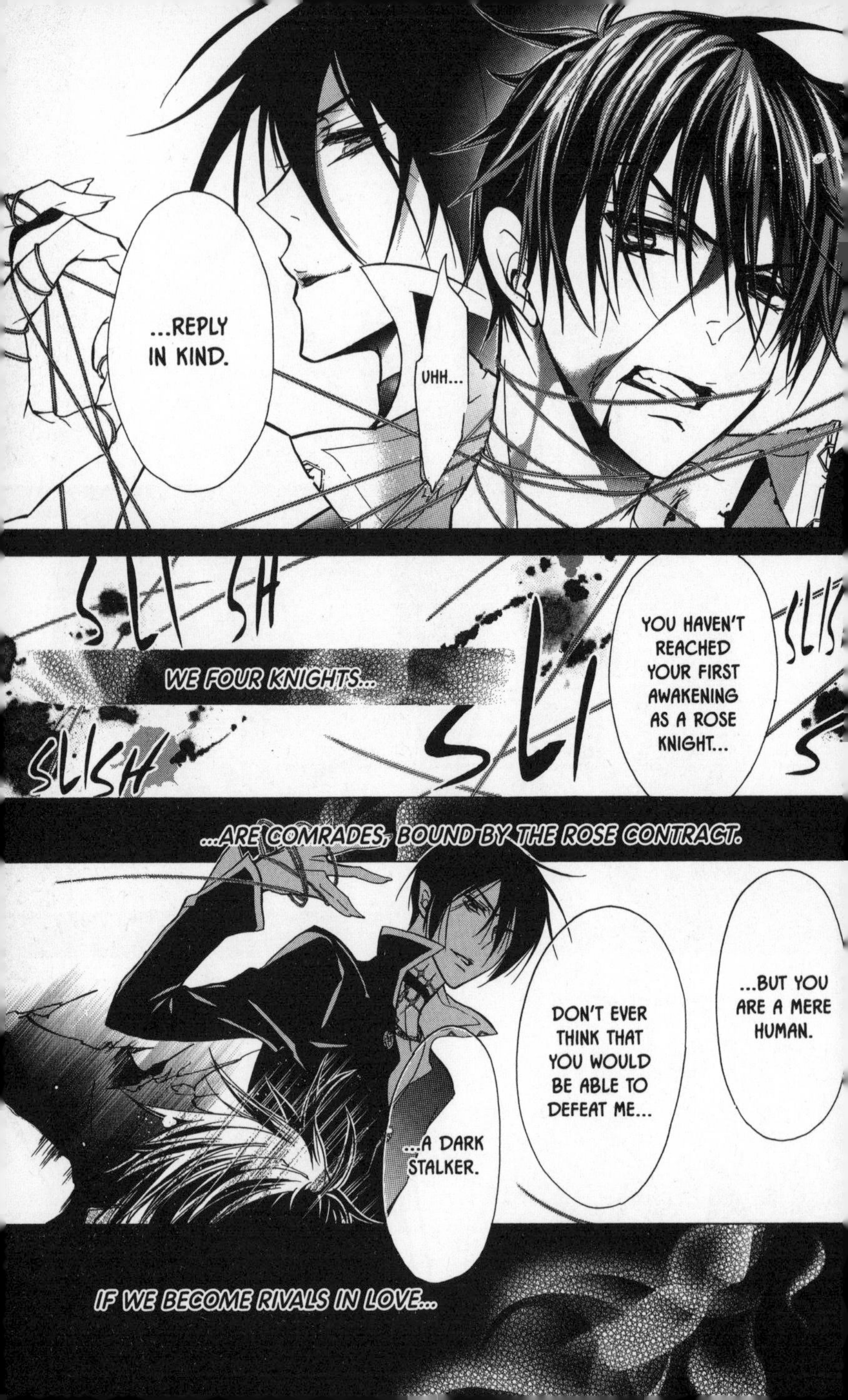
...REPLY IN KIND.
UHH...
SLIS
S
YOU HAVEN'T REACHED YOUR FIRST AWAKENING AS A ROSE KNIGHT...
SLI
SLISH
WE FOUR KNIGHTS...
SLISH
...ARE COMRADES, BOUND BY THE ROSE CONTRACT.
...BUT YOU ARE A MERE HUMAN.
DON'T EVER THINK THAT YOU WOULD BE ABLE TO DEFEAT ME...
...A DARK STALKER.
IF WE BECOME RIVALS IN LOVE...

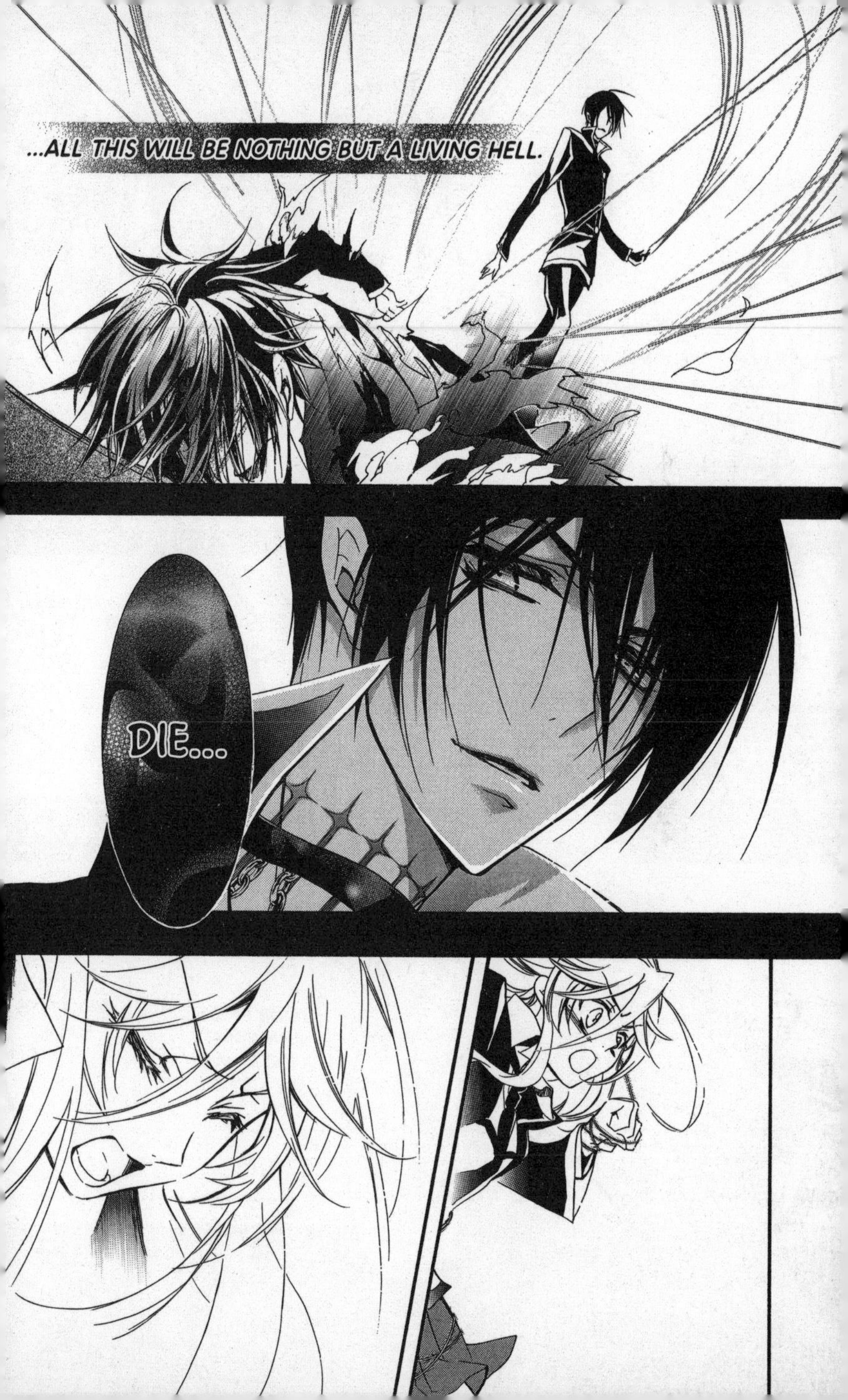
...ALL THIS WILL BE NOTHING BUT A LIVING HELL.
DIE...

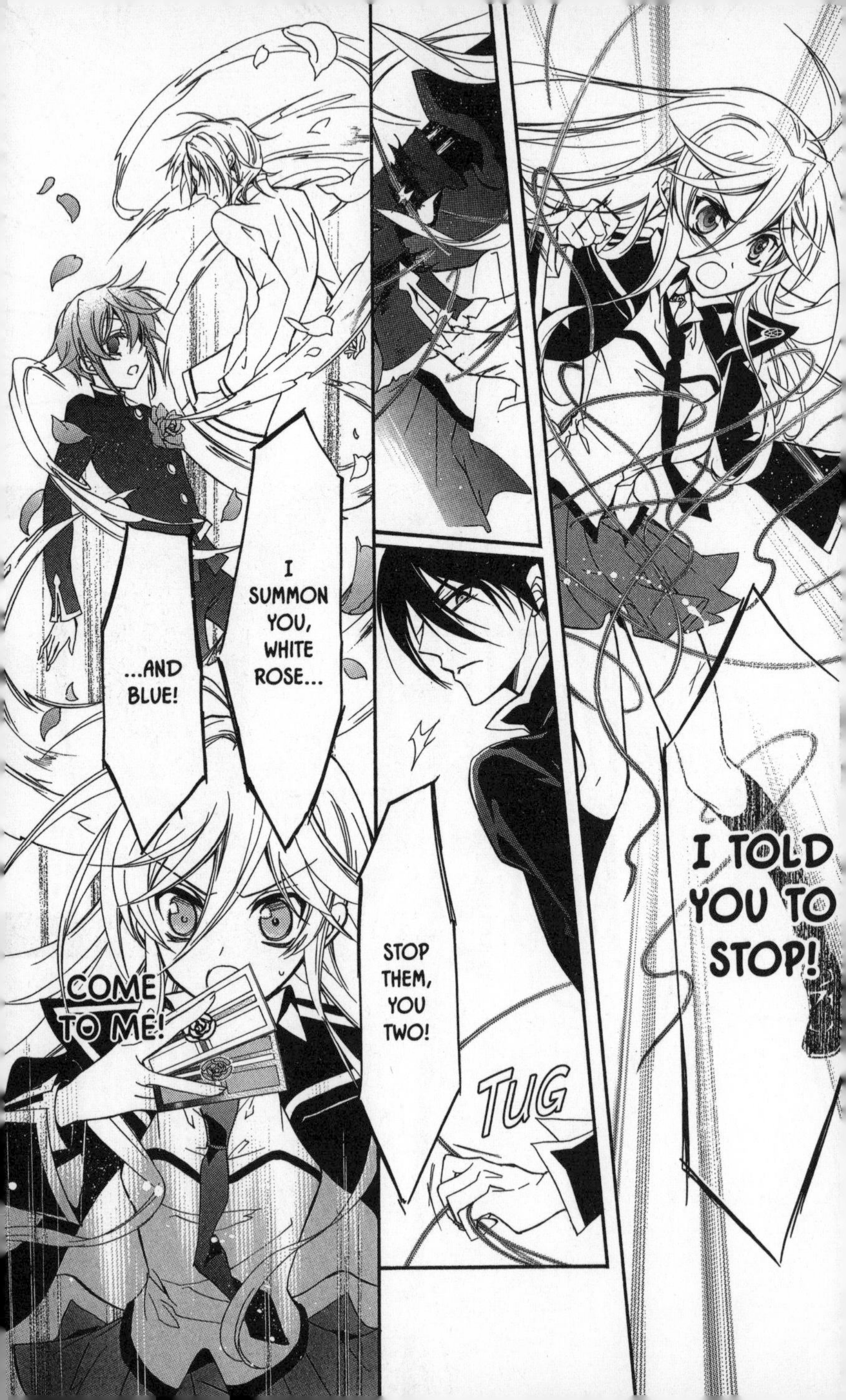
I TOLD YOU TO STOP!
STOP THEM, YOU TWO!
TUG
I SUMMON YOU, WHITE ROSE...
...AND BLUE!
COME TO ME!

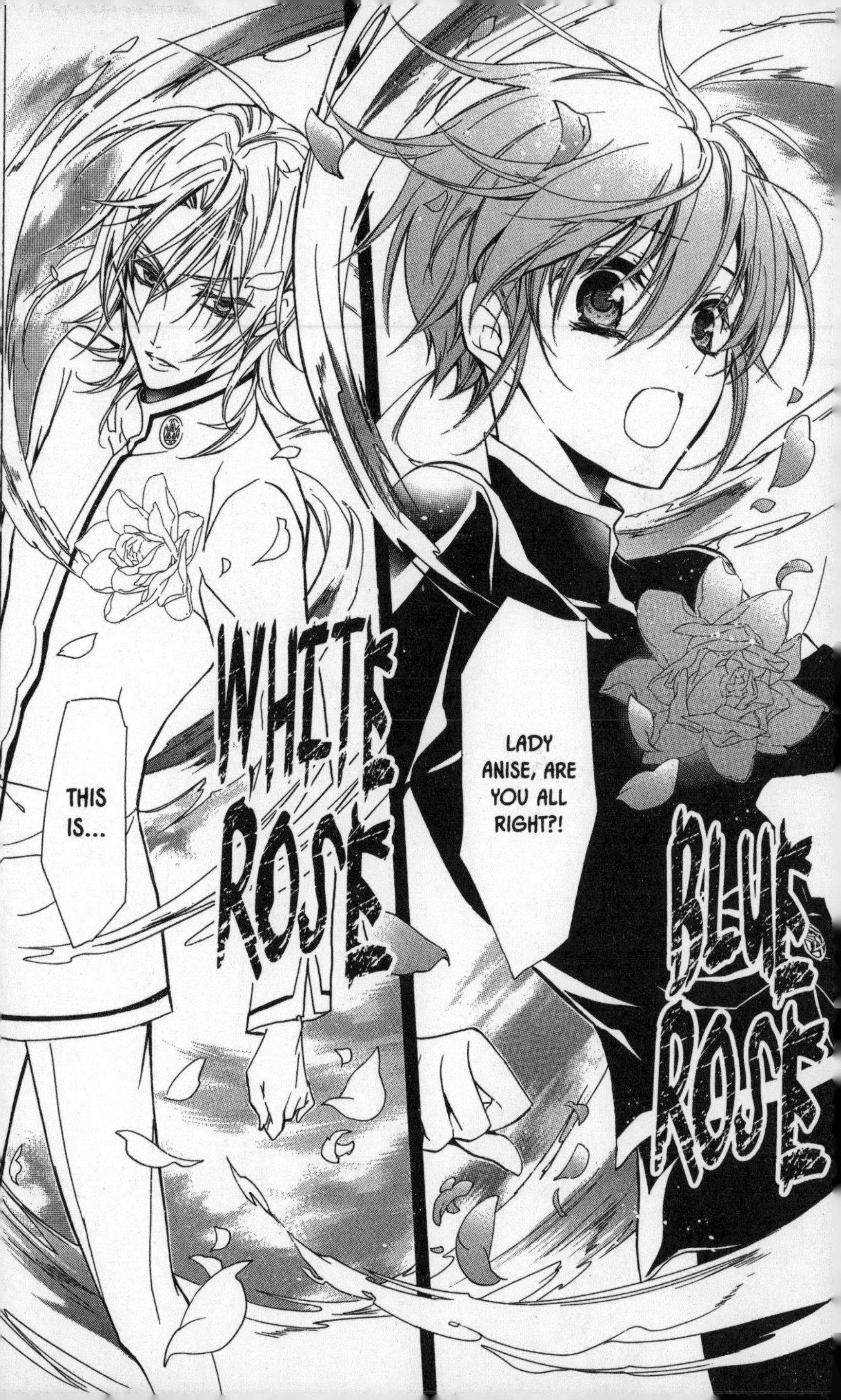
LADY ANISE, ARE YOU ALL RIGHT?!
BLUE ROSE
WHITE ROSE
THIS IS...

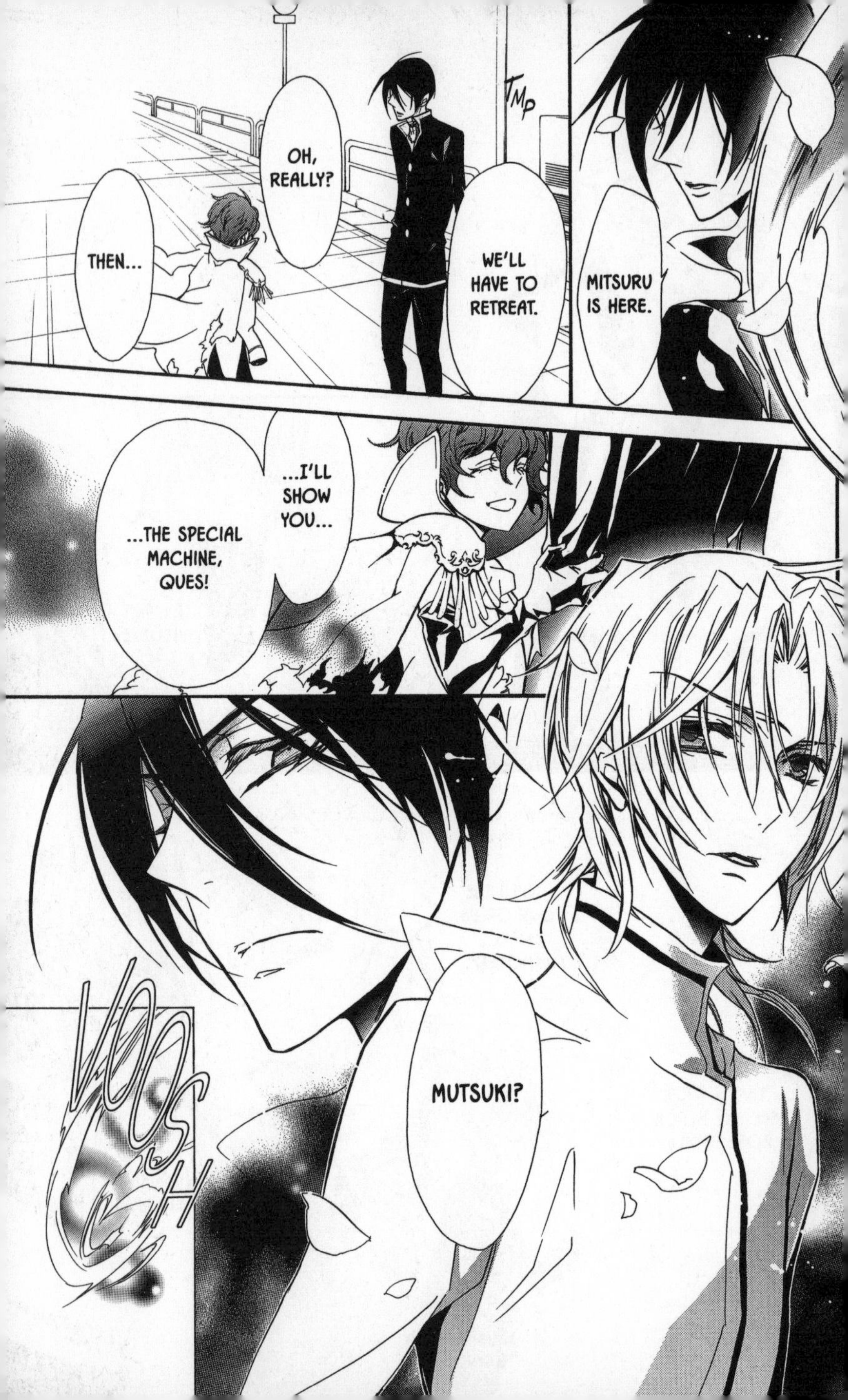
MITSURU IS HERE.
TMP
WE'LL HAVE TO RETREAT.
OH, REALLY?
THEN...
...I'LL SHOW YOU...
...THE SPECIAL MACHINE, QUES!
MUTSUKI?
VOOSH

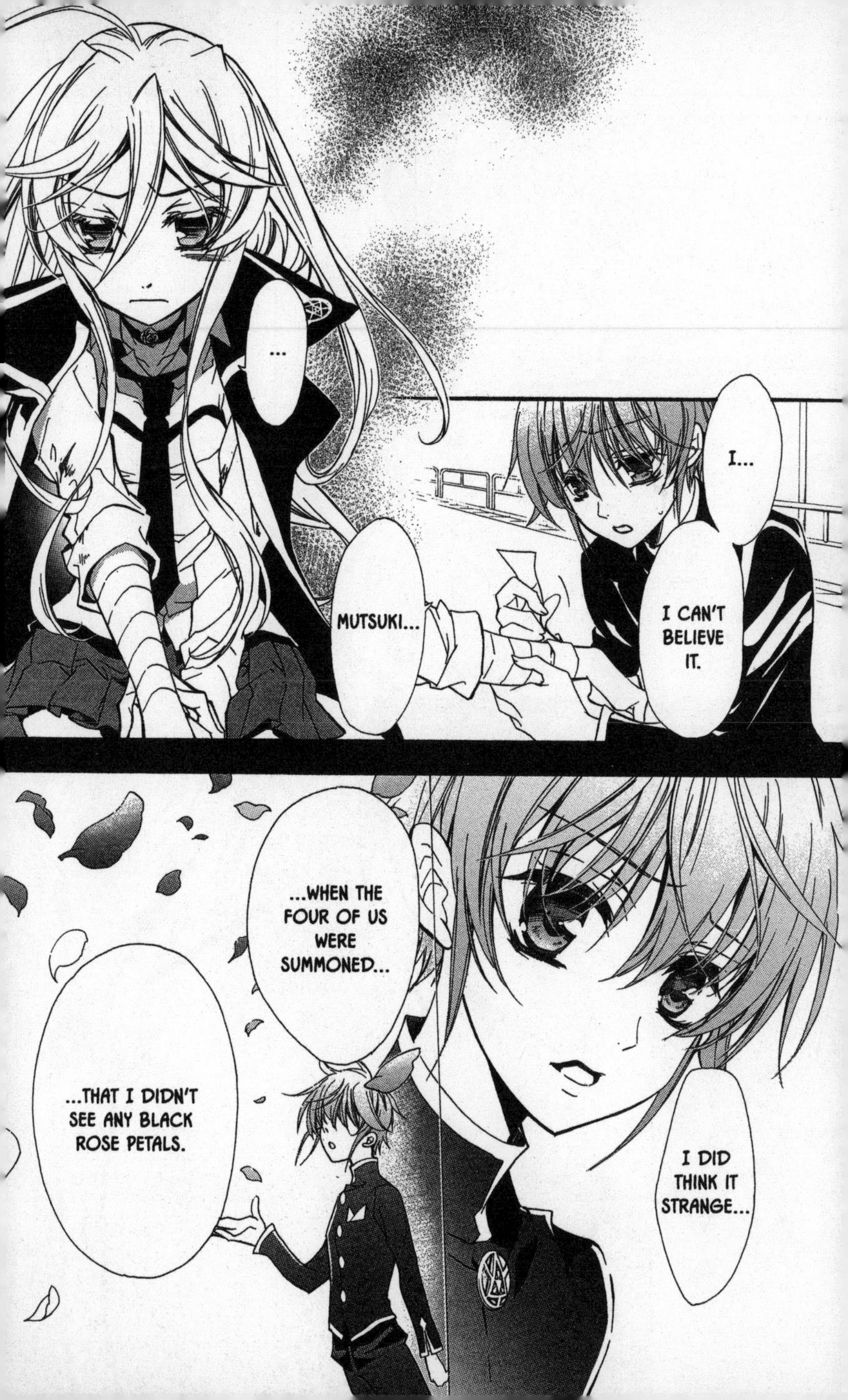
I...
I CAN'T BELIEVE IT.
MUTSUKI...
...
I DID THINK IT STRANGE...
...WHEN THE FOUR OF US WERE SUMMONED...
...THAT I DIDN'T SEE ANY BLACK ROSE PETALS.

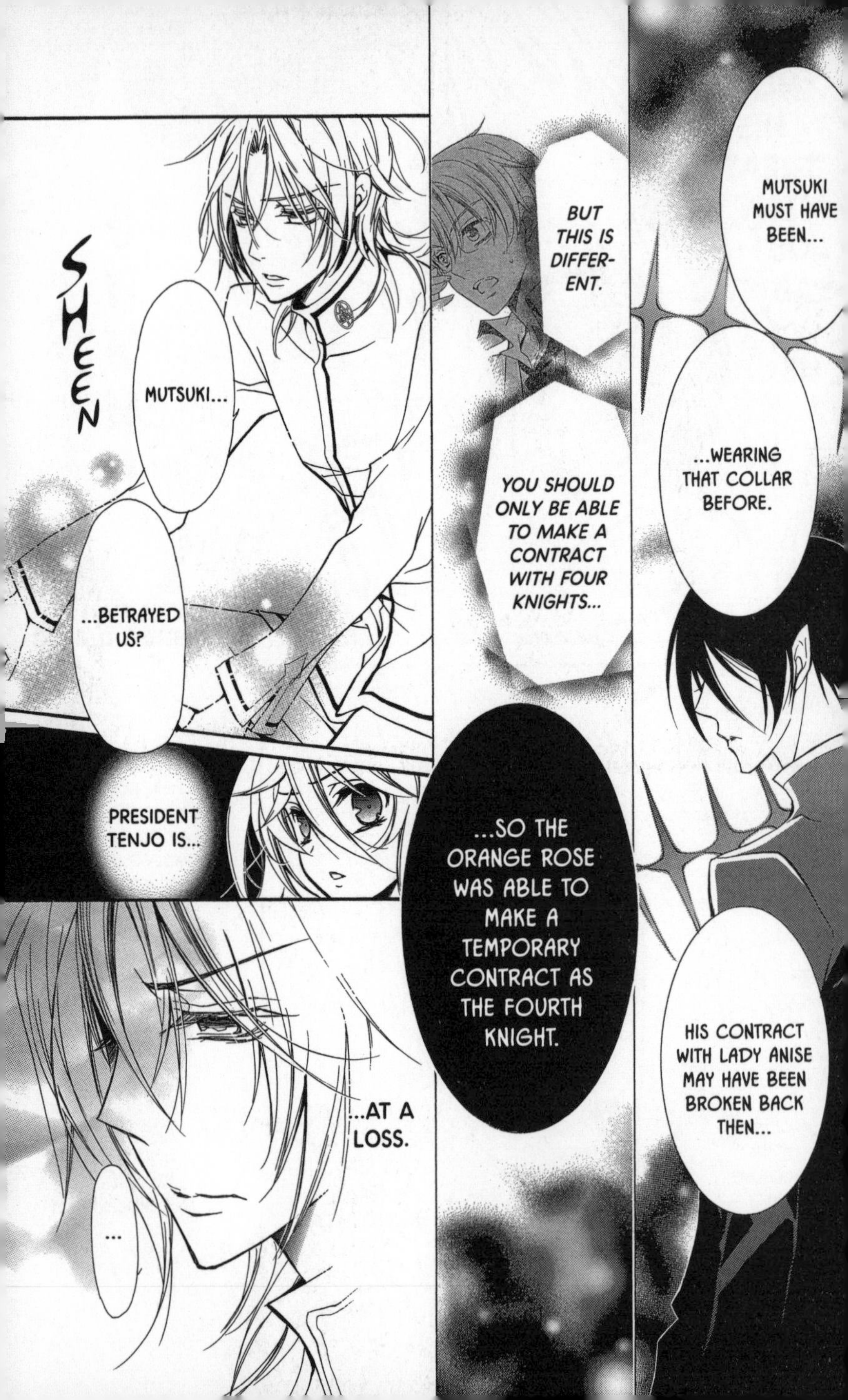
MUTSUKI MUST HAVE BEEN...
...WEARING THAT COLLAR BEFORE.
HIS CONTRACT WITH LADY ANISE MAY HAVE BEEN BROKEN BACK THEN...
BUT THIS IS DIFFER-ENT.
YOU SHOULD ONLY BE ABLE TO MAKE A CONTRACT WITH FOUR KNIGHTS...
...SO THE ORANGE ROSE WAS ABLE TO MAKE A TEMPORARY CONTRACT AS THE FOURTH KNIGHT.
MUTSUKI...
SHEEN
...BETRAYED US?
PRESIDENT TENJO IS...
...AT A LOSS.
...

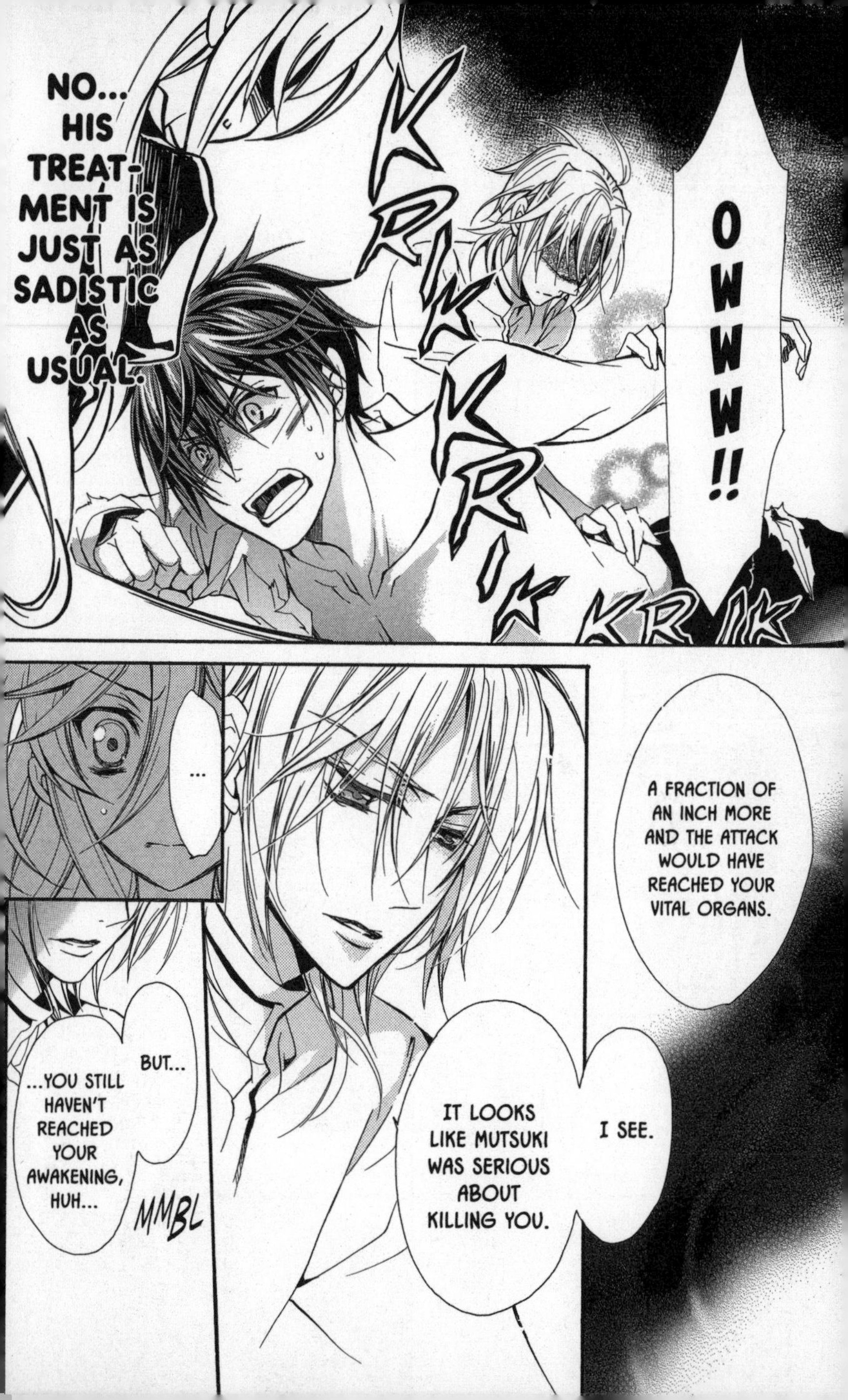

OWWW!!
KRIK KRIK KRIK
NO... HIS TREATMENT IS JUST AS SADISTIC AS USUAL.
A FRACTION OF AN INCH MORE AND THE ATTACK WOULD HAVE REACHED YOUR VITAL ORGANS.
I SEE.
IT LOOKS LIKE MUTSUKI WAS SERIOUS ABOUT KILLING YOU.
...
BUT...
...YOU STILL HAVEN'T REACHED YOUR AWAKENING, HUH...
MMBL

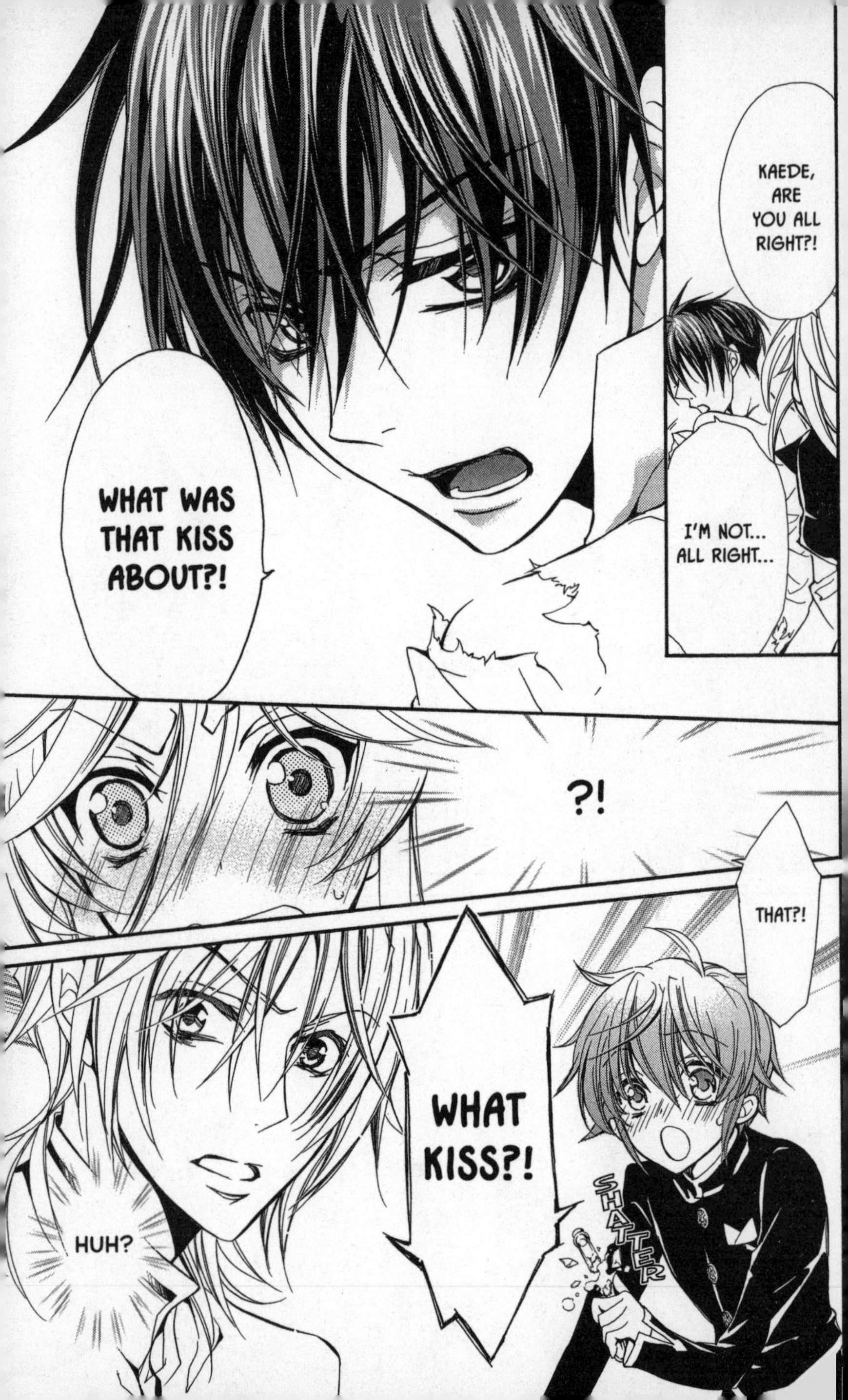
KAEDE, ARE YOU ALL RIGHT?!
I'M NOT... ALL RIGHT...
WHAT WAS THAT KISS ABOUT?!
?!
THAT?!
SHATTER
WHAT KISS?!
HUH?

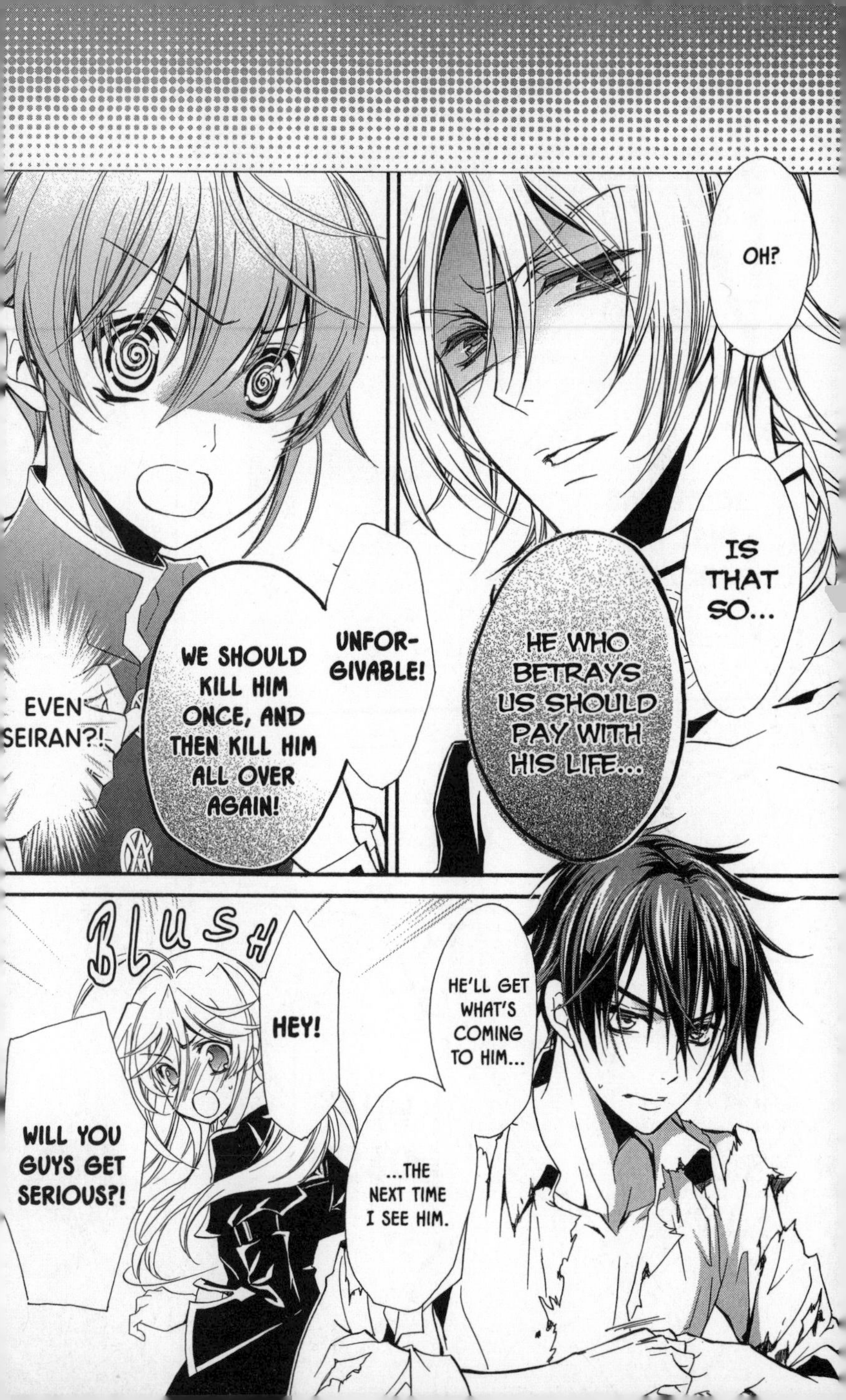
OH?
IS THAT SO...
HE WHO BETRAYS US SHOULD PAY WITH HIS LIFE...
UNFOR-GIVABLE!
WE SHOULD KILL HIM ONCE, AND THEN KILL HIM ALL OVER AGAIN!
EVEN SEIRAN?!
HE'LL GET WHAT'S COMING TO HIM...
...THE NEXT TIME I SEE HIM.
HEY!
BLUSH
WILL YOU GUYS GET SERIOUS?!

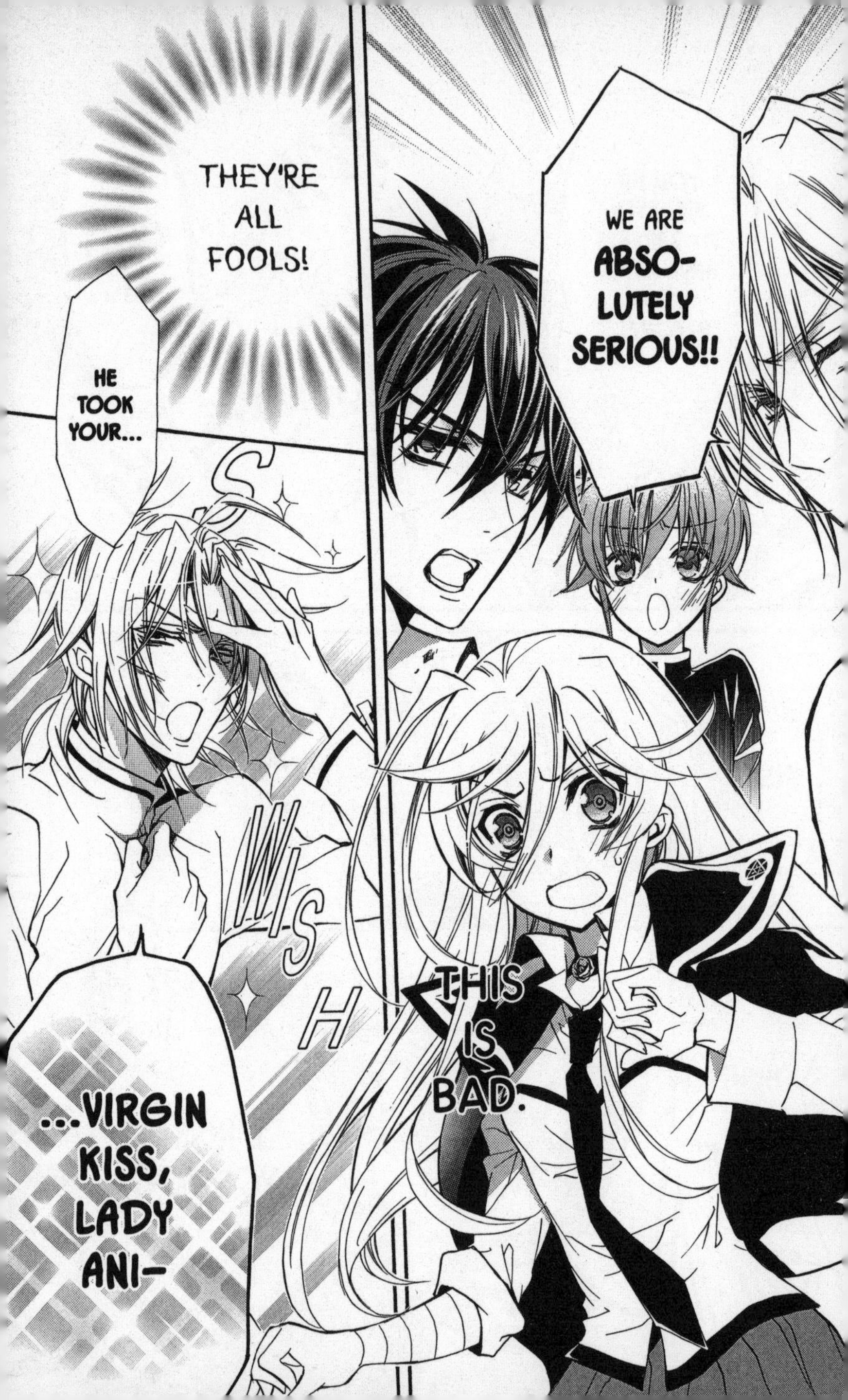
WE ARE ABSOLUTELY SERIOUS!!
THIS IS BAD.
THEY'RE ALL FOOLS!
HE TOOK YOUR...
SWISH
...VIRGIN KISS, LADY ANI-

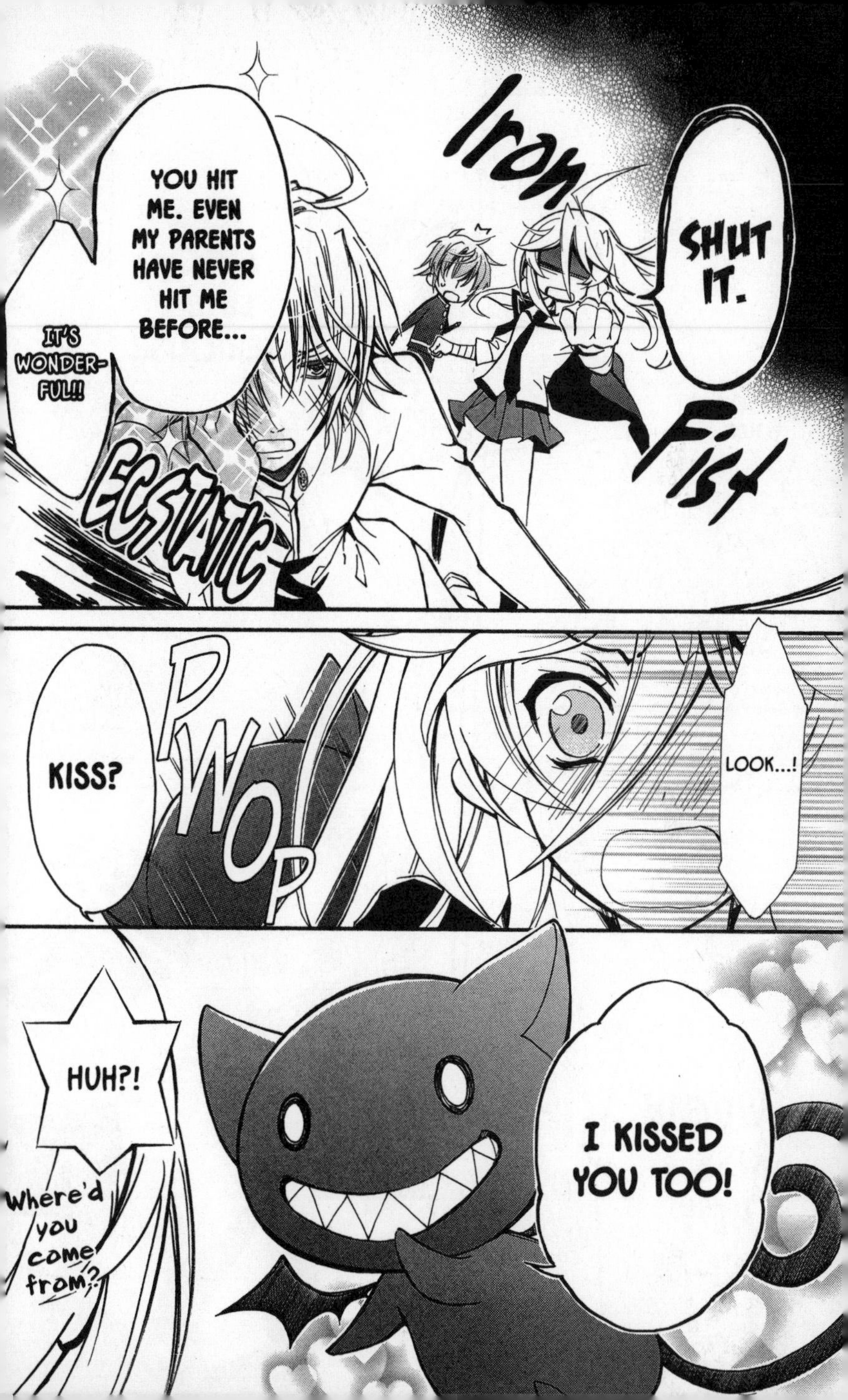
SHUT IT.
Iron Fist
YOU HIT ME. EVEN MY PARENTS HAVE NEVER HIT ME BEFORE...
IT'S WONDERFUL!!
ECSTATIC
LOOK...!
PWOP
KISS?
I KISSED YOU TOO!
HUH?!
Where'd you come from?!

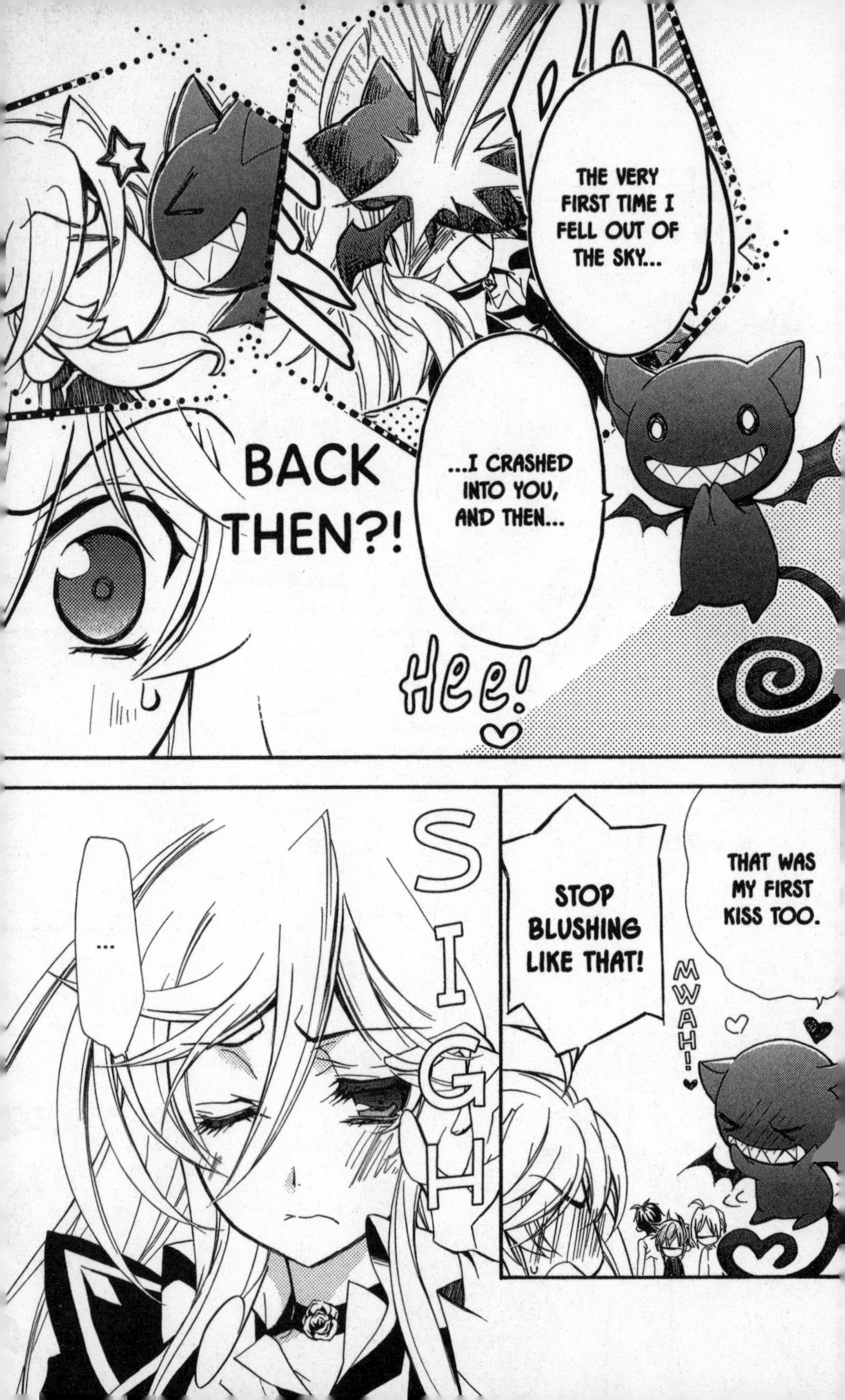
THE VERY FIRST TIME I FELL OUT OF THE SKY...
...I CRASHED INTO YOU, AND THEN...
BACK THEN?!
Hee!
THAT WAS MY FIRST KISS TOO.
STOP BLUSHING LIKE THAT!
MWAH!
SIGH
...

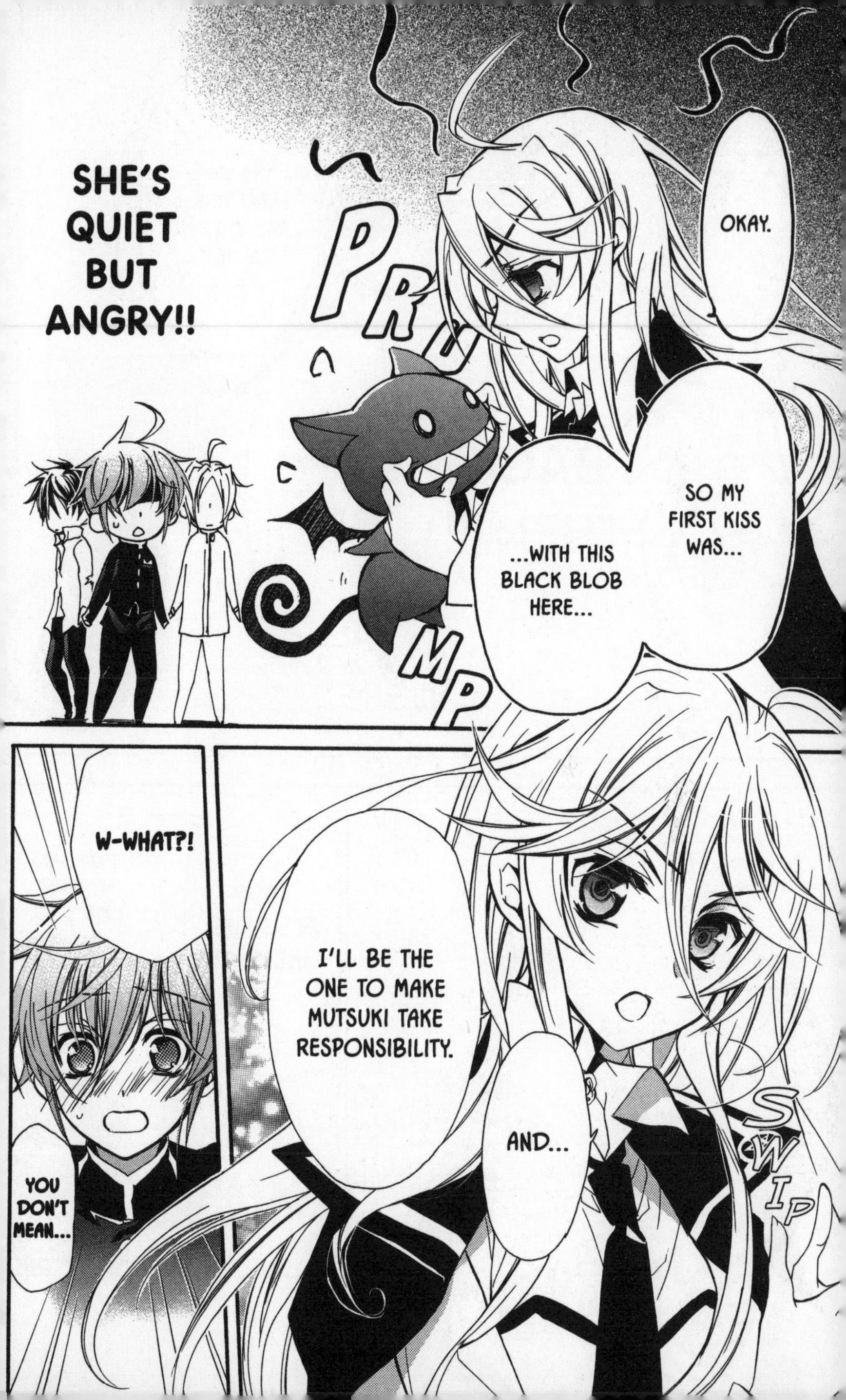
OKAY.
SO MY FIRST KISS WAS...
...WITH THIS BLACK BLOB HERE...
PRUMP
SHE'S QUIET BUT ANGRY!!
I'LL BE THE ONE TO MAKE MUTSUKI TAKE RESPONSIBILITY.
AND...
SWIP
W-WHAT?!
YOU DON'T MEAN...

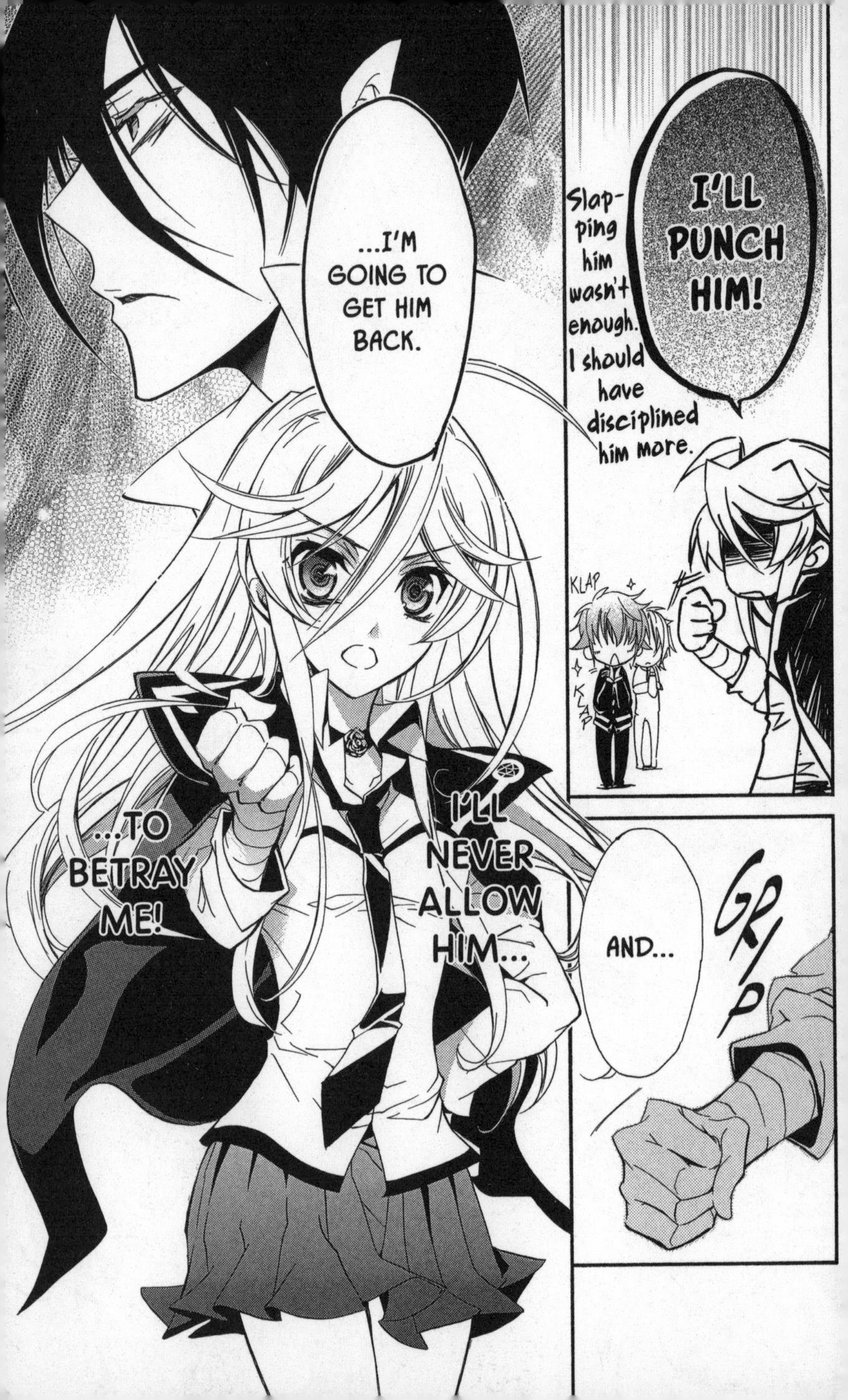
I'LL PUNCH HIM!
Slapping him wasn't enough. I should have disciplined him more.
KLAP
KLAP
GRIP
AND...
...I'M GOING TO GET HIM BACK.
I'LL NEVER ALLOW HIM...
...TO BETRAY ME!

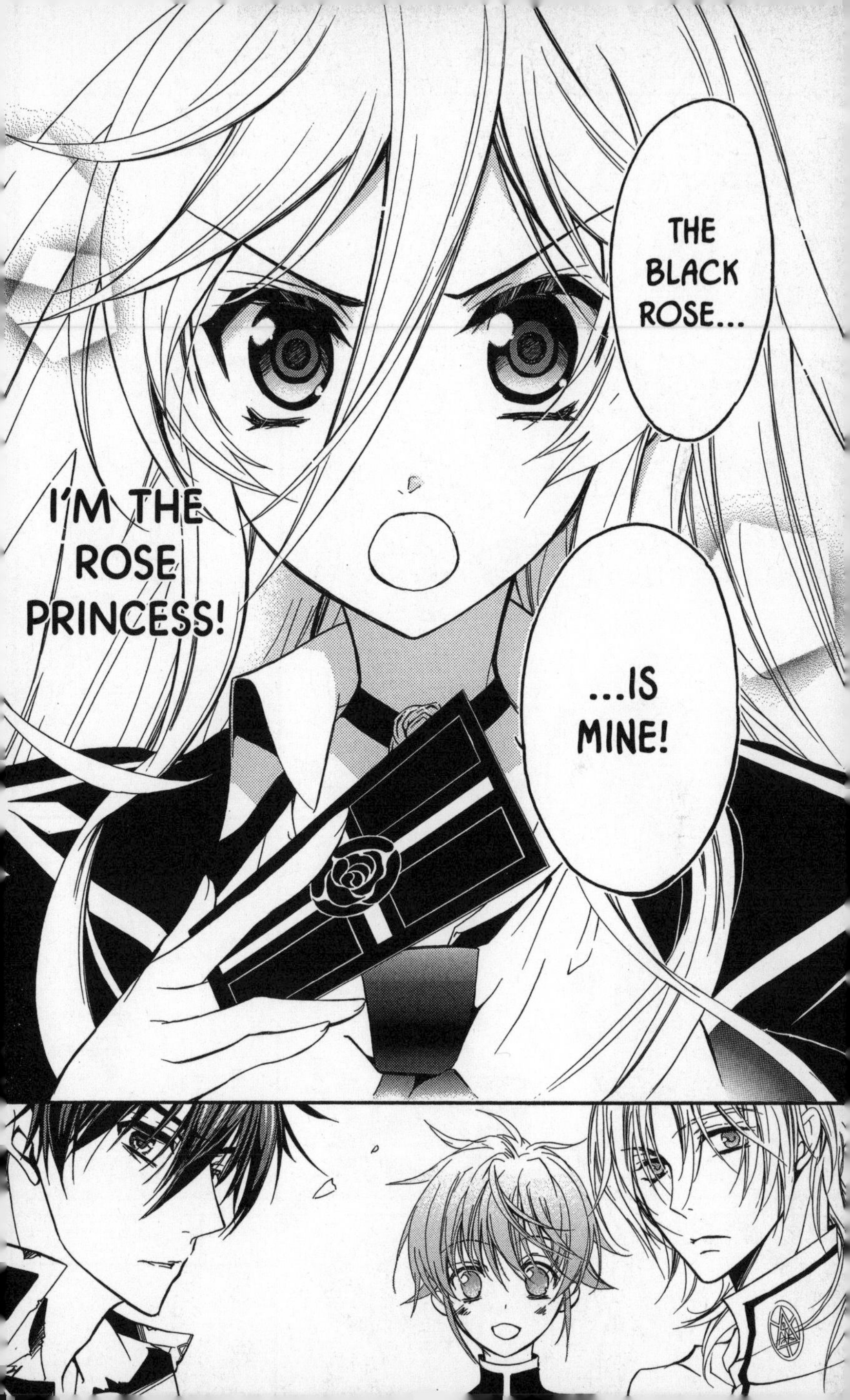
THE BLACK ROSE...
...IS MINE!
I'M THE ROSE PRINCESS!

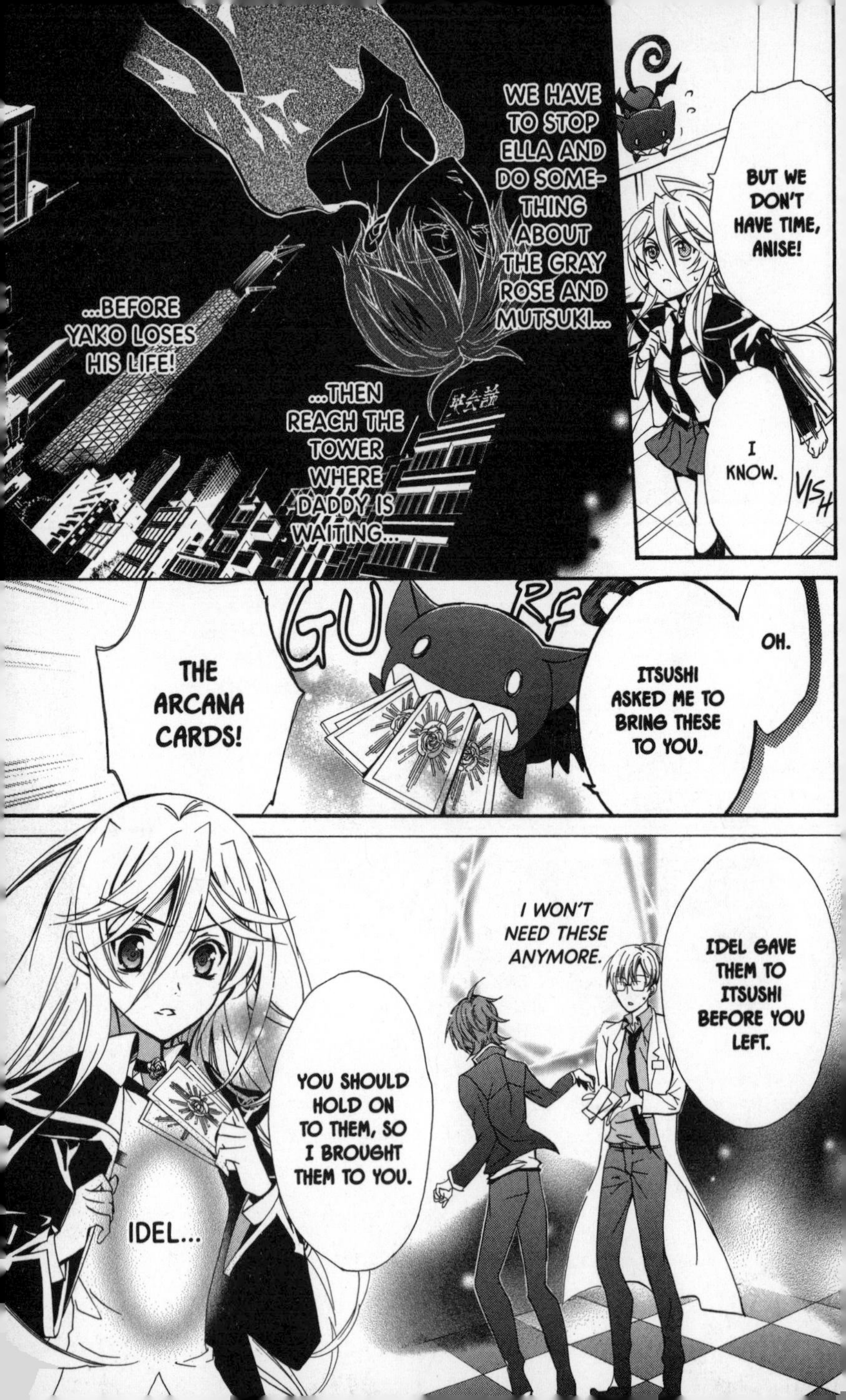
BUT WE DON'T HAVE TIME, ANISE!
I KNOW.
VISH
WE HAVE TO STOP ELLA AND DO SOME-THING ABOUT THE GRAY ROSE AND MUTSUKI...
...THEN REACH THE TOWER WHERE DADDY IS WAITING...
...BEFORE YAKO LOSES HIS LIFE!
OH.
ITSUSHI ASKED ME TO BRING THESE TO YOU.
GU RF
THE ARCANA CARDS!
IDEL GAVE THEM TO ITSUSHI BEFORE YOU LEFT.
I WON'T NEED THESE ANYMORE.
YOU SHOULD HOLD ON TO THEM, SO I BROUGHT THEM TO YOU.
IDEL...

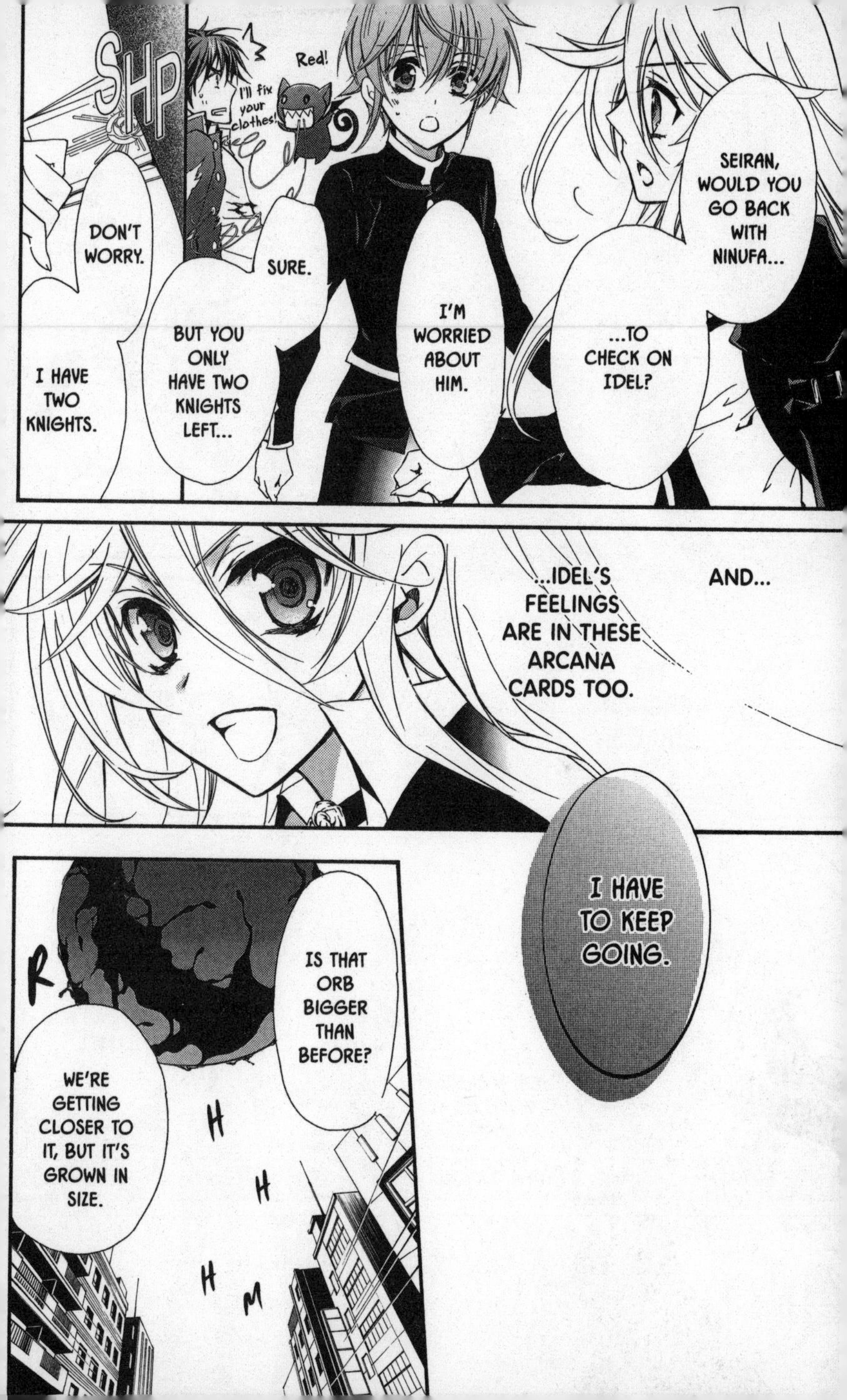
SEIRAN, WOULD YOU GO BACK WITH NINUFA...
...TO CHECK ON IDEL?
I'M WORRIED ABOUT HIM.
Red!
I'll fix your clothes!
SURE.
BUT YOU ONLY HAVE TWO KNIGHTS LEFT...
SHP
DON'T WORRY.
I HAVE TWO KNIGHTS.
AND...
...IDEL'S FEELINGS ARE IN THESE ARCANA CARDS TOO.
I HAVE TO KEEP GOING.
IS THAT ORB BIGGER THAN BEFORE?
WE'RE GETTING CLOSER TO IT, BUT IT'S GROWN IN SIZE.
RHHHM

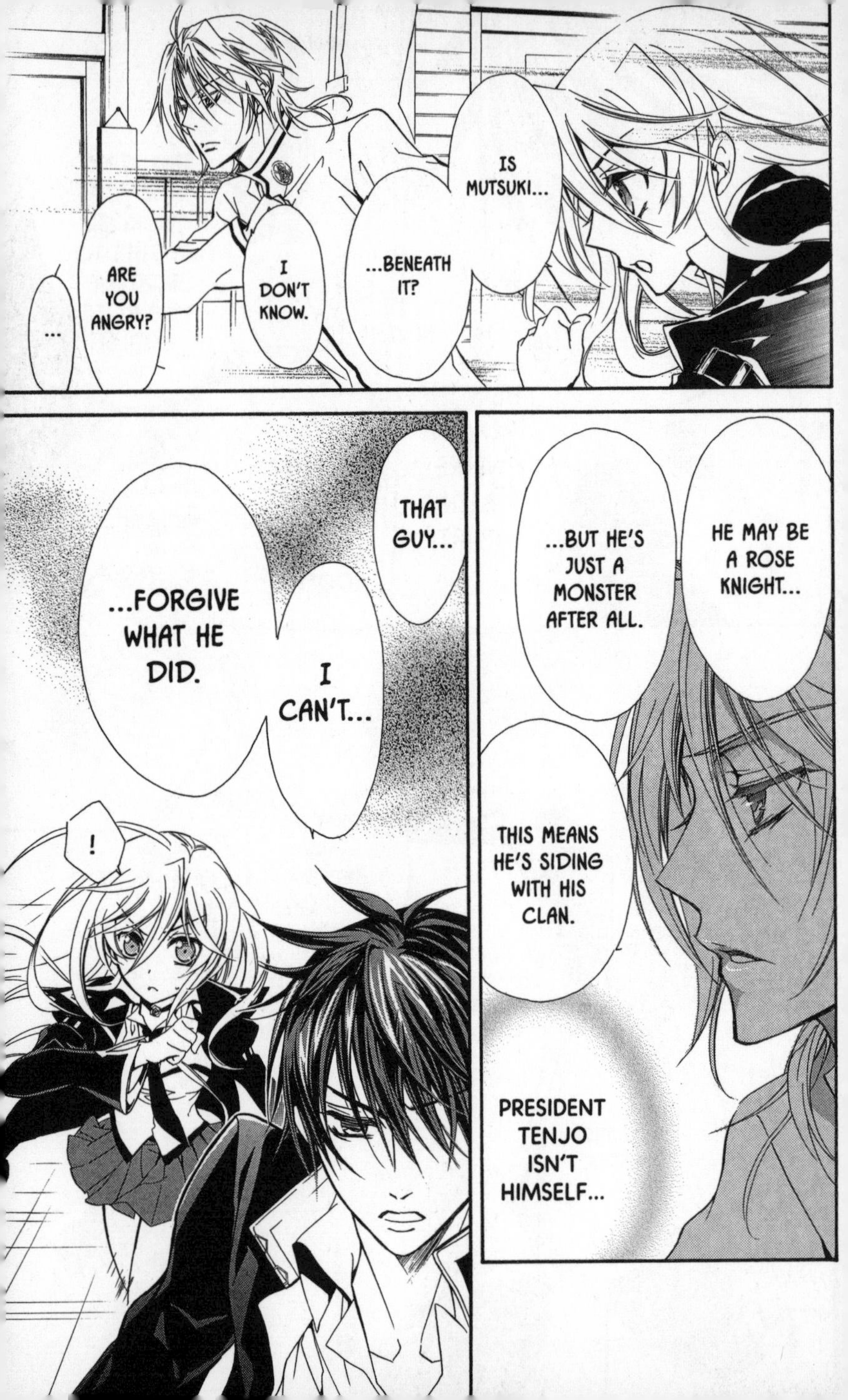
IS MUTSUKI...
...BENEATH IT?
I DON'T KNOW.
ARE YOU ANGRY?
...
HE MAY BE A ROSE KNIGHT...
...BUT HE'S JUST A MONSTER AFTER ALL.
THIS MEANS HE'S SIDING WITH HIS CLAN.
PRESIDENT TENJO ISN'T HIMSELF...
THAT GUY...
I CAN'T...
...FORGIVE WHAT HE DID.
!

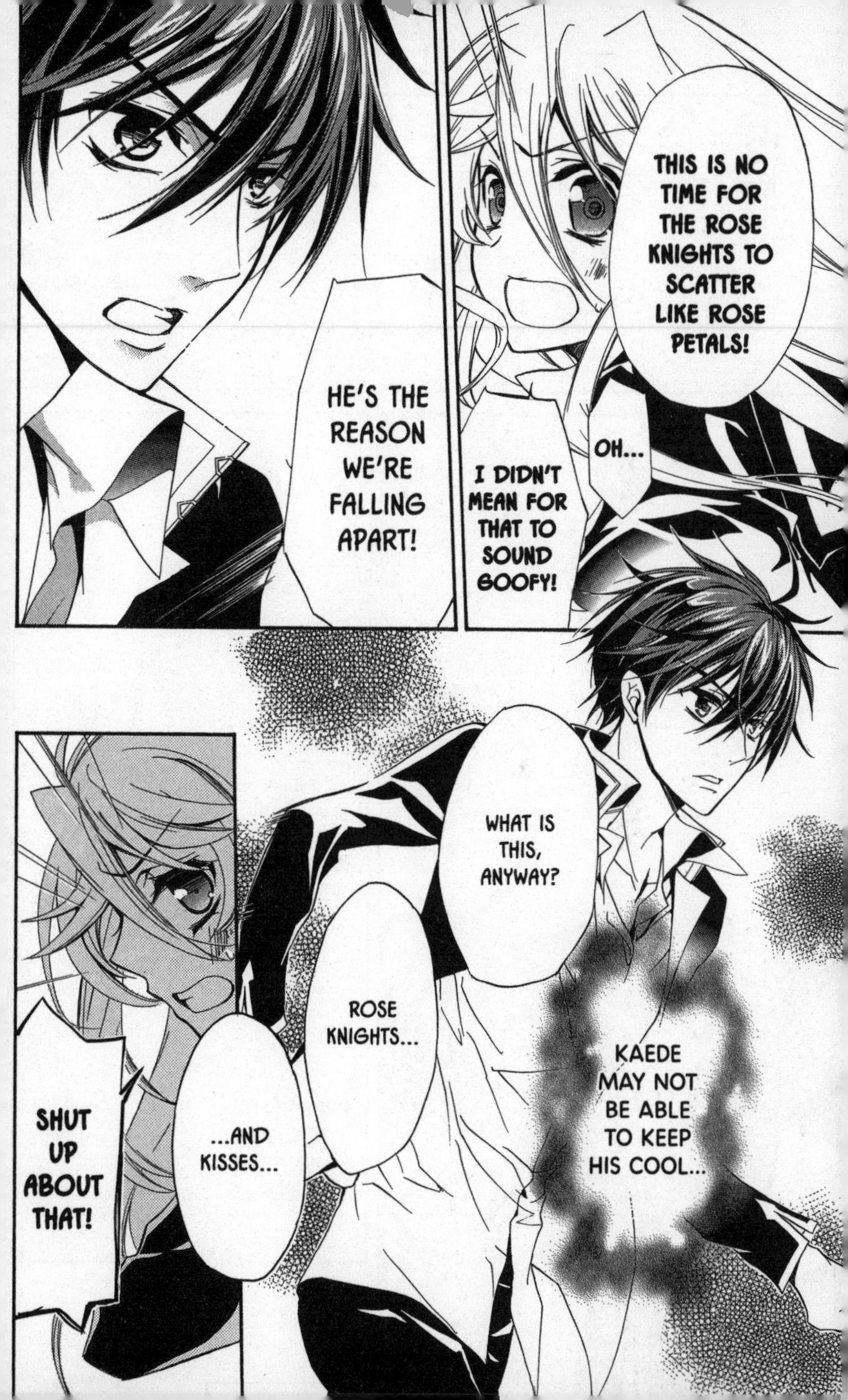
THIS IS NO TIME FOR THE ROSE KNIGHTS TO SCATTER LIKE ROSE PETALS!
OH...
I DIDN'T MEAN FOR THAT TO SOUND GOOFY!
HE'S THE REASON WE'RE FALLING APART!
WHAT IS THIS, ANYWAY?
ROSE KNIGHTS...
...AND KISSES...
SHUT UP ABOUT THAT!
KAEDE MAY NOT BE ABLE TO KEEP HIS COOL...

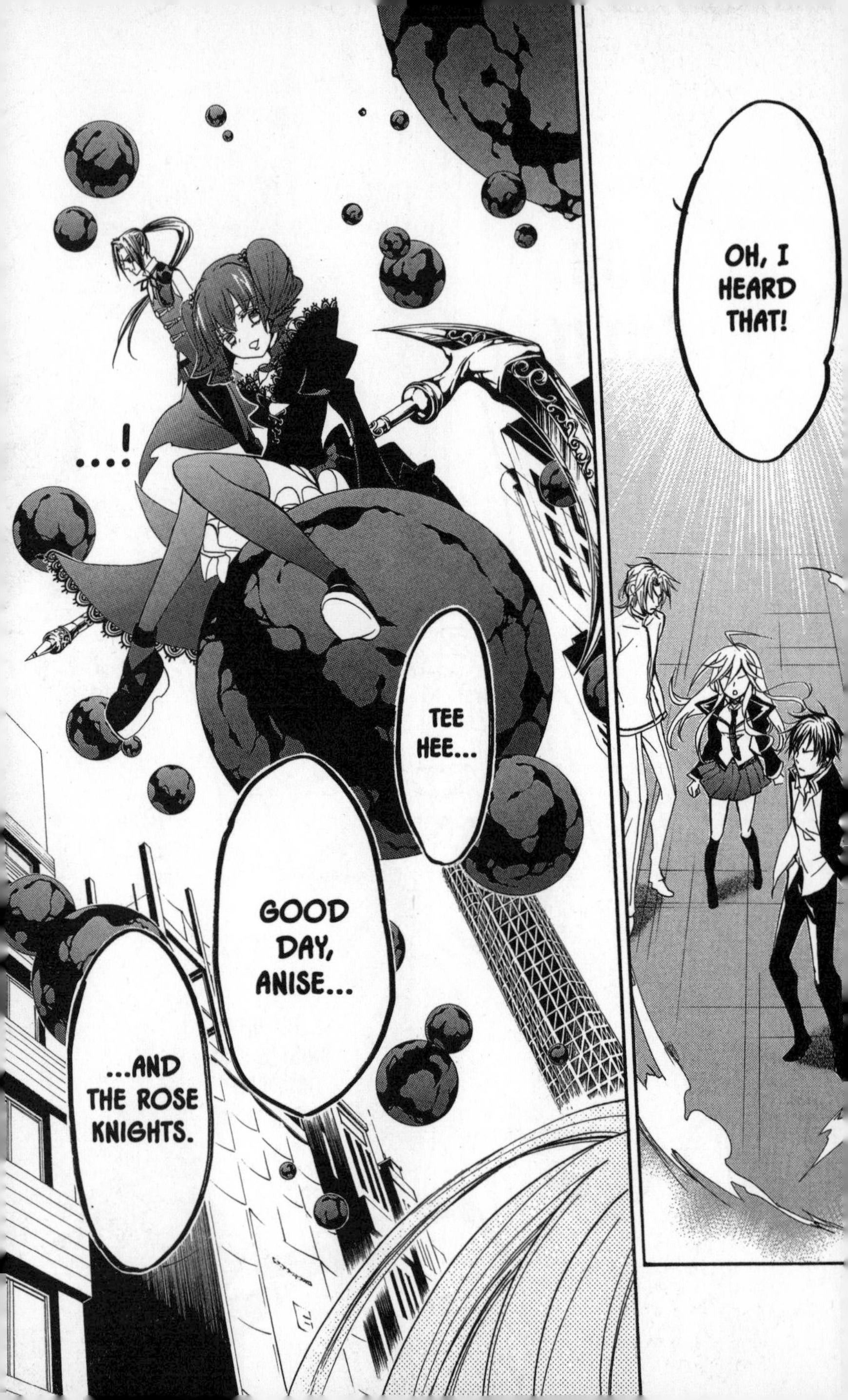
OH, I HEARD THAT!
...!
TEE HEE...
GOOD DAY, ANISE...
...AND THE ROSE KNIGHTS.

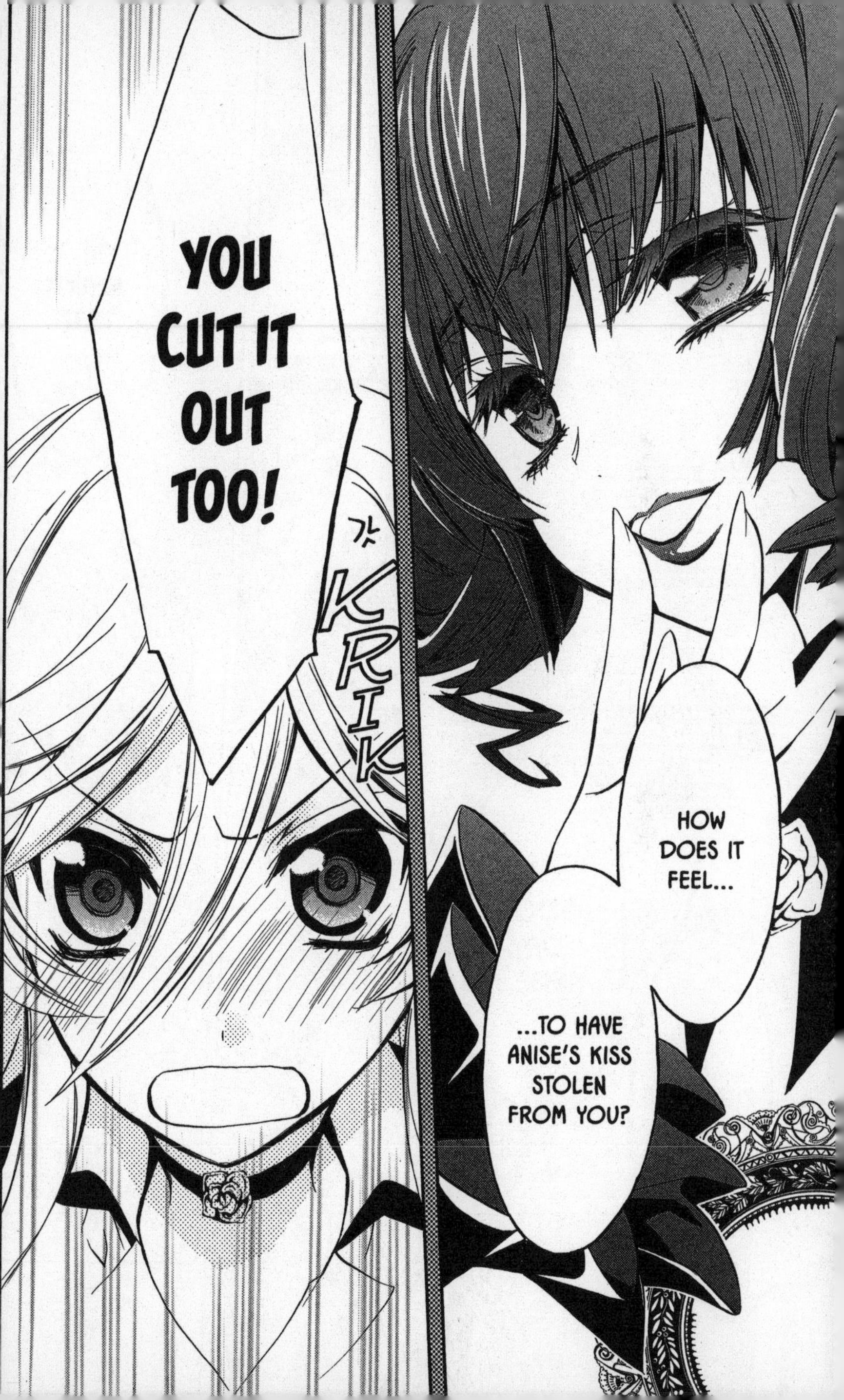
HOW DOES IT FEEL...
...TO HAVE ANISE'S KISS STOLEN FROM YOU?
YOU CUT IT OUT TOO!
각
KRIK

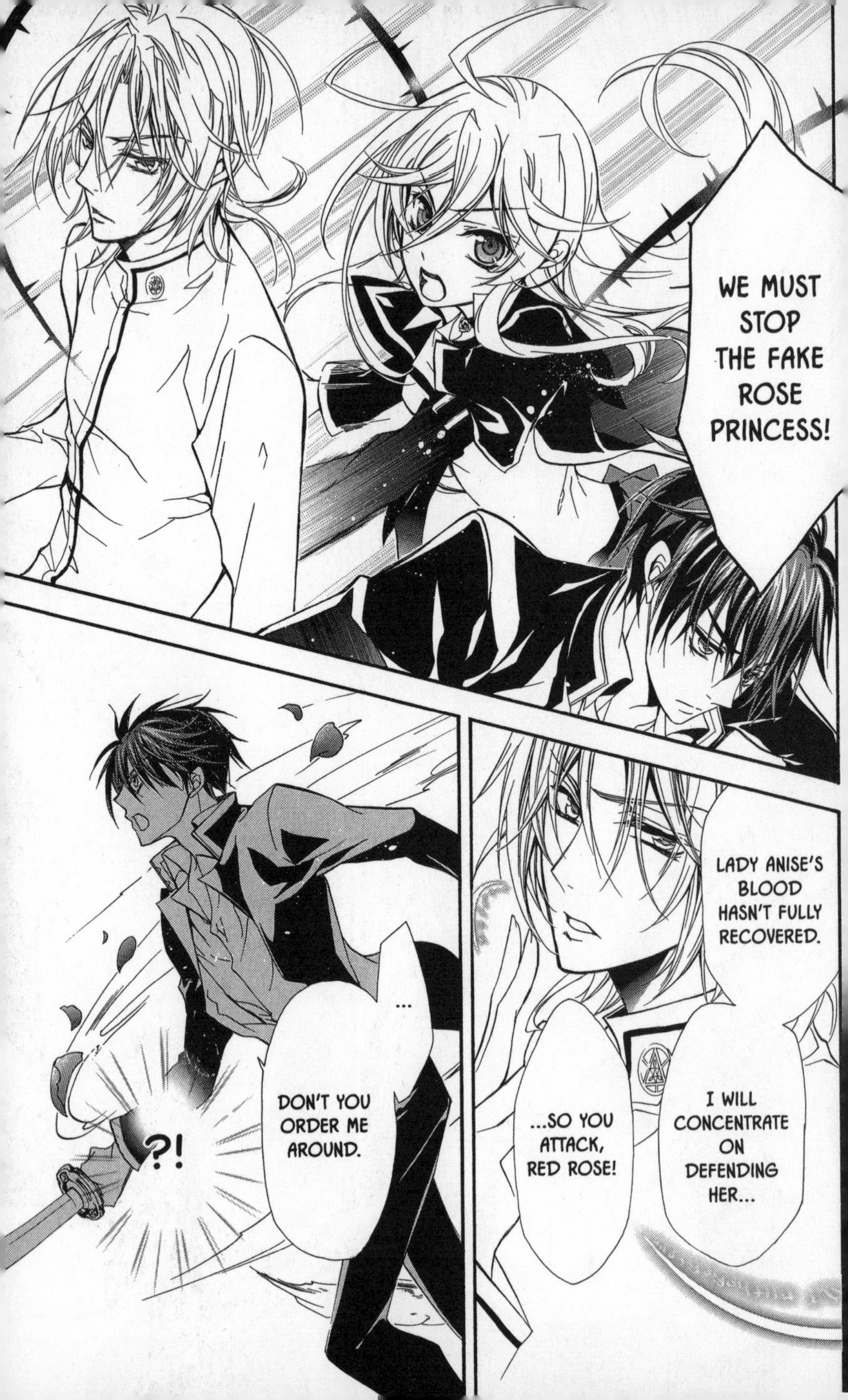
WE MUST STOP THE FAKE ROSE PRINCESS!
LADY ANISE'S BLOOD HASN'T FULLY RECOVERED.
I WILL CONCENTRATE ON DEFENDING HER...
...SO YOU ATTACK, RED ROSE!
...
DON'T YOU ORDER ME AROUND.
?!

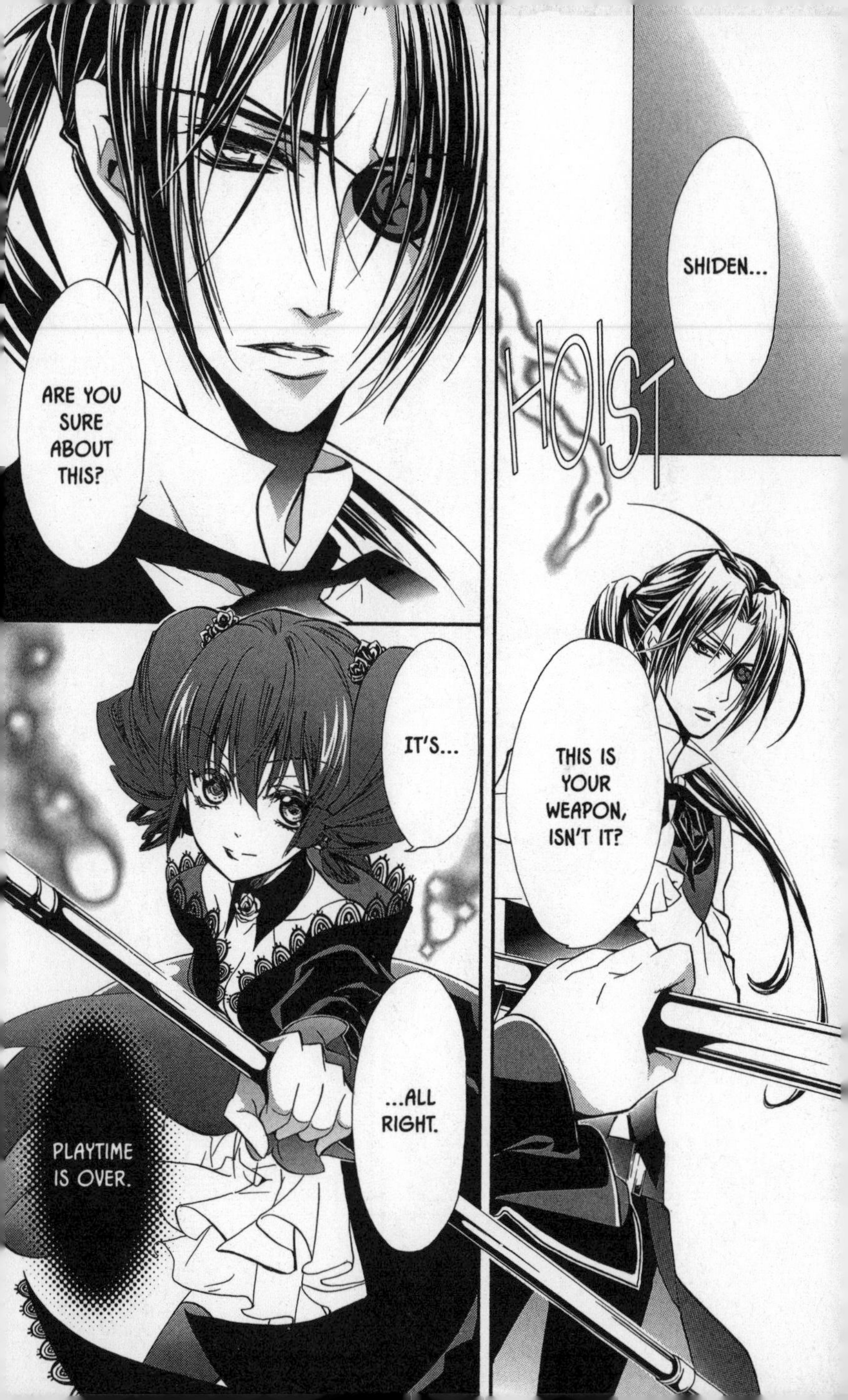
SHIDEN...
HOIST
THIS IS YOUR WEAPON, ISN'T IT?
ARE YOU SURE ABOUT THIS?
IT'S...
...ALL RIGHT.
PLAYTIME IS OVER.

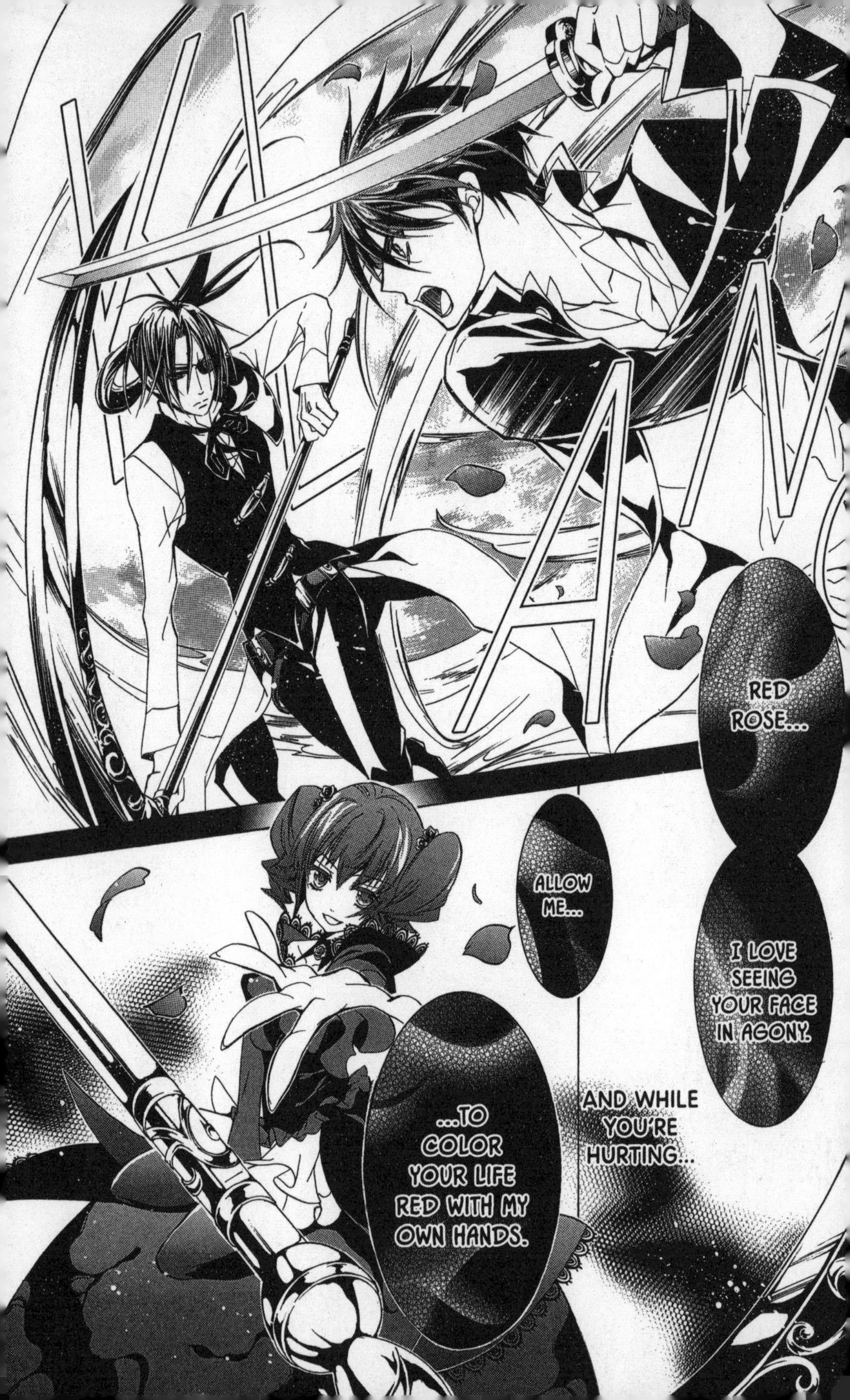
RED ROSE...
I LOVE SEEING YOUR FACE IN AGONY.
AND WHILE YOU'RE HURTING...
ALLOW ME...
...TO COLOR YOUR LIFE RED WITH MY OWN HANDS.

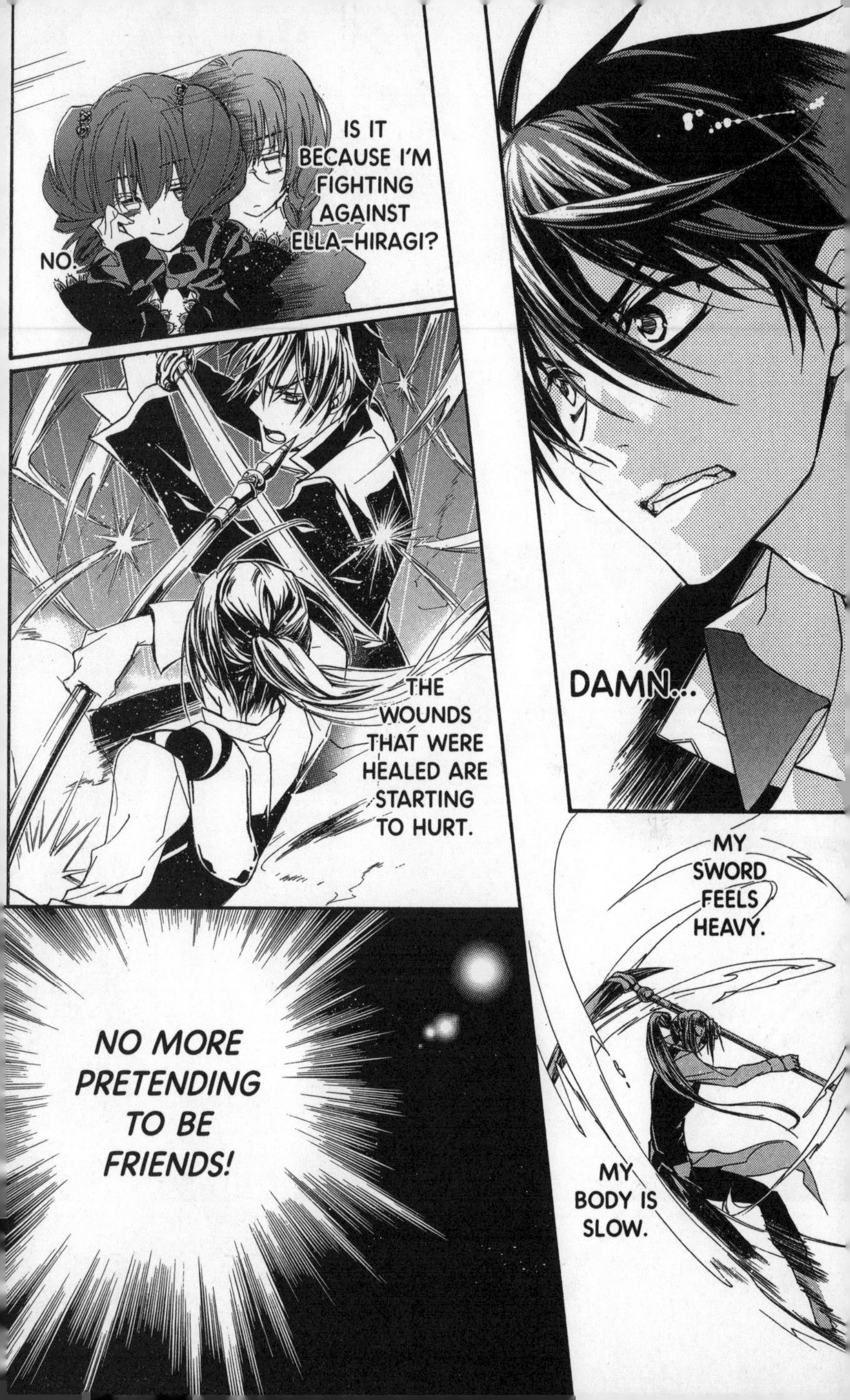
DAMN...
IS IT BECAUSE I'M FIGHTING AGAINST ELLA-HIRAGI?
NO.
THE WOUNDS THAT WERE HEALED ARE STARTING TO HURT.
MY SWORD FEELS HEAVY.
MY BODY IS SLOW.
NO MORE PRETENDING TO BE FRIENDS!

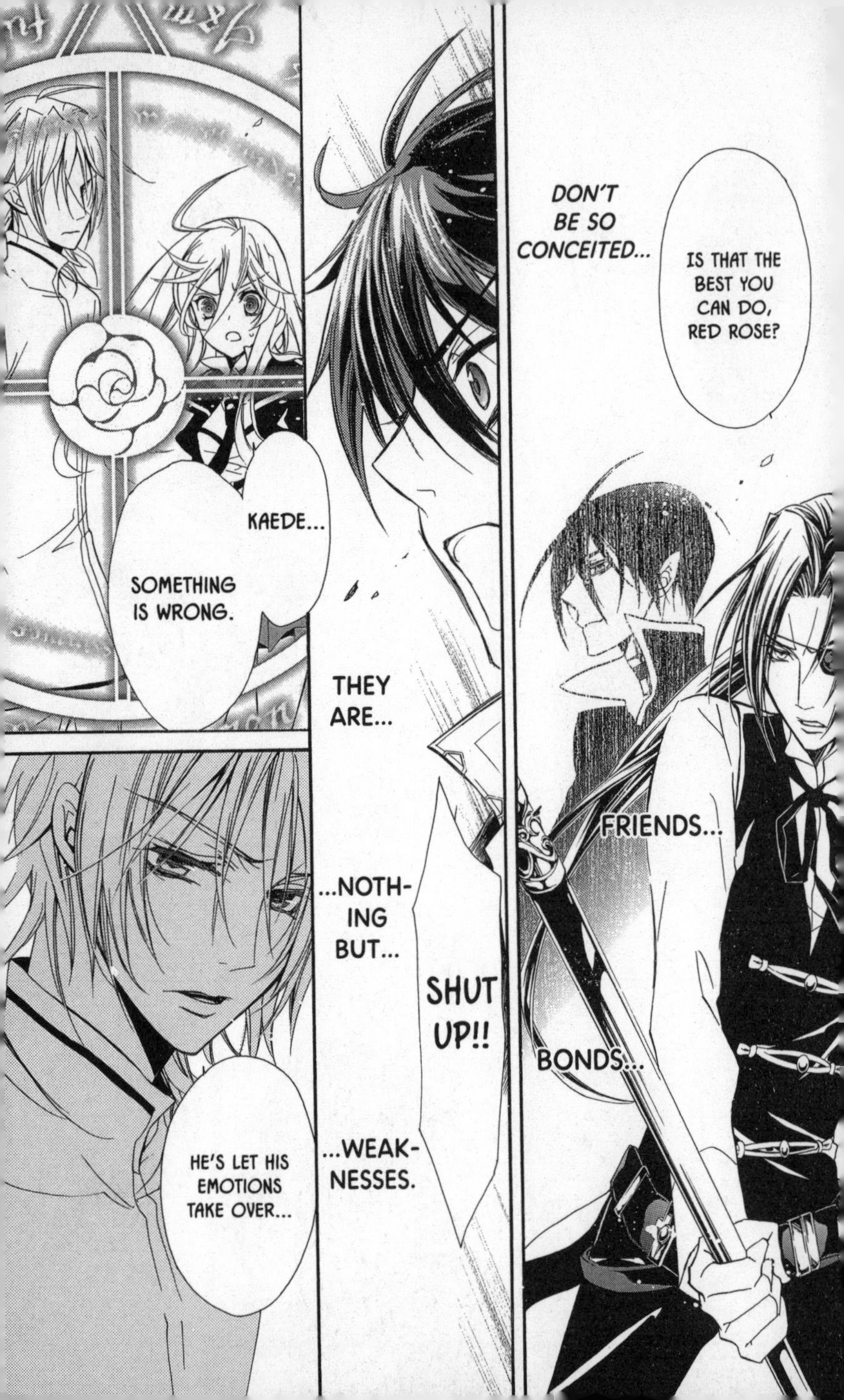
IS THAT THE BEST YOU CAN DO, RED ROSE?
DON'T BE SO CONCEITED...
FRIENDS...
BONDS...
THEY ARE...
...NOTH-ING BUT...
...WEAK-NESSES.
SHUT UP!!
KAEDE...
SOMETHING IS WRONG.
HE'S LET HIS EMOTIONS TAKE OVER...

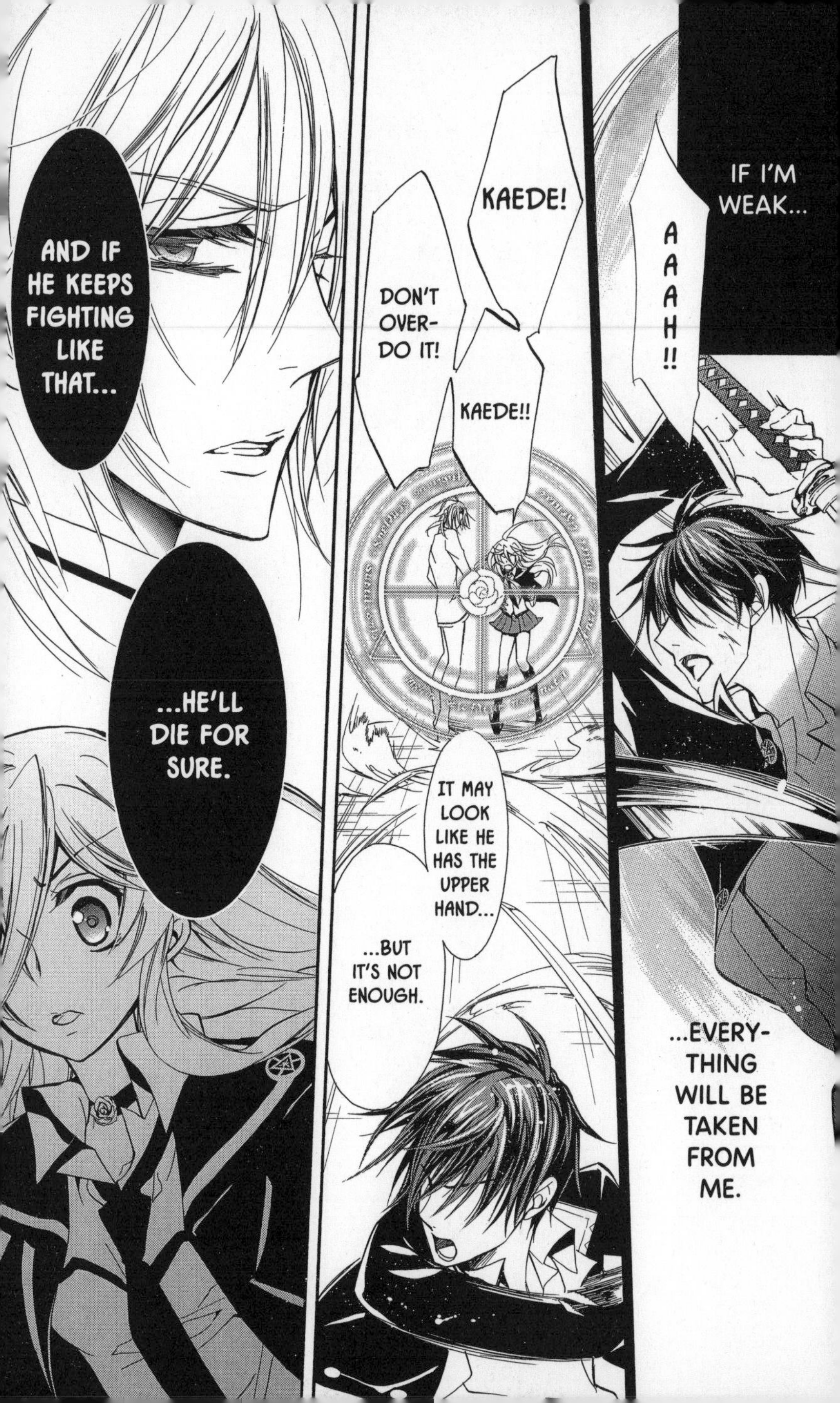
IF I'M WEAK...
AAAAH!!
...EVERYTHING WILL BE TAKEN FROM ME.
KAEDE!
DON'T OVERDO IT!
KAEDE!!
IT MAY LOOK LIKE HE HAS THE UPPER HAND...
...BUT IT'S NOT ENOUGH.
AND IF HE KEEPS FIGHTING LIKE THAT...
...HE'LL DIE FOR SURE.

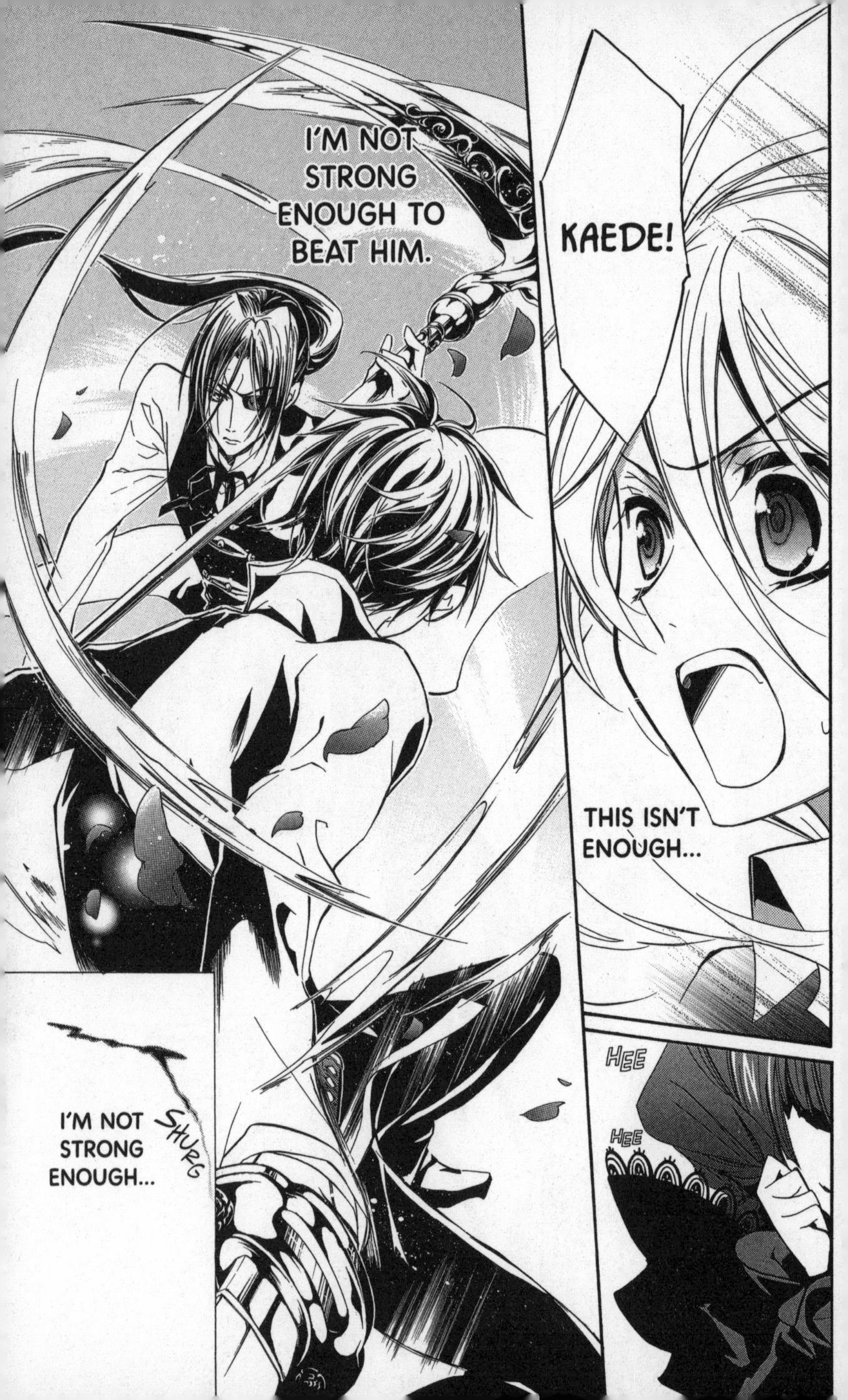
KAEDE!
THIS ISN'T ENOUGH...
I'M NOT STRONG ENOUGH TO BEAT HIM.
HEE
HEE
SHURG
I'M NOT STRONG ENOUGH...

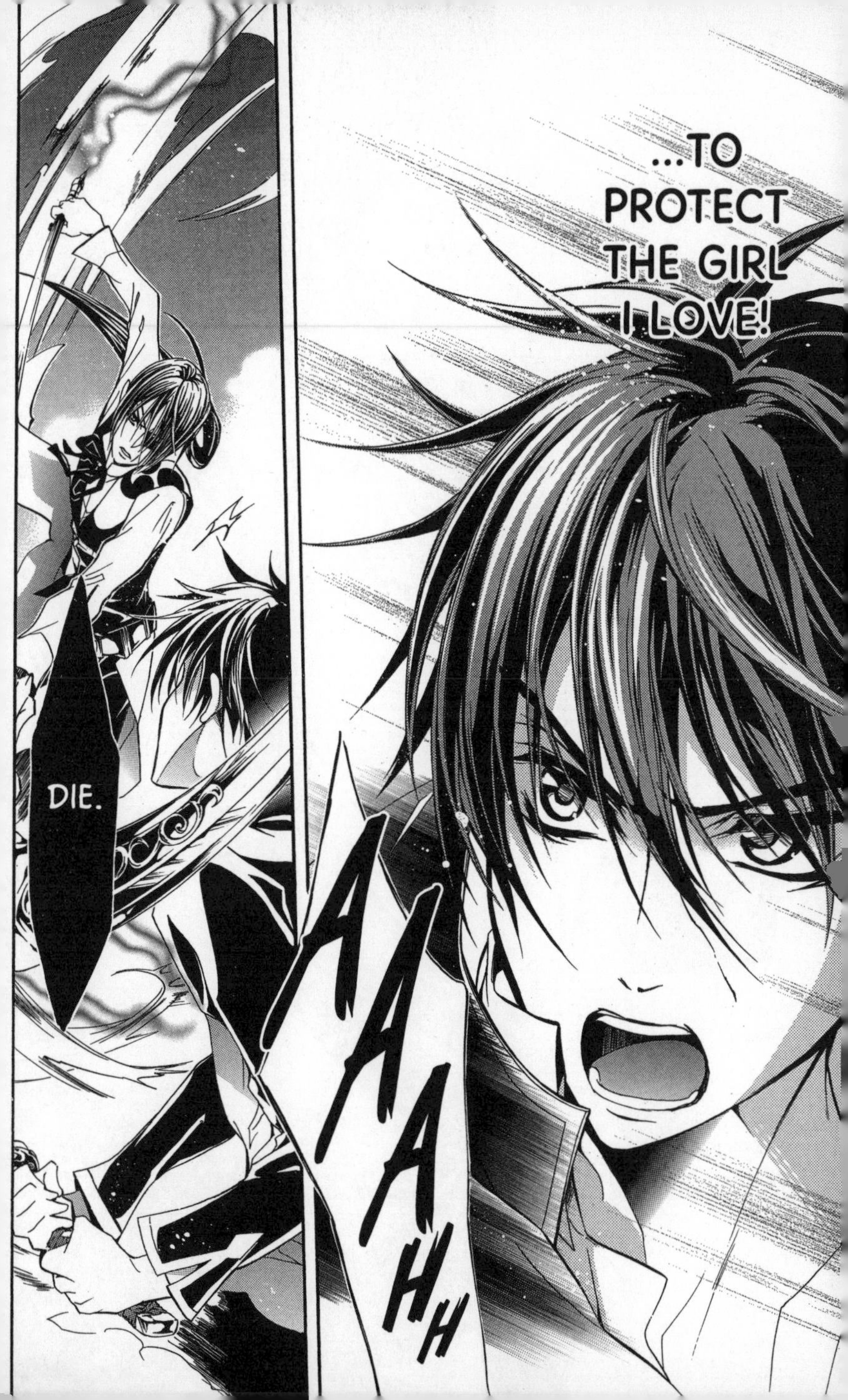
...TO PROTECT THE GIRL I LOVE!
AAAAHH
DIE.

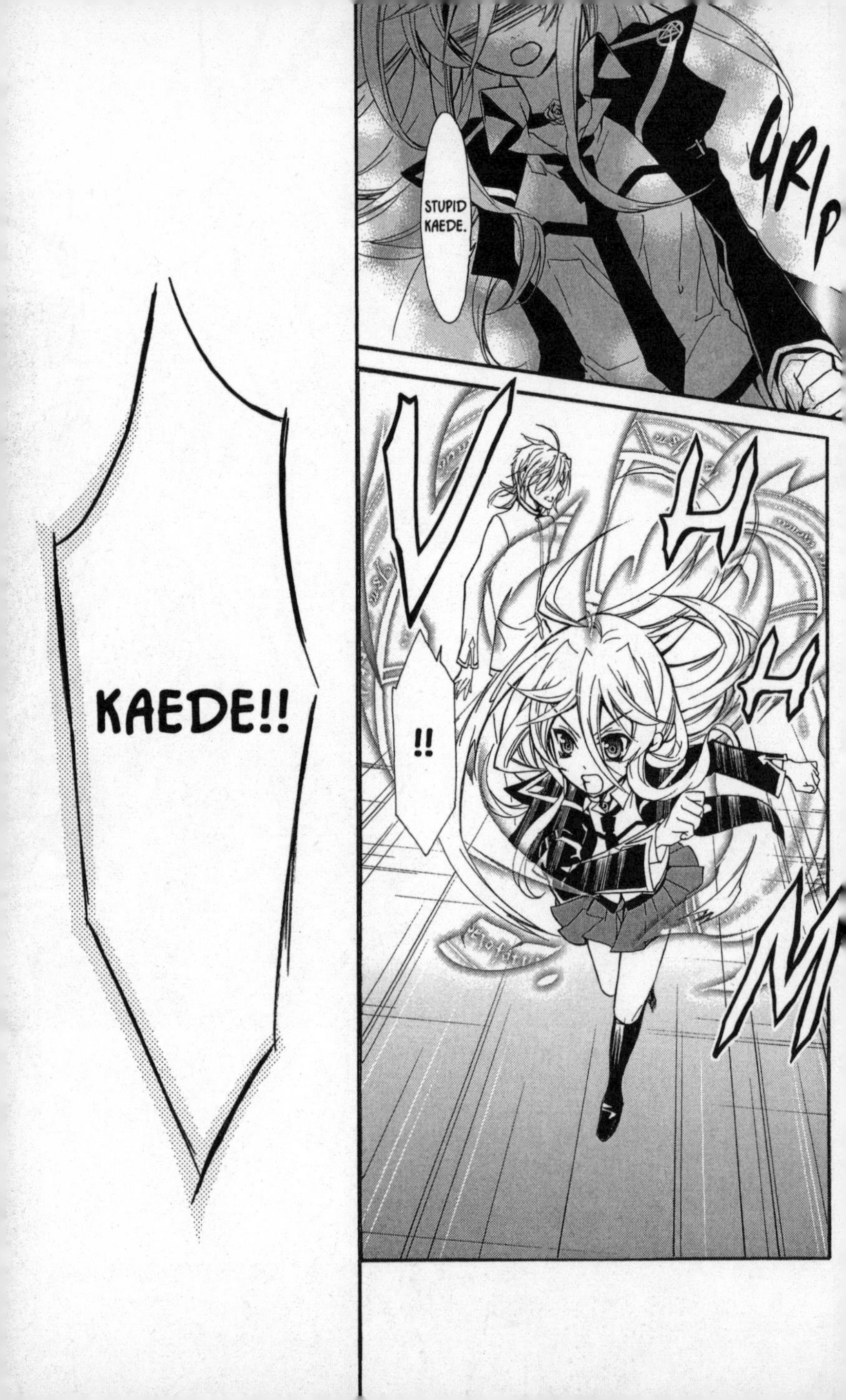
STUPID KAEDE.
GRIP
VHHM
!!
KAEDE!!

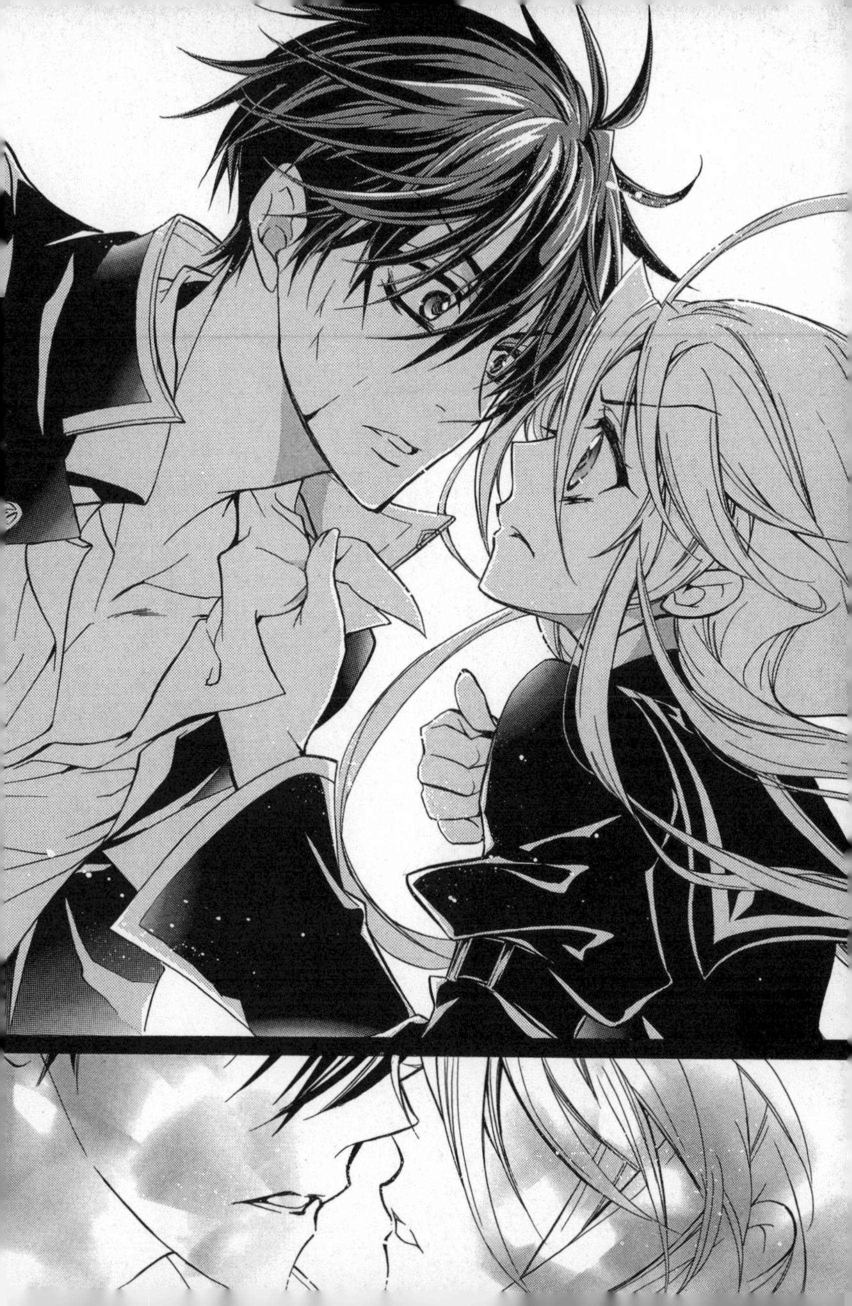

Kiss of the Rose Princess

The following bonus chapter is about President Tenjo and Mutsuki's past!

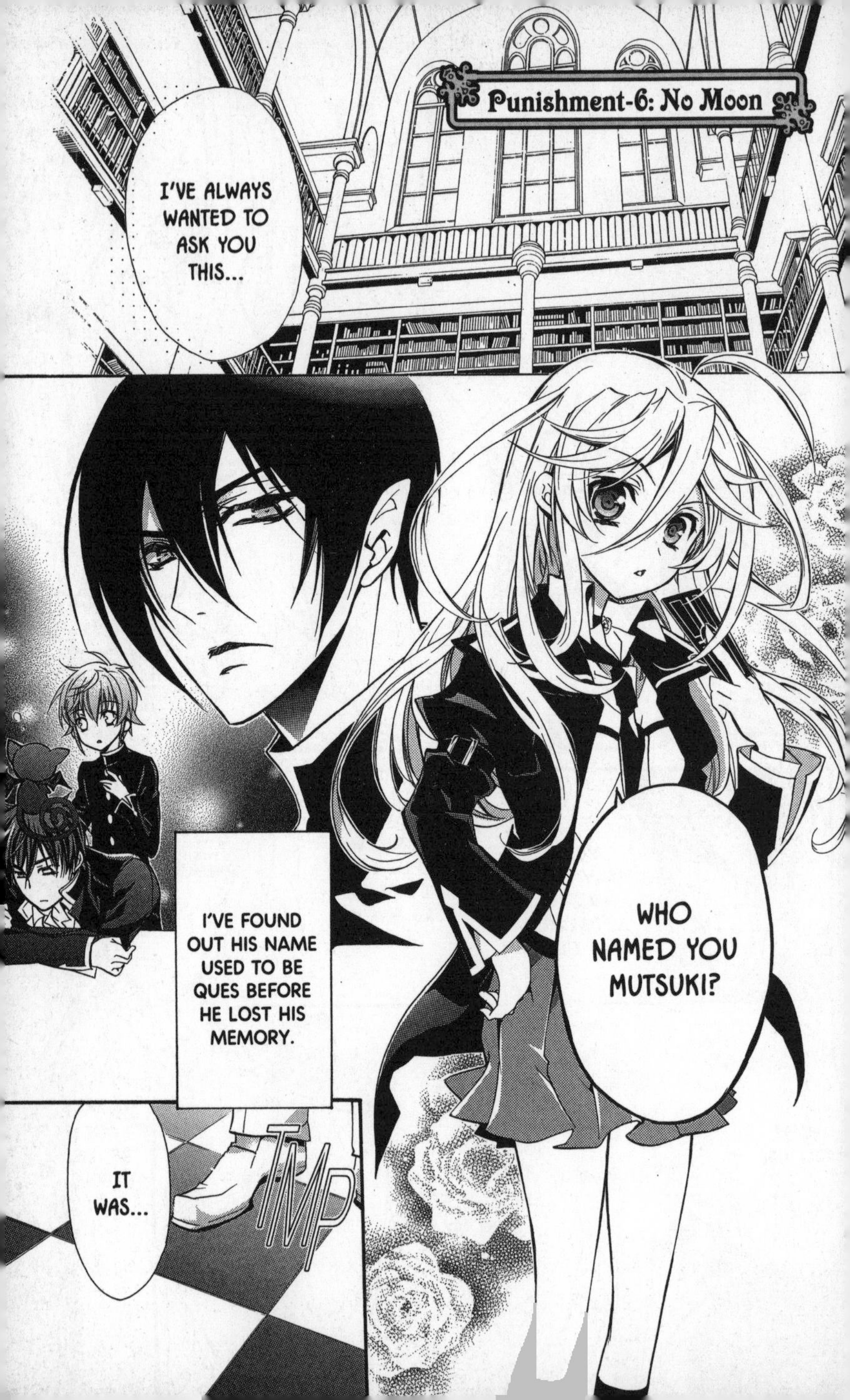
Punishment-6: No Moon
I'VE ALWAYS WANTED TO ASK YOU THIS...
WHO NAMED YOU MUTSUKI?
I'VE FOUND OUT HIS NAME USED TO BE QUES BEFORE HE LOST HIS MEMORY.
IT WAS...
TMP

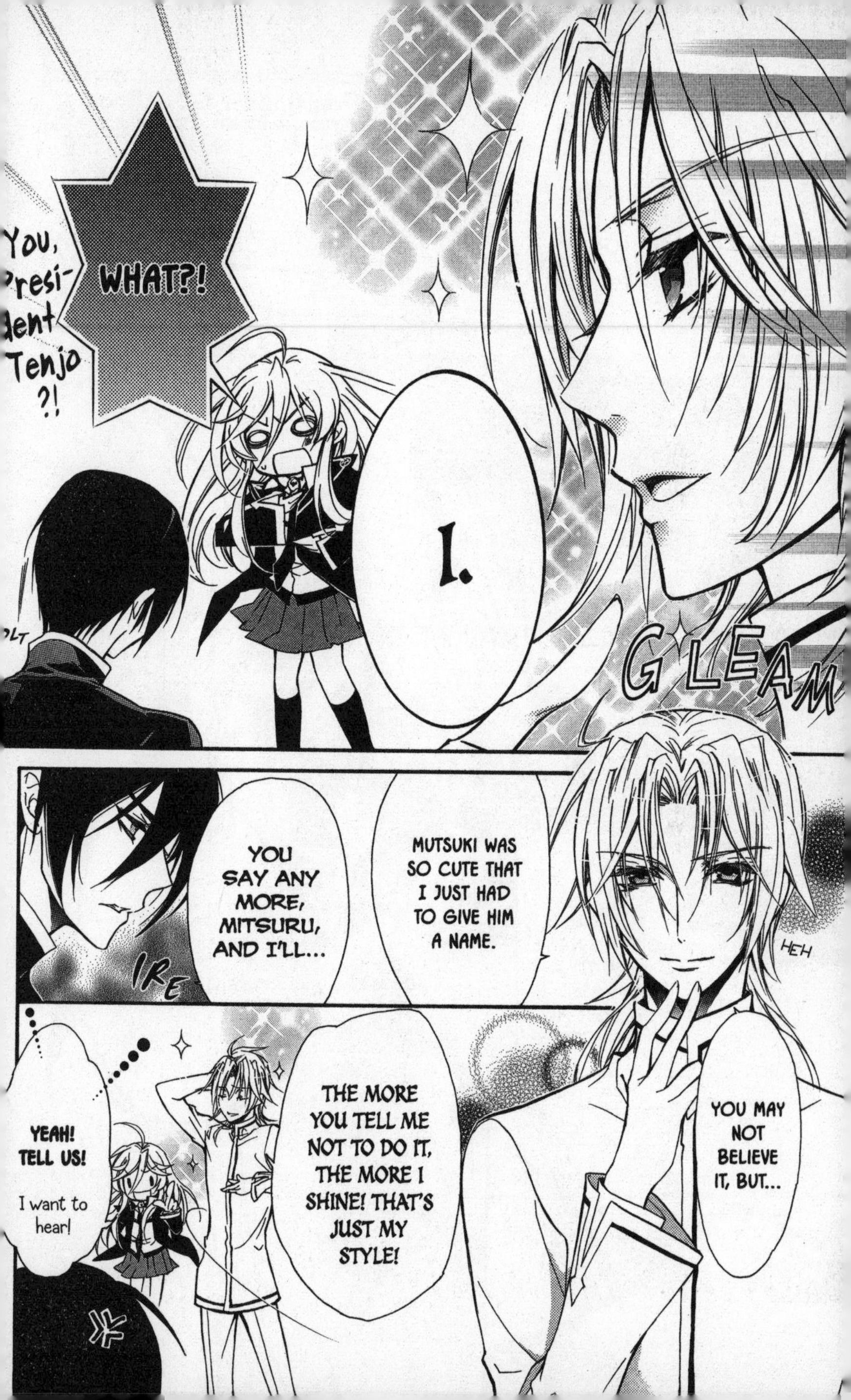
I.
GLEAM
WHAT?!
You, President Tenjo?!
MUTSUKI WAS SO CUTE THAT I JUST HAD TO GIVE HIM A NAME.
HEH
YOU SAY ANY MORE, MITSURU, AND I'LL...
IRE
YOU MAY NOT BELIEVE IT, BUT...
THE MORE YOU TELL ME NOT TO DO IT, THE MORE I SHINE! THAT'S JUST MY STYLE!
......
YEAH! TELL US!
I want to hear!

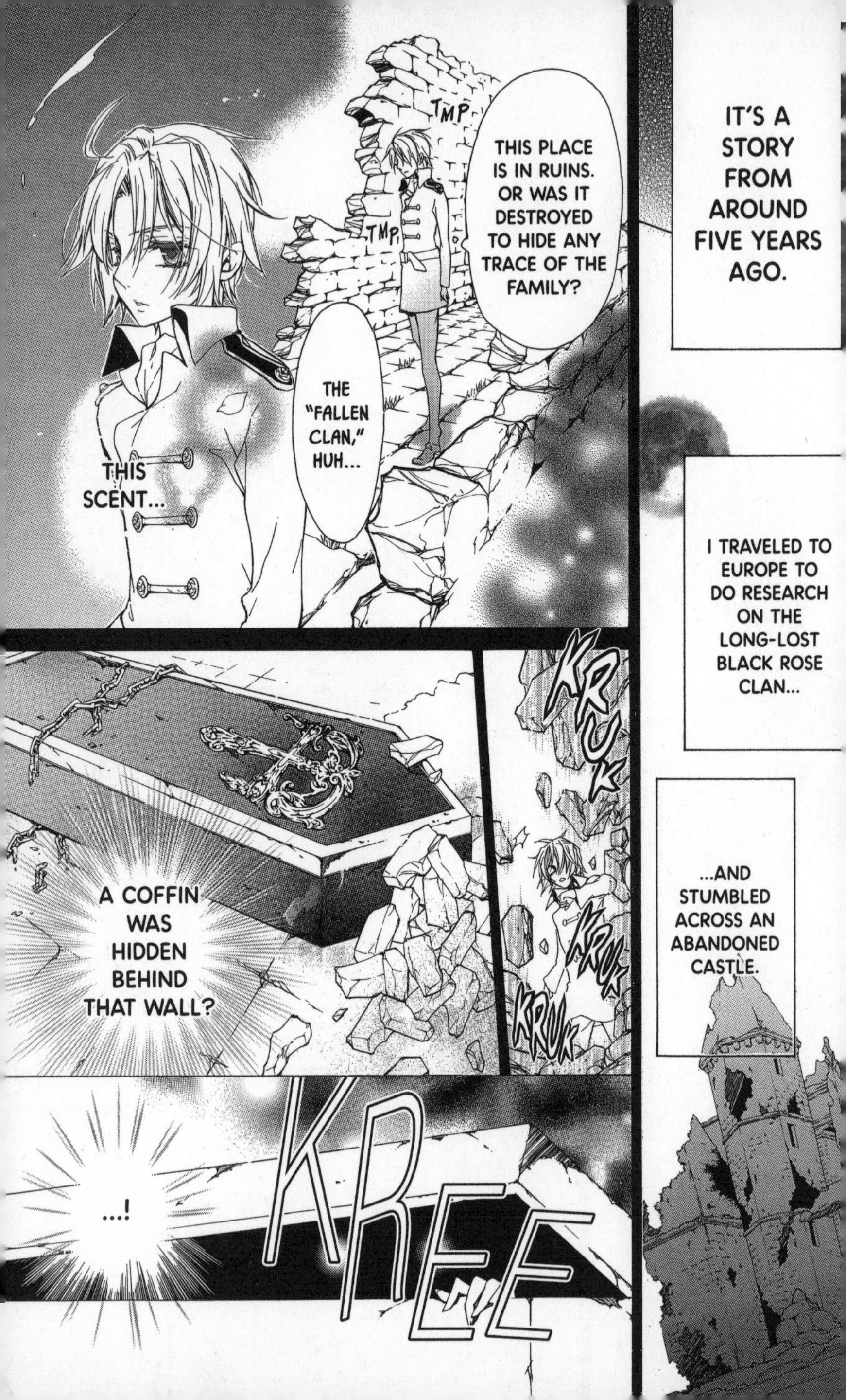
IT'S A STORY FROM AROUND FIVE YEARS AGO.
I TRAVELED TO EUROPE TO DO RESEARCH ON THE LONG-LOST BLACK ROSE CLAN...
...AND STUMBLED ACROSS AN ABANDONED CASTLE.
TMP
TMP
THIS PLACE IS IN RUINS. OR WAS IT DESTROYED TO HIDE ANY TRACE OF THE FAMILY?
THE "FALLEN CLAN," HUH...
THIS SCENT...
KRUK
KRUK
KRUK
A COFFIN WAS HIDDEN BEHIND THAT WALL?
KREE
...!

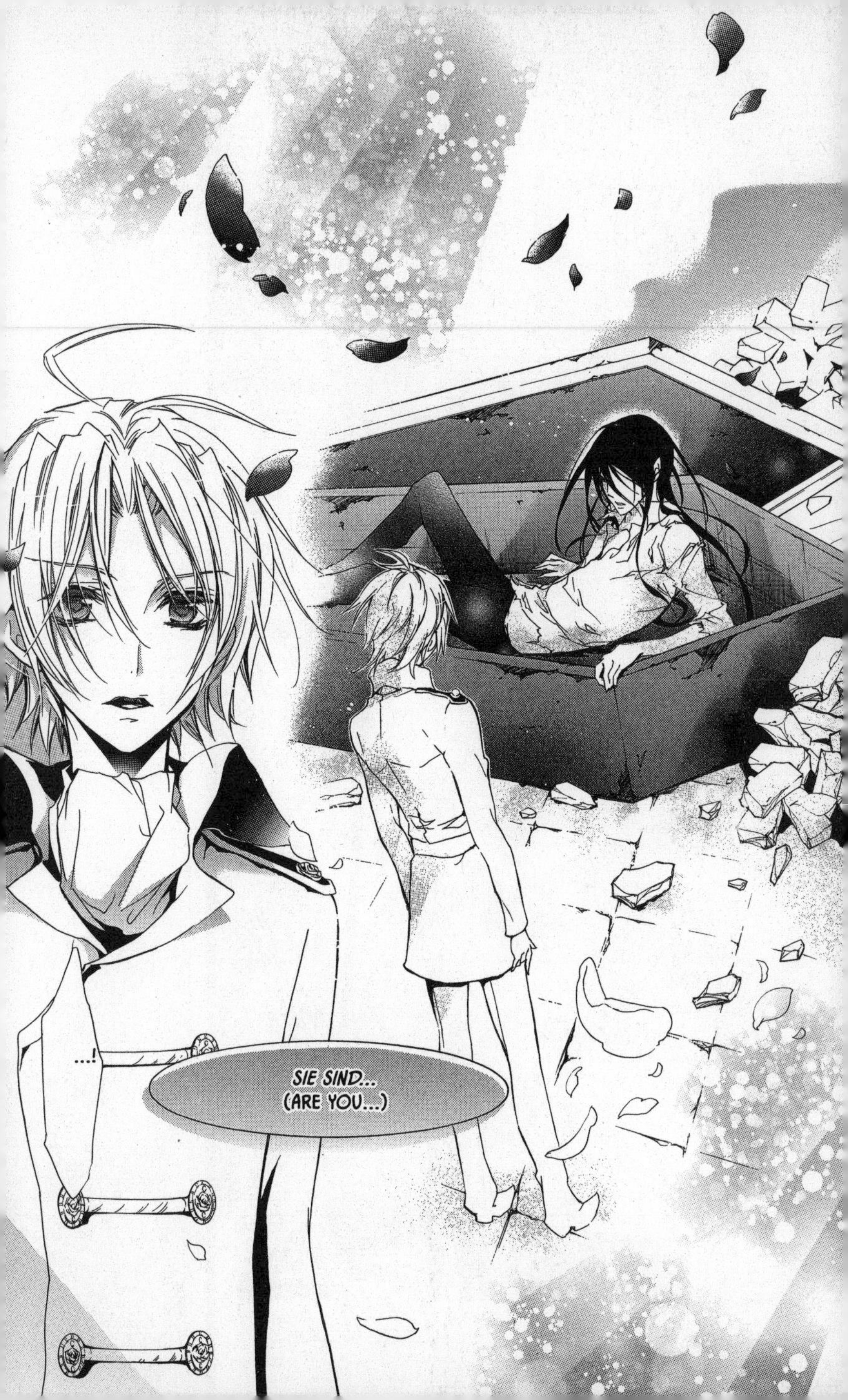
SIE SIND...
(ARE YOU...)
...!

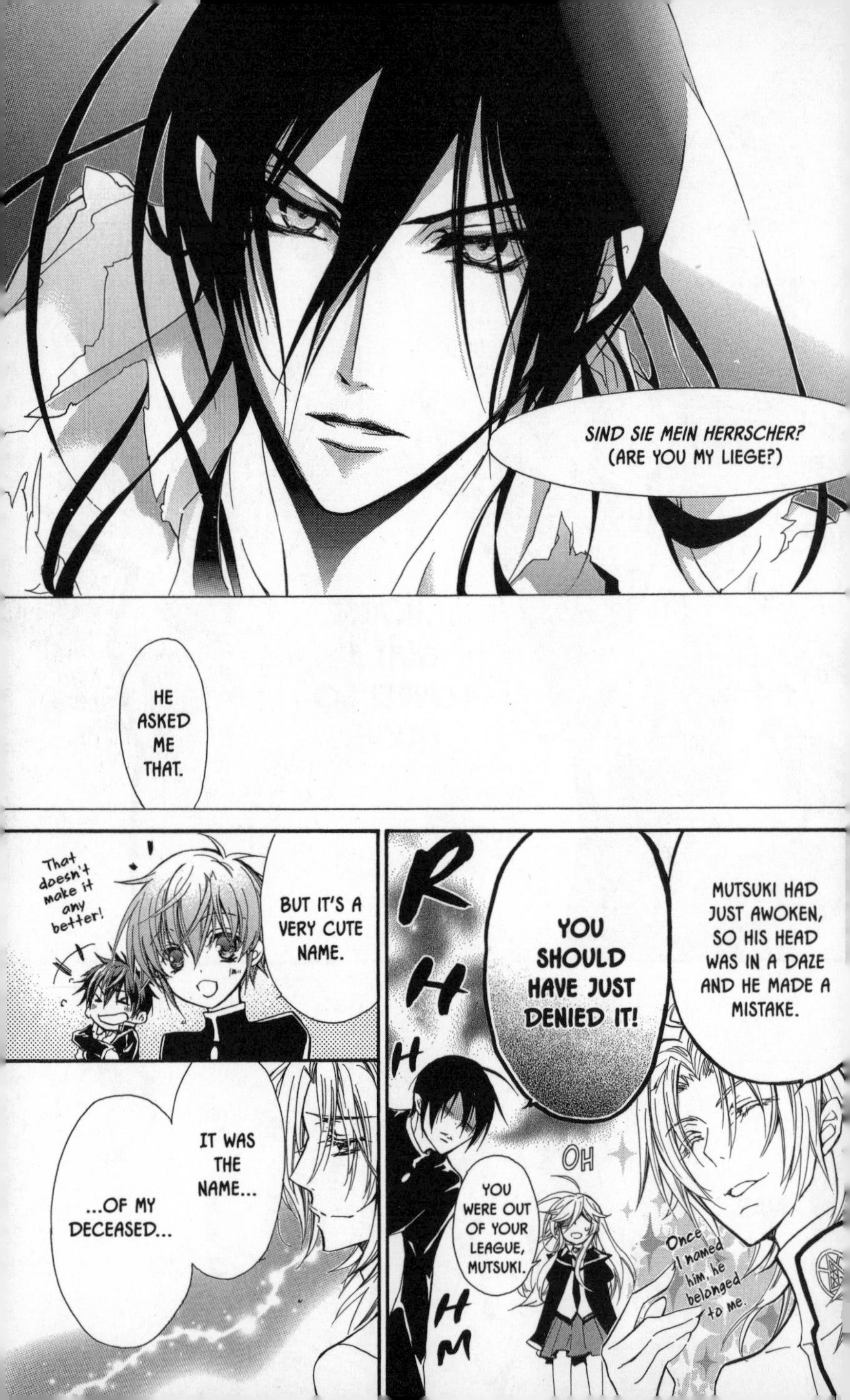
SIND SIE MEIN HERRSCHER? (ARE YOU MY LIEGE?)
HE ASKED ME THAT.
MUTSUKI HAD JUST AWOKEN, SO HIS HEAD WAS IN A DAZE AND HE MADE A MISTAKE.
YOU SHOULD HAVE JUST DENIED IT!
RHHH
OH
Once I named him, he belonged to me.
YOU WERE OUT OF YOUR LEAGUE, MUTSUKI.
HM
BUT IT'S A VERY CUTE NAME.
That doesn't make it any better!
IT WAS THE NAME...
...OF MY DECEASED...

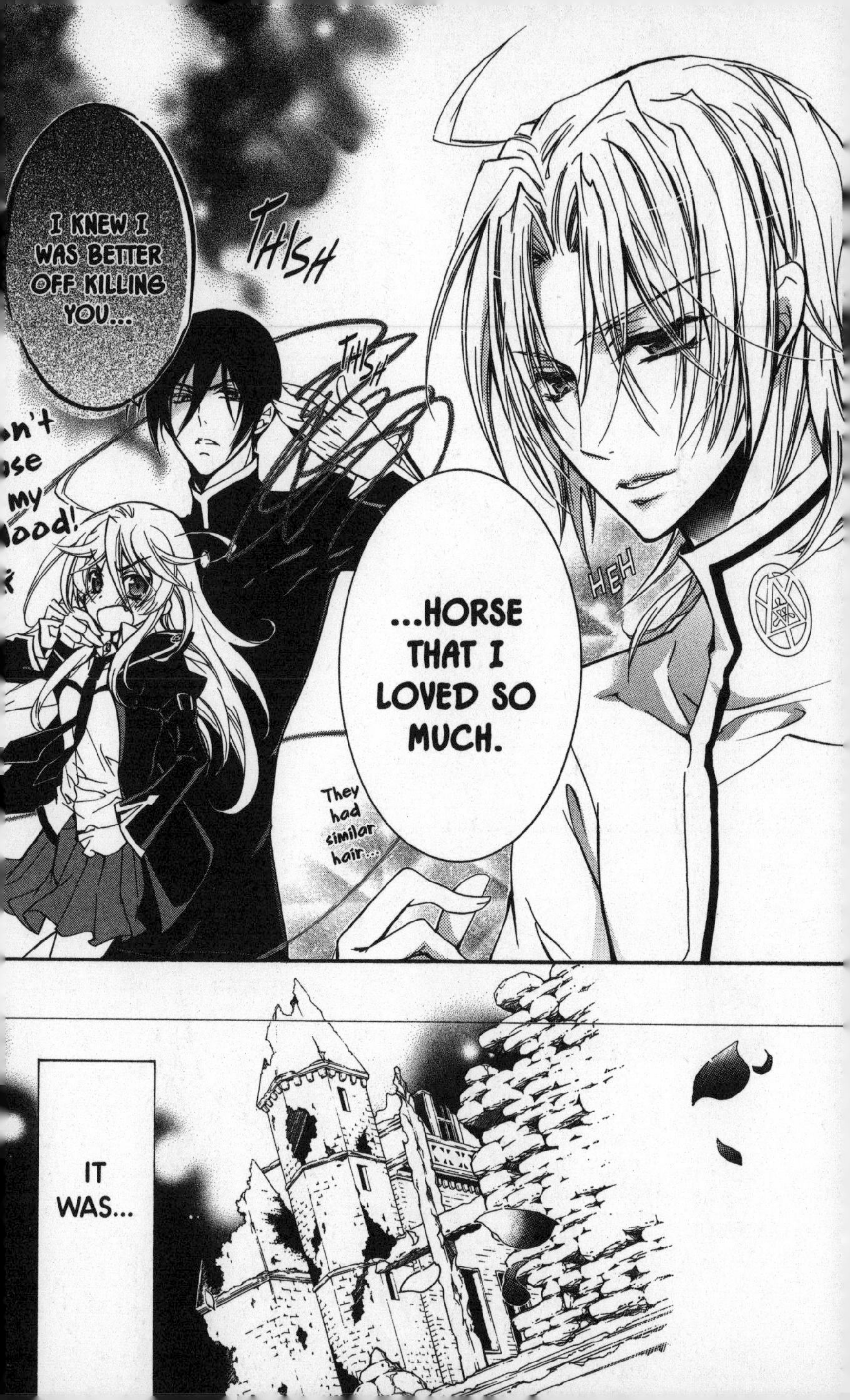
...HORSE THAT I LOVED SO MUCH.
HEH
They had similar hair...
THISH
THISH
I KNEW I WAS BETTER OFF KILLING YOU...
IT WAS...

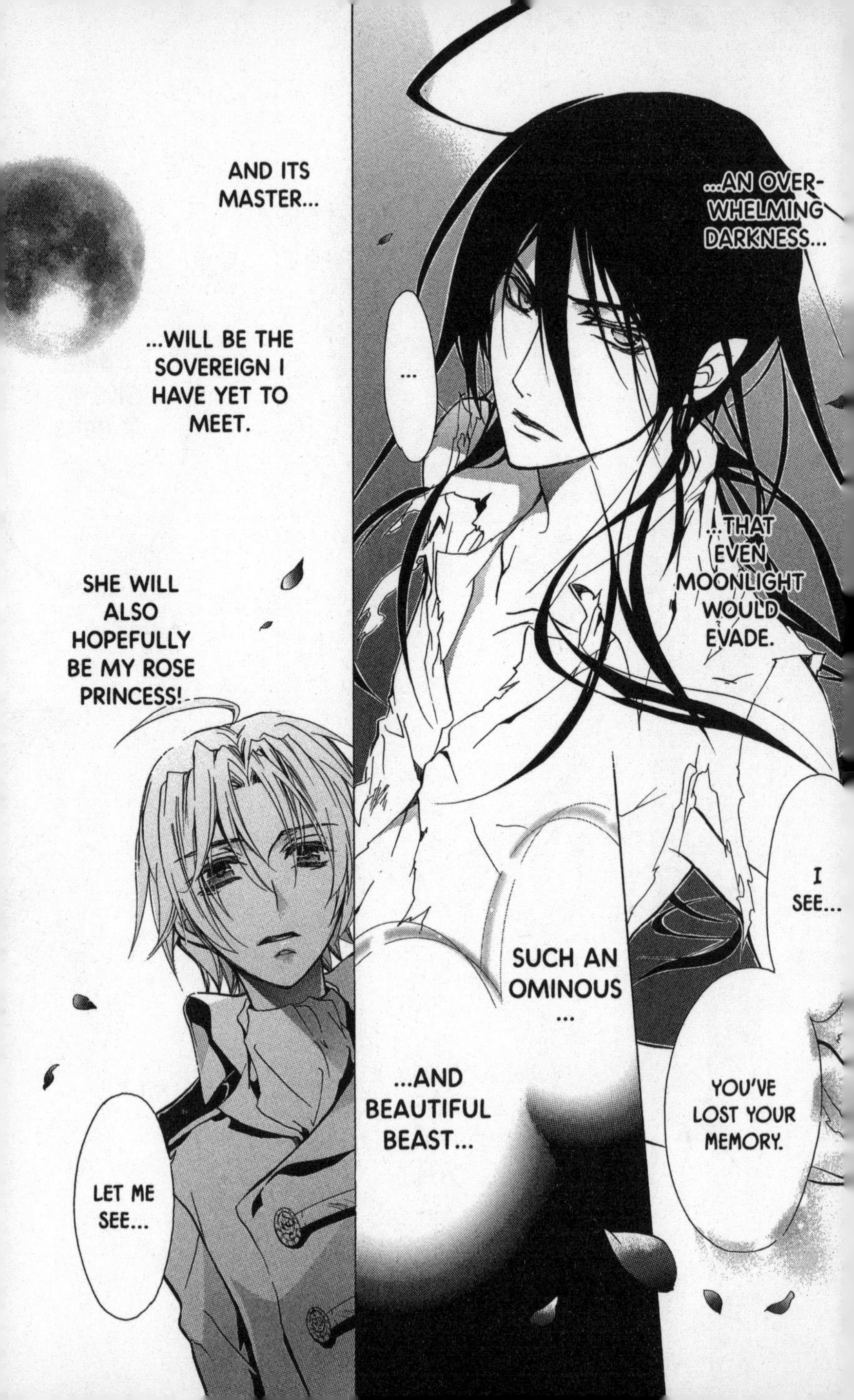
...AN OVER-WHELMING DARKNESS...
...
...THAT EVEN MOONLIGHT WOULD EVADE.
I SEE...
SUCH AN OMINOUS ...
YOU'VE LOST YOUR MEMORY.
...AND BEAUTIFUL BEAST...
AND ITS MASTER...
...WILL BE THE SOVEREIGN I HAVE YET TO MEET.
SHE WILL ALSO HOPEFULLY BE MY ROSE PRINCESS!
LET ME SEE...

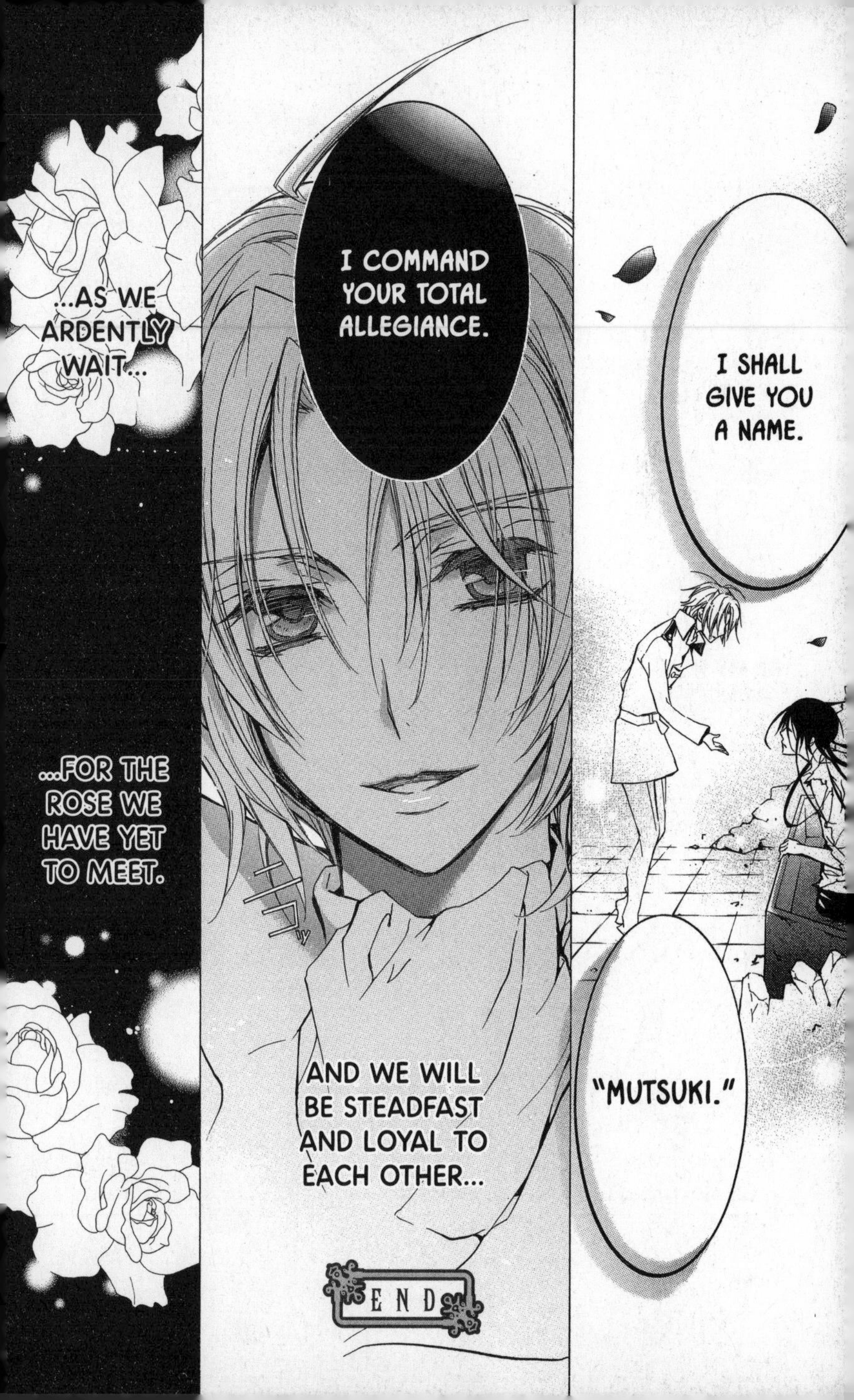
I SHALL GIVE YOU A NAME.
"MUTSUKI."
I COMMAND YOUR TOTAL ALLEGIANCE.
AND WE WILL BE STEADFAST AND LOYAL TO EACH OTHER...
END
...AS WE ARDENTLY WAIT...
...FOR THE ROSE WE HAVE YET TO MEET.

Kiss of the Rose Princess

Kiss of the Rose
Princess

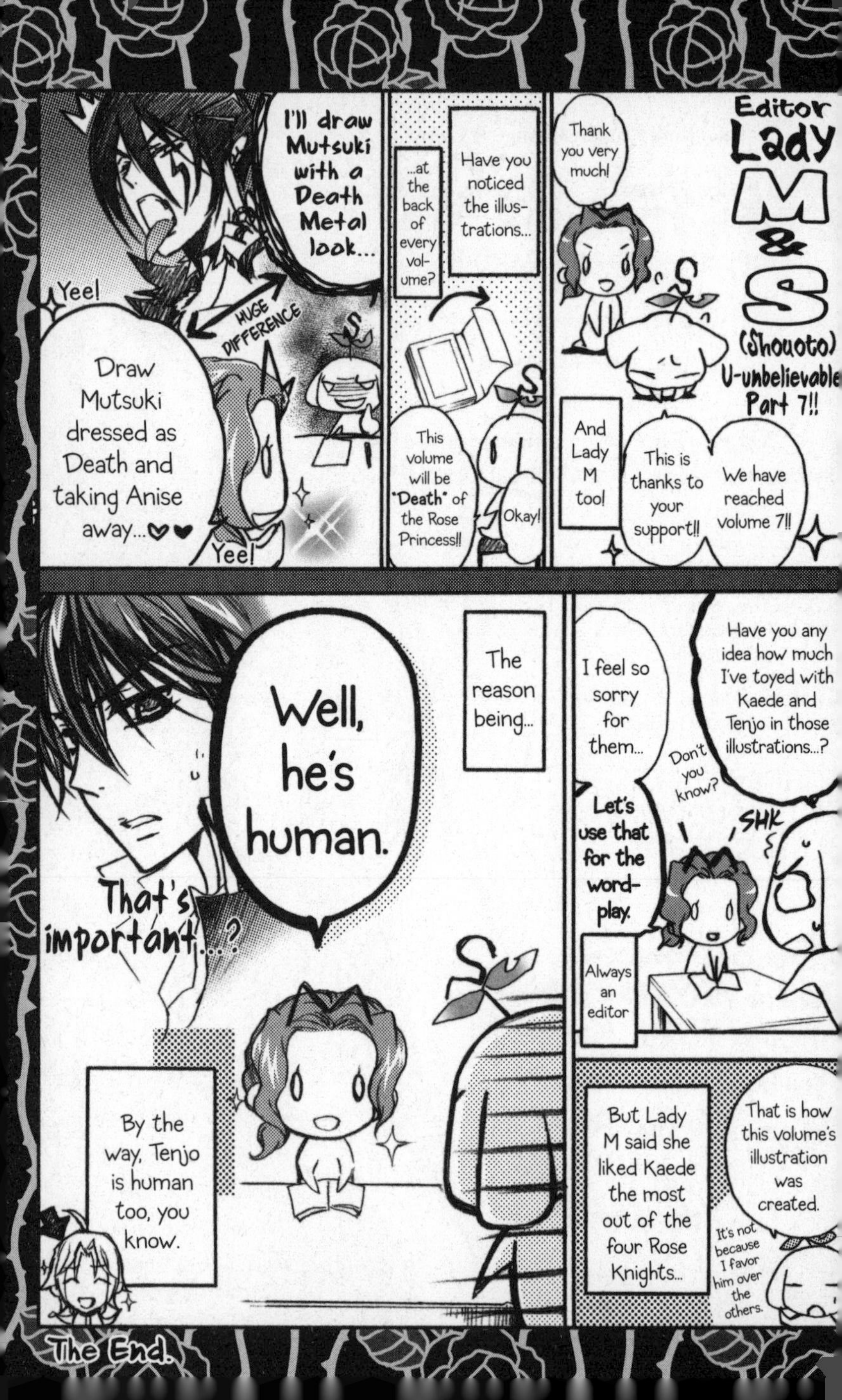
Editor Lady M & S (Shouoto) U-unbelievable Part 7!!
Thank you very much!
We have reached volume 7!!
This is thanks to your support!!
And Lady M too!
Have you noticed the illus-trations...
...at the back of every vol-ume?
This volume will be "Death" of the Rose Princess!!
Okay!
I'll draw Mutsuki with a Death Metal look...
HUGE DIFFERENCE
Yee!
Draw Mutsuki dressed as Death and taking Anise away...♥♥
Yee!
Have you any idea how much I've toyed with Kaede and Tenjo in those illustrations...?
Don't you know?
SHK
I feel so sorry for them...
Let's use that for the word-play.
Always an editor
That is how this volume's illustration was created.
But Lady M said she liked Kaede the most out of the four Rose Knights...
It's not because I favor him over the others.
The reason being...
Well, he's human.
That's important...?
By the way, Tenjo is human too, you know.
The End.

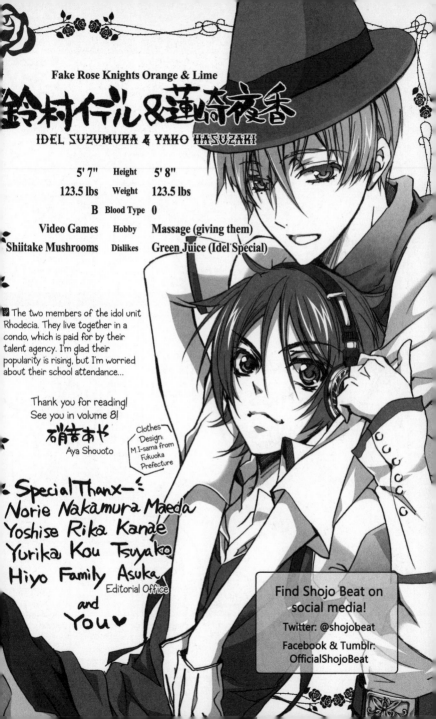

Fake Rose Knights Orange & Lime

鈴村イデル&蓮崎夜香

IDEL SUZUMURA & YAKO HASUZAKI

5' 7"	Height	5' 8"
123.5 lbs	Weight	123.5 lbs
B	Blood Type	0
Video Games	Hobby	Massage (giving them)
Shiitake Mushrooms	Dislikes	Green Juice (Idel Special)

The two members of the idol unit Rhodecia. They live together in a condo, which is paid for by their talent agency. I'm glad their popularity is rising, but I'm worried about their school attendance...

Thank you for reading!
See you in volume 8!

硝音あや
Aya Shouoto

Clothes Design: M.I-sama from Fukuoka Prefecture

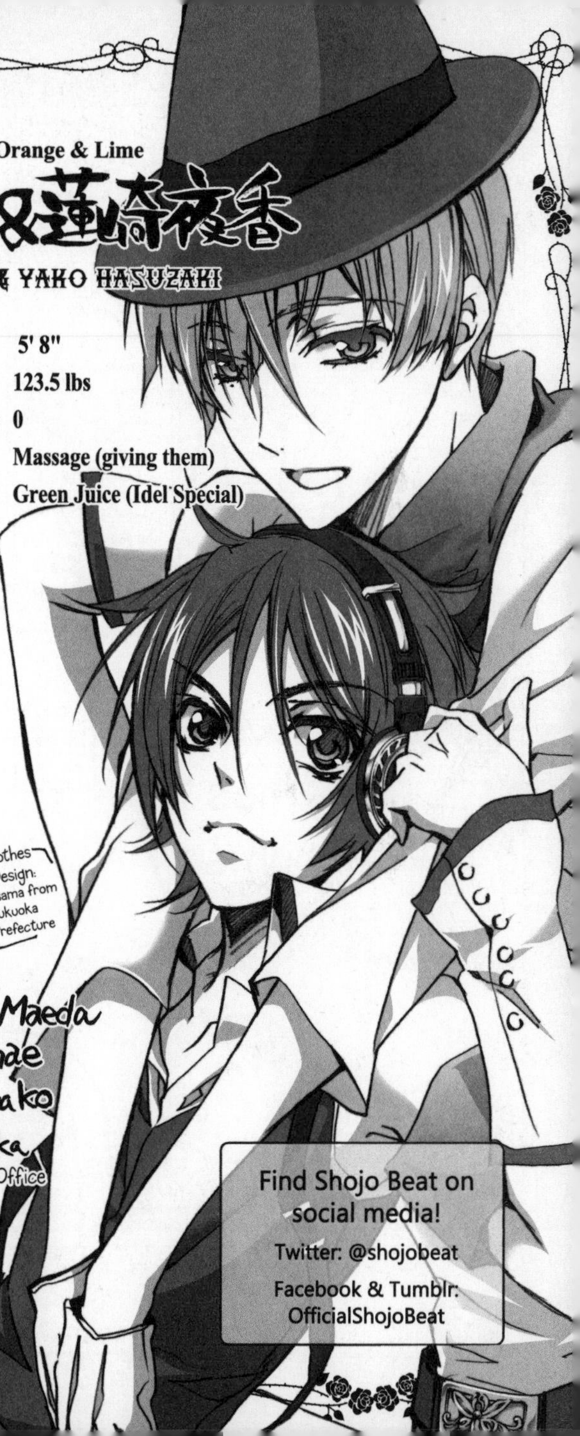

Special Thanx—
Norie Nakamura Maeda
Yoshise Rika Kanae
Yurika Kou Tsuyako
Hiyo Family Asuka
Editorial Office
and
You ♥

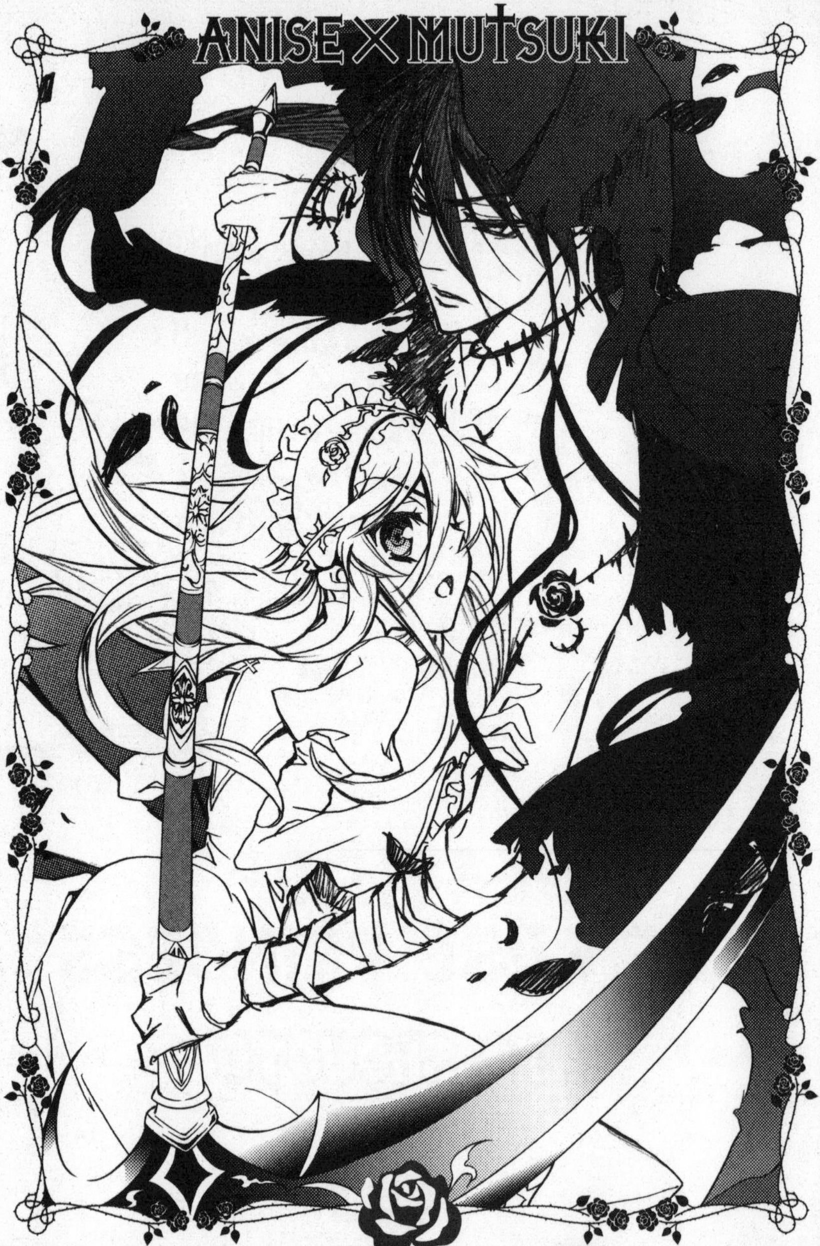
ANISE × MUTSUKI

Kiss of the Rose Princess 7 Aya Shouoto

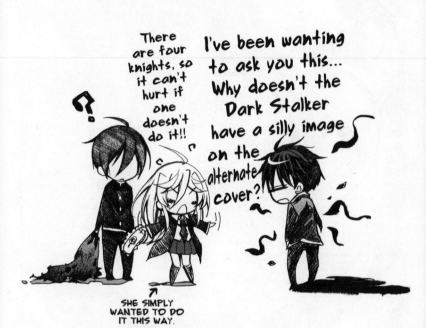

I've been wanting to ask you this... Why doesn't the Dark Stalker have a silly image on the alternate cover?
There are four knights, so it can't hurt if one doesn't do it!!
SHE SIMPLY WANTED TO DO IT THIS WAY.

DEATH OF THE ROSE PRINCESS

AYA SHOUOTO